Preaching as the Word of God

Preaching as the Word of God

Answering an Old Question with Speech-Act Theory

Sam Chan

foreword by
Graham Cole

☙PICKWICK *Publications* · Eugene, Oregon

PREACHING AS THE WORD OF GOD
Answering an Old Question with Speech-Act Theory

Copyright © 2016 Sam Chan. All rights reserved. Except for brief quotations in critical publications or reviews, no part of this book may be reproduced in any manner without prior written permission from the publisher. Write: Permissions, Wipf and Stock Publishers, 199 W. 8th Ave., Suite 3, Eugene, OR 97401.

Pickwick Publications
An Imprint of Wipf and Stock Publishers
199 W. 8th Ave., Suite 3
Eugene, OR 97401

www.wipfandstock.com

PAPERBACK ISBN: 978-1-4982-2024-8
HARDCOVER ISBN: 978-1-4982-2026-2
EBOOK ISBN: 978-1-4982-2025-5

Cataloguing-in-Publication data:

Chan, Sam.

    Preaching as the word of God : answering an old question with speech-act theory / Sam Chan; foreword by Graham Cole.

    xii + 252 pp. ; 23 cm. Includes bibliographical references and index.

    ISBN 978-1-4982-2024-8 (paperback) | ISBN 978-1-4982-2026-2 (hardback) | ISBN 978-1-4982-2025-5 (ebook)

    1. Preaching 2. Speech-Act Theory 3. Bible I. Cole, Graham. II. Title

BV4200 C310 2016

Manufactured in the U.S.A.   07/07/16

All Scripture quotations, unless otherwise indicated, are taken from the Holy Bible, New International Version®, NIV®. Copyright ©1973, 1978, 1984, 2011 by Biblica, Inc.™ Used by permission of Zondervan. All rights reserved worldwide. www.zondervan.com The "NIV" and "New International Version" are trademarks registered in the United States Patent and Trademark Office by Biblica, Inc.™

To my grandfather who taught me the joy of reading and getting up early. To my parents, Joseph and Winnie, who supported all my dreams, no matter how crazy. And to my wife, Steph, who showed me how to ski black diamond ski slopes, appreciate the beauty of karaoke, and allowed me the creative space for thinking and writing.

Contents

Foreword by Graham Cole | ix
Acknowledgments | xi
Abbreviations | xii

1 Introduction | 1

Part A—The Problem of the Reformers: When Is Preaching the Word of God?

2 Luther and Calvin: Preaching as the Word of God | 13
3 Luther and Calvin: Preaching as a Mark of the Church | 57

Part B—The Biblical Testimony: The Preached Gospel as the Word of God

4 God Speaks His Word | 81
5 The Human Messenger of God's Word | 91
6 The Message of Preaching | 113
7 The Intention and Results of Preaching | 133
8 The Preached Gospel as the Word of God | 154

Part C: A Fresh Approach: The Application of Speech-Act Theory

9 The Problem Revisited | 165
10 Speech-Act Theory, the Preached Word of God, and Discernment | 177
11 The Problem Addressed: A Final Synthesis | 210

Part D: Conclusion

Conclusion | 225

Appendix—Prophecy and Preaching | 229
Bibliography | 243
Author Index | 253
Subject Index | 257
Scripture Index | 263

Foreword

What is the status of a sermon that faithfully expounds Scripture? It is an old question. Henry Bullinger in the Reformation era argued famously that the preached Word of God is the Word of God. The Second Helvetic Confession of 1566 authored by Bullinger is evidence of that. Sam Chan explores this contention by a thorough examination of the biblical witness to the proclamation of the Word of God, and in addition to that he examines the relevant theology of sixteenth-century reformers such as Luther and Calvin. This is helpful and very well done but if that is all that he did it would be unexceptional. What makes this book noteworthy is that Chan employs a modern philosophical theory to revisit the question. That theory is speech-act theory as found in J. L. Austin and John Searle. After all a mark of a true church according to the reformers is that it is characterized by the faithful preaching of the Word of God. But what does that look like today? To make the task more focused Chan concentrates on the proclamation of the biblical gospel as the Word of God rather than the exposition of Scripture in general. The issue is how can we tell when that gospel has been faithfully proclaimed? Here speech-act theory comes to the fore. Chan concludes that, "to proclaim the gospel as the word of God is to re-locute and re-illocute the gospel message, as once locuted and illocuted by the prophets, Jesus, and the apostles, and which continues to be located and illocuted in Scripture." The mood of the work is Anselmian: faith seeking understanding. And in the case of this reader I am very much a beneficiary of Chan's project.

Professor Graham A. Cole.

Dean, Professor of Biblical and Systematic Theology,
Trinity Evangelical Divinity School, Deerfield, Illinois.

Acknowledgments

I would like to acknowledge the loving help of my wife, Stephanie, whose constant cheer made possible the completion of this project. She was an invaluable companion as we tackled five fun years of living and studying at Trinity Evangelical Divinity School, Illinois. Now that we are back in Australia, we look back on our special years together in Chicago with fondness. We will sorely miss the baseball, blues and, most of all, the hamburgers.

I would like to thank my dissertation mentor, Dr Graham A. Cole, whose insight, guidance, and contributions have been invaluable. He is a kind, godly, pastoral, generous, and wise teacher. By the grace of God, Stephanie and I were able to know him and his wife, Jules. I must also thank my Second Reader, Dr John S. Feinberg, who is a wonderful example of clear and rigorous thinking from whom I still have so much to learn, and the Program Director, Dr Willem A. VanGemeren, whose selfless love, care, and concern for international students touched the lives of Stephanie and me.

I must also mention the various members of my "theological accountability" group—including Keith, Kyle, Jon, Paul, and Jim—who helped craft my theological skills over some of Chicago's finest nutritional beverages.

My thoughts on the theology of preaching have also been shaped by preachers who are analytical, fresh, and creative communicators—such as Kirk Patston, Leigh Trevaskis, Malcolm Gill, Jon Dykes, Aaron Koh, Andrew Wong, Lawrence Tan, Morgan Powell, and Darren Hindle.

Thanks to Margaret Wilkins, Heather Pieris, and Santiago Arnaldo Jr for looking after the editing, formatting, Greek and Hebrew fonts, and proof reading for me. Thanks also to Lachlan Orr and Katherine Roberts who did the indexing for me.

Finally, I thank my mother and father, Winnie and Joseph, who raised me to fear and know the Lord. They have supported me in all my endeavors from the day that I was born. This book is a fruit of their love, support, and prayers.

Abbreviations

BECNT   Baker Exegetical Commentary of the New Testament

BST   Bible Speaks Today

CDP   *The Cambridge Dictionary of Philosophy.* Edited by Robert Audi. New York: Cambridge University Press, 1999

EBC   *The Expositor's Bible Commentary.* Edited by Frank E. Gaebelein. 12 vols. Grand Rapids: Zondervan, 1984

Institutes   John Calvin. *Institutes of the Christian Religion.* Edited by John T. McNeill. Translated by Ford Lewis Battles. 2 vols. Library of Christian Classics 20–21. Philadelphia: Westminster, 1960

LW   *Luther's Works.* Edited by Jaroslav Pelikan (vols. 1–30) and Helmut T. Lehmann (vols. 31–55). 55 vols. American ed. St. Louis and Philadelphia: Concordia and Fortress, 1955–1986

NDBT   *New Dictionary of Biblical Theology.* Edited by T. Desmond Alexander and Brian S. Rosner. Downers Grove, IL: InterVarsity, 2000

NDT   *New Dictionary of Theology.* Edited by Sinclair B. Ferguson and David F. Wright. Downers Grove, IL: InterVarsity, 1988

PNTC   The Pillar New Testament Commentary

RWML   *Reformation Writings of Martin Luther.* Edited by Bertram Lee Woolf. 2 vols. New York: Philosophical Library, 1953–1956

SBJT   *Southern Baptist Journal of Theology*

WML   *Works of Martin Luther.* 6 vols. Philadelphia: Muhlenberg, 1930–1943

— 1 —

Introduction

This book will attempt to articulate an adequate theological conceptualization of the preached gospel as the word of God. In particular, the hope is to suggest criteria for discerning whether the preached gospel is the word of God. In this introduction, the purpose is to provide an overview of the justification, purpose, method, limitations, presuppositions, and outline of this study.

Justification of Study

The "word of God" is a phrase that occurs repeatedly in the Bible. It refers to the concept that God has sovereignly revealed a divine message that is authoritative and true, for it is no less than a word *from* God. But if this is so, can a *human* proclaimer ever claim to preach the word of God? This would be an outrageous claim indeed. But this is a phenomenon to which the Bible attests, for Paul reminds the Thessalonians that they once heard the "word of God" from him (1 Thess 2:13); and Paul also exhorts Timothy to "Preach the Word" (2 Tim 4:2). But how can this phenomenon be conceptualized—a human proclaimer who claims to speak the word of God? And are there any criteria for discerning if a human is proclaiming the word of God?

These are weighty questions with important significance for the Christian church. The Reformers, when breaking away from the Roman Catholic Church, grounded the legitimacy of their church no longer upon the papal authority but upon the preached word. The Reformers argued that the true sheep recognize and gather around the voice of their Shepherd; and the voice of the Shepherd could be heard in the preaching of the word of God. As a result, the Reformers identified the preached word as a "mark" of the church. That is, when God's people meet and hear the preached word, then this is a guarantee that God's true church is indeed gathered. Thus, the legitimacy of the Reformation and Christian churches that come from the Reformation tradition was grounded upon the fact that preaching *is* the word of God.

But were the Reformers guilty of question-begging? Do the sheep really hear the voice of their Shepherd in preaching? By leaving this question unanswered, did the Reformers presume something that was not yet established? Can we conceptualize *human* proclamation to be a *divine* word? Can preaching be so readily identified as the word of God? And if so, what conditions would be necessary or sufficient to guarantee that the word of God has been preached? For surely not all preaching is the word of God. These unanswered questions demonstrate an underlying theological problem that the Reformers have raised but failed to address.

Purpose

The purpose of this book will be the exploration of the above theological problem that was raised by the Reformation, namely, how can we conceptualize preaching to be the word of God, and what conditions would be necessary or sufficient to guarantee that the word of God has been preached?

Methodology

My methodology will be to survey the theological stance of the Reformers, examine the biblical revelation regarding the phenomenon of the preached word, and utilize a contemporary philosophical tool carefully appropriated for theological use in order to answer our problem.

The philosophical tool utilized will be speech-act theory. Although there exist other appropriate philosophical tools that analyze language and communication, speech-act theory is particularly appropriate because it seeks to analyze *verbal utterances*. This is especially relevant for this project because the theological problem raised by the Reformers concerns the *preached* or *spoken* gospel (rather than the written word); the biblical phenomenon that this project will be exploring concerns the *preached* gospel; and the ultimate aim of this project is one that seeks to analyze, clarify, and suggest criteria for the theological conceptualization of the *preached* gospel.

Speech-act theory is a theory about the use of language. It was initially developed by John Langshaw Austin (1911–1960) in *How To Do Things with Words*[1] and subsequently refined and systematized by his student, John Searle (born 1932).[2] At its very heart, it proposes that a speaker is not merely uttering sounds, words, or statements, but is performing an action—hence the name, *speech act*. Over the last few decades, speech-act theory has been used to provide fresh insights in the disciplines of theological and biblical studies with many promising results. It is my hope that the use of speech-act theory may provide fresh insights in the conceptualization of the biblical phenomenon of the preached word, just as it has in other fields of theological and biblical studies. Perhaps speech-act theory will help in the understanding of how preaching is the word of God and the identification of criteria in discerning if preaching is the word of God.

Clarifications and Limitations

At this stage the task will be clarified and delimited. The term "preaching" refers to the proclamation of a message. Thus, although a message can be communicated through a wide variety of media, my task is to examine the specific medium of oral transmission, that is, the proclamation of a message. The term "word of God" in a general sense would refer to any message from God, no matter what its content would be, no matter how seemingly mundane or exciting. In this general sense, to "preach the word of God" would be to proclaim any message from God. But the term "word of God" in a special sense would refer to a salvific message from God, whose content would be the specific gospel message, which announces that Christ has come as the Savior and Lord, and that all must respond with a life of faith and obedience. In this special sense, to "preach the word of God" would be to proclaim the gospel. The focus of my task will be upon this special sense of the "word of God," that is, the specific case of preaching the gospel. This focus is warranted because, as we will discover later, the New Testament often refers to this sense; and the Reformers usually referred to this sense when they equated preaching to be the word of God. Therefore, the focus of my task will be limited to the particular concept of the *preached gospel as the word of God* (in the special sense), rather than the preached word (in the general sense) as the word of God. Thus, it is not within the scope of my present task to examine the preached word of God in its general sense, although this certainly would be a fruitful area for future research.

---

1. Austin, *How to Do Things with Words*.
2. Searle, "Austin on Locutionary and Illocutionary Acts," 405–24; Searle, *Speech Acts*; Searle, *Expression and Meaning*.

Theological Presuppositions

The book will be conducted within the following theological presuppositions. First, I acknowledge the existence of divine revelation, that is, the self-disclosure of God to humankind. Although God's revelation is a unity, it is useful to distinguish between *general* and *special* revelation.[3] General revelation refers to God's disclosure that is available to all persons at all times and places, and might include the information about God that is available by studying the natural world, history, and the human conscience. Special revelation, on the other hand, is only available to particular persons at particular times and places. It is conveyed by God's actions and words, and is most clearly demonstrated in the incarnation of the Word and the inscripturation of God's spoken word in the Bible.

Second, the Bible is the "inspired" word of God. In 2 Timothy 3:16, Paul writes, "all Scripture is God-breathed" (πᾶσα γραφή θεόπνευστος). The adjective θεόπνευστος literally means "God-breathed"[4] and refers to the revelatory activity of God in which Scripture has been "breathed-out" or "inspired" by God. But how did God "breathe-out" his Scriptures when they were written by human authors? In 2 Peter 1:19–21, the human authors of Scripture are described as being "carried" by the Holy Spirit. That is to say, the Holy Spirit sovereignly inspired the human author so that the author's thoughts and words were also what the Spirit wished to express, without necessarily dictating, and without compromising the personality of the author. Thus, in the end, the "inspired" Scriptures are the product of a dual divine-human authorship. Technically, this is usually labeled the *concursive* theory of inspiration, and can be regarded as a subset of God's special providence.

Third, Scripture is inerrant because of its divine authorship. Everything that Scripture affirms corresponds to truth and reality, not only in matters of faith and practice, but in all other matters such as history and science—for one cannot conceive how the divine author would lie or mislead. Thus, any matters of seeming inaccuracy are due to our misinterpretations of the text, the non-possession of all the facts or data, or the non-possession of the original manuscripts.

---

3. Henry notes, "While God's revelation is one, the forms of divine revelation need not be so. God does not reveal himself only in one way," in *God, Revelation and Authority*, 73.

4. The term θεόπνευστος was translated by the Old Latin, followed by the Vulgate, as *divinitus inspirata*, meaning "divinely inspired" or "breathed-by-God." A fuller treatment of θεόπνευστος can be found in Vawter's chapter "The Concept of Biblical Inspiration," in *Biblical Inspiration*, 1–19.

Fourth, a basic continuity within the canon of Scripture, between the two Testaments of Scripture, will be assumed. Old Testament themes, prophecies, and writings are understood to have been fulfilled in the person and work of Christ and the subsequent New Testament church. This is not to say that the Old Testament has been exhaustively fulfilled; but it does allow the interpreter to apply Old Testament texts to the contemporary Christian church.[5]

Fifth, Scripture should be interpreted using the grammatico-historical method. Each biblical text should be read appropriately to its language, syntax, literary genre, literary context, historical background, and cultural setting. In doing so, the aim is to bring out of the text the same meaning that the original writers intended to express, and that the original hearers or readers were expected to understand. Further, because each biblical text is ultimately authored by God, and each text has its placement in the canon according to God's providence, then each text should also be interpreted appropriately according to its canonical context.[6]

Sixth, it is possible for a reader to interpret adequately the objective meaning of Scripture. On the one hand, the finite interpreter is influenced by factors such as language, social context, and culture; further, the fallible interpreter is also influenced by the effects of the fall. On the other hand, through the tools of exegesis, the acknowledgment of one's presuppositions, the guidance of the church's interpretation, and the illuminating work of the Holy Spirit, it is possible for an interpreter to approximate the objective meaning of the text.

Finally, because God's revelation exists as both general and special revelation, it is legitimate to use a variety of sources to inform our theological discussion; further, because God's revelation exists as a unity, it is legitimate to synthesize our findings into a coherent concept. Valuable insight may be gained through recourse to reason and observation, the history of Christian

---

5. Goldsworthy notes, "The heart of the issue lies in the fact that the historical Jesus who is at the centre of the NT's message is absent from the events of the OT. Yet he claims that the OT witnesses to him. Understanding the relationship of the two Testaments involves understanding that the God who has revealed himself finally in Jesus has also revealed himself in the OT in a way that foreshadows both the structure and content of the Christian gospel," in "Relationship of Old Testament and New Testament," 89.

6. Bruce calls this "theological exegesis": "the whole canon provides a theological context within which each document may be viewed and its contribution to the record of divine revelation and of human response to that revelation may be assessed. Whereas grammatico-historical exegesis may bring out the variety of viewpoint and emphasis represented in the Bible, theological exegesis presupposes that there is an overall unity in the light of which the diversity can be appreciated in its proper perspective," in "Interpretation of the Bible," 566.

thought, experience, and philosophical tools. Nonetheless, priority is given to God's special revelation, the Bible. The Bible primarily shapes our interpretation of the other sources rather than the other way around.

Outline

The outline of my discussion will be as follows. Part A will survey the theological position of the Reformers, with particular attention to the contributions of Martin Luther and John Calvin, in order to clarify the problem. In chapter 2 I will survey the views of Luther and Calvin on preaching and the word of God, for both held very high views of preaching. They readily identified the preached word as the word of God; both claimed that one could hear God speak his words through the proclamation of a human preacher. The basis of this claim was the recognition of the source, content, and purpose of the preached word. For the source of the preached word, the human preacher, is sent by God to represent God and speak on God's behalf. The content of the preached word is the Christocentric message of the gospel, to which the term "the word" refers; this gospel is also inscripturated as the written word, which testifies to Christ; and thus the preached word is to conform to the written word. The purpose of the preached word is to achieve God's purposes of salvation and building up of his church, and this is achieved by the hidden illuminating and regenerating work of the Holy Spirit in conjunction with human preaching.

In chapter 3, I will survey how Luther's and Calvin's views of preaching were significant for their understanding of the church. Luther and Calvin both understood that the church is to be necessarily founded upon God's word. For the church is a community of saints who hear, recognize, and obey the word; they are the sheep who know the voice of their Shepherd. As a result both Luther and Calvin identified the preaching of the word of God to be a mark of the true church, which is both sufficient to guarantee and necessary for the existence of the church. In doing so, they granted the Reformation movement the legitimacy and warrant to break away from the Roman Catholic Church by founding their church upon the preached word and not upon papal authority. But all this requires that the preaching of the word of God really *is* the word of God. And even if preaching is the word of God, surely not *all* preaching can be identified as the word. This introduces our problem: when is preaching the word of God, and how is the "pure word" to be discerned?

Part B will survey and examine the biblical revelation regarding the phenomenon of preaching and the word of God, with particular reference to the preached gospel as the word of God, in order to investigate if there is any biblical support for the concept that preaching is the word of God, which is the claim of the Reformers. In chapter 4, a brief survey will find that the Bible presents God as a speaking God; God is a God of revelation who speaks his word. Thus, terms and phrases such as "word," "the word of God," or "the word of the Lord" occur frequently in the Bible. In a general sense, God's word can refer to any message from God, but as the storyline of the Bible unfolds, God's word increasingly refers specifically to its special sense, the gospel message about Christ.

In chapter 5, I will explore the phenomenon in the Bible where God chooses *human messengers* to preach his word. Moses was the paradigm of such a human messenger, and after Moses there was the expectation of another prophet "like Moses" who would faithfully preach God's word. There also developed the anticipation of an Isaianic Servant who would obediently preach God's message of salvation. In the New Testament, Jesus represents the climactic fulfillment of this expectation; he is the Prophet and Servant *par excellence*. After Jesus, the apostles are the ones commissioned by Christ to proclaim his word and continue the preaching mission of the Prophet and Servant; but after the apostles, the Christian church now collectively assumes the role and identity of the Prophet and Servant. The church collectively follows in the footsteps of Jesus by becoming the proclaimers of the word of God.

In chapter 6, the content of the preached word will be examined. In the Old Testament, the word of God could refer to a general message from God, which was usually proclaimed by one of his commissioned human messengers, such as a prophet. However, as the storyline of the Bible progressed, the content of the word of God referred increasingly to a special message of salvation where God would climactically act to save and vindicate his people, and judge and punish his enemies. In the New Testament, with the arrival of Jesus, and the inauguration of a new age of salvation-history, the word of God usually referred specifically to the gospel message. The terms "word of God" and the "gospel" were used synonymously by the New Testament writers to describe the gospel message preached by Jesus and the apostles, heard and believed by the Christian church, and now in turn preached by the Christian church.

In chapter 7, I will examine both the intention behind the preached word and the subsequent results of preaching. Regarding the intention of preaching, God's messengers are called to exhort, command, promise, warn, rebuke, or encourage their hearers, with the intent that the hearers respond with faith and obedience. This intention comes not from the preacher alone but ultimately from God, for it is God's intention that the hearers respond to the preached message. Therefore, to preach God's word is to preach on behalf of God with the divinely commissioned intention that the hearer hears God's message and responds. Regarding the results of preaching, although the preacher might faithfully preach the word, there will be mixed responses by the hearers—some will believe and obey, but others will not. Nonetheless, the status of the preached word as the word of God is not affected by the responses to it; for the word of God is still the word of God independently of how it is received. This will be explored further by examining the different roles of the preacher, the hearer, and the Holy Spirit regarding the results of the preached word.

In chapter 8, the observations from the previous chapters will be integrated in order to construct a theological understanding of preaching as the word of God, with a particular focus on the preached gospel as the word of God. Accordingly, I will grant that it is legitimate to identify preaching as the word of God, and in particular, the preached gospel as the word of God. But this leads to the related problem: assuming that preaching can be the word of God, how can we recognize preaching that is the word of God?

Part C will utilize the contemporary philosophical tool of speech-act theory, carefully appropriated for theological use, in order to provide fresh insights that might help in answering our problem. In chapter 9, I will revisit our problem by surveying different contemporary attempts at answering this question. For Klaas Runia, preaching must be a "dialectical tension" between the objective written word of God and the subjective human application of this word; for Karl Barth, human preaching becomes the word of God in the event of its witness to Jesus Christ, the Word incarnate; for Helmut Thielicke, human preaching becomes the Spirit-endowed word of God; for David Buttrick, human preaching becomes the word of God by continuing the preaching of Jesus Christ; for the expository "school" of preaching, human preaching is the word of God because it expounds the message of the written word of God; and for Peter Adam, human preaching is not the word of God, but it does convey God's message by the explanation and application of the written word of God.[7] At the end of this survey, I will conclude that each of these explanations has strengths, but ultimately fails in adequately explaining the phenomenon of preaching where human preaching *is* the word of God.

In chapter 10, I will begin by examining speech-act theory as initially developed by J. L. Austin and subsequently refined and systematized by his student, John Searle. Speech-act theory makes three important

---

7. Adam, *Speaking God's Words*, 118; Barth, *Church Dogmatics*, 1/1:124–27; Buttrick, "A Brief Theology of Preaching," 325; Runia, "What Is Preaching according to the New Testament?," 45; Thielicke, *The Evangelical Faith*, 3:94–95.

contributions: first, a speaker is not merely uttering sounds, words, or statements, but is performing an action, namely, a *speech act*; second, speech acts are composed of locution (the act *of* saying something), illocution (the act *in* saying something) and perlocution (the act performed *by* saying something); and third, speech acts require "constitutive rules" for them to *count as* an action. The recent application of speech-act theory in theological and biblical studies will then be surveyed. There is already much promise in the usefulness of speech-act theory in providing fresh insights in areas such as exegesis, hermeneutics, and the doctrine of Scripture. Finally, the tools of speech-act theory will be applied to our problem of the preached word as the word of God. In particular, I will explore the possibility of conceptualizing God as a divine speech agent, the proclaimer as a human speech agent, and the proclamation of the word of God as a speech act consisting of locutionary, illocutionary, and perlocutionary acts. I will then utilize speech-act theory to suggest "rules" or criteria for discerning if preaching is "happy" (to use the language of J. L. Austin)[8] or the "pure" preaching of the word (to use the language of the Reformers).

In chapter 11, I will summarize, refine, and synthesize the findings of the preceding chapters. The analysis of speech-act theory will help to conceptualize the preached gospel as the word of God where the gospel is a speech act, but re-performed by a preacher on behalf of God. Further speech-act theory will provide criteria for discerning what proclamation ought to be counted as a divine speech act. At the end of the discussion, my basic conclusion is *to preach the gospel as the word of God is to re-locute and re-illocute the divine speech act, the gospel, which itself was once locuted and illocuted by the prophets, Jesus, and the apostles, and which now continues to be locuted and illocuted in the canonical Scriptures.* A holistic understanding of preaching thus recognizes it as a speech act composed of its three aspects of locution, illocution, and perlocution—where God, through the Holy Spirit, is responsible for locution, illocution, and perlocution, and the preacher is responsible for locution and illocution.

In Part D, I will conclude this project. In the light of the findings in the previous chapters, speech-act theory will provide the following responses to our initial problem: first, we must recognize that there exists the real possibility that one might hear the word of God, albeit through a human preacher; second, the preacher's locution, that is p, should correspond with the p of the gospel message of Scripture; and third, the preacher's illocution, that is F, should correspond with the F of the gospel message of Scripture. If so, then that is sufficient to guarantee that the preached gospel is the word

---

8. Austin, *How to Do Things with Words*, 45.

of God. Fourth, an additional helpful criterion is if the preacher's intended perlocutionary effect corresponds with that of the gospel's, for this means that the preacher has secured illocutionary uptake and is re-illocuting the gospel with its original illocutionary force. Thus, my criteria are basically that the preacher re-locutes and re-illocutes the gospel with the same intended perlocutionary effect as that of the inscripturated gospel message, although the preacher is not responsible for the actual perlocutionary effect.

An appendix follows, which deals with the relationship between New Testament "prophecy" and preaching. In the history of Christian thought, various suggestions regarding this relationship have included prophecy as identical to preaching, prophecy as revelation, and Grudem's recent suggestion that prophecy is revelatory but under the authority of the Bible.[9] My assessment will be that prophecy is a broad and elastic term that might denote any revelatory message, but in the Pauline usage it usually refers to preaching. Thus, the referent of "prophecy" is often preaching, but it is certainly not exhausted by it.

At the end of this book, the hope is that we will have an adequate conceptualization of preaching as the word of God that will answer a theological problem raised by the Reformers. Accordingly, the end result should grant legitimacy to the Reformation and its foundation of the church upon the preached word, suggest criteria for the discernment of the preached word, and also open up fruitful lines of research for the future.

---

9. Grudem, *The Gift of Prophecy in 1 Corinthians*.

PART A

The Problem of the Reformers
When Is Preaching the Word of God?

Martin Luther and John Calvin both held exalted views of preaching. They identified preaching as no less than the word of God being proclaimed by a human preacher. In hearing the word proclaimed, one heard the "voice of God" speaking, albeit from human lips. In correspondence with such a high view of preaching, Luther and Calvin also identified "the word of God preached" as one of the marks of the true Christian church. For they believed that the church should be founded upon God's word, which does not return empty. Thus, they founded their church upon the apostolic *kerygma* rather than apostolic succession. But this move depends upon the underlying assumption that the preached word can be identified as the word of God. That is, the proclaimed word *is* the word of God. But have Luther and Calvin too readily made this equation? This introduces our problem: when is preaching the word of God?

2

Luther and Calvin

Preaching as the Word of God

Martin Luther (1483–1546) and John Calvin (1509–1564) both held high views of preaching. They readily identified the preached word as the word of God; both claimed that one could hear God speak his words through the proclamation of a human preacher. This claim was consistent with their understanding of the source, content, and purpose of the preached word. The source of the preached word is a human preacher sent by God to represent God and speak on God's behalf. The content of the preached word is the Christocentric message of the gospel, to which the term "the word" refers. This gospel is also inscripturated as the written word, which testifies to Christ; and thus the preached word is to conform to the written word. The purpose of the preached word is to achieve God's purposes of salvation and building up of his church, and this is achieved by the hidden illuminating work of the Holy Spirit in conjunction with human preaching. In this chapter, I will examine in more detail the views of Luther and Calvin regarding preaching and its relationship with the word of God.

Introduction

Martin Luther and John Calvin were both prolific preachers whose preaching shaped the course of Reformation history.[1] From 1510 onwards, Luther would preach two to three times a week to his congregation at Wittenburg, although it was not unusual for him to preach up to four times a week. On special occasions, such as Passion Week and Easter Week, he might preach up to eighteen times on eleven consecutive days.[2] Luther's output

---

1. For good discussions of this see Ferry, "Martin Luther on Preaching," 265–80; Sparn, "Preaching and the Course of the Reformation," 173–83.

2. Wood, "Luther as a Preacher," 111.

of sermons was remarkable. For example, the Weimar edition of Luther's works preserves approximately 2300 of Luther's sermons.[3] Luther ended his ministry as he began it—from a pulpit—for he preached his last sermon only four days before his death.[4]

The legacy of Luther's preaching lives on even today. It was Luther who made the sermon the centerpiece of the Protestant Christian church service. As Alfred Ernest Garvie observes, "It was [Luther] who put the sermon in Protestantism in the place held by the mass in Roman Catholicism; and made preaching the most potent influence in the churches of the Reformation."[5] Indeed, Luther's preaching shaped not only the form of the church service, it shaped the history of the church. Luther's preaching became the spearhead of the Reformation; what was later printed and read in the rest of Europe was originally preached from a pulpit in Wittenburg.[6]

Luther is remembered as first and foremost a preacher. As Luther himself notes:

> I simply taught, preached, wrote God's Word; otherwise I did nothing. And then while I slept, or drank Wittenberg beer with my Philip [Melanchthon] and with [Nicholas] Amsdorf, the Word so greatly weakened the papacy, that never a prince or emperor inflicted such damage upon it. I did nothing; the Word did it all . . . I did nothing; I left it to the Word.[7]

In 1547, one year after Luther's death, Lucas Cranach the Elder painted a panel of Luther preaching the word, which formed part of the well-known altar-piece at St Mary's, the City Church of Wittenburg. Cranach depicts Luther on a pulpit preaching to the congregation before him, with his left hand resting upon the open Bible, and his right hand pointing to a larger-than-life crucifix.[8] This is Luther, the preacher of the word.

Calvin was an equally prolific preacher. It was not uncommon for Calvin to preach regularly on weekdays and twice on each Sunday. It is estimated that Calvin preached 4,000 sermons to his congregation in Geneva; in the final fifteen years of his life, he preached over 2,000 sermons on the Old

---

3. Pless, "Martin Luther: Preacher of the Cross," 88.

4. Wood, "Luther as a Preacher," 111.

5. Garvie, *The Christian Preacher*, 130.

6. Wood, "Luther as a Preacher," 111.

7. Luther, "The Eight Wittenberg Sermons (1522)," 399–400.

8. As described by Brooks, "Luther the Preacher," 37; Pless, "Martin Luther: Preacher of the Cross," 83. A picture of this may also be found in Lose, "Luther and the Evangelical Clarity of Scripture and Sermon," 33.

Testament.⁹ Calvin also made preaching the centerpiece of the Protestant Christian church service. In a typical church service, the sermon occupied about three-quarters of the time.¹⁰

This exalted view of preaching, which was held by the Reformers Luther and Calvin,¹¹ not only shaped the form of Christian church services and the course of church history, but it continues to shape our theology of preaching and the church today. In the light of this lasting legacy of Luther and Calvin, the aim in this chapter is to explore their views on preaching and the word of God, and in the next chapter, their views on preaching as a mark of the church.

Martin Luther on Preaching

Martin Luther held an exalted view of preaching. He regarded it as no less than the voice of God speaking his word. In his comments on Malachi 2:7, which states, "For the lips of a priest guard knowledge," Luther notes:

> The Word is the channel through which the Holy Spirit is given. This is a passage against those who hold the spoken Word in contempt. The lips are the public reservoirs of the church. In them alone is kept the Word of God. You see, unless the Word is preached publicly, it slips away. The more it is preached, the more firmly it is retained. Reading it is not as profitable as hearing it, for the live voice teaches, exhorts, defends, and resists the spirit of error. Satan does not care a hoot for the written Word of God, but he flees at the speaking of the Word.¹²

Thus, for Luther, although the preacher preaches through human lips, the proclaimed words are really God's own words.¹³ The proclaimed word *is* the word of God. But why should this be? How can human words be divine

---

9. Anderson, "John Calvin: Biblical Preacher (1539–1564)," 173; Piper, "The Divine Majesty of the Word," 10; Pless, "Martin Luther: Preacher of the Cross," 173; van der Walt, "Calvin on Preaching," 326.

10. van der Walt, "Calvin on Preaching," 326.

11. A good overview of the preaching methods and styles of the Reformers, such as Martin Luther, John Calvin, Ulrich Zwingli, John Knox, and Hugh Latimer is found in Garvie, *The Christian Preacher*, 127–46.

12. *LW* 18:401.

13. When Luther himself preached, he often put words into God's mouth, as if God were directly speaking the words to the congregation. See Baue, "Luther on Preaching as Explanation and Exclamation," 412–13.

words? Luther's understanding of preaching and the word of God will now be explored in more detail.

The Content of Preaching

What is the content of preaching that is the proclaimed word of God? For Luther, the word of God is proclaimed when the message of the gospel is proclaimed. For example, in his lectures on Romans, Luther comments on Romans 1:3–4:

> When, therefore, the apostle [Paul] says of a certain brother: "whose praise is in the gospel through all the churches," this is not necessarily to be understood to refer to the Gospel of Luke but, rather, to the fact that it was his praise and distinction that he could teach the gospel, i.e., the word of God. So also Apollos and others had similar praise because they know how to preach Christ well and richly.
>
> Also the passage which says: "according to my gospel" (Rom. 2:16) does not need to be interpreted with reference to the Gospel of Luke, as if Luke had written down what Paul preached or as if what the former had written down the latter had preached. But he says "my" gospel because he himself preached the word of God "concerning his Son," as the passage we are dealing with puts it.[14]

Thus, Luther identifies Paul's "gospel," not with the written Gospel of Luke, but as the preached "word of God." And in his "Treatise on Good Works," Luther writes:

> But if the Gospel should be stirred up and be heard again, without doubt the whole world would be aroused and moved, and the greater portion of the kings, princes, bishops, doctors and clergy, and all that is great, would oppose it and rage against it, as has always happened when the Word of God has come to light; for the world cannot endure what comes from God.[15]

Here Luther uses the terms "gospel" and "word of God" synonymously. Similarly, in his commentary on 1 Peter, Luther writes regarding 1 Peter 1:23: "God lets the word, the Gospel, be scattered abroad."[16] In his comments on 2 Peter 1:16–18, Luther writes: "Therefore one concludes from

---

14. Luther, *Luther: Lectures on Romans*, 15.
15. Luther, "Treatise on Good Works (1520)," 283.
16. Luther, *Commentary on the Epistles of Peter and Jude*, 75–76.

this that the Apostles had assurance from God that their Gospel was God's word."[17] And, in his comments on 2 Peter 1:19, Luther writes: "This is God's word, even the Gospel: that we are ransomed by Christ from death, sin and hell."[18] Thus, Luther equates the "word of God" with the "gospel," and uses the terms "word" and "gospel" synonymously to refer to the message of the gospel.

Thus, in order for a preacher to preach the word of God, the message of the gospel must be preached. For example, in 1526, Luther presents his principles for "The German Mass and Order of Service," where he states that "the chief and greatest aim of any Service is to preach and teach God's Word"[19] and then proceeds to provide guidelines to ensure that the "gospel" is always preached in a church service:

> I think it would be best to direct that the sermon for the day, in whole or in part, should be read for the people out of the book, not only for the sake of the preachers who could not do any better, but also to prevent the rise of enthusiasts and sects . . . For unless spiritual knowledge and the Spirit Himself speak through the preachers (whom I do not wish hereby to limit, for the Spirit teaches better how to preach than all the postils and homilies), the final result will be that everyone preaches his own whims and instead of the Gospel and its exposition we shall again have sermons on blue ducks. This is one of the reasons why we retain the Epistles and Gospels as they are given in the postils, there are so few gifted preachers who are able to give a powerful and practical exposition of a whole evangelist or some other book of the Bible.[20]

Thus, the ideal situation for Luther would be for a gifted preacher to give a "powerful and practical exposition of a whole evangelist or some other book of the Bible," to ensure the preaching and teaching of God's word. However, if such gifted preachers are not available, Luther would prefer that a sermon be read from a book, which presents the gospel clearly, rather than have preachers who are not gifted or "enthusiasts" preaching "sermons on blue ducks." Similarly, it is not sufficient to preach only morals and fables. For example, in a sermon preached at Erfurt, in 1521, Luther complains:

> In Germany, there may be altogether perhaps three thousand pastors, but not four men of the right sort—God have mercy

---

17. Ibid., 251.
18. Ibid., 254.
19. Luther, "The German Mass and Order of Service (1526)," 176.
20. Ibid., 180.

on us in this woeful state of affairs! As soon as a good preacher appears, he deals briefly with the gospel and then follows it up with a fable of the old ass or a story about Dietrich of Bern. Or else, he dabbles in the pagan teachers, Aristotle, Plato, Socrates, and others, who are all quite contrary to the gospel. They are also contrary to God, for they have no knowledge of the light we possess.[21]

Thus, a preacher must preach the gospel, for to preach the gospel is to preach the word of God; in contrast, to talk about fables, stories, and pagan philosophers is simply to expound human wisdom but not to preach the word of God.

But what is this "gospel," that is to be preached and equated with the word of God? In his treatise "The Freedom of a Christian," Luther answers:

> You may ask, however: "What then is that word which gives such signal grace, and how shall I use it?" The answer is: It is nothing else than the message proclaimed by Jesus, as contained in the gospels; and this should be, and, in fact, is, so presented that you hear your God speak to you. It shows how all your life and labour are as nothing in God's sight, and how you and all that is in you, must eternally perish. If you truly believe this, and that you are indeed guilty, you necessarily despair of yourself; you believe that Hosea was right when he said: "O Israel, there is nought in you except your corruption, but in Me is your help." In order that you may come out of yourself and flee from yourself, i.e., escape your corruption, He sets you face to face with His beloved Son, Jesus Christ, and says to you by means of His living and comforting word: "You should surrender yourself to Him with firm faith, and trust Him gladly." Then, for your faith's sake, all your sins shall be forgiven and all your wickedness overcome. You yourself will be righteous, upright, serene, and devout. You will fulfil all commands, and be free from all things, as St. Paul says in Romans 1: "A justified Christian lives only by his faith"; and in Romans 10: "Christ is the end of the fulfilment of all commandments for them that believe in him."[22]

And similarly, in his comments on 1 Peter 1:25, Luther summarizes: "As, when I hear that Jesus Christ died to take away my sins, and has purchased heaven for me, and bestows upon me all he has, then I hear the

---

21. Luther, "Three Sermons Preached after the Summons to Worms," 113.
22. Luther, "The Freedom of a Christian," 359.

Gospel."[23] Therefore, for Luther, the "Gospel" is the message that the hearer is a sinner; but God offers salvation through his son, Jesus Christ; if the hearer responds in faith, there is forgiveness and freedom; and the redeemed believer then lives an "upright" and "devout" life, fulfilling all commands. And if one hears this gospel presented in this way, then one "hear[s] your God speak to you."

And, for Luther, the *whole* gospel must be preached; all components of the gospel must be preached. One must preach both God's wrath as well as God's mercy; and both the "law" and "grace" components. In an open letter, Luther writes:

> If we are to preach God's Word, we must preach the word that declares His wrath, as well as that which declares His mercy; we must preach of hell as well as of heaven, and help extend God's Word and judgment and work over both the righteous and the wicked, so that the wicked may be punished and the good protected.[24]

And similarly, in a response to "Goat Emser of Leipzig,"[25] Luther writes:

> It is indeed true that where only the law is preached and the letter insisted on, as in the Old Testament, and this is not followed by the preaching of the Spirit, there can be only death without life, sin without grace, anguish without comfort. Such preaching produces wretched and captive consciences, and makes men finally despair and die in their sins, and, through this preaching, be eternally damned.[26]

Thus, the gospel in its entirety must by preached. Similarly, in his treatise on "The Freedom of a Christian," Luther writes:

> [I]t is not enough just to take the life and work of Christ, and, in preaching, merely tell the story and the chronicle of events. It is even worse to pass over these altogether, and preach about ecclesiastical law or other man-made rules and doctrines. There are also many who preach and understand Christ as if they

---

23. Luther, *Commentary on the Epistles of Peter and Jude*, 77.

24. Luther, "An Open Letter Concerning the Hard Book against the Peasants (1525)," 262.

25. Jerome Emser's coat of arms displayed a goat; Emser had written a treatise against Luther, titled "Against the Unchristian Book of the Augustinian Monk Martin Luther Addressed to the German Nobility," in 1521, and placed the warning on his own title page: "Beware, the Goat will butt you."

26. Luther, "Answer to the Superchristian, Superspiritual, and Superlearned Book of Goat Emser (1521)," 359.

rather pitied Him, and were angry with the Jews; they carry on in some other childish manner ... [Instead, Christ should be preached so that] a proper explanation is given of that Christian freedom which we have from Him: how we are kings and priests with power over all things; and how everything we do is well-pleasing to and granted by God, as I have already said.[27]

Therefore, when the gospel is preached, it is preached so that a "proper explanation is given of that Christian freedom which we have from Him." Therefore, it would be inadequate if the preacher were merely to recount the story or list the events of Jesus' life; motivate the hearers to pity or anger; or teach regulations and "good deeds," or "ecclesiastical law or other man-made rules and doctrines."

In fact, for Luther, this is a criterion for how one judges whether or not the word of God is being preached—namely, that the preacher is accurately preaching the whole gospel message of Christ for the purpose of faith and repentance. In his comments on 1 Peter 4:11, Luther writes:

> Therefore whoever is now called to speak in the Church, to preach, teach and exhort, should speak what Christ has spoken and commanded on subjects relating to our personal salvation. But Christ speaks thus on this point: That he is the good Shepherd, who gives life for the sheep, who gives unto them eternal life; likewise, if any man will keep his Word, he shall never see death. He is the resurrection, and the life, whosoever believes on him though he die, yet shall he live. He is the way, the truth and the life; so that no one can come to the Father, except through him. To the Apostles however he says in Mat. 28:20: They shall teach all nations to observe all things whatsoever he commanded them; as Luke says: To preach repentance and forgiveness of sins in his name; and Mark: Whoever believes and is baptized shall be saved. Wherever this doctrine goes, there both preacher and hearer are sure, that the former speak the Word of God and that the latter hear the Word. For Christ's sheep hear his voice, and it is done unto them according to his Word.[28]

Conversely, if a preacher's message is different than the gospel, then one can confidently assert that the word of God has not been preached. For example, Luther continues:

> But is the doctrine [sic] different and even proposes another way by which to be delivered from sin than through Christ, the

---

27. Luther, "The Freedom of a Christian," 367–68.
28. Luther, *Commentary on the Epistles of Peter and Jude*, 192.

falsity of it appears at once. For such teachers do not speak the word of God, and the hearers do not hear it; hence theirs is not the true faith, and they can not be delivered from their sin, nor be saved, etc.[29]

Therefore, for Luther, an important criterion for assessing if the word of God is being preached is whether or not the preacher is accurately proclaiming the true message of the gospel.

But why should Luther so readily identify the preached gospel as the preached word of God? For Luther, the gospel is the word of God for several reasons. First, the gospel is what Christ himself proclaimed; therefore, to preach what Christ proclaimed is to preach the word of God. This is something that Luther consistently writes. For example, in his comments on 2 Peter 1:16–18, Luther writes:

> [T]he Gospel is nothing else than the preaching of Christ. Therefore we should hear no other preaching, for none other pleases the Father. "This is my beloved Son," he says; "hear ye him," he is your Doctor or Teacher; as though he had said: When ye hear him, then ye have heard me.[30]

Similarly, in the treatise on the "Freedom of a Christian," Luther writes:

> The only means, whether in heaven or on earth, whereby the soul can live, and be religious, free, and Christian, is the holy Gospel, the word of God preached by Christ. He Himself says in John 11, "I am the resurrection and the life. He that believeth in Me shall live eternally"; and John 14, "I am the way, the truth and the life"; and Matthew 4, "Man does not live by bread alone, but by every word that proceeds out of the mouth of God." . . . Christ came for no other object than to preach the word of God . . .
>
> You may ask, however: "What then is that word which gives such signal grace, and how shall I use it?" The answer is: It is nothing else than the message proclaimed by Jesus, as contained in the gospel . . .[31]

Thus, the gospel is the word of God, precisely because it is the word that was proclaimed by Christ himself, the Son of God.

Second, the gospel is the word of God because it is the message that Christ commissioned his disciples, the apostles, to proclaim. For example, Luther writes:

29. Ibid.
30. Ibid., 251.
31. Luther, "The Freedom of a Christian," 358–59.

> In Mark, the last chapter, we read that He sent out the disciples to preach. Let us hear what command He gives them, and how He sets a limit to their teaching and bridles their tongues, saying, "Go ye into all the world, and preach the Gospel to every creature. He that believeth, shall be saved," etc., Mark xvi, 15. he does not say, Go and preach what you will, or what you think to be good; but He puts His own word into their mouth, and bids them preach the Gospel.
>
> In Matthew, the last chapter, He says, "Go and make disciples of all nations, baptise them in the Name of the Father and of the Son and of the Holy Ghost; and teach them to observe all things which I have commanded you." Here, again, He does not say, Teach them to observe what you devise, but what I have commanded you. Therefore the pope and his bishops and teachers must be wolves and the apostles of the devil; it cannot be otherwise, for they teach not the commands of Christ, but their own words.[32]

And similarly, it is the message that the Old Testament prophets were called to proclaim. For example, in his comments on Romans 10:15, Luther notes:

> In chapter 1:2 the Apostle [Paul] emphasizes very strongly that the Gospel did not come into the world through any single person. It was promised long before it appeared; it is therefore not a figment of modern times. It came through many prophets of God, and indeed not only through the Word that was preached, but also through that which is in Holy Scripture.[33]

The gospel is the word of God because it is the message of God's messengers—both the Old Testament prophets and the New Testament apostles. Therefore, to preach the gospel is to preach God's own divinely commissioned message.

Third, the gospel is the word of God because it is the message about Christ. In his comments on Romans 16:25, Luther summarizes the gospel message as "the proclamation of Christ":

> By "mystery" the Apostle [Paul] here understands the mystery of Christ's incarnation. The Gospel is nothing else than the proclamation of Christ. So he himself writes in 1:1–4: "Separated unto the gospel of God . . . concerning his Son Jesus Christ our Lord, which was made of the seed of David according to the flesh; and

---

32. Luther, "That Doctrines of Men Are To Be Rejected (1522)," 449.
33. Luther, *Commentary on the Epistle to the Romans*, 133–34.

declared to be the Son of God with power, according to the spirit of holiness, by the resurrection of the dead."[34]

Therefore, if a preacher is to preach the word of God, the preacher must preach Christ. For example, Luther writes:

> Give Thy grace to all preachers, that they may preach Thy Word and Christ, to profit and salvation, in all the world. Help all who hear the preaching of Thy Word to learn Christ, and honestly to better their lives thereby. Graciously drive out of the Holy Church all strange preaching and teaching from which men do not learn Christ.[35]

And similarly, in his treatise against "Goat Emser," Luther writes:

> For the preaching of the New Testament is naught else but an offering and presentation of Christ to all men out of the pure mercy of God, in such wise [sic] that all who believe in Him receive God's grace and the Holy Spirit, by which all sin is forgiven, all law is fulfilled, they become God's children, and have eternal salvation.[36]

Thus, for Luther, to preach Christ is what it means to be a "prophet" in the New Testament age. For example, in his comments on 2 Peter 1:19, Luther writes:

> I hold indeed that we will have no more prophets, such as the Jews had in former times under the Old Testament. But a prophet eminently should he be [sic] who preaches Jesus Christ. Therefore, although many prophets in the Old Testament have foretold things to come, yet they came and were sent by God for this reason especially, that they should foretell of Christ. Those then who believe on Christ are all prophets, for they have the true central article of faith that the prophets had, although they have not the gift to foretell things to come; for as we, through the faith of our Master, are Christ's brethren, are kings and priests, so are we all through Christ also prophets. For we can all decide as to what belongs to salvation and God's honor and to a Christian life, besides we know as much of future things as is necessary for us to know, viz., that the day of judgment shall come,

---

34. Ibid., 207.

35. Luther, "A Brief Explanation of the Ten Commandments, the Creed, and the Lord's Prayer (1520)," 380.

36. Luther, "Answer to the Superchristian, Superspiritual, and Superlearned Book," 355.

and that we shall rise from the dead; besides, we understand the whole Scriptures. Of this Paul also speaks in 1 Cor. 14:31: "Ye can all prophesy, one by one." [37]

But why should the preaching of Christ be equated with the word of God? Because Christ himself is the embodiment of the message from God; he is the Word incarnate. For example, in his comments on Romans 1:1, Luther writes:

> In ancient times the prophets felt the greatest fear when they received a message from God or an angel. Even Moses could hardly endure this great terror. Since the Word had not yet become flesh, they could not understand it because of its abounding glory and their own great weakness. But now, after the Word has been made flesh, it has become very captivating and is imparted to us through men of our own flesh and blood. That, however, does not mean that we should love it less and treat it with less reverence. It is the same Word as before, even though it does not come to us with terror, but with winning love. Those who do not want to love and honor it now, must at last endure all the more anguish.[38]

Thus, the gospel is the word of God because it is God's message about Christ, as received "in ancient times" by the prophets, but now is "made flesh" in Christ himself as the incarnate "Word." Therefore, to preach about Christ, whilst urging hearers to faith and repentance, is to preach the word of God.

Fourth, the gospel is the word of God because the Holy Spirit speaks through the human proclamation of the gospel. In his comments on 1 Peter 1:12, Luther writes:

> How has grace come to us? "Through those who have preached the Gospel of Christ unto you," they had a good and faithful teacher, who taught it to them, namely, the Holy Ghost, whom Christ sent from heaven; he opened their minds to understand the holy Scriptures and to be able to minister to others through sermons and the Scriptures.[39]

Therefore, the Holy Spirit is integral to the ministry of the proclamation of the gospel. The Spirit is the "teacher" who teaches those who proclaim the "Gospel of Christ," by "open[ing] their minds to understand the

---

37. Luther, *Commentary on the Epistles of Peter and Jude*, 253.
38. Luther, *Commentary on the Epistle to the Romans*, 17.
39. Luther, *Commentary on the Epistles of Peter and Jude*, 53.

holy Scriptures" and gifting them to "minister to others through sermons and the Scriptures." Thus, the gospel is the word of God because it is the word that is taught and illuminated by the Holy Spirit.

Therefore, the proclamation of the gospel is to be equated with the proclaimed word of God because it is the same message as that proclaimed by Christ during his earthly ministry; it is the message proclaimed by God's commissioned messengers, namely, the Old Testament prophets and the New Testament apostles; it is the message about Christ, who is the incarnate Word; and it is the message taught and preached through the ministry of the Holy Spirit. As Luther himself summarizes:

> "What then is that word which gives such signal grace, and how shall I use it?" The answer is: It is nothing else than the message proclaimed by Jesus, as contained in the gospel; and this should be, and, in fact, is, so presented that you hear your God speak to you.[40]

And, for Luther, this itself becomes an important criterion for determining whether or not the word of God is being preached.

The Preached Word and the Written Word

There is a relationship between the preached word and the written word. For both proclaim the same God-commissioned, Holy-Spirit-authored, christological message. In his comments on Romans 1:2, Luther writes:

> This eternal promise was made known by the prophets in time and in human speech. It is indeed a wonderful proof of God's grace that He published this eternal promise in human words and that not merely orally, but also in writing.[41]

Thus, the gospel—the "eternal promise"—was originally proclaimed by the prophets, but then preserved in writing, in the Scriptures. As Luther elaborates in his lectures on Romans, "[The Gospel] came into the world . . . by the prophets of God and not only in form of the spoken word but also in form of the Holy Scriptures."[42] Therefore, if a preacher is to proclaim the word of God, then the preacher's message should be that of the gospel, as originally proclaimed by the Old Testament prophets and New Testament

---

40. Luther, "The Freedom of a Christian," 359.
41. Luther, *Commentary on the Epistle to the Romans*, 19.
42. Luther, *Luther: Lectures on Romans*, 297.

apostles, and now inscripturated in the Scriptures, the written word. As David J. Lose notes:

> Luther perceives that the link between Scripture and sermon rests in the unity and clarity of their gospel content, that is, the proclamation and promise of God's saving activity in Christ. The difference between the two is simply a matter of their temporal modality. The Bible bears witness to the promise and good news of God's work in Christ in the past. The sermon proclaims the promise and good news of God's ongoing and immediate work in Christ in the present ... Put most simply, preaching actualizes the Gospel that originally occasioned the Scriptures, while the Scriptures contain the Gospel that shapes and norms all preaching.[43]

For Luther, then, preaching was the expounding of this gospel message of Scripture. Preaching could not and should not deviate from this message. As Arthur Skevington Wood notes, "What strikes us most of all is the strict *Subjection* [his emphasis] of Luther's sermons to the Scripture, and the sole object of Scripture, namely, Jesus Christ ... He is bound by the Word. His preaching is never merely topical."[44] And because Luther was committed also to the clarity of Scripture, he was also committed to the clarity of preaching, for preaching should reflect this clarity of Scripture.[45] In an excerpt from his *Table Talks*, Luther comments, "In my preaching I take pains to treat a verse [of the Scriptures], to stick to it, and so to instruct the people that they can say, 'That's what the sermon was about.'"[46]

As a result, the written word is a necessary accompaniment to the preached word. The preacher relies on the Bible as the source of the apostolic message. For this reason, Luther encourages preachers to "keep to the text" of Scripture:

> Let him take care to keep to the text and attend to what is before him and make people understand that. Those preachers who say whatever comes into their mouths remind me of a maid going to market. When she meets another maid she stops and chats a while, then she meets another and talks with her, too, and then a third and a fourth, and so gets to market very slowly. So with

---

43. Lose, "Luther and the Evangelical Clarity of Scripture and Sermon," 34.

44. Wood, "Luther as a Preacher," 115.

45. And not just the clarity of Scripture but also the evangelical clarity of Scripture. For a further discussion of this, see Lose, "Luther and the Evangelical Clarity of Scripture and Sermon," 32–35.

46. *Table-Talk* no. 1650, in *LW* 54:160.

preachers who wander off the text; they would like to say everything at one time, but they can't.⁴⁷

And Luther requires that preachers support their message with appropriate references to Scripture:

> A preacher should be a logician and a rhetorician, that is, he must be able to teach, and to admonish; when he preaches touching an article, he must, first, distinguish it. Secondly, he must define, describe, and show what it is. Thirdly, he must produce sentences out of the Scriptures, therewith to prove and strengthen it. Fourthly, he must, with examples, explain and declare it. Fifthly, he must adorn it with similitudes; and, lastly, he must admonish and rouse up the lazy, earnestly reprove all the disobedient, all false doctrine, and the authors thereof; yet, not out of malice and envy, but only to God's honor, and the profit and saving health of the people.⁴⁸

Moreover, a criterion for true preaching, as opposed to heretical preaching, is that the preacher is able to corroborate the proclaimed message with the prophetic and apostolic message of Scripture:

> A heretic must present this kind of testimony for his heretical doctrine. He must also show where it was promised earlier and by whom, and then also by whom it was taught, and, finally, in what Scriptures it is to be found so as to produce also writings as witnesses.⁴⁹

Therefore, the relationship between the proclaimed word and the written word is one of continuity. The message is the same, that is, the gospel; and the written word corroborates and gives authority and authenticity to the proclaimed word.

The Preacher

Martin Luther places an emphasis upon the calling, gifting, and ordination of the preacher. According to Luther, the preacher is someone specifically called and sent by God. In his lectures on Romans, Luther comments on Romans 10:13–15:

---

47. In *Conversations with Luther*, as quoted in Luther, *A Compend of Luther's Theology*, 147–48. Also, *Table-Talk*, no. 5489, in *LW* 54:428.

48. *Table-Talk of Martin Luther*, no. 419, pp. 232–33.

49. Luther, *Luther: Lectures on Romans*, 297.

> [O]ne cannot preach if one is not sent ... The whole source and origin of salvation, therefore, is in God's sending. If he does not send them, the preachers preach falsely, and such preaching is the same as no preaching; indeed, it would be better for them not to preach at all ... Since preachers of this kind do not preach, the hearers do not believe, those who invoke God do not call upon him, and those who are to be saved are damned ... Why? Because they are not from God.[50]

But how can it be discerned if a preacher has been sent from God? Luther answers:

> We can recognize this if he proves by miracles and a testimony from heaven that he was sent (as the apostles were) or if he proves that later he is sent by apostolic authority confirmed from above and that he preaches in humble submission to this authority, always ready to stand under its judgment and to speak only what is commanded to him and not what he likes or has invented ... This is the very sharp spear by which the heretics will be pierced. For they preach without the testimony of God or without divinely confirmed authority, but from their own initiative, and they are elevated to their position by a semblance of religiousness.[51]

Therefore, one important criterion is that the preacher's message is the same message of the apostles, for the preacher "preaches in humble submission to [apostolic] authority." This is verified by the message being in line with the testimony of the Old Testament prophets and New Testament apostles:

> This is what the apostle [Paul] emphasizes so strongly in Rom. 1:2, lest one think that the gospel came into the world through a man. First, it was promised long before it came; it was no new invention. Furthermore, it came into the world not by one but by many, by the prophets of God and not only in form of the spoken word but also in form of the Holy Scriptures. A heretic must present this kind of testimony for his heretical doctrine. He must also show where it was promised earlier and by whom, and then also by whom it was taught, and, finally, in what Scriptures it is to be found so as to produce also writings as witnesses.[52]

---

50. Ibid., 296.
51. Ibid., 297.
52. Ibid.

Thus, the preacher sent by God does not preach an innovative message, but the same message of the prophets and apostles, as found in the "Holy Scriptures." Another criterion is that the gospel has taken effect in the life of the preacher:

> Hence, it is an infallible sign that one really has the word of God and that he carries it in his heart if he is not satisfied but only dissatisfied with himself and if he is troubled in all he knows, says, does, and suffers, finding pleasure only in others or in God.
>
> Conversely, it is a most evident sign that the word of God is not in one if he is satisfied with himself and rejoices in what he says, knows, does, and suffers, as if he had produced it all.[53]

Thus, the true preacher, sent by God with the word, also understands the humbling grace of the gospel. Conversely, a preacher who has not been sent by God, who does not preach the apostolic message, and takes pride in his or her own message, is a false preacher.

Having been sent by God, the preacher is also someone who has also been ordained by the congregation. In fact, this is the primary purpose of ordination, namely, that someone preaches the word to the congregation. For example, in his comments on Romans 1:5, Luther states, "In the Church of Christ no minister is ordained for his own sake, but on account of others, namely, to make them such as obey the Gospel."[54] And in "Freedom of a Christian," Luther writes, "Moreover all apostles, bishops, priests, and the whole clergy, were called and instituted only for the sake of the word."[55]

Although all Christians are "priests," there is an "office" of "priesthood" for those whose specific gifting and duty is that of preaching the word. In the "Freedom of the Christian," Luther writes:

> Should you ask: "What is the difference between the priests and the laity in Christian standing, if all are priests?" the answer is that spiritual mischief and other wrongs have been done to the little words "priest" or "pastor". These words have been taken away from the community in general and handed over to those little communities which we now call "the clergy". The Holy Scriptures make no distinction beyond calling the instructed or the consecrated, *ministros, servos, œconomos*, i.e., helpers, servants, stewards, whose duty is to preach Christ, and faith,

---

53. Ibid., 298.
54. Luther, *Commentary on the Epistle to the Romans*, 21.
55. Luther, "The Freedom of a Christian," 359.

and Christian freedom to others. For although we are all equally priests, still not all of us can serve and minister and preach.[56]

Similarly, in his treatise on the "Pagan Servitude of the Church," Luther writes:

> Now we, who have been baptized, are all uniformly priests in virtue of that very fact. The only addition received by the priests is the office of preaching, and even this with our consent. If the Romanists had to grant this point, they would have to admit that they had no right to lord it over us, except in so far as we, of our own free will, allowed them to do so. Thus it says in 1 Peter 2, "Ye are an elect race, a royal priesthood, and a priestly kingdom." It follows that all of us who are Christian are also priests. Those whom we call priests are really ministers of the word and chosen by us; they fulfil their entire office in our name. The priesthood is simply the ministry of the word. So in 1 Corinthians 4 it says: "Let a man so account of us as of ministers of Christ and stewards of the mysteries of God."
>
> That being the case, it follows (i) that any one who has been called by the church to preach the Word, but does not preach it, is in no way a priest; and (ii) that the sacrament of ordination cannot be other than the rite by which the church chooses its preacher. That is how Malachi 2 defines a priest: "The priest's lips should keep knowledge, and they should seek the law at his mouth; for he is the messenger of the Lord of Hosts." Be assured that anyone who is not a messenger of the Lord of Hosts, or any one who is called to do something other than be such a messenger is, if I may say so, by no means a priest.[57]

Therefore, Luther carefully distinguishes between the Christian "laity" and the so-called "priests" or "pastors" who are those officially recognized by the congregation to fulfill the ministry or office of preaching the word.

Indeed, only those who are recognized to be gifted should preach the word. In an "Exposition of the Eighty-Second Psalm," Luther comments:

> It is true that all Christians are priests, but all are not pastors. For to be a pastor, one must not only be a Christian and a priest, but must have an office and a field of work committed to him. This call and command make pastors and preachers. A burgher or layman may be a learned man, but this does not make him

---

56. Ibid., 367.
57. Luther, "The Pagan Servitude of the Church," 314.

a Doctor, and entitle him to teach publicly in the schools, or to assume the teaching-office, unless he is called to it.[58]

As Patrick Ferry notes, "Luther very much opposed preachers ascending the pulpit without proper authorization. He was most certainly an advocate of the doctrine of the priesthood of all believers, but Luther made a distinction in connection with the office of preaching."[59] Nonetheless, in exceptional cases, where there are no such ordained preachers, then all Christians are to heed the "call" to preach the gospel. For example, Luther writes to the congregation in Leisnig:

> Now you will say: "But, unless he has been called to do this, he dare not preach, as you yourself have repeatedly taught!" I reply: Here you must consider the Christian from a double point of view. On the one hand, when he is in a place where there are no Christians, he needs no other call than the fact that he is a Christian, inwardly called and anointed by God; he is bound by the duty of brotherly love to preach to the erring heathens or nonchristians and to teach them the Gospel, even though no one call him to this work ... But, on the other hand, when the Christian is in a place where there are Christians, who have the same power and right as he, he should not thrust himself forward, but should rather let himself be called and drawn forth to preach and teach in the stead and by the commission of the rest.[60]

Therefore, Luther recognizes that all Christians, as those called and anointed by the Spirit, have the capacity to preach the word; and all should preach the gospel in order that "heathens" hear and believe. However, there are certain Christians who are recognized by their congregation as particularly gifted to preach the word, and thus ordained to an office as a "priest" or "pastor." And it should be only such individuals who have the authority to preach the word to other Christians.

The Purpose of Preaching

For Luther, the preached word saves those who hear it and respond in faith and repentance. As Luther notes in his comments on Romans 1:16, "The

---

58. Luther, "An Exposition of the Eighty-Second Psalm (1530)," 313–14.

59. Ferry, "Martin Luther on Preaching," 269.

60. Luther, "The Right and Power of a Christian Congregation or Community to Judge (1523)," 80–81.

Gospel is a power which saves all who believe it, or, it is the Word which is powerful to rescue all who put their trust in it."[61] And in his commentary, Luther's heading for Romans 10:14–21 reads, "*Saving Faith Comes through the Preaching of the Divine Word.*"[62]

If so, then the purpose of preaching the word of God is that those who hear it might be saved. Thus, the preacher is to preach the word with the specific intent that the hearers respond with faith and obedience. Luther's comment in his treatise on "The Freedom of the Christian" is once again instructive:

> From all this we understand that it is not enough just to take the life and work of Christ, and, in preaching, merely tell the story and the chronicle of events. It is even worse to pass over these altogether, and preach about ecclesiastical law or other man-made rules and doctrines. There are also many who preach and understand Christ as if they rather pitied Him, and were angry with the Jews; they carry on in some other childish manner. But He should and must be preached in such a way that, in both you and me, faith grows out of, and is received from, the preaching. And that faith is received and grows when I am told why Christ came, how men can use and enjoy Him, and what He has brought and given me. This takes place whenever a proper explanation is given of that Christian freedom which we have from Him: how we are kings and priests with power over all things; and how everything we do is well-pleasing to and granted by God, as I have already said. For when our heart hears about Christ in this way, it must rejoice through and through. It yearns for Christ, receives consolation, and loves Him in return. Neither regulations nor good deeds can effect as much as that.[63]

Therefore, the intentionality of preaching is not merely to recount, inform, entertain, motivate, or evoke emotions, although these might be related outcomes, but it is to give a "proper explanation" of the gospel, so that "faith grows out of, and is received from, the preaching." The preacher has a responsibility to preach intentionally so that the hearer might believe and obey.

---

61. Luther, *Commentary on the Epistle to the Romans*, 23.
62. Ibid., 133.
63. Luther, "The Freedom of a Christian," 367–68.

The Holy Spirit and Preaching

Although it is a human who proclaims the word, it is God himself who speaks and saves through the proclaimed word. For example, in his comments on 1 Peter 1:25, Luther writes:

> The word is a divine and eternal power; for although the [human] voice or speech is soon gone, yet the substance remains; that is, the sense, the truth, which is conveyed by the voice. As when I put to my mouth a cup containing wine, I swallow the wine, although I do not thrust the cup down my throat.
>
> So likewise is the word which the voice conveys; it falls into our hearts and lives, while the voice remains without and passes away. Therefore it is indeed a divine power; yea, it is God himself. For thus he speaks to Moses, Ex. 4:12: "I will be with thy mouth;" and Ps. 81:10: 'Open they mouth wide, proclaim glad tidings; say thou art hungry, I will satisfy thee, I will presently speak to thee comforting things.'[64]

Thus, God speaks his word, through the instrument of human proclamation. In another sermon, Luther similarly preaches:

> His word should do the work alone, without our work. Why? Because it is not in my power to fashion the hearts of men as the potter moulds the clay, and to do with them as I please. I can get no farther than to men's ears; their hearts I cannot reach. And since I cannot pour faith into their hearts, I cannot, nor should I, force any one to have faith. That is God's work alone, who causes faith to live in the heart. Therefore we should give free course to the Word, and not add our works to it. We have the *jus verbi* [right to speak], but not the *executio* [power to do]; we should preach the Word, but the consequences must be left to God's own good pleasure.[65]

Therefore, according to Luther, it is God who speaks and works through the human proclamation of the word. The human only has the *jus verbi* but God has the *executio*. The human is obediently to preach the word, but it is God who controls the consequences according to "God's own good pleasure." Likewise, in another sermon, Luther preaches:

> And God commands this Word to be told you through men, and especially has he permitted it to be proclaimed and written for you by the Apostles; for St. Peter and St. Paul do not

---

64. Luther, *Commentary on the Epistles of Peter and Jude*, 77.
65. Luther, "The Eight Wittenberg Sermons (1522)," 397–98.

preach their own word, but God's Word, as Paul himself testifies in 1 Thess. 2:13: "When ye receive the Word of God which ye heard of us, ye received it not as the word of men, but as it is in truth, the Word of God, which effectually worketh also in you that believe." Surely, a person can preach the Word to me, but no one is able to put it into my heart except God alone, who must speak to the heart, or all is vain; for when he is silent, the Word is not spoken. Hence no one shall draw from the Word which God teaches me.[66]

Thus, it is God who sovereignly works through the proclaimed word. And unless God chooses to speak through the proclaimed word, then "the Word is not spoken." For only God can put the word into the "heart" of the hearer.

But how does God choose to work through the human proclamation of his word? This is the ministry of the Holy Spirit. For the Spirit uses the preached word to save the hearer. Luther expands upon this in his comments on 1 Peter 1:23:

> Through a seed are we born again ... But how does this take place? After this manner: God lets the word, the Gospel, be scattered abroad, and the seed falls in the hearts of men, and now wherever it sticks in the heart, the Holy Spirit is present, and makes a new man; then there will indeed be another man, of other thoughts, of other words and works. Thus you are entirely changed. All that you before avoided you now seek, and what you before sought that you now avoid. In respect to the birth of the body, it is a fact that when conception takes place the seed is changed, so that it is seed no longer. But this is a seed which cannot be changed; it remains forever. It changes me, so that I am transformed in it, and whatever is evil in me from my nature passes away. Therefore it is indeed a wonderful birth, and of extraordinary seed.[67]

Thus, the Holy Spirit uses the gospel to transform the hearer and give new birth. Similarly, Luther writes to "Goat Emser":

> Paul does not write one iota about these two senses, but declares that there are two kinds of preaching or ministries. One is that of the Old Testament, the other that of the New Testament. The Old Testament preaches the letter, the New Testament the spirit

---

66. From Luther's Gospel Sermon, Eighth Sunday after Trinity, as quoted in Luther, *A Compend of Luther's Theology*, 11–12.

67. Luther, *Commentary on the Epistles of Peter and Jude*, 75–76.

> ... We see clearly that St. Paul (2 Cor 3:3–6) speaks of two tables and two kinds of preaching. The tables of Moses were of stone, on which the law was inscribed by God's finger, Exodus xx. The tables of Christ, or the epistles of Christ, as he calls them here, are the hearts of Christians, in which are written, not letters as on Moses' tables, but the spirit of God, through the preaching of the Gospel and the ministry of the apostles. Now, just what does this mean? The letter is naught else but the divine law and commandment which is given in the Old Testament, through Moses ... But the spirit, which is divine grace, gives strength and power to the heart, yea, creates a new man, who grows to love God's commandments and does with joy all that he ought to do.[68]

According to Luther, the "spirit of God" uses the "preaching of the Gospel" to give "strength and power to the heart" and create a "new man, who grows to love God's commandments and does with joy all that he ought to do." Thus, although it is the human preacher who is to preach the word to the "ears" of the hearer, it is the Holy Spirit who speaks to the "heart."

Luther therefore begins to distinguish between "external" and "spiritual" (or internal) preaching. For example, in his comments on 1 Peter 3:19–22, an "obscure passage"[69] referring to Christ preaching to the spirits in prison, Luther comments:

> While the words only require that he be considered as speaking here of spiritual preaching, we may rest in the view, that Peter speaks of the office that Christ performs by means of external preaching. For he commanded the Apostles personally to preach the Gospel. But with the word preached he comes himself, and is spiritually present there, and speaks and preaches to the people in their hearts; just as the Apostles speak the word orally and in body to the ears, so he preaches to the spirits that lie captive in the prison-house of the devil. Therefore this also should be understood spiritually, like the preaching.[70]

Thus, human preachers, such as the apostles, "speak the word orally and in body to the ears," but it is Christ and the Spirit who preach "spiritually" to their "hearts."

---

68. Luther, "Answer to the Superchristian, Superspiritual, and Superlearned Book," 353–54.

69. Luther admits, "A wonderful text is this, and a more obscure passage perhaps than any other in the New Testament, so that I do not know for a certainty just what Peter means," in Luther, *Commentary on the Epistles of Peter and Jude*, 168.

70. Ibid., 169.

The Hearer and Preaching

On the part of the hearer, faith comes from hearing the proclaimed gospel. In his comments on Romans 10:16, Luther expands upon this:

> Verse 16 confirms also the words "How shall they believe in him of whom they have not heard?" (v. 14). He says: "Faith cometh by hearing" (v. 17). This means that unless they hear, they cannot believe. The verse moreover, confirms the statement: "How shall they hear without a preacher" (v. 14)? Hearing indeed comes only through the Word of Christ.[71]

But, at the same time, the word can only be "apprehended" by hearing it in faith. For Luther continues:

> Lastly, the verse (Romans 10:16) confirms the statement: "How beautiful are the feet of them that preach the gospel of peace" (v. 15). The Apostle here emphasizes the fact that he is speaking of a Word which no one can comprehend. It can be apprehended only by hearing it in true faith. At this Word the Jews were offended, for they sought signs and wonders.[72]

And Luther, in his comments on 1 Peter 1:25, will similarly note, "The word is quickly gone when one preaches it, but if it falls into the heart and is apprehended by faith, it can never pass away."[73] Thus, for Luther, faith comes from hearing the preached gospel, and the gospel is apprehended by faith, and the believer is saved and transformed.

Conversely, someone cannot be saved if they either do not hear the gospel proclaimed, or they hear it but fail to recognize it as the word of God speaking to them. For example, in his lectures on Romans 3:11, Luther writes:

> Therefore, they do not hear what God says nor know about it, but they think and assert that they have the word of God and demand to be listened to. This is how they go wrong in their heart and so, when they hear the voice of God, they harden their hearts as if it were not God's voice and as if it were not God speaking.[74]

---

71. Luther, *Commentary on the Epistle to the Romans*, 136.
72. Ibid.
73. Luther, *Commentary on the Epistles of Peter and Jude*, 77.
74. Luther, *Luther: Lectures on Romans*, 92.

Therefore, the hearer has the responsibility to hear and recognize the preached gospel as the word of God, and respond with faith and repentance. The hearer must not harden his or her heart as if God were not speaking.

Nonetheless, without the illuminating work of the Holy Spirit, it is not possible for the hearer to understand God's word. As Luther notes in his comments on Mary's "Magnificat":

> In order properly to understand this sacred hymn of praise, we need to bear in mind that the most blessed Virgin Mary is speaking out of her own experience, in which she was enlightened and instructed by the Holy Spirit. For no one can rightly understand God or His Word who has not received such understanding directly from the Holy Spirit.[75]

Thus, although the preacher might obediently proclaim God's word, unless the hearer responds with faith, and unless the Spirit illuminates the hearer, the hearer will fail to recognize or understand the preached word as the word of God and respond with faith and repentance. On the other hand, a hearer can apprehend the preached word in faith, and allow the Spirit to illuminate and instruct through the preached word, and be saved.

Assessment

Luther is committed to the belief that the preached word *is* God's word. According to Luther, the preached word can be identified as the word of God because the content, source, and purpose of the message are the same. The content is the apostolic christological gospel—the same message that was spoken by Christ, commissioned by Christ, and that speaks about Christ. The source of preaching is the God-commissioned and sent preacher, whose gifts have been recognized by the Christian congregation, through whom the Holy Spirit speaks the divinely authored message. And the purpose of the message is that those who hear the word should repent and obey. As Luther summarizes, "[The word] is nothing else than the message proclaimed by Jesus, as contained in the gospel; and this should be, and, in fact, is, so presented that you hear your God speak to you."[76] Conversely, if the preacher has not been sent by God, or if the message is different from the gospel, or if the intent is not that the hearers should hear and obey, then the word of God has not been preached.

---

75. Luther, "The Magnificat (1520–1)," 127.
76. Luther, "The Freedom of a Christian," 359.

According to Luther, God, the preacher, and the hearer all play their individual roles. God works through the preached word; the Holy Spirit not only speaks through the preacher, but also illuminates the hearer to recognize and understand the preached word. But the human preacher also has the responsibility to preach with the intentionality that the hearer might be able to understand and respond in faith to the proclaimed gospel message. And, finally, the hearer has the responsibility to recognize the proclamation of the gospel as nothing less than God speaking, and thus respond in faith and repentance.

Luther has suggested several criteria for assessing whether or not a preacher is preaching the word of God, namely, that the preacher is sent by God, preaches the gospel, and intends the hearers to hear and obey the message of the gospel. Out of these, Luther's main focus is on the content of the message. The preacher is to proclaim accurately the gospel, which is the same message preached by Christ, which Christ commissioned to his apostles, which speaks of Christ, and which is taught by the Holy Spirit. It is also the same message that was orally proclaimed by the Old Testament prophets and New Testament apostles, and subsequently inscripturated as the written text of the Bible. Therefore, the preacher cannot speak his or her own message, but must proclaim the divinely commissioned apostolic christological message of the Bible, and demonstrate evidence that this is indeed the biblical message through frequent appropriate references from the Bible. Similarly, the Christian congregation is not simply to accept any preached message, but must also assess if the preacher is indeed truthfully preaching the gospel, as corroborated in the Bible. It is here that we see the beginnings of the Reformation's emphasis on expository preaching as the means by which God's word is heard.

John Calvin on Preaching

John Calvin also held an exalted view of preaching. In his *Institutes*, Calvin declares, "For, among the many excellent gifts with which God has adorned the human race, it is a singular privilege that he deigns to consecrate to himself the mouths and tongues of men in order that his voice may resound in them."[77] Thus, for Calvin, through a human preacher, one hears no less than the "voice" of God speaking. Preaching *is* the word of God. Calvin's understanding of the relationship between preaching and the word of God will now be explored further.

---

77. Calvin, *Institutes*, IV.i.5.

The Content of Preaching

Like Luther, whenever Calvin discusses preaching the word, he usually is referring to the preaching of the message of the gospel. The terms "word" and "gospel" are used interchangeably. For example, in the *Institutes*, III.xxiv.1., Calvin discusses "the preaching of the gospel" by which God calls his elect. But in the subsequent point, in III.xxiv.2., Calvin describes the same activity as "the preaching of the Word." In another example, when discussing preaching as a mark of the church, Calvin notes:

> We have laid down as distinguishing marks of the church the preaching of the Word and the observance of the sacraments. These can never exist without bringing forth fruit and prospering by God's blessing. I do not say that wherever the Word is preached there will be immediate fruit; but wherever it is received and has a fixed abode, it shows its effectiveness. However it may be, where the preaching of the gospel is reverently heard and the sacraments are not neglected, there for the time being no deceitful or ambiguous form of the church is seen; and no one is permitted to spurn its authority, flout its warnings, resist its counsels, or make light of its chastisements.[78]

In this quotation, Calvin alternates between the terms "Word" and "gospel," but it is clear that he is referring to the same activity of preaching the message of the gospel.

But what is the gospel that is to be preached? Calvin's comment elsewhere in the *Institutes* is helpful:

> Paul testifies that by the true preaching of the gospel "Christ is depicted before our eyes as crucified" (Gal. 3:1 p.). What purpose did it serve for so many crosses—of wood, stone, silver, and gold—to be erected here and there in churches, if this fact had been duly and faithfully taught: that Christ died on the cross to bear our curse (Gal. 3:13), to expiate our sins by the sacrifice of his body (Heb. 10:10), to wash them by his blood (Rev. 1:5), in short, to reconcile us to God the Father (Rom. 5:10)? From this one fact they could have learned more than from a thousand crosses of wood of stone.[79]

Thus, for Calvin, the message of the gospel is the doctrine that Christ died for our sins in order to reconcile us to God the Father. Such a message

---

78. Ibid., IV.i.10.
79. Ibid., I.xi.7.

will at the same time convict people of their sins and offer the hope of salvation through Christ's redeeming work.

The Preached Word and the Written Word

The preached message is also the message of the Scriptures. In other words, the proclaimed word is the oral proclamation of the written word. Calvin summarizes:

> . . . the sole office of others is to teach what is provided and sealed in the Holy Scriptures. We therefore teach that faithful ministers are now not permitted to coin any new doctrine, but that they simply cleave to that doctrine to which God has subjected all men without exception.[80]

Thus, for Calvin, the proclaimed word is to be strictly governed by the written word. The preacher cannot change or add to any teachings that are found in Scripture. The preached word is not to be an innovative message. This is because the preached word must be continuous with God's revelation of his word from and about Christ, through the orally proclaimed, but subsequently inscripturated, message of the Old Testament prophets and the New Testament apostles.

Calvin carefully traces out the logic of this argument. First, the Old Testament prophets were strictly and accurately to proclaim only that which had been spoken to them by God.

> Ezekiel felicitously describes the general character of the prophets' power: "'O Son of man,' says the Lord, 'I have appointed you as a watchman for the house of Israel; you will therefore hear a word of my mouth and will declare it to them from me'" (Ezek. 3:17 p.). Is not he who is bidden to hear a word from the Lord's mouth forbidden to invent anything of his own? What is it to bring tidings from the Lord? So to speak that one dare confidently boast that the word he brings is not his own, but the Lord's. Jeremiah expresses the same thought in other words: "Let the prophet who has a dream tell the dream, and let him who has my word speak my true word" (Jer. 23:28 p.). Surely, he is stating a law for them all. Moreover, it is such that God does not allow anyone to teach more than he has commanded. And he afterward calls whatever has not come forth from himself alone, "chaff" (Jer. 23:28). Therefore, none of the prophets opened his mouth unless the Lord had anticipated his words.

---

80. Ibid., IV.viii.9.

Hence, it comes that these expressions are so often found among them: "the Word of the Lord," "the burden of the Lord," "Thus saith the Lord," "The mouth of the Lord has spoken."[81]

The Old Testament prophets were not allowed to teach more than what God had commanded them. Only in this way could it be that they spoke "the Word of the Lord." Similarly, the New Testament apostles were only to speak that which Christ had commanded them.

> That is, if they are "apostles," they are not to prate whatever they please, but are faithfully to report the commands of Him by whom they have been sent. And Christ's words, with which he has defined their mission, are plain enough: he commanded them to go and teach all nations everything he had enjoined (Matt. 28:19-20). But he also received this law in himself and applied it to himself so that it would be unlawful for anyone to reject it. "My teaching is not mine but his who sent me," the Father's (John 7:16). He was the sole and eternal counselor of the Father, and was appointed Lord and Master of all by the Father. Yet, because he performs the ministry of teaching, by his own example he prescribes for all his ministers what rule they ought to follow in teaching. The power of the church, therefore, is not infinite but subject to the Lord's Word and, as it were, enclosed within it.[82]

The apostles were only to preach what they had received from Christ. Likewise, Christ's own teaching was that which he had received from God the Father. Thus, by "faithfully" preaching what Christ had commanded them, the apostles would be both preaching the authoritative teachings of God the Father and following the example set by Christ's own preaching.

Second, the oral message of the prophets and apostles is now inscripturated as holy Scripture. As Calvin notes, the message of the Old Testament patriarchs was once an oral message that was to be proclaimed to each subsequent generation:

> What the patriarchs had received they handed on to their descendants. For the Lord had left it with them on this condition, that they should so propagate it. The children and children's children knew when God dictates within that what they heard was from heaven, not from earth.[83]

---

81. Ibid., IV.viii.3.
82. Ibid., IV.viii.4.
83. Ibid., IV.viii.5.

But as salvation-history progressively unfolded, it was God's will that his word was to be written as well as proclaimed:

> But where it pleased God to raise up a more visible form of the church, he willed to have his Word set down and sealed in writing, that his priests might seek from it what to teach the people, and that every doctrine to be taught should conform to that rule. Therefore, after the law has been published, the priests are bidden to teach "from the mouth of the Lord" (Mal. 2:7, cf. Vg. and Comm.) This means that they should teach nothing strange or foreign to that doctrine which God included in the law; indeed, it was unlawful for them to add to it or take away from it (Deut. 4:2; 13:1).
>
> There then followed the prophets, through whom God published new oracles which were added to the law—but not so new that they did not flow from the law and hark back to it. As for doctrine, they were only interpreters of the law and added nothing to it except predictions of things to come. Apart from these, they brought nothing forth but a pure exposition of the law. But because the Lord was pleased to reveal a clearer and fuller doctrine in order to better satisfy weak consciences, he commanded that the prophecies also be committed to writing and be accounted part of his Word. At the same time, histories were added to these, also the labor of the prophets, but composed under the Holy Spirit's dictation. I include the psalms with the prophecies, since what we attribute to the prophecies is common to them.[84]

In this way, the Old Testament Scriptures—the Law, the Prophets and the Psalms—are now the word of God. They were composed "under the Holy Spirit's dictation." And if one teaches from them, then one teaches "from the mouth of the Lord." And in the same way, the New Testament apostles also wrote the word of God, for they "were sure and genuine scribes of the Holy Spirit, and their writings are therefore to be considered oracles of God."[85] Therefore, in the writings of the prophets and apostles, the Scriptures, we have the Spirit-inspired words of God.

Third, the message of the prophets and apostles, either orally proclaimed or inscripturated, is the message that comes from Christ. Here, there is continuity because both the prophets and the apostles receive their revelation from Christ. This was the case of the Old Testament patriarchs and prophets:

---

84. Ibid., IV.viii.6.
85. Ibid., IV.viii.9.

> [I]f what Christ says is true—"No one sees the Father except the Son and anyone to whom the Son chooses to reveal him" (Matt. 11:27)—surely they who would attain the knowledge of God should always be directed by that eternal Wisdom. For how could they either have comprehended God's mysteries with the mind, or have uttered them, except by the teachings of him to whom alone the secrets of the Father are revealed? Therefore, holy men of old knew God only by beholding him in his Son as in a mirror (cf. II Cor. 3:18). When I say this, I mean that God has never manifested himself to men in any other way than through the Son, that is, his sole wisdom, light, and truth. From this fountain Adam, Noah, Abraham, Isaac, Jacob, and others drank all that they had of heavenly teaching. From the same fountain, all the prophets have also drawn every heavenly oracle that they have given forth.[86]

And it was the same case for the New Testament apostles:

> From this also we infer that the only thing granted to the apostles was that which the prophets had had of old. They were to expound the ancient Scripture and to show that what is taught there has been fulfilled in Christ. Yet they were not to do this except from the Lord, that is, with Christ's Spirit as precursor in a certain measure dictating the words. For by this condition Christ limited their embassy when he ordered them to go and teach not what they had thoughtlessly fabricated, but all that he had commanded them (Matt. 28:19–20). And nothing could be said more clearly than what he says in another place: "But you are not to be called rabbi, for you have one teacher ... the Christ" (Matt. 23:8, 10). Then to fix this more deeply upon their minds, he repeats it twice in the same place (Matt. 23:9–10). And because, on account of their ignorance, they could not grasp what they had heard and learned from the Master's lips, the Spirit of truth is promised to them, to guide them into a true understanding of all things (John 16:13). For that restriction must be carefully noted in which he assigns to the Holy Spirit the task of bringing to mind all that he has previously taught by mouth (John 14:26).[87]

Thus, both the prophets and the apostles have received their revelation from Christ. Christ was the "fountain" from which the Old Testament prophets drank and drew their teaching. And Christ was the "teacher" from

---

86. Ibid., IV.viii.5.
87. Ibid., IV.viii.8.

whom the New Testament apostles received their teaching that they are now to proclaim. But there is also a discontinuity between the prophets and the apostles. For the prophets could only behold Christ "as in a mirror." And their teachings looked forward and anticipated Christ. In contrast, the apostles received their teachings from "the Master's lips" and also had the blessing of "the Spirit of truth" who guided them in recalling Christ's teachings.

Fourth, the message of the prophets and the apostles reached its climactic fulfillment in Christ.

> But when the Wisdom of God was at length revealed in the flesh, that Wisdom heartily declared to us all that can be comprehended and ought to be pondered concerning the Heavenly Father by the human mind. Now therefore, since Christ, the Sun of Righteousness, has shone, while before there was only dim light, we have the perfect radiance of divine truth, like the wonted brilliance of midday. For truly the apostle meant to proclaim no common thing when he wrote, "In many and various ways God spoke of old to the fathers by the prophets; but in these last days he has begun to speak to us through his beloved Son" (Heb. 1:1–2 p., cf. Comm.). For Paul means, in fact, openly declares, that God will not speak hereafter as he did before, intermittently through some and through others; nor will he add prophecies to prophecies, or revelations to revelations. Rather, he has so fulfilled all functions of teaching in his Son that we must regard this as the final and eternal testimony from him. In this way this whole New Testament time, from the point that Christ appeared to us with the preaching of his gospel even to the Day of Judgment, is designated by "the last hour" (I John 2:18), "the last times" (I Tim. 4:1; I Peter 1:20), "the last days" (Acts 2:17; II Tim. 3:1; II Peter 3:3). This is done that, content with the perfection of Christ's teaching, we may learn not to fashion anything new for ourselves beyond this or to admit anything contrived by others.[88]

Christ is the climactic and final revelation from God. And because the Christ-event is the climactic and final salvation-historical act prior to the Day of Judgment, the present church age is to be understood as "the last days." For this reason, any teaching or preaching that is to be God's word is to be "content with the perfection of Christ's teaching"; it cannot go beyond it or "fashion anything new."

Therefore, fifth, any preaching by Christians in the present church age must conform to and not go beyond the Scriptures. This principle is

---

88. Ibid., IV.viii.7.

consistent with the history of God's revelation. The Old Testament prophets could not go against or add to any prior writings of the word of God.

> There then followed the prophets, through whom God published new oracles which were added to the law—but not so new that they did not flow from the law and hark back to it. As for doctrine, they were only interpreters of the law and added nothing to it except predictions of things to come. Apart from these, they brought nothing forth but a pure exposition of the law.[89]

The prophets did not "add" to the law, but expounded the law and made predictions that flowed out from the law. In the same way, the people, priests, and teachers under the Old Covenant also were to conform to the written word of God, which was "the mouth of God":

> Therefore, that whole body, put together out of law, prophecies, psalms, and histories, was the Lord's Word for the ancient people; and to this standard, priests and teachers, even to the coming of Christ, had to conform their teaching. And it was not lawful for them to turn aside either to the right or to the left (Deut. 5:32), for their whole office was limited to answering the people from the mouth of God.[90]

This principle continues to hold under the New Covenant, but even more so, because Christ is the climactic word from God.

> It was therefore with good reason that the Father by a singular privilege ordained the Son as our teacher, commanding him, and not any man, to be heard. He has, indeed, in few words commended Christ as our teacher when he says, "Hear him" (Matt. 17:5). But in these words there is more weight and force than is commonly thought. For it is as if, leading us away from all doctrines of men, he should conduct us to his Son alone; bid us seek all teaching of salvation from him alone; depend upon him, cleave to him; in short (as the words themselves pronounce), hearken to his voice alone. And what, indeed, ought we now either to expect or to hope from man, when the very Word of life has intimately and openly disclosed himself to us? But the mouths of all men should be closed when once he has spoken, in whom the Heavenly Father willed all the treasures of knowledge and wisdom to be hid (Col. 2:3), and has, indeed, so spoken as befitted the wisdom of God (which is in every part seamless (cf. John 19:23)) and the Messiah (from whom the revelation of

---

89. Ibid., IV.viii.6.
90. Ibid., IV.viii.6.

all things was awaited (John 4:25)); that is, after himself he left nothing for others to say.[91]

As a result, even the apostles could not go beyond what had been taught to them by Christ through his Spirit. Thus, even more so, those in the present Christian church are to conform to the teachings of Christ, which are now inscripturated as the written word of God.

> Let this be a firm principle: No other word is to be held as the Word of God, and given place as such in the church, than what is contained first in the Law and the Prophets, then in the writings of the apostles; and the only authorized way of teaching in the church is by the prescription and standard of his Word.[92]

Calvin's own preaching reflected this principle that the preached word is determined by the written word, for it was Calvin's custom to preach through whole books of Scripture regardless of what the church calendar might determine should be preached.[93] For example, he began preaching a series of sermons on the book of Acts on August 25, 1549, and finally finished the series in March 1554. This was followed by series of sermons on Thessalonians (46 sermons), Corinthians (186 sermons), the Pastoral epistles (86 sermons), Galatians (43 sermons), Ephesians (48 sermons), Job (159 sermons), Deuteronomy (200 sermons), Isaiah (353 sermons) and Genesis (123 sermons).[94] In another example, after preaching a sermon on Easter Day, 1538, he was banished by the City Council. On his return from exile, more than three years later in September 1541, Calvin resumed his sermon series by expounding the very next verse from where he had been interrupted.[95]

It is clear that, according to Calvin, preachers in the present church age must conform their message to the Spirit-inspired inscripturated word of God, that is, the Scriptures. The oral word is to be consistent with the written word—the oral word cannot change it or add to it. Only in this way can one say that the word of God is being preached. As Calvin himself summarizes:

> Accordingly, Peter, who was well instructed by the Master as to how much he should do, reserves nothing else for himself or others except to impart the doctrine as it has been handed down by God. "Let him who speaks," he says, "speak only the words of

---

91. Ibid., IV.viii.7.
92. Ibid., IV.viii.8.
93. van der Walt, "Calvin on Preaching," 331.
94. Piper, "The Divine Majesty of the Word," 13.
95. Ibid.

God" (1 Peter 4:11) ... What is this but to reject all inventions of the human mind (from whatever brain they have issued) in order that God's pure Word may be taught and learned in the believers' church? ...

Yet this, as I have said, is the difference between the apostles and their successors: the former were sure and genuine scribes of the Holy Spirit, and their writings are therefore to be considered oracles of God; but the sole office of others is to teach what is provided and sealed in the Holy Scriptures. We therefore teach that faithful ministers are now not permitted to coin any new doctrine, but that they simply cleave to that doctrine to which God has subjected all men without exception.[96]

The Preacher

The person who preaches the word of God has been raised to speak God's message. Under the heading, "*The Prestige of the Preaching Office in Scripture,*" Calvin writes:

> God testifies that, in raising up teachers for them, he bestows a singular benefit upon men when he bids the prophet exclaim, "Beautiful are the feet and blessed the coming of those who announce peace" (Isa. 52:7), and when he calls the apostles "the light of the world" and "the salt of the earth" (Matt. 5:13–14). And this office could not be more splendidly adorned than when he said, "He who hears you hears me, and he who rejects you rejects me" (Luke 10:16).[97]

Thus, the preacher is a person raised and sent by God to speak on behalf of God. As a result, the preacher's words are God's words.

But the preacher can only speak the message that is received from God. Therefore, if a preacher is to claim any authority, then the preacher must only proclaim the message that has been received from God. Moses is the paradigm of this:

> Moses himself, the prince of all the prophets, was to be heard above the rest; but he was previously instructed on his orders and could proclaim nothing at all except from the Lord (Ex. 3:4

---

96. Calvin, *Institutes*, IV.viii.9.
97. Ibid., IV.iii.3.

ff.). The people, therefore, embracing his teaching, "believed," it is said, "in God and in his servant Moses" (Ex. 14:31).[98]

And similarly in the present age, anyone claiming to be a messenger from God must proclaim only that which has been received from God:

> Therefore, if the priest wishes to be heard, let him show himself to be God's messenger; that is, let him faithfully communicate the commands which he has received from his Author. And as far as the hearing of them is concerned, it is expressly laid down that they are to answer according to God's law (Deut. 17:10–11).[99]

Thus, for Calvin, the preacher is someone who, like Moses, is raised and sent by God, and is entrusted with a message received from God; and thus the preacher is to "faithfully communicate the commands which he has received from his Author."

But why should God speak through a human preacher? The answer to this is found in Calvin's doctrine of accommodation:

> God has ... added these aids that he may provide for our weakness. And in order that the preaching of the gospel might flourish, he deposited this treasure in the church. He instituted "pastors and teachers" (Eph. 4:11) through whose lips he might teach his own; he furnished them with authority; finally, he omitted nothing that might make for holy agreement of faith and for right order. First of all, he instituted sacraments, which we who have experienced them feel to be highly useful aids to foster and strengthen the faith. Shut up as we are in the prison house of our flesh, we have not yet attained angelic rank. God, therefore, in his wonderful providence accommodating himself to our capacity, has prescribed a way for us, though still far off, to draw near to him.[100]

> Accordingly, after [God] forbade his people to devote themselves to auguries, divinations, magic arts, necromancy, and other superstitions (Deut. 18:10–11; Lev. 19:31), he added that he would give what ought to suffice for all: that they should never be destitute of prophets (cf. Deut. 18:15). But as he did not entrust the ancient folk to angels but raised up teachers from the earth truly to perform the angelic office, so also today it is his will to teach us through human means. As he was of old not content with the law alone, but added priests as interpreters

---

98. Ibid., IV.viii.2.
99. Ibid., IV.viii.2.
100. Ibid., IV.i.1.

from whose lips the people might ask its true meaning (cf. Mal 2:7), so today he not only desires us to be attentive to its reading, but also appoints instructors to help us by their effort. This is doubly useful. On the one hand, he proves our obedience by a very good test when we hear his ministers speaking just as if he himself spoke. On the other, he also provides for our weakness in that he prefers to address us in human fashion through interpreters in order to draw us to himself, rather than to thunder at us and drive us away. Indeed, from the dread with which God's majesty justly overwhelms them, all the pious truly feel how much this familiar sort of teaching is needed...

For, although God's power is not bound to outward means, he has nonetheless bound us to this ordinary manner of teaching.[101]

God has appointed human ministers to be "interpreters" and "instructors." On the one hand, this is a test of the hearers' faith for they are to obey the human ministers in the same way that they would if they were listening to God speak. But on the other hand, it is God's accommodation to the weakness of the hearers that they can hear God's words through ordinary human teachers.

As Calvin points out above, this preaching ministry, through which God accommodates himself, exists within the context of a God-ordained office of preaching. Calvin further explains that the preacher's authority comes not from who he or she might be, but from this Spirit-conferred office of the proclamation of God's word.

Accordingly, we must here remember that whatever authority and dignity the Spirit in Scripture accords to either priests or prophets, or apostles, or successors of apostles, it is wholly given not to the men personally, but to the ministry to which they have been appointed; or (to speak more briefly) to the Word, whose ministry is entrusted to them. For if we examine them all in order, we shall not find that they have been endowed with any authority to teach or to answer, except in the name and Word of the Lord. For, where they are called to office, it is at the same time enjoined upon them not to bring anything of themselves, but to speak from the Lord's mouth. And he himself does not bring them forth to be heard by the people before teaching them what to speak: they are to speak nothing but his Word.[102]

101. Ibid., IV.i.5.
102. Ibid., IV.viii.2.

In God's revelation of his word, throughout salvation-history, the Spirit confers authority not to the person who preaches, but to the office of preaching that is occupied by that person. This is because the authority of the preacher comes not from the person of the preacher, but from the Spirit-authored word of God that is proclaimed by the preacher.

Regarding these offices of preaching, Calvin distinguishes between four types of offices in the church: (1) the pastor, corresponding to the presbyter or bishop of the New Testament;[103] (2) the doctor or teacher;[104] (3) the deacon, who cares for the sick and the poor; and (4) the elder. The pastors and teachers are responsible for the administration of the word; whereas the elders and deacons are responsible for the administration of the community and its needs.[105] This division of offices, as Klauspeter Blaser notes, "is motivated by the diversity of spiritual gifts, and is based on the priesthood of all believers."[106] Further, regarding this fourfold division of offices, Christoph Schwöbel helpfully comments:

> Calvin was quite conscious that this rearrangement of offices in the Church cannot claim to be literally scriptural or totally in accord with the tradition. But that is not the criterion by which the offices in the Church should be judged. Their only criterion is whether they enable the Church as the community of witness to perform its ministry in the most competent manner.[107]

But to be appointed to an office of preaching, the preacher needs to be called, authorized, and ordained.[108] Regarding the calling, Calvin distinguishes between an external and internal calling:

> I am speaking of the outward and solemn call which has to do with the public order of the church. I pass over that secret call, of which each minister is conscious before God, and which does not have the church as witness. But there is the good witness of our heart that we receive the proffered office not with ambition

---

103. Calvin notes, "But in indiscriminately calling those who rule the church "bishops," "presbyters," "pastors," and "ministers," I did so according to scriptural usage, which interchanges these terms," in *Institutes*, IV.iii.8.

104. For a discussion on Calvin's use of the term "doctor," see McNeill, "John Calvin: Doctor Ecclesiae," 9–22.

105. This fourfold structure is developed in the *Institutes*, IV.iv.1. Although Schwöbel notes that there is a tension with IV.iv.1 where Calvin speaks of only three orders of the ministry, in Schwöbel, "The Creature of the Word," 146, note 55.

106. Blaser, "Calvin's Vision of the Church," 325.

107. Schwöbel, "The Creature of the Word," 146.

108. Calvin, *Institutes*, IV.iii.10–16.

or avarice, not with any other selfish desire, but with a sincere fear of God and desire to build up the church. That is indeed necessary for each one of us (as I have said) if we would have our ministry approved by God.[109]

Thus, there is a secret inner call by which God calls and gifts the minister for his service. This is a matter between the minister and God. But there is also an external formal—an "outward and solemn"—calling, by which the church congregation publicly calls the minister. The church should call only those "who are of sound doctrine and of holy life"[110] and then authorize and ordain them for a publicly recognized ministry of teaching and preaching the word.

The Purpose of Preaching

God achieves his divine purposes through the human proclamation of his word. In his comments on Romans 3:24, using the fourfold categories of causality, Calvin elaborates on this:

> There is, perhaps, no passage in the whole of Scripture which more strikingly illustrates the efficacy of this righteousness, for it shows that the mercy of God is the efficient cause, Christ with His blood the material cause, faith conceived by the Word the formal or instrumental cause, and the glory of both the divine justice and goodness the final cause.[111]

Thus, there is an intended goal of preaching, namely "faith begot from the Word," and this will ultimately glorify God.

Indeed, the intent of preaching is salvation for those who hear:

> God breathes faith into us only by the instrument of his gospel, as Paul points out that "faith comes from hearing" (Rom. 10:17). Likewise, the power to save rests with God (Rom. 1:16); but (as Paul again testifies) He displays and unfolds it in the preaching of the gospel (ibid.)[112]

The power to save comes, of course, from the sovereign God; but salvation is achieved by means of the human proclamation of the gospel.

---

109. Ibid., IV.iii.11.

110. Ibid., IV.iii.12.

111. Calvin, *Calvin's Commentaries: The Epistles of Paul the Apostle to the Romans and to the Thessalonians*, 74-75.

112. Calvin, *Institutes*, IV.i.5.

However, Calvin's main focus is upon the purpose of preaching within the context of the Christian body of believers. Here, God uses preaching for the building up of the Christian church.

> Paul writes that Christ, "that he might fill all things," appointed some to be "apostles, some prophets, some evangelists, some pastors and teachers, for the equipment of the saints, for the work of the ministry, for the building up of the body of Christ, until we all reach the unity of the faith and the knowledge of the Son of God, to perfect manhood, to the measure of the fully mature age of Christ" (Eph. 4:10–13, Comm., but cf. also Vg.). We see how God, who could in a moment perfect his own, nevertheless desires them to grow up into manhood solely under the education of the church. We see the way set for it: the preaching of the heavenly doctrine has been enjoined upon the pastors. We see that all are brought under the same regulation, that with a gentle teachable spirit they may allow themselves to be governed by teachers appointed to this function.[113]

God's will is that his church might "grow up into manhood" and be built up. But God has also sovereignly planned it so that the means by which this happens is through "the preaching of the heavenly doctrine [that] has been enjoined upon the pastors." Ultimately, then, preaching is used by God to bless his people. As Calvin later notes, "[Paul] contends that there is nothing more notable or glorious in the church than the ministry of the gospel, since it is the administration of the Spirit and of righteousness and of eternal life (II Cor. 4:6; 3:9)."[114] Thus, the Holy Spirit works through the human proclamation of the gospel to administer righteousness and eternal life to those who hear and respond with faith and obedience.

As a result, those who proclaim God's word are to do so boldly because they are performing God's actions, on his behalf, through the word:

> Here, then, is the sovereign power with which pastors of the church, by whatever name they be called, ought to be endowed. That is that they may dare boldly to do all things by God's Word; may compel all worldly power, glory, wisdom, and exaltation to yield to and obey his majesty; supported by his power, may command all from the highest even to the last; may build up Christ's household and cast down Satan's; may feed the sheep and drive away the wolves; may instruct and exhort the teachable; may accuse, rebuke, and subdue the rebellious and stubborn; may

---

113. Ibid., IV.i.5.
114. Ibid., IV.iii.3.

bind and loose; finally, if need by, may launch thunderbolts and lightnings [*sic*]; but do all things in God's Word.[115]

Thus, the intent of preaching is not merely to inform. Instead, an action is being performed, for the preachers are to "boldly . . . *do* [my emphasis] all things by God's Word." Some of these actions include compelling, commanding, building up, casting down, feeding, driving away, instructing, exhorting, accusing, rebuking, subduing, binding, loosing and "launching thunderbolts and lightnings." And all these are done "in God's Word."

The Holy Spirit and Preaching

Preaching of the word is a partnership between the human preacher and the divine Holy Spirit. The preacher is responsible for the external calling, whereas the Spirit is responsible for the internal calling of the gospel. Calvin claims that God's call to his elect "consists not only in the preaching of the Word but also in the illumination of the Spirit."[116] Calvin expands upon this:

> [T]here are two kinds of call. There is the general call, by which God invites all equally to himself through the outward preaching of the word—even those to whom he holds it out as a savor of death (cf. II Cor. 2:16), and as the occasion for severer condemnation. The other kind of call is special, which he deigns for the most part to give to the believers alone, while by the inward illumination of the Spirit he causes the preached Word to dwell in their hearts. Yet sometimes he also causes those whom he illumines only for a time to partake of it; then he justly forsakes them on account of their ungratefulness and strikes them with even greater blindness.[117]

There is, therefore, in addition to the external proclamation of the gospel, an internal witness of the Spirit that enlightens the hearer to the preached word. And all this happens according to the secret plans of God by which he calls his elect.

---

115. Ibid., IV.viii.9.
116. Ibid., III.xxiv.2.
117. Ibid., III.xxiv.8.

The Hearer and Preaching

The hearers of the preached word have the responsibility to hear the preached word and respond to it in faith and obedience. As Calvin notes:

> This, then, is the true knowledge of Christ, if we receive him as he is offered by the Father: namely, clothed with his gospel ... [T]here is a permanent relationship between faith and the Word. He could not separate one from the other any more than we could separate the rays from the sun from which they come. For this reason, God exclaims in the Book of Isaiah: "Hear me and your soul shall live" (ch. 55:3). And John shows this same wellspring of faith in these words: "These things have been written that you may believe" (John 20:31). The prophet, also, desiring to exhort the people to faith, says: "Today if you will hear his voice" (Ps. 95:7; 94:8, Vg.). "To hear" is generally understood as meaning to believe.[118]

The preached word offers a "true knowledge of Christ." And thus those who hear the gospel preached are to "hear" and receive Christ with faith. Thus, to "hear" is the same as to "believe."

But not all will be able to hear, for not all will have "ears" to hear or "eyes" to see. As Calvin discusses:

> Indeed, the Word of God is like the sun, shining upon all those to whom it is proclaimed, but with no effect among the blind. Now, all of us are blind by nature in this respect. Accordingly, it cannot penetrate into our minds unless the Spirit, as the inner teacher, through his illumination makes entry for it.[119]

Thus, although the human hearer has the responsibility to respond in faith to the preached word, the Holy Spirit also has to enlighten the hearer, so that he or she might be able to understand and receive the preached word.

Thus, the preacher is preaching to two types of hearers: one group can indeed hear and understand; but the other group without the hidden illuminating work of the Spirit is not able to understand and respond in faith to the word. As Calvin summarizes: "Therefore, when we exhort and preach to those endowed with ears, they will willingly obey, but in those who lack them is fulfilled what is written: 'Hearing, they hear not' (Isa. 6:9)."[120]

---

118. Ibid., III.ii.6.
119. Ibid., III.ii.34.
120. Ibid., III.xxiii.13.

Assessment

John Calvin's views on preaching are similar to those of Martin Luther. Calvin has an exalted view of preaching. For him, the preached word *is* the word of God. It is useful again to use the categories of the source, content, and purpose of preaching to understand Calvin's view. First, the immediate source of preaching is the preacher. However, the ultimate source of preaching is God who raises and sends the preacher to speak on his behalf. For Calvin, the authority of the preached word comes not from the person of the preacher but from the Spirit-conferred office of preaching in which the Spirit-authored word of God is proclaimed. Second, the content of preaching is strictly governed by the written word. The oral word must conform to the Scriptures; it must not change nor add to the written word. Only in this way can the preached word be identified as the word of God. Third, the purpose of preaching is that God's purposes are achieved through the proclamation of the word. Thus, the intention of preaching is not merely to inform but to perform God's actions of saving and building up his church.

Similar to Luther, Calvin's emphasis is upon the content of preaching. For Calvin, the preached word must strictly adhere to the written word. There can be no dichotomy between these two ministries of the Spirit. The ministries of the word and the Spirit belong together; they cannot be separated. Thus, the preached word can only be the word of God if it preaches the same message as Scripture. Only in this way is the preacher receiving his or her message from God. And only in this way can the preacher's voice be recognized as the voice of God.

Conclusion

We have examined the views of Martin Luther and John Calvin on preaching and the word of God. Both Luther and Calvin held very high views of preaching. They readily identified the preached word as the word of God. Through the proclamation of a human preacher, one could hear God speaking his words. The basis of this claim was the recognition of the source, content, and purpose of the preached word. The source of the preached word, the human preacher, is sent by God to represent God and speak on God's behalf. The content of the preached word is the Christocentric message of the gospel, to which the term "the word" refers. This gospel is also inscripturated as the written word, which testifies to Christ; and thus the preached word is to conform to the written word. The purpose of the preached word is to achieve God's purposes of salvation and building up of his church, and this is achieved by the hidden illuminating work of the Holy Spirit in conjunction with human preaching. But what is the significance of such an exalted view of preaching? In the next chapter I will examine how Luther's and Calvin's views of preaching were significant for their understanding of the church.

— 3 —

Luther and Calvin
Preaching as a Mark of the Church

The previous chapter examined the views of Martin Luther and John Calvin regarding the relationship between preaching and the word of God. Such a view was to become profoundly significant for the Reformers' theology of the church, since both Luther and Calvin would understand that the church was to be necessarily founded upon God's word. As a result, Luther and Calvin identified the preaching of the word of God to be a mark of the true church, which would be sufficient to guarantee and necessary for the existence of the church. In this chapter, I will explore in more detail how Luther's and Calvin's views of preaching became significant for their understanding of the true Christian church.

Introduction

Martin Luther and John Calvin identified preaching as the "word of God." When the preacher proclaims the word, God himself is heard. This would become the standard understanding of preaching during the Reformation. For example, in the Second Helvetic Confession, Heinrich Bullinger wrote the heading "*Praedicatio verbi Dei est verbum Dei*"—"The preaching of the Word of God *is* the Word of God"[1]—and then declared, "Wherefore when this word of God is now preached in the church by preachers lawfully called, we believe that the very word of God is preached, and received by the faithful."[2]

---

1. Leith, *Creeds of the Churches*, 133; Runia, "Preaching, Theology of," 528. For a discussion of Bullinger's understanding of this heading, see Scharf, "Was Bullinger Right about the Preached Word?," 3–10.

2. Leith, *Creeds of the Churches*, 133.

In the context of the Reformation, such views on preaching would necessarily also have far-reaching effects upon the understanding of the church. When the Reformers were breaking away from the established Roman Catholic Church, how could the Reformers claim to be part of the true church? And if they were the true church, then what was the status of the established Roman Catholic Church? All these questions belonged under the bigger question of what is the true church? In order to answer this, the Reformers identified what they claimed to be the "marks" of the church, which would distinguish a true church from a false one. Two marks were identified: the true preaching of the word of God and the proper observance of the sacraments, to which a third mark was often added, namely, the faithful exercise of church discipline. For example, the Second Helvetic Confession (1566),[3] under the heading "Notes or Signs of the True Church," declared:

> Now, as we acknowledge no other head of the Church than Christ, so do we not acknowledge every church to be the true Church which vaunts herself so to be; but we teach that to be the true Church indeed in which the marks and tokens of the true Church are to be found. Firstly and chiefly, the lawful and sincere preaching of the word of God as it is left unto us in the writings of the prophets and the apostles, which do all seem to lead us unto Christ ... And they that are such in the Church of God have all but one faith and one spirit; and therefore they worship but one God, and him alone they serve in spirit and in truth, loving him with all their hearts and with all their strength, praying unto him alone through Jesus Christ, the only Mediator and Intercessor ... They do withal communicate in the sacraments ordained by Christ, and delivered unto us by his apostles, using them in no other manner than as they received them from the Lord himself.[4]

Similarly, in the Thirty-Nine Articles (1563, American Revision 1801), Article XIX declared, "The visible Church of Christ is a congregation of faithful men, in which the pure Word of God is preached, and the Sacraments be duly ministered according to Christ's ordinance, in all those things

---

3. The Second Helvetic Confession is a useful creed for getting an insight into the theology of the Reformers. This confession was first written in 1561 by Heinrich Bullinger who was Zwingli's successor in Zurich; it was made public in 1566. Leith notes, "The Second Helvetic Confession appeared when the Reformed Churches were established and had reached theological maturity but before they came under the dominating influence of scholasticism ... The Second Helvetic Confession was widely accepted and can justly claim to be the most universal of Reformed creeds," in Leith, *Creeds of the Churches*, 131.

4. Ibid., 145–46.

that of necessity are requisite to the same."[5] In the Augsburg Confession (1530), Article VII equated the "one holy Christian church" as "the assembly of all believers among whom the Gospel is preached in its purity and the holy sacraments are administered according to the Gospel."[6]

Martin Luther and John Calvin were at the forefront of such Reformation understandings of preaching as a mark of the true church. Luther's and Calvin's understanding of preaching and the church will now be explored.

Martin Luther and Preaching as a Mark of the Church

Martin Luther's personal discovery of the original gospel message—that God had sent his son Jesus, through whom the work of redemption had been achieved—resulted in this gospel message becoming a primary component of his theology, life, and ministry. Such an understanding would shape not only his understanding of preaching but also his understanding of the church.

The True Church

When referring to the church, Luther uses such terms as "true," "hidden," "invisible," "visible," and "false." For Luther, the "true" church and the "hidden" (or "invisible") church are the same entity, although he prefers the term "hidden" instead of "invisible." Here, Luther's understanding that the God of Isaiah is a hidden deity (*deus absconditus*) is relevant. For this God is mysterious and inaccessible. And yet this same God paradoxically became flesh—the incarnate Word. In the same way, the true church is paradoxically at the same time hidden and yet known through the person of Christ.[7] The heart of the true or hidden church is the word of God. For Christ himself is the living Word, and the true sheep recognize the voice of their Master and gather around his word. For this reason, Luther famously defines the church in the Smalcald Articles (1537) as the "holy believers and sheep who hear the voice of their Shepherd."[8] And Christ's word can be heard through

---

5. Article XIX continued, "As the Church of Jerusalem, Alexandria, and Antioch have erred; so also the Church of Rome hath erred, not only their living and manner of Ceremonies, but also in matters of Faith." In Leith, *Creeds of the Churches*, 273.

6. Ibid., 70.

7. For this insight, see Avis, "Luther's Theology of the Church," 104–5.

8. Smalcald Articles (1537) III:xii. The broader quotation is: "[T]hank God, a seven-year-old child knows what the church is, namely, holy believers and sheep who hear

the preaching of the word, the administration of the sacraments, and the teaching of sound doctrine. In his "Against Hanswurst," in 1541, Luther writes, "[D]octrine must be straight as a plumb line, sure, and without sin. Therefore nothing must be preached in church except the sure, pure, and one word of God. Where that is missing, we no longer have the church, but the synagogue of the devil."[9]

The "false" church stands in contrast to the "true" or "hidden" church. The false church is founded upon human-made doctrines that oppose the teachings of Scripture; it is the antithesis of the true church. For Luther, the Roman Catholic Church was a concrete example of the false church, yet even here, some careful nuances are required. Mark Noll comments:

> To Luther the Roman Catholic Church was the most conspicuous locus of the false church, for it spurned the correcting word of Scripture and caused men to turn away from God's grace to their own works and religious efforts. But even the Roman church was not a wholly false church, for the mere presence of Scripture and baptism, even in perverted forms, held Roman Catholicism back from complete capitulation to human and demonic forces. The true/hidden church had the word, sacraments, and offices of God, while the false church was the church of anti-Christ; it had only Satan's aping counterfeits—anti-word, anti-sacraments, anti-offices. The true/hidden church staked all on God's grace in Christ; the false church staked all on the works of men.[10]

But what of the "visible" church and its relationship with the "true" or "hidden" church? Here, Luther's understanding that a Christian is someone who is simultaneously justified and yet still a sinner (*simul peccator et iustus*) is relevant. For if the visible church is the visible gathering of Christians then it will be necessarily mixed and imperfect. The Christians who gather will be saints who are still tainted by sin. And there may even be non-Christians or counterfeit Christians who take part in the visible gathering. Moreover, there might be only a small handful of true Christians who meet in a larger gathering of predominantly counterfeit Christians. In his lectures on Galatians, in 1535, Luther comments, "[The Church] is invisible, dwelling in the Spirit, in an 'unapproachable' place; therefore its holiness cannot be seen. God conceals and covers it with weaknesses, sins, errors, and various

---

the voice of their Shepherd. So children pray, 'I believe in one holy Christian church.' Its holiness does not consist of surplices, tonsures, albs, or other ceremonies of theirs which they have invented over and above the Holy Scriptures, but it consists of the Word of God and true faith." From Tappert, *The Book of Concord*, 315. Also in *LW* 39:xi.

9. *LW* 41:217.

10. Noll, "Martin Luther and the Concept of a 'True' Church," 81–82.

offenses and forms of the cross in such a way that it is not evident to the senses anywhere."[11] But there must also be a visible church. As Luther also writes, "The church must appear in the world. But it can only appear in a covering (larva), a veil, a shell, or some kind of clothes which a man can grasp, otherwise it can never be found."[12]

The visible church is related to the hidden church by means of the word. For true Christians, whenever they gather, can participate in the hidden church through the supernatural word, which is administered through the human proclamation of the word and administration of the visible sacraments: "The church is universal throughout the world, wherever the Gospel of God and the sacraments are present."[13] As Noll observes:

> The Word of God, baptism, and the Lord's Supper were gifts from God; where men received these they participated in the true/hidden church. The true/hidden church, however, revealed itself only to the eyes of faith. Since the sacraments of the church and the Word were supernatural gifts of God, they could only be truly apprehended and appropriated by the supernatural gift of faith. Since, on the other hand, Christians were creatures of the natural realm as well as of the supernatural, the gifts belonging to the true/hidden church would only be apprehended in the naturalness of the visible church.[14]

The Marks of the Church

The true church, although hidden, is identifiable by its "marks." Here, the analogy of Christ's incarnation is helpful. For although God is hidden, he appeared on earth as the incarnate Christ, in a visible and recognizable form. In the same way, the church ought to be visible and identifiable by its "marks." For Luther, if the true church is founded upon Christ and his gospel, rather than human-made doctrine, then it should be recognizable by visible marks that demonstrate this. In his treatise "On the Councils and the Church," in 1539, Luther elaborates upon seven such marks: the word of God, baptism, the Lord's Supper, the offices of the keys, the pastoral office, prayer, and cross-bearing.[15]

11. *LW* 24:84.
12. From *D. Martin Luthers Werke* (Weimar edition), Briefwechsel 9:608, as cited by Noll, "Martin Luther and the Concept of a 'True' Church," 83.
13. From Luther's comments on Gal 1:2, in *LW* 26:25.
14. Noll, "Martin Luther and the Concept of a 'True' Church," 83.
15. Avis, "Luther's Theology of the Church," 106; Klug, "Luther's Understanding of

But the two key marks are the preaching of the word and the administration of the sacraments, of which the preaching of the word is the primary mark. For Luther, a true church consists of a congregation of Christian believers who are gathered around the preaching of the gospel. For example, in 1523, in a treatise to a congregation in Leisnig, Luther writes:

> It is necessary, first of all, to know where and what a Christian congregation is, so that men may not engage in purely human affairs under cover of the name of a Christian congregation, as has always been the custom of non-christians. Now the certain mark of the Christian congregation is the preaching of the gospel in its purity. For as one can tell by the army standard, as by a sure sign, what leader and what army have taken the field, so one may surely know by the gospel where Christ and His army are stationed. Of this we have God's sure promise in Isaiah lv. "My word," He says, "that goeth forth out of my mouth, shall not return unto me void; but as the rain cometh down from heaven and watereth the earth, so shall my word accomplish all things whereto I send it." Hence we are certain that where the Gospel is preached, there must be Christians, no matter how few in number or how sinful and frail they be; just as where the Gospel is not preached and the doctrines of men hold sway, there can be no Christians but only heathens, no matter how great their numbers or how saintly and good their lives.[16]

Thus, "the preaching of the Gospel in its purity" is a "sure sign" or "certain mark of the Christian congregation." It is a sufficient condition, for "no matter how few in number or how sinful and frail" the Christians might be in that church, "where the Gospel is preached, there must be Christians." But Luther, in this above excerpt, goes further and claims that the preaching of the gospel is also necessary, for "where the Gospel is not preached and the doctrines of men hold sway, there can be no Christians but only heathens."

This is confirmed by Luther's later writing, the treatise "On the Councils and the Churches," in 1539:

> We speak, however, of the external Word orally preached by men like you and me. For Christ left this behind Him as an outward sign whereby His Church, His Christian, holy people in the world, was to be recognized. We speak too of this oral Word as it is earnestly believed and publicly confessed before the world, as He says, "He that confesseth me before men, him will

---

'Church' in His Treatise *On the Councils and the Church* of 1539," 35–37.

16. Luther, "The Right and Power of a Christian Congregation," 75.

I confess before my Father and His angels"; for there are many who know it secretly, but will not confess it. Many have it and do not believe in it or act by it, for those who believe in it and act by it are few, as the parable of the seed, in Matthew xiii, tells us: three parts of the field get it and have it, but only the fourth part, the fine, good field, "bringeth forth fruit with patience."

Wherever, therefore, you hear or see this Word preached, believed, confessed, and acted on, there do not doubt that there must be a true *ecclesia sancta catholica*, a Christian, holy people, even though it be small in number; for God's Word does not go away empty (Isaiah lv), but must have at least a fourth part, or a piece of the field. If there were no other mark than this one alone, it would still be enough to show that there must be a Christian church there; for God's Word cannot be present without God's people, and God's people cannot be without God's Word. Who would preach or listen to preaching, if no people of God were there? And what could or would God's people believe, if God's Word were not there?[17]

Thus, the preaching of the word alone is sufficient to demonstrate that there is a Christian congregation: "If there were no other mark than this alone, it would still be enough to show that there must be a Christian church there." Indeed, it is an "outward sign" left behind by Christ, whereby the Christian church might be recognized. Moreover, it guarantees the presence of a true *ecclesia sancta catholica*, for "God's Word cannot be present without God's people"; and Luther cites Isaiah 55, where God's word will not go away empty.

In identifying the preaching of the word as sufficient, and even necessary, condition for identifying the Christian church, Luther bases the Christian church upon the foundation of the proclaimed word of God; the Christian church does not receive its legitimacy from its attachment to papal authority or Roman Catholic ecclesiastical structure. In order to emphasize this, Luther also writes to the congregation in Leisnig:

> [Christ] takes from the bishops, theologians and councils both the right and the power to judge doctrine, and confers them upon all men, and upon all Christians in particular. He does this when He says in John x, "My sheep hear my voice"; and, "My sheep do not follow a stranger, but flee from him; for they know not the voice of strangers. As many as have come are thieves and robbers; but the sheep did not hear them." Here you see plainly who has the right to judge teaching. Bishops, pope, theologians,

---

17. Luther, "On the Councils and the Churches (1539)," 271.

and any one else have the power to teach; but the sheep are to judge whether what they teach is the voice of Christ or the voice of strangers . . . We therefore let bishops and councils decide and decree what they please; but when we have God's Word on our side, it shall be for us, and not for them, to say whether it is right or wrong, and they shall yield to us and obey our word.[18]

We conclude, then, that where there is a Christian congregation which has the Gospel, it not only has the right and the power, but it is in duty bound, according to the obedience it pledged to Christ in Baptism, and under pain of forfeiting its salvation, to shun, to flee, to put down, to withdraw from, the authority which our bishops, abbots, monastic houses, foundations, and the like exercise today; since it is plainly to be seen that their teaching and rule are opposed to God and His Word. Thus our first point is established certainly and firmly enough, and we should depend upon it that to put down or to shun such bishops, abbots, monasteries, and the like rule, is a divine right and necessary for the salvation of souls.[19]

Thus, the Christian congregation, which is gathered around the preaching of the word, can exist separately from the established Roman Catholic Church; it has the "right and power" to do this, for its foundation of the word has authority over that of the established ecclesial hierarchy. But it is more than this, for if the Christian congregation has the word, then it has the power to judge whether the established ecclesial hierarchy is right or wrong, based upon the word. Furthermore, if the Christian congregation has the gospel, then it is also "duty bound" to withdraw from whatever "bishops, abbots, monastic houses, foundations, and the like" who are opposed to the word.

Therefore, according to Luther, the marks of the church, particularly the preaching of the word, are sufficient to guarantee the existence of a true church. Moreover, the preaching of the word is necessary if a gathering is to be defined as the true church. Thus, there is a true gathering of believers, whenever the word is preached, even in the midst of a false church. But the preaching of the word also grants a gathering of believers the legitimacy to call itself the true church, for they are the sheep who recognize the voice of their Master.[20]

18. Luther, "The Right and Power of a Christian Congregation," 76–77.//
19. Ibid., 79.//
20. For further discussion and comments on Luther's understanding of the marks of the church, see Allister, "Ecclesiology: A Reformed Understanding of the Church," 249–61; Avis, "Luther's Theology of the Church," 104–11; Kistner and Buthelezi, "The

The Church and the Preached Word

The church is the work of God (*opus Dei*) and not of humankind (*opus hominum*). Specifically, the church is a creature of God's word (*creatura verbi divini*).[21] As Luther notes, "For since the Church owes its birth to the Word, is nourished, aided and strengthened by it, it is obvious that it cannot be without the Word. If it is without the Word it ceases to be a Church."[22]

For Luther, this word is primarily an oral word. Luther famously says, "The church is not a pen-house but a mouth house."[23] Or, similarly, "The Gospel should not be written but screamed."[24] In a sermon on July 21, 1532, Luther preaches that Christians would profit more from hearing a sermon in church than by reading the Bible at home alone, "[E]ven if they do read it, it is not as fruitful or powerful as it is through a public preacher whom God has ordained to say and preach this."[25]

Luther sees little place for the reading of the written word in a church gathering unless it is also accompanied by the preached word. In 1523, Luther writes "Concerning the Ordering of Divine Worship in the Congregation," in which he states:

> Now in order to do away with these misuses, it is necessary to know, first of all, that the Christian congregation never should assemble unless God's Word is preached and prayer is made, no matter for how brief a time this may be. See Psalm 101—When the king and the people assemble for God's grace, they are to proclaim God's Name and praise. And Paul in I Corinthians 14 says, that in the congregation there is to be prophesying, teaching and admonishing. Therefore where God's Word is not preached, it is better that one neither sing nor read, nor even come together.[26]

Proclamation of the Gospel and Other Marks of the Church," 21–32; Klug, "Luther's Understanding of 'Church' in His Treatise *On the Councils and the Church* of 1539," 27–38; Klug, "Luther on the Church," 193–207; Lewis, "Ecclesia ex Auditu," 13–31; Noll, "Martin Luther and the Concept of a 'True' Church," 79–85; Rogge, "Luther and the One Church," 100–109; Schwöbel, "The Creature of the Word," 110–55; Westphal, "The Marks of the Church," 91–100; Williamson, "The Marks of the Church," 24–34.

21. A good discussion of this is found in Schwöbel, "The Creature of the Word," 110–55.

22. *LW* 40:37.

23. *LW* companion volume: 63.

24. Ibid., 63–64.

25. Ibid., 64n66.

26. Luther, "Concerning the Ordering of Divine Worship in the Congregation (1523)," 60–61.

Or as P. Z. Strodach comments regarding the liturgical writings of Luther:

> Of course, all of Luther's activities in this field were bound and colored by the doctrine which he espoused. The centralization of the Word and the constant and great emphasis—almost amounting to over-emphasis—which he placed upon it quite naturally forced him to break with the practices of the Roman Church which centralized and constantly emphasized the sacrificial. While Luther does not neglect the Mass—the celebration of Holy Communion—or over-shroud it, he does place a tremendous importance on the preaching of the Word. The read Word, of course, has its place, which in all respects remains quite normal to Roman use—and Luther never breaks with Roman use without definite reason and deliberate purpose—but the read Word is never to appear unless accompanied by exposition or preaching. In fact a constantly reiterated principle is that the congregation is not to gather for worship unless the Word be preached, and the idealized service of Divine Worship is just this in which the Word is centralized.[27]

Therefore, the Christian congregation gathers around the word of God, through the exposition of the written word. Moreover, there is a primacy of preaching, so that it is a necessary requirement for any Christian gathering, even above that of the reading of the written word alone.

Assessment

Luther's understanding of the church was profoundly shaped by his understanding of the gospel. Paul Avis helpfully comments:

> Luther's understanding of the church . . . was essentially and fundamentally evangelical and Christological: evangelical in the sense that the evangel, the gospel, constituted the reality of the church and was the one thing needful to ensure its existence; Christological in the sense that the church was the mode of Christ's saving presence in the world, communicating his life to men through its ministries and sacraments.[28]

---

27. Strodach, "Luther's Liturgical Writings," 22.
28. Avis, "Luther's Theology of the Church," 104–5.

An important component of Luther's understanding of the gospel was the doctrine of justification by faith. This too shaped Luther's understanding of the nature of the church. Here, Eugene F. Klug's insights are helpful:

> [Luther] had moved away from *theologica gloriae*, which placed the emphasis on man's efforts in gaining God's favor, as in the monastic system, to *theologica crucis*, which focused on Christ's redemptory, vicarious sacrifice for all sins and all sinners. This was the heart and content of the saving Gospel which underlay membership in Christ's church.[29]

As a result, the church is always to be recognized as a work of God rather than a work of humankind. It is a creature of God, given birth through the word of God, rather than a creation of human works.

This word of God, from which the church was born, is heard through the preaching of the word, for when a Christian congregation gathers to hear preaching, they hear no less than God's voice speaking to them. As a result, Luther identifies the preaching of the word as a mark of the true church. It is this belief that gives Martin Luther not only the legitimacy but the warrant to break away from the established ecclesiastical hierarchy of the Roman Catholic Church. For, where God's voice is heard, through the faithful preaching of the word, God's people are there also; the sheep recognize the voice of the Shepherd.

If Luther can be faulted, then it is in the overstatement of his case. For while the preached word might identify a congregation of faithful Christian believers, it does not follow that it is *necessary* to identify such a congregation. If God could speak his word through Balaam's donkey, then God can speak through other means besides a preacher. Preaching does not have to be the only means by which God's word is heard. For example, in the New Testament, Christian wives are to win their husbands over to the gospel by their behavior "without words" (1 Pet 3:1); and the visual and sensual medium of the Lord's Supper is sufficient to "proclaim (καταγγέλλω) the Lord's death until he comes" (1 Cor 11:26).[30] Therefore, the Christian congregation can still gather around and "hear" the word of God, but not necessarily only through the preached word, but also through other media

---

29. Klug, "Luther on the Church," 194.

30. For example, Luther also believed that the Lord's Supper must be accompanied by the preaching of the Word. One can understand that Luther feared that the meaning of the Lord's Supper without explanation could be obscured; but the possibility of an obscured meaning does not mean that the word has not been "proclaimed." For God's word is God's word whether or not it is understood by the recipient. For example, Jesus often proclaimed the word, whilst the meaning was obscured to the listeners (e.g., Mark 4:10–13), yet one would still want to say that God's word was preached.

such as singing, the Lord's Supper, and the reading of the written word. One suspects that Luther's comments were largely shaped by his polemic against the Roman Catholic Church at the time, for Luther in the end did place great emphasis upon singing and reading the written word, as evidenced by his output of hymns in the German vernacular and translation of the Bible into the German language.

Nonetheless, Luther has established the church upon the word, for the church is born from the word and membership comes through hearing and recognizing the word. And if this word is heard through the oral proclamation of a preacher, then Luther has elevated preaching to a place of central significance in the church. So much so, that it becomes a visible mark of the true church.

John Calvin and Preaching as a Mark of the Church

Martin Luther's theology of the church emerged during the historical context of his conflict with the established Roman Catholic Church. In contrast, John Calvin's theology of the church emerged during the consolidation of the Reformation movement against the radical wing of the Reformation.[31] As Owen Chadwick notes, "Luther married an ex-nun, Calvin the widow of an Anabaptist; and the difference is symbolic."[32] Despite these different contexts, Calvin's understanding of the church will find remarkable similarities with Luther's.

The True Church

Calvin distinguishes between the "invisible" church and the "visible" church.[33] The "invisible" church refers to

> that which is actually in God's presence, into which no persons are received but those who are children of God by grace of adoption and true members of Christ by sanctification of the Holy Spirit. Then, indeed, the church includes not only the saints

---

31. Schwöbel, "The Creature of the Word," 118.

32. As cited by Schwöbel, "The Creature of the Word," 139. Or as Nestingen notes, "Perhaps it is also appropriate to think of [Calvin's] work as Lutheranism done over from the perspective of the city manager," in Nestingen, "Challenges and Responses in the Reformation," 257.

33. Calvin's heading for his *Institutes*, IV.i.7, reads, "Invisible and Visible Church."

presently living on earth, but all the elect from the beginning of the world.[34]

Thus, the invisible church consists of the "true members of Christ"; it is composed of "all the elect from the beginning of the world." It is, therefore, the whole church of God, including the elect who have already died. It is this church that is "actually in God's presence." It is this church that is the "holy catholic church" of the creed.[35] Here, Calvin's doctrine of election is helpful for understanding his concept of the church. For the elect are the true saints, but it is a mystery whom God has secretly elected:

> We must thus consider both God's secret election and his inner call. For he alone "knows who are his" (II Tim. 2:19), and as Paul says, encloses them under his seal (Eph. 1:13), except that they bear his insignia by which they may be distinguished from the reprobate. But because a small and contemptible number are hidden in a huge multitude and a few grains of wheat are covered by a pile of chaff, we must leave to God alone the knowledge of his church, whose foundation is the secret election.[36]

Thus, the church is founded upon God's secret work of election, in which God draws his elect saints to him, through the efficacious work of the Spirit and his inner call; and the Spirit calls the elect to the saving work of Christ through the word. It is entirely the work of God.[37]

The "visible" church refers to "the whole multitude of men spread over the earth who profess to worship one God and Christ."[38] Within this visible church, there will be true believers: "By baptism we are initiated into faith in him; by partaking in the Lord's Supper we attest our unity in true doctrine and love; in the Word of the Lord we have agreement, and for the preaching of the Word the ministry instituted by Christ is preserved."[39] But this visible church is not perfect; instead, it is mixed with imperfection and even false

---

34. Calvin, *Institutes*, IV.i.7.

35. Calvin discusses this in his *Institutes*, IV.i.1–4. For further discussion, see McNeill, "John Calvin: Doctor Ecclesiae," 14–15; Schwöbel, "The Creature of the Word," 139.

36. Calvin, *Institutes*, IV.i.2.

37. For further insights on the foundation of the church upon God's election, see Blaser, "Calvin's Vision of the Church," 316–27; Schwöbel, "The Creature of the Word," 139–40.

38. Calvin, *Institutes*, IV.i.7.

39. Ibid.

believers: "In this church are mingled many hypocrites who have nothing of Christ but the name and outward appearance."[40]

Calvin also distinguishes between the "false" and "true" churches. The "false" church exists where false doctrine is taught:

> But, as soon as falsehood breaks into the citadel of religion and the sum of necessary doctrine is overturned and the use of the sacraments is destroyed, surely the death of the church follows—just as a man's life is ended when his throat is pierced or his heart mortally wounded. And that is clearly evident from Paul's words when he teaches that the church is founded upon the teaching of the apostles and prophets, with Christ himself the chief cornerstone (Eph. 2:20). If the foundation of the church is the teaching of the prophets and apostles, which bids believers entrust their salvation to Christ alone—then take away that teaching, and how will the building continue to stand? Therefore, the church must tumble down when that sum of religion dies which alone can sustain it. Again, if the true church is the pillar and foundation of truth (I Tim. 3:15), it is certain that no church can exist where lying and falsehood have gained sway.[41]

Thus, the false church is no longer founded upon true doctrine, which is "founded upon the teaching of the apostles and prophets." This is the basis upon which Calvin condemns the Roman Catholic Church:

> Instead of the ministry of the Word, a perverse government compounded of lies rules there, which partly extinguishes the pure light, partly chokes it. The foulest sacrilege has been introduced in place of the Lord's Supper. The worship of God has been deformed by a diverse and unbearable mass of superstitions. Doctrine (apart from which Christianity cannot stand) has been entirely buried and driven out. Public assemblies have become schools of idolatry and ungodliness.[42]

In contrast, the "true" church is the antithesis to the "false" church. The "true" church is founded upon true doctrine:

> Paul reminds us that the church was founded not upon men's judgments, not upon priesthoods, but upon the teaching of apostles and prophets (Eph. 2:20). Nay, Jerusalem is to be distinguished from Babylon, Christ's church from Satan's cabal, by

---

40. Ibid.
41. Ibid., IV.ii.1.
42. Ibid., IV.ii.2.

the very difference with which Christ distinguishes between them. He says: "He who is of God hears the words of God. The reason why you do not hear them is that you are not of God." (John 8:47.)[43]

And this true doctrine is to be found in the teachings of the apostles and prophets.[44] Therefore, the word is a key part of the identity of the true church, for the true church correctly hears and recognizes the true word of God, but the false church teaches and practices false doctrine, which is not the true word of God.

The Marks of the Church

Calvin is now faced with the issue of how one might identify the true church. Like Luther, Calvin answers this by suggesting visible "marks"[45] by which the true church might be identified:

> From this the face of the church comes forth and becomes visible to our eyes. Wherever we see the Word of God purely preached and heard, and the sacraments administered according to Christ's institution, there, it is not to be doubted, a church of God exists (cf. Eph. 2:20).[46]

Calvin thus identifies two recognizable marks: the preaching of the word of God and the administration of the sacraments, of which preaching has the primary role, and the sacraments a subordinate role under preaching.[47] These marks are sufficient to guarantee the existence of the true church. As Calvin adds, "The pure ministry of the Word and pure mode of celebrating the sacraments are, as we say, sufficient pledge and guarantee

---

43. Ibid., IV.ii.4.

44. True doctrine distinguished a true church from a false church. Yet Calvin was also careful to distinguish between fundamental and nonfundamental doctrines. The fundamentals are the doctrines necessary for salvation, and one should separate from a false church that denied such beliefs. However, one could disagree with nonfundamentals without risking separation. For a full discussion on this, see Klauber, "Calvin on Fundamental Articles and Ecclesiastical Union," 341–48.

45. Calvin's heading for his *Institutes*, IV.i.9, reads, "The Marks of the Church and Our Application of Them to Judgment."

46. Calvin, *Institutes*, IV.i.9.

47. For "a sacrament is never without a preceding promise but is joined to it as a sort of appendix, with the purpose of confirming and sealing the promise itself," in *Institutes*, IV.xiv.3. For a discussion on the primacy of preaching and the subordinate role of the sacraments, see Torrance, "*Mysterium Christi* and *Mysterium Ecclesiae*," 459–67.

that we may safely embrace as church any society in which both these marks exist."[48]

The marks are sufficient because God's word is efficacious. As Calvin reasons, "For his promise cannot fail: 'Wherever two or three are gathered in my name, there I am in the midst of them (Matt. 18:20).'"[49] Indeed, God's word is so efficacious that one must not leave a church if these marks exist. For one would be leaving the communion of the true church:

> We have laid down as distinguishing marks of the church the preaching of the Word and the observance of the sacraments. These can never exist without bringing forth fruit and prospering by God's blessing. I do not say that wherever the Word is preached there will be immediate fruit; but wherever it is received and has a fixed abode, it shows its effectiveness. However it may be, where the preaching of the gospel is reverently heard and the sacraments are not neglected, there for the time being no deceitful or ambiguous form of the church is seen; and no one is permitted to spurn its authority, flout its warnings, resist its counsels, or make light of its chastisements—much less to desert it and break its unity. For the Lord esteems the communion of his church so highly that he counts as a traitor and apostate from Christianity anyone who arrogantly leaves any Christian society, provided it cherishes the true ministry of Word and sacraments.[50]

Thus, according to Calvin, by necessity, the preaching of the word and the administration of the sacraments are sufficient to guarantee that there is a gathering of the true church, no matter how mixed with imperfections it might be. As Calvin adds, "The principle [of the marks] extends to the point that we must not reject [any church] so long as it retains them, even if it otherwise swarms with many faults."[51]

But, like Luther, Calvin goes further than this, for the marks are not only sufficient for a true church but they are also necessary for a true church. Calvin continues in his discussion upon the marks:

> For, in order that the title "church" may not deceive us, every congregation that claims the name "church" must be tested by this standard as by a touchstone. If in word and sacraments it has the order approved by the Lord, it will not deceive; let us,

---

48. Calvin, *Institutes*, IV.i.12.
49. Ibid., IV.i.9.
50. Ibid., IV.i.10.
51. Ibid., IV.i.12.

then, confidently pay to it the honor due to churches. But again, if, devoid of Word and sacraments, it advertises the name of church, we must just as scrupulously beware such deceits, as we must avoid rashness and pride on the other side.[52]

The marks not only identify a true church, but they define the true church by distinguishing it from the false church. Conversely, if a gathering is "devoid of Word and sacraments," then it cannot claim to be a true church. As Calvin also notes, "For the Lord nowhere recognizes any temple as his save where his Word is heard and scrupulously observed."[53]

In so defining the church, Calvin has founded the church exclusively upon the word of God. Like Luther, a key concept for Calvin is that the true sheep recognize and gather around the voice of their Shepherd.[54] For Calvin, preaching and the sacraments are the means by which the Shepherd's voice is heard.

The Church and the Preached Word

Calvin has founded the church upon the word of God. Calvin states this clearly, "[S]ince the church is Christ's Kingdom, and he reigns by his Word alone, will it not be clear to any man that those are lying words (cf. Jer. 7:4) by which the Kingdom of Christ is imagined to exist apart from his scepter (that is, his most holy Word)?"[55] The church requires the word not only for its very existence but for its governance. For the word is the "scepter" of Christ. John D. Morrison helpfully comments:

> For Calvin, then, the reign of Christ must, in great measure, be understood as the spiritual, transcendent and heavenly reign which Christ exercises over his people by means of the gospel message, his own Word . . . Such Lordship is *not* then mediated *through* humanity (the human hierarchy of the 'papal church') but *to* humanity by the Spirit of Christ through his Word [his emphasis].[56]

---

52. Ibid., IV.i.11.
53. Ibid., IV.ii.3.
54. "For this is the abiding mark with which our Lord has sealed his own: 'Everyone who is of the truth hears my voice' (John 18:37). Likewise: 'I am the Good Shepherd; I know my sheep, and they know me.' (John 10:14.) 'My sheep hear my voice, and I know them, and they follow me.' (John 10:27)," in *Institutes*, IV.ii.4.
55. Calvin, *Institutes*, IV.ii.4.
56. Morrison, "John Calvin's Christological Assertion of Word Authority," 482–83.

As a result, preaching the word is necessary for the existence and well-being of the church. God provides ministers whose primary role is "to feed the people with the Word of God."[57] Further, preaching the word is necessary for governing the church. Calvin elaborates:

> Now we must speak of the order by which the Lord willed his church to be governed. He alone should rule and reign in the church as well as have authority or pre-eminence in it, and this authority should be exercised and administered by his Word alone. Nevertheless, because he does not dwell among us in visible presence (Matt. 26:11), we have said that he uses the ministry of men to declare openly his will to us by mouth, as a sort of delegated work, not by transferring to them his right and honor, but only that through their mouths he may do his own work—just as a workman uses a tool to do his work.[58]

The church needs preaching to hear God "declare openly his will to us by mouth." And the church submits to the authority of this preached word.[59]

And Calvin would suggest that it is *only* by preaching that the church can be edified and governed:

> We must hold to what we have quoted from Paul (II Cor. 4:6)—that the church is built up solely by outward preaching, and that the saints are held together by one bond only: that with common accord, through learning and advancement, they keep the church order established by God (cf. Eph. 4:12).[60]

Therefore, it is necessary for the church to maintain the public preaching of the word since the purpose of gathering as a congregation of saints is to gather around the preached word—"there is no other bond." And this is the only divinely ordained way for the church to be instructed and edified.

Moreover, for Calvin, in preaching, "the glory of God shines in the face of Christ."[61] Therefore, hearing the public preaching of the word at church is to be preferred over the private reading of the word at home:

> Those who think the authority of the Word is dragged down by the baseness of the men called to teach it disclose their own

---

57. Calvin, *Institutes*, IV.iv.3.

58. Ibid., IV.iii.1.

59. Notice that the authority resides in the preached word and not the preacher, since the preached word is the "tool" provided by God and the preacher is only the "workman."

60. Calvin, *Institutes*, IV.i.5.

61. Ibid., IV.i.5.

ungratefulness. For, among the many excellent gifts with which God has adorned the human race, it is a singular privilege that he deigns to consecrate to himself the mouths and tongues of men in order that his voice may resound in them. Let us accordingly not in turn dislike to embrace obediently the doctrine of salvation put forth by his command and by his own mouth. For, although God's power is not bound to outward means, he has nonetheless bound us to this ordinary manner of teachings. Fanatical men, refusing to hold fast to it, entangle themselves in many deadly snares. Many are led either by pride, dislike, or rivalry to the conviction that they can profit enough from private reading and meditation; hence they despise public assemblies and deem preaching superfluous.[62]

Thus, Calvin speaks against those "[f]anatical men" who would cease attending church, claiming that preaching is superfluous, and that they can profit equally from private reading and meditation. Calvin's response is that, although God is not limited to only one external means, God has chosen to speak through the proclamation of his word, by human preachers, among the public gathering of his people.

Assessment

Similar to Luther, Calvin's understanding of the church is shaped by his understanding of the gospel. The doctrine of election is an important component in his ecclesiology as well as his soteriology, for the true church is the communion of the saints—the elect from all time. Thus, the church is founded upon God's sovereign work of election. But the church is also a creature of God's efficacious word. The elect are those who hear the external call of the proclaimed gospel and respond to the inner call of the Holy Spirit. As a result, the true church exists and is governed by the word. Thus, like Luther, Calvin identifies preaching as a mark of the church. The proclamation of God's word is both sufficient and necessary for a church to be recognized as the true church.

But this is not without its problems. Is the preaching of the word *sufficient* to guarantee the existence of the true church? For the externally preached word is only efficacious in combination with the internal call of the Spirit. Yet the "mark" of preaching only identifies the external calling through the human proclamation of the gospel; but it cannot identify the internal call of the Spirit, for the activity of the Spirit is hidden, secret, and

62. Ibid.

mysterious. In other words, the mere external proclamation of the gospel by itself cannot guarantee that the hearer has received the word.[63] As Edmund P. Clowney observes, "A preacher proclaiming the gospel in a market-place does not fulfil the New Testament description of the church . . ."[64] Both Luther and Calvin are aware of this problem, for Luther qualifies his mark: "Wherever, therefore, you hear or see this Word preached, *believed, confessed* and *acted* on . . ."[65] Similarly, Calvin qualifies his mark: "Wherever we see the Word of God purely preached *and heard* . . ."[66] Likewise, other Reformers add church discipline as a third mark. Thus, Luther, Calvin, and other Reformers also recognize the need to hear, believe, confess, and obey the word of God through the inner work of the Spirit, in addition to the external proclamation of the gospel. But how can this inner work of the Spirit be visible? Surely something like this cannot be externally seen or heard as Luther and Calvin claim.

And is the preaching of the word *necessary* for the existence of the true church? The Reformers may have correctly located the authority of the church in God's word. But God's word can be heard through many other media besides preaching. Thus, although it can be granted that the word is necessary for the existence of the church, it does not have to be granted that preaching—that is, oral proclamation—is the only means by which this word is heard. This word can also be sung, read, and acted.[67] For example, the prophets in the Old Testament often communicated their message from God through prophetic speech-acts[68] rather than an oral proclamation.

The above are internal questions regarding the marks of the church and are not the real focus of our investigation. However, there are also external

---

63. Moore argues therefore that we need both "operative" and "receptive" aspects for the marks of the church. For a further discussion see Moore, "The Pastor's Glory and Crown," 61–80. Williamson calls this the "Protestant Dilemma": "The crux of the problem was not the evangelical marks *per se*. The New Testament did affirm that by the foolishness of preaching men should be saved . . . The problem, rather, was that the Reformers excluded on principle the requirement that the response of the obedient individual had anything to do with the identity of the Church," in Williamson, "The Marks of the Church," 27–28.

64. Clowney, *The Church*, 103.

65. Luther, "On the Councils and the Churches (1539)," 271; my emphasis.

66. Calvin, *Institutes*, IV.i.9; my emphasis.

67. Kistner and Buthelezi recognize this problem and therefore argue for a broader interpretation of what it means to "preach the Gospel" that is not restricted to only the speaking of words, in Kistner and Buthelezi, "The Proclamation of the Gospel and Other Marks of the Church," 21–32.

68. Here I am referring to *prophetic* speech-acts, such as Isaiah's dressing as a captive (Isaiah 20), Ezekiel's symbolic actions (Ezekiel 4–5) and Jeremiah's bearing of a yoke (Jeremiah 27), rather than to Austin's technical use of the term "speech-acts."

questions that do concern us. Both Luther and Calvin identify preaching as a mark of the church because they also equate preaching as the word of God—that is, the preaching of the word of God *is* the word of God. But can preaching be so readily equated with the word of God? And is *all* preaching to be so identified as the word of God? Both Luther and Calvin acknowledge that this cannot be the case. For whenever they identify preaching as a mark of the church, they are also required to qualify what they mean by preaching. For example, Luther writes, "Therefore nothing must be preached in the church except the *sure, pure, and one* word of God." [69] And Calvin employs phrases such as the "*true* ministry of the Word";[70] "the Word of God *purely* preached";[71] and the "*pure* ministry of the Word."[72] And this is something that the other Reformers recognize. For, in the Augsburg Confession (1530), Article VII uses the phrase, "the Gospel is preached in its *purity.*"[73] Similarly, in the Thirty-Nine Articles (1536), Article XIX uses the phrase "the *pure* Word of God is preached" [74] to describe the mark of the church. Likewise, the Second Helvetic Confession (1566) describes the "*lawful* and *sincere* preaching of the word of God" as a mark of the church.[75] Thus, the Reformers are required to use terms such as "pure," "true," and "sincere" to qualify what is meant by "preaching" that is to be identified as the mark of the church. In doing so, the Reformers acknowledge that not all preaching is the word of God.

Conclusion

Luther and Calvin both held high views of preaching: the preaching of the word of God *is* the word of God. They also understood that the church is to be necessarily founded upon God's word; for the church is a creature of God, created through the word. And the church is a community of saints—elected by God and justified through faith—who hear, recognize, and obey the word. They are the sheep who know the voice of their Master. As a result,

---

69. *LW* 41:217; my emphasis.
70. Calvin, *Institutes*, IV.i.10; my emphasis.
71. Ibid., IV.i.9; my emphasis.
72. Ibid., IV.i.12; my emphasis.
73. Leith, *Creeds of the Churches*, 70; my emphasis.
74. Ibid., 273; my emphasis. Article XIX continues by distinguishing such "pure" preaching from impure preaching: "As the Church of Jerusalem, Alexandria, and Antioch have erred; so also the Church of Rome hath erred, not only their living and manner of Ceremonies, but also in matters of Faith."
75. Ibid., 145–46.

both Luther and Calvin identified the preaching of the word of God to be a mark of the true church, which is both sufficient to guarantee and necessary for the existence of the church. In doing so, they granted the Reformation movement the legitimacy and warrant to break away from the Roman Catholic Church that was founded no longer upon the preached word but upon papal authority. But all this requires that the preaching of the word of God really *is* the word of God. And even if preaching is the word of God, surely not *all* preaching can be identified as the word. This introduces our problem: when is preaching the word of God, and how is the "pure Word" to be discerned?

PART B

The Biblical Testimony
The Preached Gospel as the Word of God

The previous part examined how Martin Luther and John Calvin equated the preached word as the word of God. For them, preaching *is* the word of God. This resulted in not only a high view of preaching, but it also became a foundational concept for their concept of the church, for they identified the preached word as a mark of the true church. But did the Reformers too readily equate preaching with the word of God? This introduced our problem: when is preaching the word of God? In this part, I will examine if, in the biblical testimony, there is any support for the concept that preaching is the word of God, which is the prior question. In particular, the focus will be upon the more specific question of whether or not the preached gospel can be identified as the word of God.

4

God Speaks His Word

As explored in the previous section, the Reformers identified preaching as the word of God. When one listens to a preacher, one is listening to the voice of God through human lips. This was a foundational concept for Martin Luther, John Calvin, and other Reformers who established preaching as a mark of the church. But can preaching be so readily identified as the word of God? In this chapter, I will begin answering this question by exploring how the biblical testimony presents the concept that God speaks his word.

God Speaks

The biblical testimony is quite clear that God, who reveals himself to us in the Bible, is the God *who speaks*. The letter to the Hebrews begins with this introduction:

> In the past *God spoke* to our forefathers through the prophets at many times and in various ways, but in these last days *he has spoken* to us by his Son, whom he appointed heir of all things, and through whom he made the universe. [My emphasis] (Heb 1:1–2)

Thus, in this opening paragraph, the writer of Hebrews introduces God as the God who speaks. This is a foundational argument for the letter of Hebrews. And it is a major concept in the Bible.[1] Right from the beginning,

---

1. For example, the phrase "this is what the Lord says" (כֹּה אָמַר יהוה) occurs in more than four hundred and twenty verses in the Bible. Similarly, "the word of the Lord" or "the words of the Lord" (דְּבַר יְהוָה ; ὁ λόγος τοῦ κυρίου and τὸ ῥῆμα τοῦ κυρίου) occur in over two hundred and forty verses, "the word of God" or "the words of God" (דְּבַר אֱלֹהִים ; ὁ λόγος τοῦ θεοῦ and τὸ ῥῆμα τοῦ θεοῦ) in over forty verses, "the Lord said"

God is presented as a speaking God. The canon of the Bible begins with the words, "And God said" (וַיֹּאמֶר אֱלֹהִים). The creation account of Genesis 1 can be understood as a six-part sermon preached by God, where God preaches the heavens and earth into existence.[2] After this, God continues to speak throughout the biblical narrative. God calls out to Adam and Eve in the garden (Gen 3:9); to Abraham (Gen 12:1–3); to Moses from a burning bush (Exod 3); to Samuel in the temple (1 Sam 3); and to Elijah in a whisper (1 Kgs 19:13). God declares Jesus to be his Son at his baptism (Mark 1:11) and transfiguration (Mark 9:7). The canon of the Bible closes with a final vision in the book of Revelation in which God makes a pronouncement from his throne (Rev 21:5–8). The God of the Bible is revealed to us as a speaking God.

The Bible uses many concepts, images, and metaphors to depict God as a God who speaks. For example, the Bible refers to God commanding, promising, blessing, warning, or cursing. The Bible also figuratively refers to God as having a "mouth" (1 Kgs 8:15; 2 Chr 6:4; Pss 33:6; 138:4; Prov 2:6; Isa 1:20; 34:16; 40:5; 58:14; 62:2; Jer 9:20; 23:16; Acts 22:14), "lips" (Job 11:5; Isa 30:27), or "voice" (Exod 15:26; 19:19; Num 7:89; Deut 4:12, 33; 5:22–26; 18:16; 30:20; 2 Sam 22:14; Job 37:5; 40:9; Pss 18:13; 29:3–9; 95:7; Isa 6:8; 30:30–31; Ezek 10:5; 43:2; Hag 1:12; John 5:25; Acts 7:31; 2 Pet 1:17; Rev 1:10).[3]

As the God who speaks, God is the one true God who is to be distinguished from all other gods. God stands in contrast to the idols or false gods who cannot speak. The Psalmist declares, "Our God is in heaven; he does whatever pleases him. But their idols are silver and gold, made by the hands of men. They have mouths, *but cannot speak*, eyes, but they cannot see" (Ps 115:3–5). In Isaiah, God boasts:

> Gather together and come;
>
> assemble, you fugitives from the nations.
>
> Ignorant are those who carry about idols of wood,
>
> who pray to gods that cannot save.
>
> Declare what is to be, present it—

(וַיְדַבֵּר יְהוָה; וַיֹּאמֶר יְהוָה; and ὁ κύριος εἶπεν) in three hundred verses, "God said" (וַיֹּאמֶר אֱלֹהִים and ὁ θεὸς εἶπεν) in more than fifty verses, "the Lord has spoken" (or "the Lord has not spoken"; דְּבַר יהוה) in twenty-five verses, "for the Lord has spoken" or "for the mouth of the Lord has spoken" (כִּי יְהוָה דִּבֵּר) in fourteen verses, and "declares the Lord" (נְאֻם יְהוָה and λέγει κύριος) in over three hundred and forty verses. (These figures were obtained using a GRAMCORD search.)

2. Carefull, as quoted by Adam, *Speaking God's Words*, 15.

3. As discussed in Fanning, "Word," 848.

let them take counsel together.
Who foretold this long ago,
who declared it from the distant past?
Was it not I, the Lord?
And there is no God apart from me,
a righteous God and a Savior;
there is none but me. [My emphasis] (Isa 45:20-21)[4]

In Jeremiah, God ridicules his people's idols, because "like a scarecrow in a melon patch, their idols cannot speak" (Jer 10:5). Thus, in contrast to false gods, God is the true God—the true God who speaks.[5] A corollary of this is that the people of God are distinguished from other peoples because they are the people who worship a God who speaks. Moses reminds the Israelites that they are different than other nations because they have "*heard the voice of God*" (Deut 4:33, 35-36, 39). Thus, the people of God are distinct, not only because they have been uniquely blessed by God, but because they worship a unique God who speaks and they have been privileged in hearing him speak.

The God of the Bible is also a trinitarian God and all three persons of the Trinity are presented as speaking persons in the biblical narrative. For example, God the Father makes declarations at significant stages of Jesus' ministry, such as at his baptism (Mark 1:11) and transfiguration (Mark 9:7). God the Father is also heard in a voice from heaven that pronounces, "I have glorified [my name], and will glorify it again" (John 12:28). God the Son makes preaching a central part of his earthly ministry (Mark 1:14-15; 1:38-39; 2:2; Luke 4:16-21). As the risen Son, Jesus also appears to Saul in a bright light and loud voice, asking, "Saul, Saul, why do you persecute me?" (Acts 9:3-6). In fact, the Son embodies the speaking God by being the "Word" incarnate (John 1:14). God the Spirit also speaks. The writer of Hebrews quotes Psalm 95 and writes to his readers, "So, as the Holy Spirit *says*: 'Today if you hear his voice, do not harden your hearts'" (Heb 3:7). Paul begins his instructions to Timothy by saying, "The Spirit clearly *says* . . ." (1 Tim 4:1). In the book of Revelation, each of the seven letters to the

---

4. This is a key argument in Isaiah 40-48, where there is an extended polemic against idols, in which the idols are compared with God. God's ability to speak is one characteristic that distinguishes him from the idols; other distinguishing characteristics are God's sovereignty and ability to act, save, create, rule over history, and know the future.

5. "This satire of the 'mute idols' . . . emphasizes one of the most characteristic traits of the living God in biblical revelation. *God speaks to man* [my emphasis]" in Feuillet and Grelot, "Word of God," 666.

churches ends with the exhortation, "He who has an ear, let him hear what the Spirit *says* to the churches" (Rev 2:7, 11, 17, 29; 3:6, 13, 22). Significantly, the canon of the Bible ends its narrative with all three persons of the Trinity speaking—God the Father makes his pronouncement from his throne (Rev 21:5), God the Son announces that he will come soon (Rev 22:7, 12–16, 20) and God the Spirit cries out with the bride, saying, "Come!" (Rev 22:17).

And importantly, God is the God who continues to speak. He is not a deistic God who might have once spoken in the past but no longer speaks in the present. On the contrary, he is the God who continues to speak even today. For example, in the letter to the Hebrews, when the writer of Hebrews quotes passages from Scripture, the writer often uses the present tense for the introductory formulae "God says," "Jesus says," or "the Holy Spirit says," because God's words in Scripture continue to speak to hearers today. In Hebrews 3:7–11, the writer quotes Psalm 95, and attributes the words to the Holy Spirit, in which the Holy Spirit is speaking to the present readers and saying, "*Today*, if you hear his voice . . ."[6]

God Speaks His Word: The Word of God

As explored above, God is a God who speaks. But what is it that God speaks? The biblical testimony reveals that God is a God who speaks *his word*, namely, the "word of God." In the Bible, terms such as אָמַר, דָּבָר, λόγος, ῥῆμα and their cognates, and phrases such as "the word," "the word of God," and "the word of the Lord" are used to describe God's revelation.[7] But it is more than this, for the concept of God speaking his word cannot be limited to the occurrences of certain terms or phrases in the Bible; instead, the concept of God speaking his word is itself foundational to both the understanding that God is a God of revelation and the biblical storyline. But what is it that God reveals? What is the message or referent of the word of God?

---

6. The Holy Spirit is indeed speaking these words, through the Psalmist, to the contemporary readers of the letter to the Hebrews. The "rest" to which the Psalmist refers is the "rest" that is available to the contemporary readers (4:1, 8–11); and the Psalmist's reference to "Today" refers to the present days in which the readers are situated (4:7; cf. 3:13). Although the words were once proclaimed in the past and recorded in OT Scripture, they have a referent and an application for the present readers. Thus, the Holy Spirit continues to speak to the present readers.

7. For detailed analyses and statistics regarding the occurrences of these terms and phrases, see Ames, "dbr," 912–15; J. Bergman, et al., "dabhar," 84–125; Haarbeck et al., "Word, Tongue, Utterance," 1078–146.

A General Message from God

In a general sense, the "word" refers to *any* message that comes from God. In some cases, God might directly speak his word. For example, in Deuteronomy, Moses recounts God's meeting with Israel at Mount Sinai, "Then the Lord spoke to you out of the fire. You heard the sound of words but saw no form; there was only a voice . . . [A]nd you heard his words from out of the fire" (Deut 4:12–33). But in other cases, God might indirectly speak his word, through perhaps a human messenger. For example, in Deuteronomy, Moses also recounts, "At that time I stood between the Lord and you to declare to you the word of the Lord" (Deut 5:5). Thus, an important phenomenon in the Bible is where "the word of the Lord" is said to come to a prophet who will then orally convey "the word of the Lord" to the people (e.g., Jer 2:2, 4; Ezek 6:1–3).[8] But in either case, whether directly or indirectly through a human messenger, the "word" refers to a revealed message from God.

God's word also expresses his will. And because God is the Creator, his word is therefore effective. That is, God achieves his will, as expressed by his word. For example, the opening act of God in the Bible consists of his word commanding creation into existence: "By the word of the Lord were the heavens made, their starry host by the breath of his mouth" (Ps 33:6). Similarly, God promises that his plans for salvation will be fulfilled, because:

> As the rain and the snow
> come down from heaven,
> and do not return to it
> without watering the earth
> and making it bud and flourish . . .
> *so is my word that goes out from my mouth:*
> *It will not return to me empty,*
> *but will accomplish what I desire*
> *and achieve the purpose for which I sent it.*
> [My emphasis] (Isa 55:10–11)

Thus, God's word is effective, because it expresses the will of the sovereign God.[9]

---

8. This is the so-called "word-event formula," as noted in Edwards, "Word," 1102.

9. The effective "power" of the word does not rest upon some supposed magical power inherent to the word. Rather, as Ruth B. Edwards notes, "[T]he effectiveness of God's word depends ultimately on the biblical concept of His character rather than

Similarly, because God is the Creator, his word is also authoritative and normative. All who hear his word are commanded to obey its message. Thus, God's word can be also conceived as his law. For example, the Ten Commandments are summarized as the "ten words"—the Decalogue (Exod 34:28; Deut 4:13; 10:4). And in poetic and prophetic passages of the Old Testament, the terms "law" and "word" are often used in synonymous parallelism (e.g., Isa 2:3).[10]

Because God's word is authoritative and normative, it is accompanied with an exhortation to "hear!" (e.g., Deut 6:4; Isa 1:2, 10); and to "hear" God's word is to believe and conform to it. Those who hear and obey God's word will be blessed; but those who refuse to hear God's word are judged. For example, at the conclusion of Moses' sermons in Deuteronomy, there is an exhortation to "listen" to the voice of God (Deut 30:20; cf. 32:1–2) accompanied by a recital of the blessings for obeying and curses for disobeying God's word (Deuteronomy 27–28). Thus, a recurring paradigm in the Bible is the need to hear God and trust his word. In the Garden of Eden, the serpent tempts Eve by asking, "Did God really say . . . ?" (Gen 3:1). Adam and Eve succumb to the serpent's temptation by not knowing, not trusting, and not obeying God's word and thus incur God's judgment and curses. This becomes the paradigm of sin and its consequences. In contrast, when God's word comes to Abraham, Abraham hears and obeys (Gen 12:1–7; cf. 22:1–18); this becomes the paradigm of a faithful servant of God who receives God's blessings for hearing and obeying the word of God.

When God did speak his revelation through a human messenger, this "word" could be either orally conveyed or written.[11] There are many examples of God's messengers orally conveying the word of God—for example, Moses (Exod 4:22; 5:1; 7:17; 8:1, 20; 9:1, 13; 10:3; 11:4; 32:27), Joshua (Josh 24:2), Elijah (1 Kgs 17:14, 24) and the prophets. But there are also examples where God's messengers or their disciples are commanded to write God's message—for example, Moses (Exod 34:27; Deut 31:9, 24), Isaiah (Isa 30:8), Jeremiah (Jer 30:1; 36:27–32), and Daniel (Dan 12:4)—thus inscripturating God's word. Thus, in the Psalms, where there are many references to

---

anything intrinsic to words themselves," in Edwards, "Word," 4:1102–3. Thiselton also provides an in-depth critique of this supposed power of the words in the Old Testament, and suggests that the effectiveness of the words comes from its "performance utterance," in "The Supposed Power of Words in the Biblical Writings." A useful summary of this issue is also found in Fretheim, "Word of God," 961–62.

10. Edwards, "Word," 1103.

11. Thus, Adam observes that the three biblical foundations of preaching are that God has spoken, God's word is written and God's word is preached. In *Speaking God's Words*, 15–56.

the "word of the Lord" or the "word," sometimes the "word" refers to the spoken word—spoken either directly or indirectly through human messengers (e.g., Ps 33:6; 68:11)—but sometimes it refers to God's written word as found in the law (e.g., Pss 119:9–16; 147:19–20).

The purpose of writing God's message was so that it might be preserved so subsequent generations could still hear God's word, through the reading of Scripture. What was originally proclaimed was inscripturated and preserved for later readers (e.g., Deut 31:9–13). This is the purpose of Scripture, namely, to continue to speak God's word for subsequent generations. For this reason, in Stephen's speech in Acts, he recounts, "[Moses] received living words to pass on to us" (Acts 7:38). Thus, while God's word was significant for its original recipients, it remains significant for contemporary readers of Scripture; God continues to speak a contemporary word to present readers of Scripture, through words once proclaimed to past hearers but now inscripturated.

As a result, present readers must also "hear" the words of Scripture and obey them, for they are no less than God's word for them. For example, when Josiah discovers the "Book of Law" or the "Book of the Covenant" and reads it himself and in the presence of the people, there is the recognition that God is speaking to them (2 Kings 22–23). When Ezra reads the "Book of the Law of Moses" to the assembled people, they understood that "the words ... had been made known *to them*" (Neh 8:12). Similarly, in the New Testament, Jesus admonishes the Sadducees, "[H]ave you not read what *God said to you* ...?" (Matt 22:31, quoting Exod 3:6). Paul encourages his readers in Rome, "[E]verything that was written in the past was written *to teach us*, so that through endurance and the encouragement of the Scriptures we might have hope" (Rom 15:4). And to his readers in Corinth, Paul writes, "Now these things occurred as examples *to keep us from* setting our hearts on evil things as they did" (1 Cor 10:6, referring to the events of the "Exodus" generation of Israelites). Thus, although it was once proclaimed in the past, the written word of God speaks a contemporary word to present readers of Scripture; and it must be "heard" and obeyed today.[12]

---

12. As Adam notes, "God speaks to us today by the words he spoke long ago, to them, for us, so that Scripture is God's contemporary Word to us today," in "The Preacher and the Sufficient Word," 33. See also Grudem's survey of the biblical witness to this phenomenon in "Scripture's Self-Attestation and the Problem of Formulating a Doctrine of Scripture," 19–59.

A Special Message from God

But as the stages of salvation-history passed, and God's progressive revelation gradually unfolded, God's "word" had a more specific referent.[13] In the Old Testament, the word of God as spoken through the prophets increasingly referred to a specific message of eschatological hope and salvation. Examples of this message of eschatological salvation are found in the oracles and writings of the so-called Writing Prophets and the Psalms. This message was a two-edged sword. On the one hand, God would vindicate his people and establish his kingdom, which would be ruled by the Messiah; but on the other hand, God would also judge and punish those who had opposed him and his people.

In the New Testament, at the incarnation, "the Word" becomes a title for Christ (John 1:1–18; cf. Rev 19:13); he is the Word who becomes flesh.[14] In one sense, Christ is the Word because he is the Word *from* God; he is the climactic revelation from God. As the Son sent by God, he speaks the Father's message on the Father's behalf; as God incarnate, his words are also God's words. But in another sense, Christ is the Word because he himself is the message. The message from God is *about* Christ; the referent of the word is Christ himself—his person, work, and message. He is the fulfillment of the Old Testament message of eschatological salvation; he is the Messiah who will usher in the kingdom of God and bring salvation and vindication for God's faithful people.

In other sections of the New Testament, the "word" will often refer to the gospel message about Christ. For example, in the Synoptic Gospels, Jesus proclaims the "word" (e.g., Mark 2:2; 4:33; Luke 5:1). Similarly, the book of Acts uses the phrases "the word of the Lord spread" or "the word of God spread" to describe how the message of the gospel was not only proclaimed by the apostles from place to place, but accompanied by fruitful results (e.g., Acts 6:7; 12:24; 13:49; 19:20).

Importantly, this message is now Christocentric: it is the message *from* Christ and it is the message *about* Christ, for it is the message from Christ— given by Christ to his disciples to preach on his behalf (e.g., Luke 9:1–6; 10:1–20). And it is the message about Christ—the disciples are to proclaim the coming of the kingdom of God and the dawning of God's eschatological age of salvation that is inaugurated through the arrival of the person and work of Christ (e.g., Luke 24:45–49).

---

13. Chapter 6 will discuss in more detail the issues raised by these next few paragraphs, namely, *the content* of the preached word.

14. For extended treatments of John's use of "Word" as a title for Christ, see Johnson, "Logos," 481–84; Morris, *The Gospel according to John*, 102–11.

This message is also trinitarian: it is proclaimed by all three persons of the Trinity, for the Father (e.g., John 5:37; 8:18) and the Spirit (e.g., John 15:26) also testify to the Son. This is exemplified at Jesus' baptism and his transfiguration. At Jesus' baptism, the Father publicly declares, "You are my Son" and the Spirit publicly marks out Jesus as the Anointed One (Mark 1:9–11). Similarly, at the transfiguration, the Father declares, "This is my Son, whom I love. Listen to him!" thus bearing testimony to Jesus (Mark 9:7).

This message is also the message of the apostles; the apostles proclaim the gospel message about Jesus Christ. The book of Acts frequently uses the phrases "the word of the Lord" or "the word of God" to refer to the gospel message proclaimed by the apostles (e.g., Acts 4:31; 6:2, 7; 8:25; 12:24; 13:5, 7, 44, 46, 48, 49; 15:35, 36; 16:32; 17:13; 18:11; 19:10, 20). The gospel message about Christ is the apostolic word or *kerygma*. For example, in the book of Acts, although the context and audience might require different forms of presentation, the content of the preached apostolic message is the same, namely, Christ (e.g., Acts 2:14–41; 3:11–26; 4:8–20; 10:34–43; 13:16–48; 14:14–17; 17:22–31; etc.). For this reason, Paul sums up his apostolic message as "we preach Christ crucified" (1 Cor 1:23).

Also, this message is both written and proclaimed. The written Scriptures testify to the Son (e.g., John 5:39); thus both Christ (Luke 24:27, 44) and the apostles (e.g., Acts 8:35; 28:23; Rom 3:21; 16:25–26; cf. 1 Pet 1:10–12) use the Scriptures to testify to Christ. Similarly, the proclamation of the gospel also testifies to the Son; thus both Christ (e.g., Mark 1:15) and the apostles (Mark 6:12) proclaim the gospel message to announce the arrival of the Messiah. Importantly, this proclamation of Christ and the apostles is also subsequently inscripturated so that their proclamation is preserved for subsequent generations (e.g., Luke 1:1–4; John 20:30–31; 1 John 1:1–4; Rev 1:1–2; 21:5).

And this is a message that demands a response. Both Christ and the apostles proclaim the word for the purpose of salvation; and this message and its intent demand a response from the hearer. The word is always accompanied by an exhortation to "hear" and "repent!" (e.g., Mark 1:15; 4:9; 6:12; Acts 2:38). For the gospel is a two-edged message. It is accompanied by a promise of blessings and a warning of curses; there is salvation for all who repent and believe this message, but there is judgment for all who refuse to hear and obey.

Conclusion

This brief survey has found that the Bible presents God as a speaking God. In contrast to false gods or idols, God is not silent. Instead, he is a God of revelation. God is a God who speaks his word. Thus, terms and phrases such as "word," "the word of God," or "the word of the Lord" occur frequently in the Bible; and the concept of God speaking his word is foundational to both the concept of a God of revelation and the Bible's storyline. In a general sense, God's word can refer to any message from God. But as the storyline of the Bible unfolds, God's word is used increasingly in its special sense, by referring specifically to the gospel message, namely, the news that God's eschatological salvation has come in the person and work of Christ. This gospel message, then, is an important component of the word of God. This word is a Christocentric word, for it is from Christ and about Christ; it is a trinitarian word, for all three persons of the Trinity proclaim it; it is the apostolic word, for the content of the apostolic *kerygma* is Christ; it is an oral and written word, for it is both proclaimed and inscripturated by the prophets and apostles, so that it can be heard by subsequent generations; and it is an authoritative word that demands a response of faith and repentance from the hearer.[15]

But how can God's word be proclaimed by *human* messengers? Can God's voice really be heard through the lips of finite and fallible humans? The Bible's presentation of this phenomenon will be explored in the next chapter.

---

15. This relationship between the gospel message and the word of God will be explored in more detail when I examine the message of preaching in Chapter 6.

5

The Human Messenger of God's Word

The previous chapter explored the Bible's presentation of God as the God who speaks his word. It was also explored how this word, in a general sense, refers to any message from God, but in a more specific sense, it often refers to the gospel message about Christ. But how might this word of God be proclaimed?

In the Bible, God proclaims his word through a variety of means. Sometimes God speaks through dreams (e.g., Gen 20:3–7; 31:10–13, 24; Num 12:6; 1 Kgs 3:5; Joel 2:28), visions (e.g., Gen 15:1; 46:2; Num 12:6; 1 Sam 3:1; Ps 89:19; Isa 1:1; Ezek 1:1; Dan 7; Obad 1:1; Mic 1:1; Joel 2:28; Acts 9:10; 2 Cor 12:1), angels (Gen 16:7–13; 21:17–19; 22:11–12; 31:11–13; Judg 2:4; 6:11–12; 2 Kgs 1:3–4; Zech 1:14; 3:6–7; Matt 1:20; 2:13; 28:5–7; Luke 1:13–17; 2:9–12; Acts 8:26; 10:3–6; 27:23–24; Heb 2:2; Rev 1:1), a voice (Num 7:89; Deut 4:12; 5:22; Mark 1:11; 9:7; John 12:28; 2 Pet 1:17–18), and even a donkey (Num 22:28). Thus, God sovereignly chooses his own way to reveal his word; he is not restricted to only one way.

But in addition to the above means, God also uses human messengers to speak his word. For example, the prophets often introduce their message with the formula, "This is what the Lord says." In another example, when the prophet Nathan conveys God's promise of an everlasting covenant to King David (2 Sam 7:4–17), David responds by identifying Nathan's message as God's own words (2 Sam 7:28). Later, King Solomon looks back to Nathan's message and declares, "And now, O God of Israel, let your word that you promised your servant David my father come true" (1 Kgs 8:26; 2 Chr 6:16), thus also identifying Nathan's message as God's own words. Therefore, the Bible testifies to the phenomenon of God speaking his word through the proclamation of humans. The purpose of this chapter is to explore in more detail how the Bible presents this specific phenomenon of human messengers who proclaim the word of God.

Moses

In the Old Testament, Moses is *the paradigm* of a human messenger who proclaims the word of God; as we will explore later, Moses becomes the model for subsequent prophets or servants who speak the word of God. There are certain characteristics that are associated with Moses' ministry of proclamation. First, Moses is anointed by the Spirit of God. In an interesting episode in Moses' life, we learn that Moses is anointed by God's Spirit (רוּחַ; Num 11:17–30) and it is the Spirit who is responsible for empowering Moses in his ministry as a prophet:

> Then the Lord came down in the cloud and spoke with [Moses], and *he took of the Spirit that was on him* and put the Spirit on the seventy elders. When the Spirit rested on them, they prophesied, but they did not do so again. However, two men, whose names were Eldad and Medad, had remained in the camp ... Yet the Spirit also rested on them, and they prophesied in the camp ... Joshua son of Nun, who had been Moses' assistant since youth, spoke up and said, "Moses, my lord, stop them!" But Moses replied, "Are you jealous for my sake? I wish that all the Lord's people were prophets and that the Lord would put his Spirit on them!" [My emphasis] (Num 11:25–29)

Thus, in this episode we learn that God's Spirit is responsible for empowering Moses and the other prophets to "prophesy," that is, to speak God's words. Conversely, without the Spirit, it is impossible for anyone to speak God's words. We also learn that, in the Old Testament, only a few privileged people are gifted with God's Spirit. Not all of God's people are blessed with an endowment of the Spirit. Instead, only Moses and those whom God chooses to serve him in a special role, such as that of a prophet, receive God's Spirit.

Second, Moses is commissioned and sent by God to speak on God's behalf. At the beginning of Moses' ministry, in Exodus chapters 3–4, God appears to Moses at Mount Horeb and commissions him to be a prophet to his people:

> God said to Moses, "I am who I am. This is what you are to say to the Israelites: 'I am has sent me to you.'" God also said to Moses, "Say to the Israelites, 'The Lord, the God of your fathers—the

God of Abraham, the God of Isaac and the God of Jacob—*has sent me to you.*" [My emphasis] (Exod 3:14–15a)

Thus, Moses is the human messenger commissioned and sent by God (cf. Exod 5:23); he speaks on God's behalf and his words have the same authority as the word of God. For this reason, Moses can speak in God's name with God's authority.

Third, Moses receives his message from God. Moses does not author his own message; rather, he receives his message as authored by God. For example, when Moses is reluctant to fulfill his commission, because he is not "eloquent" and is "slow of speech and tongue" (Exod 4:10), the LORD replies:

> "Who gave man his mouth? . . . Is it not I, the Lord? Now go; I will help you speak and will teach you what to say." But Moses said, "O Lord, please send someone else to do it." Then the Lord's anger burned against Moses and he said, "What about your brother, Aaron the Levite? . . . *You shall speak to him and put words in his mouth*; I will help both of you speak and will teach you what to do. *He will speak to the people for you, and it will be as if he were your mouth and as if you were God to him.*" [My emphasis] (Exod 4:11–16)
>
> Now when God spoke to Moses in Egypt, he said to him, "I am the Lord. Tell Pharaoh king of Egypt everything I tell you." But Moses said to the Lord, "Since I speak with faltering lips, why would Pharaoh listen to me?" Then the Lord said to Moses, "*See, I have made you like God to Pharaoh, and your brother Aaron will be your prophet.* You are to say everything I command you, and your brother Aaron is to tell Pharaoh to let the Israelites go out of his country." [My emphasis] (Exod 6:28–7:2)

In this episode, due to Moses' reluctance, Aaron can speak in his place. God tells Moses to "speak to" Aaron and "put words in his mouth," and Aaron will be the "mouth" of Moses. God points out that this models the way that he deals with his prophets, where he speaks to his prophets and puts words in their mouths, so that when they speak, they are his "mouth." Moses is as "God" and Aaron is as his "mouth" (Exod 4:16) and "prophet" (Exod 7:1). Thus, a prophet is someone to whom God has spoken and given his words, becoming the "mouth" of God who speaks on behalf of God. That is, the prophet's message is not his own; instead, it is God's message.

Fourth, Moses faithfully proclaims the message that he has received from God. That is, Moses truthfully proclaims the divinely authored message without modifying it. Nor does he proclaim his own innovative message. Instead, the message is the same message as that received from God, and now truthfully proclaimed without modification. For example, in Moses' ministry, God repeatedly commands Moses to "Go . . . and say . . ." (Exod 3:16, 18; 6:11; 7:15–16; 8:1; 9:1; 19:21; Deut 5:30) or "Say" (Exod 3:15; 4:22; 6:6; 7:2,16; 8:1, 20; 9:13;19:3; 30:31; 31:13; Lev 1:2; etc.). In response, Moses obediently proclaims the message that he has received. For this reason, Moses repeatedly uses the formula "This is what the Lord says" (Exod 4:22; 5:1; 7:17; 8:1, 20; 9:1, 13; 10:3; 11:4; 32:27) to introduce his message.

Therefore, Moses is the Spirit-anointed, God-commissioned, faithful proclaimer of the divinely authored message received from God. Moses becomes the paradigm of a human messenger who proclaims the word of God.[1] He is called a *prophet* of God, for at the end of his life, it is said, "no prophet (נָבִיא) has risen in Israel like Moses, whom the Lord knew face to face" (Deut 34:10). And he is called a *servant* of God, for God calls Moses his faithful "servant" (עֶבֶד), with whom he speaks clearly "face to face" (Num 12:7–8). Moses will be the model of a faithful servant-prophet who anticipates other servant-prophets who will also proclaim God's word; Moses is the paradigm in whose footsteps subsequent human messengers will follow. For this reason, Willem A. VanGemeren calls Moses the "fountainhead" of the prophets, and notes:

> Moses has a special place in redemptive history (Heb 3:1–5). In God's administration of his people, which lasted till the coming of the Son of God, Moses was God's servant. He was also the fountainhead of the prophets. The prophetic message was rooted in the Mosaic revelation, just as the apostolic teaching (*paradosis* or "tradition") was rooted in Jesus' teaching.[2]

The Eschatological Prophet of Deuteronomy 18

In Deuteronomy 18:15–22 there is a key passage that records the expectation that God would raise up an *eschatological prophet* "like Moses." The purpose of this is so that the people can hear "the voice of the Lord our God" (cf. v. 16). In other words, this prophet will be the human messenger who will proclaim the word of God.

---

1. Grudem similarly identifies the following two features of a "prophet" in the Pentateuch: "A messenger empowered by the Spirit of God" and "The prophets' message is not their own," that is, "the prophet has no message of his own but can only report the message God has given him," in "Prophecy, Prophets," 701.

2. VanGemeren, *Interpreting the Prophetic Word*, 28.

Importantly, this eschatological prophet will be someone who follows in the pattern established by Moses.³ The prophet will share the same characteristics of Moses' ministry that was noted earlier in my survey of Moses. First, this prophet will be commissioned by God: "The Lord your God will raise up for you a prophet" (vv. 15, 18). Second, this prophet will receive words from God: "I will put my words in his mouth" (v. 18). Third, although it is not directly mentioned, this prophet will be anointed by the Spirit of God. This is implied because the prophet will be "like Moses" (vv. 15, 18) and will have received the Spirit-authored words of God. Fourth, this prophet will faithfully and truthfully proclaim the message received from God: "he will tell them everything I command him" (v. 18). For these reasons, the eschatological prophet is someone who "speaks in the name" of the Lord (e.g., v. 19; cf. vv. 20, 22). The prophet's message is God's message; his words are God's words.

Thus, Deuteronomy 18 sets up the anticipation that God will once again act in salvation-history by raising up an eschatological prophet like Moses—Spirit-anointed and commissioned by God, who faithfully proclaims the divinely authored message that he has received from God. As the storyline of the Bible unfolds, in each successive salvation-historical stage, God does indeed raise major salvation-historical figures who proclaim the word of God. All these proclaimers follow in the footsteps of Moses and fulfill the eschatological expectation of Deuteronomy 18 of a prophet "like Moses." For example, major salvation-historical figures such as Joshua, Samuel, King David, King Solomon, Nathan, Elijah, Elisha, the other court prophets, and the so-called writing prophets are God's commissioned, Spirit-anointed, recipients and faithful proclaimers of his word.⁴

But as each salvation-historical stage passes, there remains the expectation that the promise of Deuteronomy 18 still awaits a future fulfillment; each salvation-historical figure anticipates another greater figure who is still to come. For example, Malachi foretells the coming of another "Elijah" who will usher in the eschatological Day of the Lord. But it is more than this, because there is also the expectation of a plurality of prophets, for there will be an eschatological Spirit-anointed community. For example, the prophet Joel anticipates a future day when God will pour out his Spirit upon his people

---

3. Schmitt, "Prophecy (Preexilic)," 482.

4. Nonetheless, the editorial comment of Deut 34:10—"no prophet has risen in Israel like Moses"—cautions against too readily identifying subsequent OT prophets as those who fulfill the expectation of Deuteronomy 18. This heightens the eschatological anticipation of a future prophet "like Moses." For a more detailed discussion on the relationship between Deuteronomy chapters 18 and 34, consult Christensen, *Deuteronomy 21:10—34:10*, 873.

and servants, so that they will dream dreams, see visions and prophesy (נָבָא; Joel 2:28–32).[5] Thus, there is an anticipation that in a future salvation-historical era the whole of God's community will enjoy Spirit-empowered proclamation, rather than individual major salvation-historical figures.

The Eschatological Isaianic Servant

In Isaiah, there is the additional promise of an *eschatological Spirit-anointed faithful servant of God* who heralds the arrival of God's reign, the restoration of his people, and the establishment of his kingdom. What is important for this investigation is that this eschatological Isaianic servant will follow in the pattern of Moses—the faithful "servant" (Num 12:7)—and the prophet of Deuteronomy 18. For this servant will also be the preacher of God's news of salvation (Isa 61:1–3).[6] This servant-preacher will be anointed by God's Spirit (61:1), sent by God (61:2) to "preach good news" and to "proclaim" (61:1–2). His ministry will be a holistic ministry that not only preaches God's good news of salvation, but also one that cares for the broken-hearted, the captives, the prisoners, and those who mourn (Isa 61:1–3). This servant-preacher is probably the same person as the eschatological messenger, in Isaiah 40:9 and 41:27, who announces, "Here is your God!"

However, Isaiah also develops this eschatological expectation from a *single* servant-preacher to a *plurality* of Spirit-endowed servant-preachers. There is reference not only to the servant but also to his "offspring" (זֶרַע).

---

5. This builds upon the pre-existing longing, established by Moses, that all of God's people would one day be Spirit-anointed proclaimers in the model of Moses: "I wish that all the Lord's people were prophets and that the Lord would put his Spirit on them!" (Num 11:29).

6. Thus, I am identifying the preacher of Isaiah 61 as the servant of Isaiah. I understand that the preacher of Isaiah 61 is a somewhat anonymous figure whose exact identity is not immediately apparent. The preacher could be the prophet Isaiah himself, speaking in the first person, but this is unlikely because the section commonly called "Third Isaiah" (chapters 56–66) never presents Isaiah speaking in the first person. Perhaps the preacher could be identified as the eschatological Messianic King, but we should not so readily do this, for other eschatological figures were to be similarly anointed and Spirit-endowed. In addition, unlike other messianic passages, there is no attempt in Isaiah 61 to identify the person as a Davidic figure. Moreover, in "Second" and "Third Isaiah," there is no mention of a messianic figure.

Therefore, it is best to identify the preacher of Isaiah 61 as the servant from "Second Isaiah." Although the preacher is never called "servant," the preacher shares many similarities with and best reflects the complexity of the servant of Isaiah. Childs comments, "[T]he relation of chapter 61 to the servant remains a very subtle one, but fits in clearly with the major theme of Third Isaiah in linking the suffering servant of Second Isaiah with the servants of chapters 56–66 who are his offspring," in *Isaiah*, 505.

This progression is developed in several ways. First, there is the progression from a single servant to a plurality of servants. Towards the end of Isaiah, Isaiah begins to speak of a plurality of "offspring" (זֶרַע; 59:21; 61:9; 65:9; 65:23; 66:22) and of "servants" (עֲבָדִים; 54:17; 56:6; 63:17; 65:8, 9, 13, 14, 15, 66:14) rather than a single servant. Second, there is the progression from God placing his Spirit upon his faithful servant (42:1–4; cf. 48:16) to God pouring out his Spirit upon the servant Jacob's (44:1) "offspring" (זֶרַע; 44:3).[7] Significantly, one result of this Spirit endowment is the concomitant gifting of the words of the Lord in the mouths of the people (59:21). Third, there is the progression from a single servant-preacher-messenger whom God would "send" (שָׁלַח) to preach good news (40:1–5; 41:27; 42:19; 48:16; 61:1–11), to the expectation of a large number of faithful servant-preachers or proclaimers of God's message "sent" by God (43:21; 44:26; 52:7).[8]

Thus, in Isaiah, there is the eschatological expectation of not only a single servant-preacher but a plurality of faithful servant-preachers sent by God to preach his message to not only Israel but the nations. These faithful servant-preachers will be anointed by God's Spirit. They are God's redeemed covenant community who enjoy God's reign in his restored kingdom and their preaching heralds the arrival of God's eschatological age of salvation. This expectation complements the already existing expectation of an eschatological prophet "like Moses," set up by Deuteronomy 18.

Jesus

The New Testament presents Jesus as the one who fulfills the Old Testament's anticipation of the prophet of Deuteronomy 18 "like Moses" and the faithful Isaianic servant.

---

7. And there is the progression from God anointing a single messianic-deliverer with his Spirit (11:1–3) to God pouring out his Spirit upon all of his "people" (עַם) who would dwell in a kingdom of Edenic harmony (32:15–20). In fact, the Lord's Spirit is to come upon his people and their "descendants" (זֶרַע), and it will be a manifestation of God's eternal covenant with them (59:21). These Spirit-endowed people are the restored righteous covenant community, who share links with the righteous people of 60:21–22 and 61:8–9 and the Spirit-endowed preacher of 61:1–11.

8. For example, God will "send" (שָׁלַח) survivors to the nations who will proclaim his glory among the nations (66:19). God refers to his own people as his "witnesses" (עֵדִים; 43:10, 12) who might proclaim his praise (43:21).

Jesus the Prophet

Jesus comes in the pattern of Moses the prophet. First, like Moses, Jesus is anointed by God's Spirit (Mark 1:9-13; Matt 3:16—4:1; Luke 3:22; 4:1, 18), but is set apart and empowered by the Spirit in a way never before described in the Old Testament.[9] His ministry is empowered by the Spirit (Luke 4:14; 10:21), so that he can preach good news (Luke 4:18). Thus, to reject Jesus and his message is to blaspheme against the Spirit (Mark 3:29; Matt 12:31-32; cf. Luke 12:10). Second, Jesus is commissioned by God. For Jesus is "sent" by God to be the prophet to his people (Mark 9:37; 12:6; Matt 10:40; 15:24; 21:37; Luke 4:43; 10:16; 20:13). In the parable of the disobedient tenants, Jesus teaches that he follows in the tradition of the Old Testament prophets who are sent by God on his behalf with his message; but as the son of the vineyard-owner, he is the final climactic messenger (Mark 12:1-12; Matt 21:33-46; Luke 20:9-19). This is an especially prominent theme in John's Gospel, where Jesus has been "sent" (ἀποστέλλω) by God the Father.[10] For this reason, Jesus' words are to be identified as the word of God (John 3:34) because Jesus has been sent and commissioned to speak for God the Father—"the One who sent me" (ὁ πέμψας με).[11] Thus, to believe in Jesus is the same as believing in God the Father, the one who sent him (John 5:24; 12:44). Third, Jesus receives his message from God. His words come from God the Father (John 3:34; 14:10; 17:14). Fourth, Jesus faithfully proclaims God's message to the people. At the conclusion of his ministry on earth, Jesus declares to the Father that, not only did he receive his words from him, but that he faithfully proclaimed them: "I have given them your word" (John 17:14).

As a result, the Synoptic Gospels present Jesus as the eschatological prophet of Deuteronomy 18. The Old Testament prophets foreshadow Jesus, who is the prophet *par excellence*, as Jesus himself notes, "The men of Nineveh will stand up at the judgment with this generation and condemn it; for they repented at the preaching of Jonah, and now one greater than Jonah is here" (Matt 12:41; Luke 11:32). Jesus is the prophet of a new climactic stage

---

9. For example, he is conceived by the Holy Spirit and born from a virgin woman (Matt 1:18, 20; Luke 1:35); he will be a Spirit-baptizer (Mark 1:8; Matt 3:11; Luke 3:16); he is led and "driven" (ἐκβάλλω) by the Spirit (Mark 1:12; Matt 4:1; Luke 4:1); and he drives out demons by the Spirit (Matt 12:28).

10. John 3:17, 34; 5:36-38; 6:29, 57; 7:29, 8:42; 10:36; 11:42; 17:3-25; 20:21.

11. John 4:34; 5:23-24, 30, 37; 6:38-39, 44; 7:16-33; 8:14-18, 26-29; 9:4; 12:44-50; 13:20; 14:24; 15:21; 16:5; 20:21.

in salvation-history, in the pattern of Moses[12] and Elijah.[13] This is demonstrated at Jesus' transfiguration, when he stands alongside Moses and Elijah (Mark 9:2–8), thus identifying with them, but also demonstrating that he is the final fulfillment of what was anticipated by Moses and Elijah.

Similarly, John's Gospel also presents Jesus as the eschatological prophet.[14] He is identified as "a prophet" (John 4:19; 7:52; 9:17) and there is speculation as to whether he is "the prophet" (John 6:14; 7:40, 52).[15] After

12. In Matthew, Jesus is not only a prophet but also the prophet in the pattern of Moses. In the same way that Moses went up Mount Sinai to receive and proclaim the word of God to his people (Exod 19; Deut 4:10–14; 5:23–32), Jesus goes up the mountain and proclaims his words to his disciples (Matt 5–7). At this Sermon on the Mount, Jesus preaches with authority, so much so that he juxtaposes his own words with the word of God as found in the Old Testament law, using the formula: "You have heard that it was said to the people long ago . . . But I tell you that . . ." (Matt 5:21, 27, 31–32, 33–34, 38–39, 43–44). Jesus concludes his sermon with an exhortation and a warning to hear and obey his words (Matt 7:24–27), in the same manner that Moses and subsequent Old Testament prophets exhorted and warned God's people to hear and obey the word of God with pronouncements of blessings and curses (e.g., Lev 26; Deut 28).

13. In the Synoptics, Jesus comes in the pattern of Elijah: anointed by the Spirit, just as Elijah was (Mark 1:9–14; Luke 3:21–22; Matt 3:13–17); his rejection is paralleled by the Israelites' rejection of Elijah and Elisha (Luke 4:24–27); his ministry mirrors that of Elijah and Elisha—Jesus raises a widow's dead son (Luke 7:12–17; cf. 1 Kgs 17:17–24; 2 Kgs 4:8–37), feeds five thousand men (Mark 6:30–44; cf. 2 Kgs 4:42–44), heals people from leprosy (Mark 1:40–45; cf. 2 Kgs 5), and preaches the word of God (Mark 2:2; cf. 1 Kgs 17:2, 8, 14, 16, 24; 2 Kgs 2:21–22)—so that the crowds declare, "A great prophet has appeared among us. God has come to help his people" (Luke 7:16; cf. 1 Kgs 17:24). But what of John the Baptist, who is also portrayed as the Elijah who was to come, the last of the Old Covenant prophets, who heralds the arrival of God's eschatological kingdom (Matt 11:11–15; cf. Matt 17:11–13)? John the Baptist begins his ministry in the pattern of the anticipated prophet of Deuteronomy 18 and the prophet Elijah: filled with the Spirit—"in the spirit and power of Elijah" (Luke 1:15–17); the word of God comes upon him (Luke 3:2); and he preaches "a baptism of repentance for the forgiveness of sins" and the gospel to prepare the way for the Christ (Luke 3:2–18; Mark 1:1–8). Even his appearance resembles that of Elijah (Mark 1:6; cf. 2 Kgs 1:8). He is also presented as the eschatological messenger of good news as foretold in Isaiah and Malachi (Mark 1:2; Matt 11:10; Luke 3:4–6; 7:27; quoting Isa 40:1–5 and Mal 3:1). But John the Baptist is a transitional figure between the Old and New Covenant eras: he anticipates a greater salvation-historical figure who is still to come (Matt 3:11–12; Mark 1:7–8; Luke 3:15–17; John 1:6–9, 15, 19–27; 3:27–30), namely, Jesus the Christ (John 1:29–34).

14. For example, Jesus is anointed by God's Spirit at his baptism (John 1:32–33). Jesus is addressed as "Teacher" (διδάσκαλος; John 8:4) or "Rabbi" (ῥαββί; John 1:38, 49; 3:2; 4:31; 6:25; 9:2; 11:8; 20:16). He introduces his sayings with the formula, "Truly, truly I say to you" (ἀμὴν ἀμὴν λέγω ὑμῖν; e.g., John 3:3, 5; 5:19, 24, 25; etc.).

15. In John 7:52, the term "the prophet" occurs in two early manuscripts, although the majority of texts have "a prophet" (no definite article). For a more detailed discussion of this text critical issue, consult Carson, *The Gospel according to John*, 332–33; Metzger, *A Textual Commentary on the Greek New Testament*, 187; Morris, *The Gospel*

Jesus feeds the five thousand, the crowds hope that he might be the one whom Moses foreshadowed (John 6:30–34). The people's rejection of Jesus' message is mirrored by the people's rejection of the prophet Isaiah's message in his time (John 12:38–41).

Jesus the Servant

The New Testament also presents Jesus as the faithful servant-preacher, as foretold by Isaiah. This is especially prominent in the Gospels of Luke and Matthew, where Jesus receives a public anointing by God's Spirit (Luke 3:21–22; Matt 3:13–17) at which God echoes the words of Psalm 2 and Isa 42:1, which announce the arrival of God's messianic king and faithful servant respectively, "You are my Son, whom I love; with you I am well pleased."[16] This announcement will be repeated at Jesus' transfiguration, but with the important additional command to "listen" to Jesus (Luke 9:35; Matt 17:5). Luke and Matthew also use the language of Isaiah's servant to describe Jesus as the "light" (Matt 4:16; in reference to Isa 9:2) and the "light . . . to the Gentiles" (Luke 2:32; in reference to Isa 42:6 and 49:6). Matthew explicitly states that Jesus is Isaiah's Spirit-anointed servant-preacher (Matt 12:18–21; quoting Isa 42:1–4).[17] And the climax of Jesus' Isaianic servant-preacher ministry comes with his suffering and death on the cross, which Jesus sees as a fulfillment of the servant passage of Isaiah 53 (Luke 22:37).

As a proclaimer of God's message of salvation, Jesus fulfills the role of the servant-preacher. For example, Paul notes, "[Jesus] came and preached peace to you who were far away and peace to those who were near" (Eph 2:17) thus referring to Isa 57:19 and the so-called servant passage of Isa 52:7.[18] Moreover, in Luke, Jesus begins his public ministry by preaching in the synagogue at which he claims to be the eschatological servant-preacher of Isaiah 61 (Luke 4:16–21):

> The Spirit of the Lord is on me,

---

according to John, 385n115.

16. So also Carson, who notes, "These words from heaven link Jesus with the Suffering Servant at the very beginning of his ministry," in "Matthew," 109.

17. Leske also concludes that, in Matthew, Jesus' preaching and healing ministry "clearly points to Jesus fulfilling the role of the Servant, the Anointed One of Isaiah 61:1," in "Isaiah and Matthew," 164.

18. But *when* did Christ "come and proclaim peace"? Is the reference to his incarnation, ministry, death, resurrection, post-resurrection appearances, his proclamation as the Christ through the apostles by the Spirit, or a telescoping of the entire "Christ event"? This is a notorious crux. For a summary of the different positions, see Lincoln, *Ephesians*, 148–49; O'Brien, *The Letter to the Ephesians*, 205–8.

because he has anointed me

to preach good news to the poor.

He has sent me to proclaim freedom for the prisoners

and recovery of sight for the blind,

to release the oppressed,

to proclaim the year of the Lord's favor.

(Luke 4:18-19)

This servant passage in Isaiah 61 then becomes programmatic for Jesus' preaching ministry in the rest of Luke's Gospel.[19] For, after preaching in the synagogue, Jesus begins his Isaianic servant ministry by preaching, teaching, and healing (Luke 4:31-44), which will continue to characterize his entire ministry (Luke 4:31-44; 5:15, 17; 6:6, 17-19; 7:22; 9:11; 13:10-13, 22, 32-33; 19:47; 20:1; 21:37-38). When John the Baptist doubts the identity of Jesus, Jesus reinforces his claim to be the Isaianic servant-preacher by deliberately alluding again to Isaiah 61 (Luke 7:21-22; Matt 11:4-5; alluding to Isaiah 61 and possibly also to Isa 35:5-6; 26:19; 29:18-19) and cites, as part of his evidence, that "the good news is preached to the poor."[20]

Therefore, Jesus is the Spirit-anointed, commissioned, faithful proclaimer of God's message. He follows in the footsteps of Moses the prophet-servant. In doing so, he fulfills the eschatological anticipations of the prophet of Deuteronomy 18 and the Isaianic servant-preacher. In Jesus, the prophet and the servant become one identity. But it is more than this. Because Jesus is now the prophet *par excellence*. Jesus is not only *like* Moses; Jesus *replaces* Moses as the paradigm of the servant-preacher.[21] As a result, in the New

---

19. Childs gives a good discussion on the New Testament's use of the Isaianic servant passage of Isaiah 61, in which he notes, "Jesus identifies himself with the Old Testament promise of the one coming to preach the gospel, to free the captives, and to heal the infirmed—activities all sharing the language of Second Isaiah's servant. Above all, Jesus proclaims the 'acceptable year of the Lord,' the eschatological event of God's outpouring of his favor foreshadowed in the ancient Jubilee year (Leviticus 25). He announces that the promise has been fulfilled now in his presence. 'Today' is fulfilled time. The new age of the salvation has arrived," in *Isaiah*, 507. Thus, Hawthorne's view that Jesus, in quoting Isaiah 61, is *only* identifying himself as a prophet and not the servant is too restrictive, in Hawthorne, "Prophets, Prophecy," 640.

20. Preaching seems to be a neglected aspect of Jesus' servant ministry, with most commentators choosing to concentrate on the suffering aspect. However, the New Testament writers understood this to be an important aspect of Jesus' servant ministry. VanGemeren helpfully notes, "The apostles showed an understanding of Jesus' teaching on his servant role (see Matt. 8:17 [Isa. 53:4]; Matt. 12:18-21 [Isa. 42:1-4]; Luke 22:37 [Isa. 53:12])," in *The Progress of Redemption*, 356.

21. This is consistent with the *a fortiori* argument that runs through the Letter to the

Testament, Jesus becomes the model of a proclaimer of the word of God for the apostles and the Christian church.

Jesus the Son

Nonetheless, despite the continuity between Jesus and the Old Testament prophets and the anticipation of an eschatological prophet in the model of Moses, or a servant-preacher as foretold by Isaiah, there is also a discontinuity. For there is a uniqueness about Jesus that sets him apart from other OT prophets and the subsequent NT apostles and church. It is not enough to identify Jesus as "Elijah" or "one of the prophets" (Mark 8:28; cf. Matt 16:14; Luke 9:19).

For Jesus is also the Son of God. Indeed, the purpose of the Gospel writers is to demonstrate that Jesus is both the Christ and the Son of God (e.g., John 20:31; Mark 1:1; 15:39; Matt 16:16; Luke 1:32–35).[22] As a result, he is the unique messenger of the word of God in several ways. First, the Son is a unique category of messenger. In the parable of the disobedient tenants (Mark 12:1–12; Matt 21:33–46; Luke 20:9–19), although Jesus follows in the line of the prophets, he is unique because he is the *son* of the vineyard-owner. The Gospel of John notes that Jesus "comes from above," in contrast to a human messenger such as John the Baptist who is "from the earth" and "speaks as one from the earth" (John 3:31). In the prologue to the Letter to the Hebrews, the writer notes, "In the past God spoke . . . through the prophets, *but*[23] in these last days he has spoken to us *by his Son*" (Heb 1:1–2). Although there is a salvation-historical difference between Christ and the prophets ("in these last days"), there is also a difference in identity, for Christ is the "Son."[24] In the ensuing *a fortiori* argument of the Letter to

---

Hebrews. The "how much more" element of the *a fortiori* argument in the Letter to the Hebrews relies upon the premise that Jesus is greater than, and has replaced, the Old Covenant system, which consisted of Moses, Joshua, rest in Canaan, the Temple, the priesthood, and the animal sacrifices.

22. The term "Son of God" or its equivalents (e.g., "the Son," "my Son," etc.) occurs more than 124 times in the NT. It has both messianic and divine overtones. My purpose here is to explore the relationship between Jesus' identity as the divine Son of God and his proclamation of the word of God. For a more detailed analysis of Jesus as the "Son of God," consult Bauer, "Son of God," 769–75; Ladd, *A Theology of the New Testament*, 158–69.

23. The NIV and the RSV insert "but" in their translations. Although it is not present in the Greek, it is necessary in English because of the vivid contrast between verse 1 and verse 2.

24. Attridge notes, "The expression ['through a Son'], without a definite article . . . emphasizes the exalted status of the final agent . . . As the following chapters will

the Hebrews, Jesus does not only follow in the model of Moses, but he is greater than Moses because, whereas Moses was only a "servant," Christ is a "son" over God's house (Heb 3:5-6).

Second, as the Son, Jesus has a unique relationship with God the Father.[25] In the Synoptics, Jesus stunningly exclaims, "All things have been committed to me by my Father. No one knows the Son except the Father, and *no one knows the Father except the Son* and those to whom the Son chooses to reveal him" (Matt 11:27; cf. Luke 10:21-22). Thus, Jesus' privileged identity as the Son allows him to reveal God in a way that would otherwise be impossible. As George Eldon Ladd notes, "In the process of revelation, the Son fills an indispensable role . . . Because Jesus is the Son of God, he is able to receive all things from his Father that he may reveal them to others. The messianic mission of revelation thus rests upon the antecedent sonship."[26] In the prologue of John's Gospel, the writer John declares, "No one has ever seen God, but God the One and Only,[27] who is at the Father's side,[28] has made him known[29]" (John 1:18; cf. 6:46). Thus, the Son, who intimately knows the Father, is able to reveal and make known the Father (e.g., John 14:6-10).[30] And, as a result, the words that the Son speaks are the words of the Father (John 14:10; 17:8).

---

indicate, that Son, seated at God's right hand, is superior to all other agents through whom God's word has come, particularly to the angels, to Moses, to Joshua, and to Aaron," in *The Epistle to the Hebrews*, 39. Koester similarly comments, "The absence of a definite article . . . highlights the singularity of God's Son (cf. 3:6; 5:8; 7:28) in contrast to the multitude of prophets," in *Hebrews*, 177.

25. The divine sonship of Jesus is unique. In John's Gospel, the disciples are never called "sons," nor do they address God as "Father," and Jesus distinguishes between "my Father" (his unique relationship with the Father) and "your Father" (the disciples' relationship with the Father). Similarly, in the Synoptics, Jesus distinguishes between "my Father" and "your Father," and never uses "our Father" (except in the Lord's Prayer which is what the disciples were to say). See also Bauer, "Son of God," 772, 75.

26. Ladd, *A Theology of the New Testament*, 165.

27. μονογενῆ θεος. Though some manuscripts have ὁ μονογενῆ υἱός. For a discussion regarding the textual variants, consult Metzger, *A Textual Commentary on the Greek New Testament*, 169-70. μονογενής is better translated as "one of a kind" (so the NIV's "one and only") rather than "only begotten." For a review of the linguistic reasons, see Feinberg, *No One Like Him*, 490-91.

28. εἰς τὸν κόλπον, which literally means "into the bosom." This expression "brings out the closeness of the Father and the Son," in Morris, *The Gospel according to John*, 101.

29. ἐξηγήσατο. The English word "exegesis" is derived from this Greek word.

30. As Carson notes, "It is this intimacy that makes it possible for Jesus to know and speak about heavenly things (3:12-13; cf. Mt. 11:27)," in Carson, *The Gospel according to John*, 135.

Third, as the Son, Jesus has a unique relationship with the Spirit and the word. For example, in John's Gospel, the writer John notes, "For the one whom God has sent speaks the words of God, for God[31] gives the Spirit without limit" (John 3:34). Thus, Jesus speaks "the words of God," not only because he has been sent by God, but because he has received the Spirit from the Father "without limit." As Carson comments:

> Throughout redemptive history, God spoke to his people through many accredited messengers. Each received that measure of the Spirit that was required for his or her assigned task ... Not so to Jesus: to him *God gives the Spirit without limit*.[32]

Fourth, as the Son, Jesus himself is the message. In the programmatic prologue, John's Gospel presents Jesus as the Word, God incarnate (John 1:1–18). Jesus does not merely proclaim the word of God. Jesus *is* the Word—the supreme revelation from the Father. As D. A. Carson notes, "[W]e might almost say that Jesus is the exegesis of God."[33] As a result, Jesus' spoken word will save those who believe in him (John 15:3) and judge those who reject him (John 12:48). Thus, the correct response is to hear Jesus' words and "believe" (πιστεύω) in Jesus, the Word himself (John 3:36; 4:41–42; 7:40; 8:31, 51; 14:23; 17:6). The true followers are those who recognize Jesus' words as the voice of their Shepherd (John 10:27). For example, in John's Gospel, Peter's pivotal declaration identifies Jesus as the one with the words of life—"Lord, to whom shall we go? You have the words of eternal life." (John 6:68). Conversely, those who reject Jesus, reject him because they do not hear and obey his word (John 8:37, 43; 14:24; 15:20).

Fifth, as the Son, Jesus is the one who commissions his apostles to speak on his behalf. For it is now the Son who sends them into the world (John 17:18). And it is the Son who anoints them with the Spirit (John 20:22)[34] and commissions them with his authority (John 20:23).

As the Son, then, Jesus' ministry is unique from that of the preceding OT prophets and the subsequent apostles and the church. Although there is a continuity with other divinely commissioned human messengers, there

---

31. The Greek does not have "God," but only has the verb δίδωσιν in the third person masculine singular and the subject is not specified. The NIV inserts the word "God" to make it explicit that it is the Father (rather than the Son or the Spirit) who gives the Spirit to the Son. For a discussion on this, consult Carson, *The Gospel according to John*, 213n1; Morris, *The Gospel according to John*, 218–19.

32. Carson, *The Gospel according to John*, 213; his emphasis.

33. Ibid., 135, commenting on John 1:18.

34. Ibid., 649–55, for a discussion regarding the relationship between this event and Pentecost in Acts 2.

is an important discontinuity because Jesus is the Son who reveals God in a way that is impossible for any other messenger. As the unique and divine Son of God, Jesus speaks the word of God because he is *from* the Father, whose words are divine; he himself *is* God; and the word is *about* him, the divine Son of God. For this reason, at both Jesus' baptism and transfiguration, which designate key moments in his public ministry, God declares of Jesus, "This is my Son, whom I love. *Listen to him*" (Mark 1:11; 9:7; Matt 3:17; 17:5; Luke 3:22; 10:35).

Therefore, in this survey, Jesus is the Spirit-anointed, commissioned, faithful proclaimer of God's message. He follows in the footsteps of Moses the prophet-servant. In doing so, he fulfills the eschatological anticipations of the prophet of Deuteronomy 18 and the Isaianic servant-preacher. In Jesus, the prophet and the servant become one identity. But it is more than this. Because Jesus is now the prophet *par excellence*. Jesus is not only *like* Moses; Jesus *replaces* Moses as the paradigm of the servant-preacher. As a result, in the New Testament, Jesus becomes the model of a proclaimer of the word of God for the apostles and the Christian church. Nonetheless, we also need to recognize the uniqueness of Jesus as the Son of God. His word is the word of God because he himself is divine.

The Apostles

The apostles are called by Jesus to become "fishers of men," for their role will be to "catch" men into the kingdom through the proclamation of the gospel (Mark 1:17; Matt 4:19; Luke 5:8–11).[35] They will follow in the footsteps of Jesus; Jesus' ministry as a preacher will become their ministry.[36]

---

35. The call to become "fishers of men" establishes a major theme for the followers of Jesus. For Jesus will also call his followers to be "salt" (Matt 5:13; Luke 14:34) and "light" (Matt 5:14–16), and to "preach the good news of the kingdom" (Matt 10:6–42). This call finds its culmination at the Great Commission, where Jesus commands his disciples to "make disciples" (Matt 28:19), "preach" repentance and forgiveness of sins, and to be "witnesses" (Luke 24:47–48). As Carson notes, "[T]here is a straight line from this commission to the Great Commission," in Carson, "Matthew," 119–20. The phrase "fishers of men" may contain a further allusion to Jer 16:16, where God sends "fishermen" to gather his people for the exile. In contrast, Jesus is sending his "fishermen" to gather his people from the exile—for they will proclaim the end of the exile and the beginning of the messianic age. In doing so, Jesus is pronouncing the end of the exile, and the inauguration of the eschatological messianic reign. See Carson, "Matthew," 119.

36. The same concepts and language used to describe the mission of Jesus are used to describe that of the disciples. In Mark (Mark 3:13–18; 6:6–13; cf. 1:14–15, 34, 38–39), both missions consist of "proclaiming" (κηρύσσω), "driving out the demons" (ἐκβάλλωand τά δαιμόνια), "healing" (θεραπεύω), and preaching for "repentance"

The Apostles as the Prophet

The apostles assume the role and identity of the prophet of Deuteronomy 18. First, just as Jesus was anointed and empowered by the Spirit to proclaim the word of God, the disciples will now be anointed and empowered by God's Spirit. Jesus the "Spirit-baptizer" (Mark 1:8; Matt 3:11; Luke 3:16) promises that his disciples would be empowered by the Spirit so that they will be able to speak the word of God (Matt 10:19–20; Mark 13:11; Luke 12:12; John 15:26–27). At the end of Jesus' earthly ministry, he commissions his disciples by promising to send them the Holy Spirit: "I am going to send you what my Father has promised" (Luke 24:49). Second, just as Jesus was commissioned and sent by the Father, the disciples are now commissioned and "sent" by Jesus (Mark 3:14; 6:7; Matt 10:5, 16; Luke 9:2; 10:1–3; John 13:16, 20); the disciples are the "workers" whom God sends into "the harvest field" (Matt 9:37–38; Luke 10:2). And so, just as Jesus spoke with God's "authority,"[37] the disciples will now speak with Jesus' "authority" (Mark 6:7; Matt 28:18–20; Luke 9:1–2). When Jesus gives the Great Commission, he explains to his disciples that they will be preaching "in his name" (Luke 24:47). Conversely, just as the listeners rejected God by rejecting Jesus (e.g., Mark 9:37; Luke 9:48), now the listeners will be rejecting Jesus if they reject his disciples (Matt 10:40–42; Luke 10:16).[38] Third, the apostles receive their message from God. For their message is given to them by Jesus; it was not human-made or received from a human (John 17:6–8, 14, 18; Gal 1:11–12).

(μετανοέω). In Matthew (10:1–4, 5–42; 28:16–20; cf. 4:23; 9:35; 11:1, 5), both missions consist of "preaching" (κηρύσσω) the "kingdom" (ἡ βασιλεία), "healing" (θεραπεύω) "every disease and sickness" (πᾶσα νόσος καί πᾶσα μαλακία), "raising" (ἐγείρω) the "dead" (νεκροί), and "cleansing" (καθαρίζω) "those who have leprosy" (λεπροί). In Luke (6:12–16; 9:1–6; 10:1–24; 24:45–49; cf. 4:18–19, 43–44; 7:22; 8:1; 20:1), both missions consist of "preaching" (κηρύσσω) "the kingdom of God" (ἡ βασιλεία τοῦ θεοῦ), and "preaching the gospel" (εὐαγγελίζω).

37. As the one sent by God, Jesus had authority because his authority came from God who sent him. Thus, in the Synoptic Gospels, there is an emphasis on how Jesus spoke with authority—for his message was not his own, but God's (Mark 1:22, 27; 11:28–33; Matt 7:29; 21:23–27; Luke 4:32, 36; 20:2–8).

38. And in being rejected by the people the apostles follow in the footsteps of the OT prophets who were similarly rejected (Luke 11:48–49). Notice how Jesus lists the "apostles" alongside the "prophets." The apostles are in *continuity* with the OT prophets because both preach the word of God and are rejected. But the apostles are also in *discontinuity*, and are thus listed separately from the prophets, because they belong to a new salvation-historical age, having been with Christ from the Baptist's time, and seen him risen (or as in the case of Paul, only having seen him risen).

Fourth, the apostles faithfully proclaim this message, by obeying Jesus and truthfully proclaiming the message that they have received from him.[39]

The Apostles as the Servant

The apostles also assume the role and identity of the Isaianic servant-preacher. In the Synoptic Gospels, the apostles demonstrate this through their preaching and healing (Mark 3:14–15; 6:12–13; Matt 10:1, 7–8; 28:18–20; Luke 9:2, 6; 10:9; 24:47–48), and call to a life of suffering and persecution (Mark 13:9–11; Matt 24:9–14; Luke 21:12–15). The Synoptic Gospels use words and concepts from the Isaianic servant—such as "servant," "witness," and the "light of the Gentiles" who brings "salvation to the ends of the earth"—to describe the followers of Christ.[40] For, the disciples will become Jesus' "witnesses" before kings, governors, and the Gentiles on account of his name (Mark 13:9; Luke 21:13; Matt 10:18). Jesus calls his disciples to be a "light of the world" who are to let their "light shine before men" (Matt 5:14–16); and in the Great Commission, Jesus sends his disciples as his "witnesses" to the nations (Luke 24:48).[41]

In Acts, there are several allusions to Jesus as the "servant" (ὁ παῖς; e.g., Acts 3:13, 26; 4:27, 30). But the apostles also identify themselves as the "servants" (ὁ δοῦλος; e.g., Acts 4:29; cf. 16:17) and assume the role and identity

39. The apostle Paul especially fits the paradigm of the prophet. For a detailed analysis of Paul as a prophet, see Evans, "Prophet, Paul as," 763–65.

40. In Isaiah, words and concepts such as "servant" (עֶבֶד; LXX παῖς, δοῦλος, θεραπεύω, σέβομαι; Isa 41:8–9; 42:1, 19; 43:10–12; 44:1–2, 21, 26; 45:4; 48:20; 49:3–7; 50:10; 52:13; 53:11; 54:17; 63:17; 65:8–9, 13–15; 66:14), "witness" (עֵד; LXX μάρτυς; Isa 43:10–12; 44:8; 55:4–5), "light to the Gentiles" (אוֹר גּוֹיִם; LXX τὸ φῶς ἐθνῶν; Isa 42:6; 49:6), and bringing "salvation to the ends of the earth" (עַד־קְצֵה הָאָרֶץ; LXX τό ἔσχατος τῆς γῆς; Isa 49:6; cf. 41:9; 42:10; 48:20; 52:10) are used to describe the identity and role of the Servant and servants of the Lord.

41. Jesus also tells his disciples that they must be "servants" just as the Son of Man also came to "serve" and give his life as a "ransom" for many (Mark 10:43–45; Matt 20:26–28), which may be a reference to the Servant Passage of Isaiah 53. Interestingly, many of Jesus' parables portray Jesus or God as the master or king and his followers as the "servants" (Mark 12:1–11; 13:32–37; Matt 13:24–30; 18:23–35; 21:33–42; 22:1–14; 24:42–51; 25:14–30; Luke 12:35–48; 14:15–24; 16:13; 17:7–10; 19:11–27). In the parables of the talents and the minas, the faithful follower of Jesus is called the "good and faithful servant" (Matt 25:21, 23; Luke 19:17). Luke also uses the term "servant" to describe Mary (Luke 1:38; 46–48), Israel (1:54), King David (1:69), and Simeon (2:29). In Luke's prologue there is also an interesting reference to the "eyewitnesses (αὐτόπτης) and servants (ὑπηρέτης) of the word (ὁ λόγος)" (Luke 1:2). According to Luke, he has received his account of Jesus and the church from these "eyewitnesses and servants of the word," who are the apostles and proclaimers of the gospel, in the manner of the Isaianic servant-preacher.

of the Isaianic servant. This is anticipated by the programmatic prologue of Acts (Acts 1:4–8) in which Jesus announces that the apostles will be his Spirit-anointed "witnesses" who will proclaim his gospel to "the ends of the earth." The rest of the book of Acts will confirm the prologue: the apostles are indeed Spirit-anointed (e.g., Acts 2:4); they are "witnesses" of Christ and his resurrection (e.g., Acts 1:21–22; 2:32; 3:15; 4:33; 5:32; 8:25; 10:39–43; 13:31; 14:3; 20:24; 22:14–15, 20; 23:11; 26:16); they faithfully endure suffering for the sake of the gospel (Acts 5:41; 9:16); and ultimately they do bring the message of salvation to the "ends of the earth" (τὸ ἔσχατος τῆς γῆς; Acts 1:8; 13:47). In doing so, they are portrayed as the Isaianic servant—the Spirit-empowered witness of God's message of salvation to the ends of the earth (cf. Isa 52:7–10; 61:1–3; 62:10–12).

Paul, who dominates the second half of the narrative in Acts, is the one who most prominently assumes the role of the Isaianic servant by becoming the "light to the Gentiles" (τὸ φῶς ἐθνῶν). After Paul's dramatic conversion along the road to Damascus, the risen Jesus appears to his faithful follower Ananias:

> But the Lord said to Ananias, "Go! This man [Paul] is my chosen instrument to carry my name before the Gentiles and their kings and before the people of Israel. I will show him how much he must suffer for my name." (Acts 9:15–16)

Here, the risen Jesus uses the language of the Isaianic servant to announce his commissioning of Paul to be his "chosen" one (cf. Isa 41:8–9; 42:1; 43:10; 44:1, 2; 45:4; 49:7), who will "suffer" (cf. Isa 52:13—53:12) and go as the messenger of the Lord before the "nations" and their "kings" (cf. Isa 42:1; 43:9–10; 49:1, 6–7, 22–23; 52:15; 55:5; 61:6, 9, 11; 66:19–20).[42]

At Pisidian Antioch, Paul and Barnabas quote from an Isaianic servant passage and identify themselves as the servant who is the "light for the Gentiles," who brings "salvation to the ends of the earth" (Acts 13:47; cf. Isa 49:6). Later, at Paul's appearance before King Agrippa, he makes a similar claim:

> Then I asked, "Who are you, Lord?"
> "I am Jesus, whom you are persecuting," the Lord replied. "Now get up and stand on your feet. I have appeared to you *to appoint you as a servant and as a witness* of what you have seen of me and what I will show you. I will rescue you from your own people and from the Gentiles. I am sending you *to them to open*

---

42. This is a prominent theme in the sections of "Second" and "Third" Isaiah: God's glory, salvation, and judgment will be displayed to all the nations and their kings (e.g., 45:1; 52:10; 60:3, 10–16; 62:2, 10; 64:2; 66:12, 18–19).

their eyes and turn them from darkness to light, and from the power of Satan to God, so that they may receive forgiveness of sins and a place among those who are sanctified by faith in me." [My emphasis] (Acts 26:15–18)

Thus, Paul believes that he has been commissioned by the risen Jesus to be the Isaianic servant, especially with his reference to being appointed as a "servant," "witness," and the one who turns people, both Jews and Gentiles, from "darkness" to "light" (which also has allusions to Isa 9:2 and 42:7, 16). Moreover, Paul understands that his mission as the Isaianic-servant is in continuity with that of Jesus, who was the servant *par excellence*, who proclaimed "light to his own people and to the Gentiles" (Acts 26:23). But Paul now identifies himself as the one who has been commissioned by Jesus to be his servant. And this becomes a driving motif for the second half of the book of Acts. The second half of Acts is dominated by the missionary journeys of Paul and his associates, who proclaim the gospel to both the Jews and the Gentiles, bringing "light" and announcing God's salvation to the ends of the earth, in fulfillment of Isaianic servant passages such as Isaiah 42:6–7 and 49:6.[43]

The Christian Church

Subsequent to the apostles, the Christian church also assumes the role and identity of the human proclaimer of God's word. In other words, the Christian church collectively follows in the footsteps of Jesus and the apostles as the prophet and servant-preacher.

First, like Jesus, Christians are anointed by the Spirit. At the Day of Pentecost, when God poured out his Spirit upon the apostles, Peter claims that this marks the fulfillment of Joel's prophecy that in the last days all of God's people would similarly have the Spirit and be empowered to prophesy (Acts 2:16–21). Second, Christians are commissioned to preach God's word. For example, at the end of Matthew's Gospel, Jesus gives his disciples and all subsequent Christians a commission to "go and make disciples of all nations . . . teaching them to obey everything I have commanded you" (Matt 28:19–20). This commission remains in effect until "the very end of the

43. Paul's understanding of himself in the role of the Isaianic servant-preacher is also demonstrated in his writings. For example, Wagner, in his study of Paul's use of Isaiah 51–55 in Romans, observes, "Paul finds in Isaiah a prefiguration or pre-announcement of his own proclamation of the gospel of Christ to Jew and Gentile alike, wherever Christ is not yet known," in "The Heralds of Isaiah and the Mission of Paul," 194. Thus, Paul is more explicit in his identification as the Isaianic servant than Kruse suggests in "Servant, Service," 870.

age" (Matt 28:20). Third, Christians are those who have heard and received the word of God. Peter reminds his readers that they have been born again of an imperishable seed, which is, namely, "the word that was preached to you" (1 Pet 1:23–25). Similarly, in Jesus' parable of the sower, he describes the genuine believers as those who "heard the word" and "accept it" (Mark 4:20). And the writer to the Hebrews describes believers as those "who have tasted the goodness of the word of God" (Heb 6:5). Importantly, Christians receive this word, no longer directly from Christ, but from the preaching of the apostles, either proclaimed or as written Scripture (Eph 1:13; 1 Thess 1:4–6; 2:13; 1 John 1:1–5). Fourth, Christians are those who proclaim the word of God. Peter tells his Christian readers, who have received the word (1 Pet 1:23–25) that they are now "a chosen people, a royal priesthood, a holy nation, a people belonging to God" whose identity and role is to "declare the praises of him who called you out of darkness into his wonderful light" (1 Pet 2:9). Similarly, Paul tells the Ephesian church that, though it was once his role to "preach to the Gentiles the unsearchable riches of Christ, and to make plain to everyone the administration of this mystery" (Eph 3:8–9), God's purpose is now that his "manifold wisdom" should be made known "through the church" (Eph 3:10). Paul also famously appeals to his Roman readers to become the "feet" of the Isaianic servant who brings good news (Rom 10:15; cf. Isa 52:7).[44] Thus, the New Testament apostles begin to use the language and concepts of the prophet of Deuteronomy 18 and the Isaianic servant, and apply them to the role and identity of the Christian church.[45]

But although the Christian church collectively becomes God's prophet and faithful servant-preacher, God also particularly gifts certain individuals to preach his word. The New Testament writers provide various lists of gifts in Romans 12:6–8, 1 Corinthians 12:1–11, 28–31, Ephesians 4:11–12 and 1 Peter 4:10–11. On the one hand, each of the lists is slightly different, and probably shows that the lists are not meant to be exhaustive;[46] but on the

---

44. Wagner comments on Paul's use of the Isaianic servant passages in Romans 10: "Paul transforms the lone herald of the LXX (πόδες εὐαγγελιζομένου) into multiple preachers of the good news (οἱ πόδες τῶν εὐαγγελιζομένων) . . . The effect of this change is to make explicit Paul's identification of the heralds of Isaiah 52:7 (οἱ εὐαγγελιζόμενοι) with the Christian preachers (κηρύσσοντες) mentioned in Romans 10:8, 14–15," in Wagner, "The Heralds of Isaiah and the Mission of Paul," 207.

45. Thus, Hugenberger suggests the principle of the "preacherhood of all believers," in Hugenberger, "Preach," 943.

46. O'Brien comments, "The New Testament contains five such lists (Rom. 12:6–8; 1 Cor. 12:8–10, 28–30; Eph. 4:11–12; cf. 1 Pet. 4:10–11) which between them number more than twenty different gifts, some of which are not particularly spectacular (cf. Rom. 12:8). Each list diverges significantly from the others. None is complete, but each

other hand, there is also a prominence of "word gifts" in each of the lists, which are to be used to build up the church, in a context of love, towards maturity in Christ.[47] Those individuals who are particularly gifted by God for the proclamation of his word are recognized as such by other Christians and set aside for this special role. For example, one such individual is Timothy. Paul commissions Timothy to assume the role of the preacher of the gospel, "So do not be ashamed to testify about our Lord, or ashamed of me his prisoner. But join with me in suffering for the gospel, by the power of God" (2 Tim 1:8). Thus, Paul encourages Timothy to join with him in his divinely commissioned, suffering-servant ministry of faithful gospel proclamation. As part of this ministry, Timothy is to "present [himself] to God as one approved . . . who correctly handles the word of truth" (2 Tim 2:15) and to "preach the Word" (2 Tim 4:2). Paul is commissioning Timothy to teach and preach[48] faithfully the gospel to the members of his church. But Timothy is also in turn to pass on to the next generation of Christian leaders this same ministry (2 Tim 2:2). In the same way that Timothy has been entrusted with the ministry of gospel proclamation by Paul, Timothy is also to entrust this same ministry to worthy and faithful successors.[49]

---

is selective and illustrative, with no effort to force the various gifts into a neat scheme. Even together all five do not present a full catalogue of gifts," *The Letter to the Ephesians*, 298.

47. Parenthetically, in the list of gifts, Paul uses the word "prophecy" (Rom 12:6; 1 Cor 12:10, 28; Eph 4:11; cf. 1 Thess 5:19–21; 1 Cor 14:1–5, 22–25, 39). But to what is this word "prophecy" referring? And what is its relationship with preaching? This is no simple discussion, and thus it will be the subject of an appendix that follows the conclusion of this book.

48. We should not make too much of a distinction between "teaching" and "preaching." Although in the early twentieth century, C. H. Dodd popularized the thesis that "teaching" is ethical instruction whereas "preaching" is the public proclamation of Christianity to non-Christians, this view is now largely out of favor. Runia helpfully notes, "[I]t is impossible to make a clear-cut distinction between the two terms. In the first place, the terms are often used together . . . Secondly, the content of both terms is also essentially the same," in "What Is Preaching According to the New Testament?," 14. Similarly, Polhill comments, "It is highly unlikely that preaching and teaching were ever entirely separated in early Christianity. Kerygma and didache belong together. To set one over against the other would be a loss for the church and an abandonment of the NT pattern," in "Kerygma and Didache," 628.

49. Paul also states this commissioning of Christians and the Christian church in other ways. For example, Paul uses the language of being κλητός "called." In Rom 1:1 he introduces himself as the one "called" to be an apostle and "set apart" for the gospel of God; but then Paul is not only the one "called" but also the one who does the "calling" on God's behalf (Rom 1:5), through his commissioned preaching of the gospel. And then Paul immediately applies the same concept to the Roman Christians by addressing them as the ones κλητός "called" to belong to Jesus Christ (Rom 1:6) and "called" to be ἅγιοι "saints" or "holy" (Rom 1:7). Similarly, in 1 Corinthians, Paul introduces

Conclusion

This chapter has explored the phenomenon in the Bible where God chooses *human messengers* to preach his word. Moses was the paradigm of such a human messenger, for he was anointed by the Spirit, commissioned by God, received his words from God, and he faithfully proclaimed this word by truthfully proclaiming it. He did not modify the message; and he did not preach his own message, but God's message. After Moses, there was the expectation of another prophet "like Moses" who would faithfully preach God's word. This expectation was fulfilled in each subsequent salvation-historical stage by major salvation-historical individual figures, most prominently Samuel, David, Solomon, Elijah, and the other court prophets and writing prophets. There also developed the anticipation of an Isaianic servant who would obediently preach God's message of salvation. In the New Testament, Jesus represents the climactic fulfillment of this expectation. He is the prophet and servant *par excellence*. But he is more than this, for he is also the divine Son of God whose words are God's words. After Jesus, the apostles are the ones commissioned by Christ to proclaim his word and continue the preaching mission of the prophet and servant. But after the apostles, the Christian church now collectively assumes the role and identity of the prophet and servant. They are to follow in the footsteps of Jesus by becoming the Spirit-anointed, commissioned, faithful proclaimers of the word of God. But what is the content of this proclamation? This question will be addressed in the next chapter.

---

himself as the one κλητός "called" to be an apostle (1 Cor 1:1), but then applies the same concept to the Corinthian Christians by addressing them as the ones κλητός "called" to be ἅγιοι "saints" or "holy" (1 Cor 1:2). Therefore, just as Paul was called to serve God, so the Christians have also been called to a life of service to God, which of course is not limited to, but surely includes, the preaching of the gospel.

6

The Message of Preaching

The previous chapter explored the phenomenon in the Bible where God chooses human messengers to preach his word. It was concluded that God sovereignly chooses to speak his word through his Spirit-anointed, divinely commissioned messengers who faithfully proclaim the message that they receive from God. But what is this message that is to be received from God and proclaimed by the human messengers? Although this was briefly overviewed in a previous chapter, the purpose of this chapter is to examine in more detail the content of the preached word by human messengers in the biblical testimony.

A General Message from God

When a preacher in the Old Testament proclaims the word of God, in a general sense, it can refer to any message from God. Prophets might even precede such messages with the formula, "This is what the Lord says..." (כֹּה אָמַר יהוה). For example, Nathan's word from God to King David rebukes and punishes David for his sin of adultery with Bathsheba (2 Sam 12:7–10). Elijah's word from God to the widow at Zarephath is that her jar of flour will not be used up and the jug of oil will not run dry (1 Kgs 17:14). Isaiah's word from God to King Hezekiah is that he will be healed (2 Kgs 20:5–6).

There were several criteria for assessing if a prophet's message was indeed from God or not. First, if the message instructs its hearers to worship other gods, then it is not the word of God. Deuteronomy 13 warns:

> If a prophet, or one who foretells by dreams, appears among you and announces to you a miraculous sign or wonder, and if the sign or wonder of which he has spoken takes place, and he says, "Let us follow other gods" (gods you have not known) "and

let us worship them," you must not listen to the words of that prophet or dreamer. (Deut 13:1–3)

Second, if the message does not come true, then it is not the word of God. Deuteronomy 18 warns, "If what a prophet proclaims in the name of the Lord does not take place or come true, that is a message the Lord has not spoken" (Deut 18:22). Thus, in both these warnings, the criteria concern the content rather than the form of the message. While the message might come through a variety of means—for example, dreams, miracles, or proclamation—its content must correspond with the truth. The message must not turn people away from the true God to false gods, and it must come true.

A Special Message from God

By the time of the so-called writing prophets, in a more specific sense, the word from God often refers to a special message of salvation. In this message, on an eschatological "Day of the Lord," God would climactically act to save and vindicate his people; conversely, God would climactically act to judge and punish his enemies and the enemies of his people. Moreover, this would be achieved through his chosen Davidic Messiah, who would establish the eternal reign of his kingdom, which would be characterized by peace, justice, and salvation. This is the dominant message of the prophets who proclaim the word from God.[1] Willem VanGemeren provides this useful summary:

> By the eighth century the prophetic function was enlarged to that of *preacher*, whose inspired message was cast into distinct forms of prophetic speech. The prophet was a *covenant prosecutor*, commissioned by the Lord to indict Judah, declare it guilty, and forewarn it of the coming judgments of the Lord. The prophet was also a *visionary*, speaking of a new age. This message of another day was marked by comfort, hope, and a call for an individual response of love for the Lord, with whom is mercy and forgiveness.[2]

---

1. For a more detailed analysis of the content of the prophets' message, see Smith, "Prophet; Prophecy," 999–1000.

2. VanGemeren, *The Progress of Redemption*, 269; his italics.

The Word of God in the New Testament

With the arrival of Jesus, a new salvation-historical age is inaugurated.[3] Increasingly, the word of God refers specifically to the gospel message that is proclaimed by Christ and about Christ.[4] This subsequently becomes the message proclaimed by the apostles, and is the same message that the Christian church hears and believes, and in turn proclaims. This section will explore how the gospel message in the New Testament is an important component of the word of God.

Jesus

Jesus is presented as the paradigmatic preacher of the word of God. But what is the content of his preached word? In the Synoptic Gospels, a variety of terms are used to refer to the content of Jesus' proclamation.[5] To preach "the word" is to preach the "gospel" or the message of "the kingdom."[6] Mark uses the terms "word" and "gospel" interchangeably to refer to the news that the kingdom of God comes in the person of the Christ;[7] this is

---

3. "Although the continuities between the preaching of John [the Baptist] and of Jesus are evident, it is also clear that in the person, work, and words of Jesus a new era begins. The reign of God has broken in and continues to do so," Craddock, "Preaching," 452.

4. This is not to say that the "word of God" in the New Testament refers exclusively to the gospel message (e.g., 1 Thess 4:15), but that, increasingly, the referent of "word of God" would be the gospel message.

5. The "word" (ὁ λόγος; Mark 2:2; 4:14, 33; Luke 10:39); "the word of God" (ὁ λόγος τοῦ θεοῦ; Luke 5:1; 8:11; 11:28); "the gospel" (the verb εὐαγγελίζω; Luke 4:18; 7:22; 20:1; cf. Luke 9:6; Matt 11:5); "the gospel" (the noun τό εὐαγγέλιον; Mark 1:14–15; cf. Mark 13:10; 14:9; Matt 24:14; 26:13); "the kingdom of God" (ἡ βασιλεία τοῦ θεοῦ; Luke 9:11; cf. 9:2, 60); "the gospel of the kingdom" (τό εὐαγγέλιον τῆς βασιλείας; Matt 4:23; 9:35; Luke 4:43; 8:1; cf. Matt 24:14; Luke 16:16); "the kingdom of heaven [or God] is near" ἡ βασιλεία and ἐγγίζω; Matt 3:2; Mark 1:15; cf. Matt 10:7; Luke 10:9); and "the word of the kingdom" (ὁ λόγος τῆς βασιλείας; Matt 13:19).

6. For a detailed discussion of the concept of "the kingdom," see Ladd, *A Theology of the New Testament*, 54–132; Ladd, "Kingdom of God," 23–29. For an alternative understanding of "kingdom," from the perspective of dispensational theology, consult Ryrie, *Dispensationalism*, 153–58.

7. Cranfield provides this useful analysis of Jesus' preaching about the kingdom of God: "[The kingdom of God] is intimately connected with [Jesus'] own person. It is in his activity . . . words and works and person that the kingdom has come. In fact, we may actually go as far as to say that the kingdom of God *is* Jesus and that he *is* the kingdom . . . He is himself the fulfilment of God's promises, God's royal intervention in judgement and mercy . . . [The kingdom of God is, for the evangelists, identical with Jesus himself . . . The kingdom has both come and is still to come, because Jesus has come and

the word that must be "heard" (Mark 4:9), and the correct response is to "repent and believe the gospel" (Mark 1:14–15).[8] Matthew, similarly, uses the terms "word" and "gospel" to refer to the news that the kingdom of God[9] comes in the person of the Christ.[10] And Luke, like Matthew and Mark, uses the terms "gospel," "word," and "word of God" to describe the content of Jesus' preaching, which consists of the message that the kingdom of God is nearing through the person and work of Christ.[11]

---

is to come again," in *The Gospel according to Saint Mark*, 66.

8. For example, Mark describes Jesus commencing his public preaching ministry by "proclaiming the gospel of God" (κηρύσσωand τόευάγγελιον; Mark 1:14) in which he announces, "The kingdom of God is near" (ἡ βασιλεία τοῦ θεοῦand ἐγγίζω) to which the hearers need to respond by repenting and believing the "gospel" (τόευάγγελιον; Mark 1:15). Thus, the gospel message consists of the news that the kingdom of God is arriving in the person of Jesus, and this sets the paradigm for the rest of Jesus' preaching.

Earlier, in Mark 1:1, Mark uses "gospel" (τό εὐαγγέλιον) to introduce his account of the life, person, and ministry of Jesus the Christ, the Son of God. The ensuing quotation of Isaiah 40 and Malachi 3 (Mark 1:2–3) shows that the "gospel" refers to news about the impending arrival of God's eschatological age of salvation, through the arrival of the "Lord," whom we will find out is the person Jesus Christ. But after Mark 1:14–15 uses the term "gospel," Mark 2:2 uses "word" (ὁ λόγος) to describe the content of Jesus' preaching (Mark 2:2; 4:14, 33). In the paradigmatic parable of the sower, the sower sows the "word" (Mark 4:14, 15, 16, 17, 18, 19, 20). Further, Mark 4:14 and 4:33 act as inclusios, by bracketing Mark's collection of Jesus' parables in Mark 4; Mark thus categorizes Jesus' parables, in which he teaches "the kingdom of God" (Mark 4:26, 30), as a form of "speaking the word."

9. The terms "kingdom of heaven" and "kingdom of God" refer to the same kingdom—they do not refer to two different kingdoms. Matthew uses both terms, whereas Mark and Luke only use "kingdom of God." Matthew will often use "kingdom of heaven" where Luke and Mark will use "kingdom of God" in the same account (e.g., Matt 4:17 and Mark 1:15; Matt 10:7–8 and Luke 9:2; Matt 11:11 and Luke 7:28; Matt 13:11 and Mark 4:11). As Ladd notes, "Although [classic] dispensational theology has customarily made a theological distinction between these two terms, the simple fact is that they are quite interchangeable . . . In Jewish rabbinic literature, the common phrase is 'the kingdom of the heavens' . . . In Jewish idiom, 'heaven' or some similar term was often used in place of the holy name (see Lk. 15:18; Mk. 15:61)," in "Kingdom of God," 3:24. So also Cranfield, *The Gospel according to Saint Mark*, 64.

10. In Matthew, Jesus commences his public preaching ministry by preaching, "Repent, the kingdom of heaven is near" (Matt 4:17), but omitting the term "gospel," which Mark uses (Mark 1:14). For Matthew, the content of Jesus' preaching is "the gospel of the kingdom" (τό εὐαγγέλιον τῆς βασιλείας; Matt 4:23; 9:35) and "the word of the kingdom" (ὁ λόγος τῆς βασιλείας; Matt 13:19). Whereas the sower sowed the "word" in Mark, the sower sows "the word of the kingdom" (ὁ λόγος τῆς βασιλείας) in Matthew 13:19, which he equates with the "word" (ὁ λόγος) in the rest of the explanation of the parable (Matt 13:20, 21, 22, 23). The parable of the sower also introduces Matthew's collection of Jesus' "kingdom of heaven" parables (Matt 13:24, 31, 33, 44, 45, 47, 52).

11. In Luke, Jesus commences his public preaching ministry by claiming to be the Isaianic servant-preacher who "preaches the gospel" (εὐαγγελίζω; Luke 4:18), which

In John's Gospel, Jesus is not only the preacher of God's word—he *is* God's "Word" incarnate (John 1:1-18). Thus, everyone (e.g., the Father, the Spirit, the Son, John the Baptist, and the disciples) and everything (e.g., Scripture, Jesus' works) "testify" to Jesus. The word, God's testimony, is Christocentric: Christ is the word from God; he is the "testimony" from the Father; and he is the climactic revelation from God—God the Son becoming flesh and dwelling among his people.

The Apostles

In the Synoptic Gospels, the disciples preach the same message as Jesus' message. The content of the preaching is the same—that is, the gospel. The Synoptic Gospels describe the disciples' message as "the gospel" (the verb εὐαγγελίζω; Luke 9:6); "the gospel" (the noun τό εὐαγγέλιον; Mark 13:10; Matt 24:14); "the kingdom of God" (ἡ βασιλεία τοῦ θεοῦ; Luke 9:2, 60); "the gospel of the kingdom" (τό εὐαγγέλιον τῆς βασιλείας; Matt 24:14; Luke 16:16); and "the kingdom of heaven [or God] is near" (ἤγγικεν ἡ βασιλεία τῶν οὐρανῶν; Matt 10:7; Luke 10:9). The disciples' preaching is that "people should repent" (Mark 6:12), just as Jesus had also preached (Mark 1:15).

In John's Gospel, the paradigm of a follower of Jesus is a "witness." For example, John the Baptist is a faithful witness of Christ (John 1:6-8, 15); and in John 4, the Samaritan woman bears "testimony" to Jesus (John 4:39-41). John, the Gospel writer, is another example of a faithful "witness" (John 19:35; 20:31; 21:24); and the Gospel of John itself represents a written testimony of Jesus Christ (John 21:24). Thus, a disciple of Christ is someone who faithfully "testifies" to the Word—that is, Jesus the Christ.

In Acts, the role of the apostles as the eschatological preacher who preaches the word of God is prominent.[12] But what is the content of this

---

establishes the paradigm for the rest of Jesus' preaching (Luke 7:22; 20:1). However, Luke also uses the term "the word of God" (ὁ λόγος τοῦ θεοῦ) to describe the specific content of this preaching (Luke 5:1; 11:28). In his account of the parable of the sower, the sower is sowing "the word of God" (ὁ λόγος τοῦ θεοῦ; Luke 8:11), which he equates with "the word" (ὁ λόγος) in the rest of the explanation of the parable (Luke 8:12, 13, 15). Luke also describes Jesus preaching "the kingdom of God" (ἡ βασιλεία τοῦ θεοῦ; Luke 9:11).

12. Words such as κηρύσσω (Acts 8:5; 9:20; 10:37, 42; 15:21; 19:13; 20:25; 28:31), εὐαγγελίζω (Acts 5:42; 8:4, 12, 25, 35, 40; 10:36; 11:20; 13:32; 14:7, 15, 21; 15:35; 16:10; 17:18), μαρτυρέω (Acts 6:3; 10:43; 13:22; 14:3; 15:8; 23:11), διαμαρτύρομαι (Acts 2:40; 8:25; 10:42; 18:5; 20:21; 23:11; 28:23), καταγγέλλω (Acts 3:24; 4:2; 13:5, 38; 15:36; 16:17; 17:3, 13, 23; 26:23), ἀναγγέλλω (Acts 14:27; 15:4; 20:20, 27), ἀπαγγέλλω (Acts 26:20), διδάσκω (Acts 1:1; 4:2, 18; 5:21, 25, 28, 42; 11:26; 15:35; 18:11, 25; 20:20; 21:21, 28; 28:31), λαλέω (2:11; 4:1, 17, 20, 29; 4:31; 5:20, 40; 6:10; 8:25; 10:44; 11:14-15, 19,

apostolic preaching? The preaching, or the *kerygma*, of the apostles is the message that Jesus is the Christ who has come, died, and has been raised and vindicated by God, so that all must now repent and obey him.[13] Peter, the paradigmatic apostle of the first half of Acts, summarizes this message as:

> Therefore, let all Israel be assured of this: God has made this Jesus, whom you crucified, both Lord and Christ . . . Repent and be baptized, every one of you, in the name of Jesus Christ for the forgiveness of your sins. And you will receive the gift of the Holy Spirit. (Acts 2:36, 38)

And Paul, the paradigmatic apostle in the second half of Acts, similarly summarizes the message as, "I have declared to both Jews and Greeks that they must turn to God in repentance and have faith in our Lord Jesus" (Acts 20:21). Often Luke, the writer of Acts, will record a summary of the apostolic speeches that contains this essential *kerygma*.[14] Other times, Luke will abbreviate the message and simply say that the apostles preached about "Jesus," "Christ," or his resurrection.[15] At other times, Luke will use various terms to describe the content of the apostolic preaching—including terms

---

20; 13:42, 45, 46; 14:1, 9, 25; 16:6, 13, 14, 32; 17:19; 18:9, 25; 26:22, 26), ἐκτίθημι (18:26; 28:23), and παρρησιάζομαι (9:27, 28; 13:46; 14:3; 18:26; 19:8; 26:26) describe the activity of preaching. This demonstrates that Luke uses a variety of terms to describe preaching; it also reinforces that the concept of preaching cannot be restricted to a few word groups.

13. In a famous and influential study, C. H. Dodd summarized the essential elements of the "primitive preaching," the *kerygma*, of the apostles as: (i) the age of fulfillment has dawned; (ii) this has taken place through the ministry, death, and resurrection of Jesus; (iii) by virtue of his resurrection, Jesus is the messianic head of the new Israel; (iv) the outpouring of the Holy Spirit in the church is a sign of Christ's present power and glory; (v) the Messianic Age will shortly reach its consummation in the return of Christ; and (vi) all should repent and receive the offer of forgiveness, the Holy Spirit, and the promise of salvation. Dodd, *The Apostolic Preaching and Its Developments,*, 21–24. Dodd's work was also largely a response to Rudolf Bultmann's existential understanding of Paul's *kerygma*. For a summary and analysis of this debate regarding the apostolic *kerygma* in NT studies, see Mounce, "Preaching, Kerygma," 736–37.

Although we should probably resist the temptation to reconstruct the *kerygma* from the summary of the sermons in Acts, for such attempts can be overly rigid and narrow, nonetheless, in all the sermons in Acts, the important elements of proclamation are Christ's death for sins, his resurrection as a fulfillment of God's plan, and the need to repent accordingly. For a more extensive treatment of the apostolic *kerygma*, see Polhill, "Kerygma and Didache," 626–29.

14. E.g., Acts 2:14–41; 3:12–26; 4:8–12; 7:2–53; 10:34–43; 13:16–41; 14:15–17; 17:3, 22–31; 22:1–21; 26:2–23.

15. E.g., Acts 4:33; 5:42; 8:5, 12, 35; 9:20, 22; 11:20; 17:3, 7, 18; 18:5, 25, 28; 19:4; 24:24; 25:19; 28:23, 31.

such as "the word of God" (ὁ λόγος τοῦ θεοῦ), "the good news that Jesus is the Christ" (εὐαγγελίζτόν χριστόν Ἰησοῦ), "the Christ" (ὁ Χριστός), "the good news of the kingdom of God" (εὐαγγελίζωπερὶ τῆς βασιλείας τοῦθεοῦ), and "the word of the gospel" (ὁ λόγος τοῦ εὐαγγελίου)—all of which refer to the gospel.[16] And sometimes Luke personifies "the word" so that "the word of God spread" (6:7), "the word of God continued to increase and spread" (12:24), "the word of the Lord spread through the whole region" (13:49), and "the word of the Lord spread widely and grew in power" (19:20)—in such cases, Luke is referring to the whole event of gospel proclamation. Thus, Luke uses a variety of terms to describe or summarize the content of the apostolic preaching, and one primary term is the preaching of "the word." But these terms are all synonymous for the *kerygma*, or the gospel, that is, the proclaimed message that Jesus is the risen Christ. Thus, in Acts, to preach the gospel is to preach the word.

Likewise, in Acts, the role of the apostles is also to be the Isaianic servant—the "witness." But to what are the apostles "testifying"? A key passage is when Peter proclaims to Cornelius:

> We are witnesses of everything he did in the country of the Jews and in Jerusalem. They killed him by hanging him on a tree, but God raised him from the dead on the third day and caused him to be seen. He was not seen by all the people, but by witnesses

---

16. Additional examples include "the wonders of God" (τὰ μεγαλεῖα τοῦ θεοῦ; Acts 2:11), "in Jesus" (ἐν τῷἸησοῦ; 4:2), "the resurrection of the dead" (ἡ ἀνάστασις ἐκ νεκρῶν; 4:2; 17:18, 32), "the word" (ὁ λόγος; 4:4, 29; 6:4; 8:4; 10:36, 44; 11:19; 14:25; 16:6; 17:11; 18:5; 20:7), "in the name of Jesus" (ἐπί τῷ ὀνόματιτοῦἸησοῦ; 4:18; 5:28, 40; 9:27, 28; 19:13), "the word of God" (ὁ λόγος τοῦ θεοῦ; 4:31; 6:2, 7; 8:14; 11:1; 12:24; 13:5, 7, 46; 17:13; 18:11), "the full message of this new life" (πάντα τά ῥήματα τῆς ζωῆς ταύτης; 5:20), "the good news that Jesus is the Christ" (εὐαγγελίζω τόν χριστόνἸησοῦ; 5:42; 17:3), "the Christ" (ὁ Χριστός; 8:5), "the good news of the kingdom of God" (εὐαγγελίζω περὶ τῆς βασιλείας τοῦ θεοῦ; 8:12; 19:8; 28:23, 31), "the name of Jesus Christ" (τό ὄνομαἸησοῦ Χριστοῦ; 8:12), "the word of the Lord" (ὁ λόγος τοῦ κυρίου; 8:25; 13:44, 48, 49; 15:35, 36; 16:32; 19:10, 20), "the good news about Jesus" (εὐαγγελίζω τόνἸησοῦν; 8:35; 11:20; 17:18), "the gospel" or "good news" (εὐαγγελίζω; 8:40; 13:32; 14:7, 15, 21; 16:10), "Jesus is the Son of God" (ὁἸησοῦς ὅτι οὗτός ἐστιν ὁ υἱός τοῦ θεοῦ; 9:20), "the good news of peace through Jesus Christ" (εὐαγγελίζω εἰρήνην διὰ Ἰησοῦ Χριστοῦ; 10:36), "the word of salvation" (ὁ λόγος τῆς σωτηρίας; 13:26), "the forgiveness of sins" (ἡ ἄφεσις ἁμαρτιῶν; 13:38), "the word of grace" (ὁ λόγος τῆς χάριτος; 14:3), "the word of the gospel" (ὁ λόγος τοῦ εὐαγγέλιον; 15:7), "the way of salvation" (ἡ ὁδός σωτηρίας; 16:17), "Jesus is the Christ" (ἐστιν ὁ ΧριστόςἸησοῦ; 17:3; 18:5), "the way of God" (ἡ ὁδός τοῦ θεοῦ; 18:26), "the gospel of God's grace" (τό εὐαγγέλιον τῆς χάριτος τοῦ θεοῦ; 20:24), "the kingdom" (ἡ βασιλεία; 20:25), "the whole will of God" (πᾶσα ἡ βουλή τοῦ θεοῦ; 20:27), "the word of his grace" (ὁ λογος τῆς χάριτος αὐτοῦ; 20:32), "faith in Christ Jesus" (εἰς ΧριστόνἸησοῦν πίστις; 24:24), and "repentance and turning back" (μετανοέωκαί ἐπιστρέφω; 26:20).

whom God had already chosen—by us who ate and drank with him after he rose from the dead. He commanded us to preach to the people and to testify that he is the one whom God appointed as judge of the living and the dead. All the prophets testify about him that everyone who believes in him receives forgiveness of sins through his name. (Acts 10:39–43)

The content of Peter's Christocentric "testimony" is that Christ is the risen and vindicated Messiah, whom God has appointed to be judge, and thus all must repent and believe in him, in order to receive forgiveness of sins (vv. 39–42). Peter's testimony is specifically Christocentric; and Peter earlier calls it "the message (ὁ λόγος) God sent to the people of Israel, telling the good news (εὐαγγελίζω) of peace" (Acts 10:36). And this Christocentric "testimony" is the consistent "testimony" of all the apostles throughout the book of Acts (cf. Acts 2:32; 3:15; 4:33; 5:30–32; 10:39–43; 13:30–31; 20:21). And although Luke might employ many different terms to describe the content of the apostolic "witness,"[17] they are terms used synonymously for "the word" or "the gospel"—the message that Christ is the risen King and Savior to whom all must repent and obey. Therefore, in Acts, the apostles "testify" to Christ by proclaiming the gospel. As a result, although not all have been able to see physically the risen Christ (Acts 10:41), nonetheless they are able to know the risen Christ through the "witness" of those who have seen, namely, the apostles (v. 42).

Moreover, the apostles' Christocentric "testimony" is consistent with the "testimony" of the Old Testament prophets who also "testified" that Jesus is the one through whom forgiveness of sins is found (Acts 10:43). That is, the Old Testament prophets and the Old Testament canonical Scriptures also testified about Christ through their proclaimed and written words— and a consistent theme in Acts is how the apostles regularly appealed to the OT Scriptures' testimony to demonstrate the validity of their own testimony (e.g., Acts 3:18, 21, 24; 13:27, 32–33; 15:15; 26:22; 28:23).[18] Thus, there is continuity in the apostles' Christocentric "testimony" with that of the OT prophets and canon; the apostles' "testimony" is the message that

---

17. The "witness" of the apostles is the "word" or "the gospel" of God. In other passages in Acts, the "witness" of the apostles is associated with "proclaiming the word of the Lord" (λαλέω and ὁ λόγος τοῦ κυρίου) and "preaching the gospel" (εὐαγγελίζω; Acts 8:25); "the message of salvation" (ὁ λόγος τῆς σωτηρίας; Acts 13:26); "the good news" (ἡ ἐπαγγελία; Acts 13:32); "the message of his grace" (ὁ λόγος τῆς χάριτος αὐτοῦ; Acts 14:3); "the gospel of God's grace" (τό εὐαγγέλιον τῆς χάριτος τοῦ θεοῦ; Acts 20:24); and "the kingdom of God" (ἡ βασιλεία τοῦ θεοῦ; Acts 28:28).

18. This was also an important theme in the book of Luke (e.g., Luke 24:27, 44–49).

the eschatological messianic reign, as anticipated by the OT prophets and canonical writings, has begun.

In Paul's epistles, the content of his preached message is specifically the gospel. Paul sometimes uses the terms εὐαγγελίζω and εὐαγγελιον to refer to this activity of preaching the gospel, but at other times he will use a wide variety of phrases—such as ὁ λόγος, τό κήρυγμα, τό μαρτήριον, τό μυστήριον, and τό ῥῆμα—to refer to this preached gospel message, either in its entirety or some aspect of it.[19] Sometimes Paul will provide a summary of this gospel in the form of a creed, tradition, or hymn (e.g., 1 Cor 15:1-8, Phil 2:6-11; 2 Tim 2:11-13). For Paul, to preach the message of the gospel is to preach the "word." In the Letters to the Corinthians, Paul expounds this in more detail. Paul has been commissioned by God to preach the gospel: "For Christ did not send me to baptize, but to preach the gospel—not with words of human wisdom, lest the cross of Christ be emptied of its power" (1 Cor 1:17). Thus, not only has Paul been commissioned to preach, but his message is to be specifically that of the gospel. In the first two chapters of 1 Corinthians, Paul explains that he preaches "Christ crucified" (1 Cor 1:23; 2:2). Although this message seems weak and foolish (1:18-25), and unaccompanied by eloquence, "superior wisdom," and "wise and persuasive words" (2:1-4), it comes with a demonstration of the Spirit's power (2:4)

---

19. For example, Paul refers to the preached message of the gospel as τό ῥῆμα τῆς πίστεως "the word of faith" (Rom 10:8); ῥῆμα Χριστοῦ "the word of Christ" (Rom 10:17); τό κήρυγμα Ἰησοῦ Χριστοῦ "the proclamation of Jesus Christ" (Rom 16:25); ὁ λόγος ὁ τοῦ σταυροῦ "the message of the cross" (1 Cor 1:18); Χριστός ἐσταυρωμένος "Christ crucified" (1 Cor 1:23; 2:2); τό μαρτήριον τοῦ θεοῦ "the testimony about God" (1 Cor 2:1); αἱ παραδόσει "the traditions" (1 Cor 11:2; 2 Thess 2:15; 3:6); παραδίδωμι ὑμῖν "[the tradition] I passed onto you" (1 Cor 11:2, 23; 15:3); Χριστός κηρύσσεται ὅτι ἐκ νεκρῶν ἐγήγερται "it is preached that Christ has been raised from the dead" (1 Cor 15:12); ὁ λόγος τοῦ θεοῦ "the word of God" (2 Cor 2:17; 4:2; Phil 1:14; 2 Tim 2:9; 1 Thess 2:13); Ἰησοῦς Χριστός κύριος "Christ as Lord" (2 Cor 4:5); ὁ λόγος τῆς καταλλαγῆς "the message of reconciliation" (2 Cor 5:19); ὁ υἱός αὐτοῦ "[God's] Son (Gal 1:16); ὁ λόγος τῆς ἀληθείας, τό εὐαγγέλιον τῆς σωτηρίας ὑμῶν "the word of truth, the gospel of your salvation" (Eph 1:13; Col 1:5); τό μυστήριον τοῦ Χριστοῦ "the mystery of Christ" (Eph 3:4; Col 4:3); τό ἀνεξιχνίαστον πλοῦτος τοῦ Χριστοῦ "the unsearchable riches of Christ" (Eph 3:8); τό μυστήριον τοῦ εὐαγγελίου "the mystery of the gospel" (Eph 6:19); ὁ Χριστός "Christ" (Phil 1:15-18); λόγος ζωῆς "the word of life" (Phil 2:16); ὁ λόγος τοῦ θεοῦ; τό μυστήριον "the word of God ... the mystery" (Col 1:25); Christ (Col 1:28; 1 Tim 3:16); ὁ λόγος τοῦ Χριστοῦ "the word of Christ" (Col 3:16); ὁ λόγος "the word" (Col 4:3; 1 Thess 1:6; 2 Tim 4:2); ὁ λόγος τοῦ κυρίου "the word of the Lord" (1 Thess 1:8; 2 Thess 3:1); οἱ λόγοι τῆς πίστεως "the words of the faith" (1 Tim 4:6); τό μαρτύριον τοῦ κυρίου ἡμῶν "the testimony about our Lord" (2 Tim 1:8); ὁ λόγος τῆς ἀληθείας "the word of truth" (2 Tim 2:15); τό κήρυγμα "the message" (2 Tim 4:17); ὁ λόγος αὐτοῦ "[God's] word" (Titus 1:3); and πιστός λόγος "the trustworthy message" (Titus 1:9). These terms are synonymous for the preaching of the gospel message. So also Mounce, "Preaching, Kerygma," 735.

and is nothing less than God's secret, hidden, but now revealed, wisdom (2:6-10). Thus, it is not the form of the message that determines if the word of God is preached but its content, namely, the gospel; and the content has priority over the form of the message, for the form must not obscure or detract from the gospel. Conversely, Paul argues in Gal 1:6-9 that if the gospel message is replaced with a different gospel, then the word of God has not been preached, no matter how convincing its form or messenger (cf. 2 Cor 11:4).

God has spoken this Christocentric message of the gospel in the past to his people through his Old Testament prophets. Paul begins his Letter to the Romans: "[T]he gospel [God] promised beforehand through his prophets in the Holy Scriptures regarding his Son" (Rom 1:2-3a).[20] Similarly, in the body of the letter, Paul announces, "But now a righteousness from God, apart from law, has been made known, to which the Law and the Prophets testify" (Rom 3:21).[21] In the conclusion of the Letter to the Romans, Paul states that the gospel is "now revealed and made known through the prophetic writings by the command of the eternal God" (Rom 16:26). Thus, for Paul, God spoke and revealed his word, the gospel, through the proclamation and writings of the OT prophets, whose words have been inscripturated and continue to speak to the present audience through OT Scripture. However, God also continues his revelation through the proclamation by Jesus Christ, and subsequently by the New Testament apostles. Thus, there is continuity between the OT prophets, Jesus, and the NT apostles, because all are proclaiming the same God-revealed, Christocentric message of the gospel.[22]

---

20. Moo comments on these verses, "Paul further defines the gospel as something promised in the OT. In a manner typical of Paul's emphasis throughout Romans, he draws a line of continuity between the new work of God in his Son, the content of the gospel (vv. 3-4), and the OT . . . It is doubtful whether Paul has any particular OT passages in mind here; his purpose is general and principial, to allay possible suspicion about 'his' gospel as new and innovative by asserting its organic relationship to the OT," in *The Epistle to the Romans*, 43-44.

21. The term "righteousness of God" refers back to Rom 1:17; it is the aspect of the gospel in which God justifies the Christian believer. For an extensive treatment of the contemporary debate regarding this term, see Moo's treatment in *The Epistle to the Romans*, 63-90. Of relevance for us is the continuity of this aspect of the gospel with the OT—it is testified to by the Law and the Prophets; but there is also a discontinuity—it is "apart from law."

22. There is also continuity between the OT prophets, Jesus, and the NT apostles in the way that they are rejected by their people. Paul notes this in his letter to the Thessalonians: "You suffered from your own countrymen the same things those churches suffered from the Jews, who killed the Lord Jesus and the prophets and also drove us out" (1 Thess 2:14b-15a).

But there is also a discontinuity between the Old Testament prophets and the New Testament apostles because of God's progressive revelation through the different stages of salvation-history. Paul expresses this continuity and discontinuity between the OT prophets and the NT apostles through his use of the term "mystery" (μυστήριον).[23] For example, Paul writes in his conclusion to Romans:

> Now to him who is able to establish you by my gospel and the proclamation of Jesus Christ, according to the revelation of the *mystery* hidden for long ages past, but now revealed and made known through the prophetic writings by the command of the eternal God, so that all nations might believe and obey him ... [my emphasis] (Rom 16:25-26)[24]

There is continuity between Paul's "gospel" (εὐαγγέλιον), the "proclamation" (κήρυγμα) of Christ, and the Old Testament "prophetic writings" (γραφαί προφητικαί), for it is the prophetic writings that "reveal" (φανερόω) this gospel. But there is also discontinuity, for although this gospel was referred to by the OT prophetic writings, and thus already present in the OT Scriptures, it was a "mystery" (μυστήριον) that was "hidden" (σιγάω; or "kept secret") and is only now "revealed" (ἀποκάλυψις) and made known by the command of God.[25] Paul accordingly uses the term "mystery" to refer

---

23. The term "mystery" occurs twenty-one times in Paul's writings. For an extensive treatment of Paul's use of this term, see O'Brien, "Mystery," 621–23.

24. There is a text critical issue involving Rom 16:25-27; the editors of UBS4 give this text a "C" rating. Metzger writes on behalf of the Editorial Committee of the United Bible Societies' Greek New Testament, "While recognizing the possibility that the doxology may not have been part of the original form of the epistle, on the strength of impressive manuscript evidence (P61 a B C D 81 1739 itd, 61 vg syrp copsa, bo eth Clement *al*) the Committee decided to include the verses at their traditional place in the epistle," in Metzger, *A Textual Commentary on the Greek New Testament*, 540. More detailed discussions regarding the final chapter of Romans can be found in ibid., 533–36; Moo, *The Epistle to the Romans*, 936n2.

25. Paul also refers to this "mystery" in Eph 3:1-13, where he states that he has been commissioned by God—"God's grace ... was given to me for you" (vv. 2, 7, 8)—to proclaim the gospel—"to preach to the Gentiles the unsearchable riches of Christ ... " (v. 8b). Paul uses the term "mystery" (μυστήριον) to refer to a particular aspect of the gospel message—that "through the gospel the Gentiles are heirs together with Israel, members together of one body, and sharers together in the promise in Christ Jesus" (v. 6). Although elements of this message might be continuous with that of the OT prophets, it is largely discontinuous because this "mystery" was "made known" (γνωρίζω) to Paul by "revelation" (ἀποκάλυψις; v. 3). Thus, there is a hiddenness about this mystery, for it was "not made known" (οὐκ γνωρίζω) to people from past generations (v. 5a) and only "now" (νῦν) has been "revealed" (ἀποκαλύπτω) by the Spirit of God through the apostles and prophets (v. 5b)—νῦν occurs twice in this passage (vv. 5, 10) to emphasize the discontinuity and newness in what God is doing in the present salvation-historical

to either the whole gospel, or an aspect of it, which was "hidden" in the previous salvation-historical ages, even though it was proclaimed and inscripturated by the OT prophets, but has only now been "revealed" by God and his Spirit, through the proclamation of the apostles and the writings of the prophets, in this present salvation-historical age. As such, the term "mystery" demonstrates both a continuity and discontinuity between the gospel ministry of the OT prophets and the NT apostles: the proclamation ministry of the OT prophets and the NT apostles is continuous because they are proclaiming the same Christocentric gospel; but also discontinuous because they belong to different salvation-historical eras and different stages in God's progressive revelation.[26]

Therefore, by the time of the apostles, the content of the apostolic preached word of God is increasingly the Christocentric message of the gospel. Ruth B. Edwards agrees: "It is a short step from describing Jesus' own preaching as the word of God to describing the early Christian preaching about Him as the word of God."[27] Similarly, Buist M. Fanning notes:

> In Acts and the epistles, the emphasis moves away from the word of God through Jesus to the word of God about Jesus. The phrases "word of God," "word of the Lord," and simply "the word" are used mostly to denote the gospel, the message about God's work of salvation through the death and resurrection of Jesus Christ. This is the word preached by the apostles and the

---

era by revealing this mystery. Prior to this, "for ages past" (ἀπό τῶν αἰώνων), this mystery was "kept hidden" (ἀποκρύπτω) in God, but has now been "made plain" (φωτίζω; or "brought to light"; v. 9).

Similarly, in Col 1:24–27, Paul states that he has been commissioned by God, to be a servant of the church, to present the word of God in its fullness (v. 25). Paul calls this word of God "the mystery" (τό μυστήριον). This "mystery" had been "kept hidden" (ἀποκρύπτω) "for ages" (ἀπό τῶν αἰώνων) and generations, but only "now" (νῦν δὲ) has been "disclosed" (φανερόω) by God to the saints (vv. 26–27).

26. This is consistent with Paul's understanding of the gospel in his other letters. For example, in 2 Timothy, Paul speaks of the "grace" that was "given us in Christ Jesus before the beginning of time, but . . . now revealed through the appearing of our Savior, Christ Jesus" (2 Tim 1:9b–10a). Thus, although the message of the gospel was always present, even before the beginning of time, it was only progressively revealed by God through each successive stage of salvation-history, reaching its climactic revelation in the person of Christ.

27. Edwards, "Word," 4:1105. So also Runia, who observes, "[A]fter [Jesus'] resurrection and the outpouring of the Spirit Jesus himself is the main content of the apostolic proclamation . . . The apostles, commissioned by the risen Lord, preached this message as the very word of God . . . In the apostolic message (the emphasis being always on *the content*) the voice of the living God is being heard," in "Preaching, Theology of," 527–28.

early church as they went out as Spirit-empowered witnesses to Jesus.[28]

And it is the content of the preached message that determines whether or not the message is the word of God, rather than its form or messenger.

The Christian Church

In the New Testament, the church is composed of individual Christians who have heard and believed the word of God proclaimed, and who in turn now proclaim the word. In Acts, individuals (Acts 21:8) or the whole church (Acts 8:4) would engage in gospel proclamation. In Paul's epistles, Christians are commissioned and called to a ministry of proclaiming the word of God. For example, Paul charges Timothy to "preach the Word" (2 Tim 4:2). But what is this word? In the same way that Paul has been appointed a "herald" of the "gospel" (τό εὐαγγέλιον; 2 Tim 1:8–11), Paul appoints Timothy to join him in testifying "about our Lord" and "suffering for the gospel" (2 Tim 1:8). Therefore, the "word" that is to be preached by Timothy is the message of the gospel, which is:

> [God] has saved us and called us to a holy life—not because of anything we have done but because of his own purpose and grace. This grace was given us in Christ Jesus before the beginning of time, but it has now been revealed through the appearing of our Savior, Christ Jesus, who has destroyed death and has brought life and immortality to light through the gospel. (2 Tim 1:9–10)[29]

In Peter's epistles, the word of God is the gospel message that the Christian readers have heard and believed. For example, in 1 Peter 1:10–12, Peter reminds his readers of the "salvation" (v. 10), of which the Old Testament prophets "spoke" (v. 12)—in their proclamation and subsequent inscripturation as OT Scripture[30]—but which came to them through the proclamation of "those who preached the gospel to you" (v. 12). Thus, the word of God is still heard today through the inscripturated words of Scripture and

---

28. Fanning, "Word," 851.

29. Stott, commenting on 2 Timothy 4:2, notes, "Timothy is to 'preach' this word, himself to speak what God has spoken . . . It is good news of salvation for sinners. So he is to proclaim it like a herald in the market-place," in *Guard the Gospel*, 106.

30. In Peter's epistles, God's word is both proclaimed and inscripturated. For example, in 2 Pet 1:19–21, the message of God is proclaimed, for "men *spoke* from God" (ἐλάλησαν ἀπὸ θεοῦ ἄνθρωποι; v. 21). But it is also inscripturated, for Peter also refers to the "prophecy *of Scripture*" (προφητεία γραφῆς; v. 20).

the proclamation of the gospel.³¹ In another example, in 1 Peter 1:18–25, Peter reminds his readers of how the revelation of Christ came to them through hearing "the word of God" (ὁ λόγος θεοῦ; v. 23) or "the word of the Lord" (τό ῥῆμα κυρίου; v. 25) that was preached to them (v. 25b).³² In this context, the "word" refers to the gospel message—as it does later in 1 Pet 3:1 (ὁ λόγος). And the readers became Christians when they heard and believed the preached word, and were "born again" (v. 23; cf. 1 Pet 1:3). Thus, people become Christians through hearing and believing the proclaimed word (cf. 1 Pet 4:6); and the Christians stand in contrast to those who hear the word but do not believe (e.g., 1 Pet 3:1). Moreover, the Christian readers have eternal security because the word, which they heard and believed, will never pass away (1 Pet 1:23–25).³³

In the Letter to the Hebrews, an important component of the overarching argument of the letter is that God continues to speak his word today through the human proclamation of the gospel:

---

31. Michaels, commenting on 1 Peter 1:10–12, notes, "The 'sufferings destined for Christ and the glorious events that would follow' are here identified as the gospel recently proclaimed in Asia Minor to Peter's readers. Their knowledge of these things is by no means solely dependent on the witness of ancient prophets. They have heard the message for themselves, proclaimed afresh in their own time. Although Peter does not say so, this fresh proclamation and fresh hearing are what actually define the message as the gospel of Jesus Christ, supplying for its content his suffering and vindication. This, for the hearers, is the decisive revelation; the ministry of the prophets simply confirms it," *1 Peter*, 46.

32. Thus, Michaels comments on 1 Peter 1:25, "Not content to leave the interpretation of ῥῆμα κυρίου merely implicit, Peter attaches a comment identifying it with 'the message of the gospel that has been proclaimed to you.' To Peter, the message of Jesus and the message about Jesus are the same message, just as they are to Mark (1:1, 14–15) and to the author of Hebrews (2:3–4)." Then Michaels adds, "The passive participle τὸ εὐαγγελισθεν may have been prompted by the active participle ὁ εὐαγγελιζόμενος, which occurs twice in Isa 40:9. Peter does not extend the quotation to v 9 because his attention is focused not on the messengers . . . but on the message. The occurrence of εὐαγγελίζεσθαι in Isaiah's context . . . affords him an excellent opportunity to identify the eternal word of God with the gospel proclaimed in Asia Minor," *1 Peter*, 79.

33. In 1 Peter 4, Peter also notes, "For this is the reason the gospel was preached even to those who are now dead, so that they might be judged according to men in regard to the body, but live according to God in regard to the spirit" (v. 6). Thus, the gospel is preached (εὐαγγελίζω) so that people's lives might be transformed. This is because the gospel message presents the Christ who suffered for sins, and the one who believes will be done with sin (vv. 1–2). This is similar to the argument here in 1 Peter 1:22–24 where Christians have "purified" themselves because they have been born again through the living and enduring "word of God," which was "preached" to them. Thus, for Peter, the "preaching of the word of God" and the "preaching of the gospel" are different terms for the same concept.

> For we also have had the gospel preached to us, just as they did; but the message they heard was of no value to them, because those who heard did not combine it with faith. Now we who have believed enter that rest . . . [my emphasis] (Heb 4:2-3a)

The writer states that both the Exodus generation and the present readers have had "the gospel preached to us" (εὐαγγελίζω); both generations have heard the word (ὁ λόγος τῆς ἀκοῆς; 4:2; cf. 4:6)—God's "voice" (φωνή; cf. 3:7, 15; 4:7) preached the gospel (εὐαγγελίζω) to them. God's "voice"—the gospel—came to the Exodus generation directly from Mount Sinai and indirectly through the proclamation of Moses (cf. Deut 5:23, 27).[34] But how have the *present* readers heard God's "voice" speaking to them? It was through the human proclamation of the gospel.[35] Notice that this is what the writer earlier argues:

> We must pay more careful attention, therefore, to what we have heard, so that we do not drift away. For if the message [λόγος] spoken by angels was binding, and every violation and disobedience received its just punishment, how shall we escape if we ignore such a great salvation [σωτηρία]? *This salvation, which was first announced by the Lord, was confirmed to us by those who heard him.* God also testified to it by signs, wonders and various miracles, and gifts of the Holy Spirit distributed according to his will. [My emphasis] (Heb 2:1-4)

---

34. Bruce comments, "The good news which was proclaimed to [the Israelites], summarized in such Old Testament passages as Ex. 19:3-6; 23:20-33, told them how the God of their fathers, who had delivered them from Egypt, would bring them safely to the promised land and give them possession of it, and would make them 'a kingdom of priests, and a holy nation' to himself, if only they would obey his voice and keep his covenant." Bruce also notes that A. T. Hanson argues that the "gospel" the Israelites received in the wilderness was the identical gospel of Christ received by the recipients of this Letter to the Hebrews, in *The Epistle to the Hebrews*, 105. Hanson's view might be a bit rigid. Nonetheless, both these views (Bruce's and Hanson's) are not incompatible with each other. For, as the writer of Hebrews argues, the Old Testament events, such as the deliverance from Egypt and entrance into the promised land, were anticipations of the salvation that would come through the arrival of Jesus Christ. Thus, the "gospel," which the Israelites heard, was anticipatory of the gospel of Christ. Koester agrees, "Good news came to Moses' generation as a promise that God would deliver them from slavery and bring them to Canaan (Exod 3:16-17; 4:27-31; cf. 6:1-9). In Hebrews these promises foreshadow the deliverance and rest that come through Christ—something that was not apparent to previous generations," in *Hebrews*, 269.

35. Certainly, the readers have heard God's voice through the reading of Old Testament Scriptures, but the readers have also heard God's "voice" through the proclamation of the gospel.

But from whom have the readers "heard" the "message of salvation" (ὁ λόγος... σωτηρίας)—the gospel—as "first announced by the Lord and confirmed by those who heard him"?[36] Unless the readers were present at the time of Jesus' earthly ministry, they would have heard the message of salvation through the proclamation of the gospel from the apostles and other Christians.[37] If so, then God speaks his "voice" to the readers "today," through the human proclamation of the gospel.[38] Therefore, Heb 4:12 concludes this early section by stating:

> For *the word of God* is living and active. Sharper than any double-edged sword, it penetrates even to dividing soul and spirit, joints and marrow; it judges the thoughts and attitudes of the heart. [My emphasis] (Heb 4:12)

But what is this "word of God" (ὁ λόγος τοῦ θεοῦ), which is personified as "living and active"? Certainly, it would at least refer to the text of Psalm 95 that has been repeatedly quoted by the writer in the preceding section.[39] However, because 4:12–13 concludes the argument of 3:1—4:13, the "word of God" could refer more broadly to "God's voice" (3:7, 15; 4:7)—the gospel that was proclaimed and heard by the present readers.[40]

---

36. Notice that the gospel was "first announced by the Lord," that is, it was proclaimed by Jesus during his earthly ministry. This message has been subsequently "confirmed" by "those who heard him," namely, the apostles and others who heard Jesus' preaching. In addition, God testified to this message with signs, wonders, and various miracles, and gifts of the Holy Spirit. Interestingly, instead of an emphasis on "seeing" the ministry of Jesus, the emphasis is upon "hearing" the proclamation of Jesus.

37. Lane comments, "The message of salvation was proclaimed to those who did not have the privilege of hearing the Lord by those who had been witnesses to his word and deed... By speaking of 'the hearers'... all interest is concentrated on the message, not the office, of those who had brought the word of redemption to the community," *Hebrews 1–8*, 39.

38. That the human proclamation of the gospel *is* God's "voice" speaking to the readers is a key component of the *a fortiori* argument that runs throughout the letter. For if the Exodus generation heard and disobeyed God's voice, and were subsequently punished, then *how much more* will the present readers be punished if they also heard and yet disobey God's voice, which now comes through the climactic revelation of his Son, Jesus Christ, as proclaimed through the gospel.

39. For example, Lane identifies the "word of God" in Heb 4:12 as "the text of Scripture," in Lane, *Hebrews 1–8*, 102–3.

40. The "word of God" as the proclaimed gospel is consistent with the usage of the phrases the "word of God" in Heb 2:1–4; 5:12; 6:5; 13:7 and "word of Christ" in Heb 6:1. And, as Koester notes, "The author has focused on God's word as a spoken word, not an abstract concept... Of principal concern is the effect that the word has when it addressed people, whether through the biblical text or through the exhortations that Christians address to one another (13:22; cf. 3:13)," *Hebrews*, 280. So also, Bruce who identifies "God's word" as "that word which fell on disobedient ears in the wilderness

This argument comes to its climax in Hebrews 12:18–27, where the present readers gather, no longer at a physical mountain, such as the Mount Sinai of the Exodus generation, but at the eschatological heavenly reality of Mount Zion; the present readers gather around this "heavenly Jerusalem" whenever they gather on earth.[41] And, whereas the Exodus generation heard the "voice" (φωνή) of God coming from Mount Sinai (v. 19), the readers now hear "him who speaks," namely, God, "the one who warns us from heaven" (v. 25).[42] But how do the present readers hear this "voice"? Since the argument of chapter 12 is a recapitulation and extension of the argument from chapters 3–4,[43] then the "voice" from God, from heaven, comes through the written testimony of Scripture and the proclamation of the gospel.[44] Thus, the present readership are the people of God who gather on earth, but also in anticipation of the eschatological reality of a heavenly gathering of saints and angels around God at the heavenly Mount Zion. Moreover, just as the Exodus generation once gathered around the "voice" of God from Mount Sinai, the present generation gathers around the "voice" of God, as heard now through the written testimony of Scripture and the proclamation of the gospel.[45]

---

and which has been sounded out again in these days of fulfilment," in *The Epistle to the Hebrews*, 111.

41. Earlier, in Hebrews 10:19–25, the writer has argued that because the readers can enter the presence of God in heaven, through the work of Jesus (vv. 19–22), they should make every effort to gather together on earth to encourage each other (vv. 23–25). Thus, although there is a future anticipation of a gathering in heaven, it is also a present reality. So also, Lane, *Hebrews 9–13*, 466–67. Contra Koester, *Hebrews*, 550. Peterson concludes, "Christians are still pilgrims, still treading the road to that heavenly city, yet through Christ we may enjoy the fellowship of that joyful assembly in advance," in *Engaging with God*, 254.

42. Verse 25a only refers to one speaking as "him who speaks." But verse 25b further specifies the one speaking as "him who [warns] us from heaven." This, most likely then, refers to God in heaven. Bruce comments, "But if it was from an earthly hill that God proclaimed the statutes which formed the basis of the old covenant, it is from the heavenly Zion, from his unseen throne, that he speaks in the gospel," in *The Epistle to the Hebrews*, 363.

43. Both sections are introduced with the same imperative, "See to it . . ." (βλέπετε; 3:12; 12:25), and employ similar phrases, exhortation and *a fortiori* argument.

44. Koester agrees, "In an ultimate sense, the one who is speaking is God, but those addressed by Hebrews do not hear God speak in an unmediated way. Therefore, the appeal not to refuse the word of God calls for attention to the human speaker who delivers the word," in *Hebrews*, 552.

45. The *a fortiori* argument is operating here. To disobey the gospel, as "heard" through the Scriptures and human proclamation, is worse than disobeying the "voice" of God that once thundered from the earthly Mount Sinai.

Therefore, in the series of final brief exhortations of the letter, the writer provides an encouragement to the readers to: "Remember your leaders, who spoke the word of God to you" (Heb 13:7). But how did these leaders speak "the word of God"? In the preceding chapters, for the writer of Hebrews, God has spoken through the written testimony of Scripture and the proclamation of the gospel. The "leaders[46] who spoke the word of God" refers, then, to those who originally proclaimed the gospel[47] to the present readers and led them to the Christian faith.[48]

In the Letter of Revelation, one major motif is that the Christians are to be faithful witnesses of Christ.[49] The specific ministry of the Christian church, in its role of the faithful witness and servant, is one that involves bearing witness to "the word of God and the testimony of Jesus" (Rev 1:2, 9; 20:4; cf. 6:9; 19:10). The juxtaposition of "the word of God" and "the testimony of Jesus" implies that these are complementary ways of describing the gospel message—that is, the testimony about what God has achieved through the life and ministry of his Son Jesus Christ.[50] Thus, the Christian

---

46. Verse 17 further identifies the "leaders" as those who are in authority over the readers. These leaders "keep watch" over the souls of the readers, and must give an account, presumably to God. Bruce comments that the leaders are probably the same persons referred to in Hebrews 2:3, where the gospel "was delivered to us with assurance by those who heard him." *The Epistle to the Hebrews*, 375.

47. This understanding of "word of God" as the gospel of Christ would be consistent with the other brief exhortations in the concluding section. For example, in 13:9, the writer also exhorts the readers: "Do not be carried away by all kinds of strange teachings." These "strange teachings" would be teachings that are inconsistent with the "word of God," namely, the gospel that was originally proclaimed by the leaders.

48. So also Lane, *Hebrews 9–13*, 526–27.

49. As Trites notes, "In the Apocalypse the stress seems to fall on Christ, 'the faithful and true witness', who serves as the archetype for the faithful band of believers who must maintain the same testimony even at the sacrifice of life itself," in "Witness, Testimony (part)," 1047.

50. So also Beale who comments, "καὶ τὴν μαρτυρίαν Ιησοῦ Χριστοῦ ('the witness of Jesus Christ') is parallel with τὸν λόγον τοῦ θεοῦ ('the word of God') and clarifies its precise content. The revelatory 'word about God' concerns what he has carried through Jesus Christ," in *The Book of Revelation*, 184. Similarly, Osborne notes, "The two aspects, 'word of God' and 'testimony of Jesus,' are not separate but complementary descriptions . . . Due to their frequent appearance in the book [of Revelation], they become a semitechnical formula for gospel truth and faithful Christian witness to it." Osborne adds, "Τὸν λόγον τοῦ θεου (*ton logon tou theou*, the word of God) is used in Scripture for prophetic utterances as well as for the apostolic message. The phrase occurs seven times in Revelation (1:2, 9; 6:9; 17:17; 19:9, 13; 20:4). In 1:2, 9; 6:9; 20:4 the phrase has the same force it has in Acts (cf. 4:31; 6:2; 8:14; 11:1), referring to Christian witness to and proclamation of the gospel message (in 17:17 and 19:9 it refers to the revealed message of this book)," in *Revelation*, 56.

church fulfills its role as the eschatological Isaianic servant by proclaiming the "word of God," which is the gospel message about Jesus Christ.

Conclusion

This chapter has examined the content of the preached word. In the Old Testament, the word of God could refer to a general message from God, which was usually proclaimed by one of his commissioned human messengers, such as a prophet. However, as the storyline of the Bible progressed, the content of the word of God referred increasingly to a special message of salvation where God would climactically act to save and vindicate his people, and judge and punish his enemies. In the New Testament, with the arrival of Jesus, and the inauguration of a new age of salvation-history, the word of God usually referred specifically to the gospel message. The terms "word of God" and the "gospel" were used synonymously by the New Testament writers to describe the gospel message preached by Jesus and the apostles, heard and believed by the Christian church, and now in turn preached by the Christian church. In the New Testament, the content of the preached word was usually the special message of the gospel. And the content was more important than the form. For it was the content that determined if the preacher was preaching the word of God or not; and the content had priority over the form of the message, lest the form obscure or detract from the content. Conversely, if the preacher was preaching a message that contradicted the gospel, then that message was not to be accepted as the word of God, no matter how convincing the form or the messenger might be. The content of the preached word, the gospel, was also continuous with the message of the Old Testament prophets, which is now inscripturated as Old Testament Scriptures. Thus, there is a continuity between the New Testament apostolic message and the Old Testament Scriptures. And the New Testament apostles frequently referred to this continuity to demonstrate the legitimacy of their message. But the gospel message was also discontinuous with the Old Testament prophets because its message was once "hidden" but only now "revealed."

Our exploration in this chapter suggests that, by the time of the New Testament, the content of the preached word was often the special message of the gospel. Of course this does not mean that the message of the word of God was *only* the gospel, for any general message from God would still be the "word of God" (for example, the prophecy by Agabus in Acts 11:28); thus it would not be *necessary* to preach the gospel to preach the word of God. But it does demonstrate that an important component, or subset, of the message of the word of God in the New Testament was the special message of the gospel; thus it would be *sufficient* to preach the gospel in order to preach the word of God. In other words, to preach the gospel *is* to preach the word of God.

However, this leads to the next subject for investigation. For, when Jesus, the apostles, and the Christian church preached the word of God, they were not attempting only to present the message of the gospel. That is, they were not only trying to convey information to their audience. Instead, there was an intentionality behind their preaching. They were preaching for an intended result. But what was this intentionality? This will be the subject of the next chapter.

— 7 —

The Intention and Results of Preaching

The previous chapter examined the preached word and found that its content, by the time of the New Testament, was often the special message of the gospel. To preach the gospel message was the same as preaching the word. But this leads to two important and related questions. First, what was the intention behind preaching the word? For the human proclaimers, when they were proclaiming God's word, were never only conveying information; there was an intention behind their preaching. Second, how do the actual results of preaching relate to the proclamation of the word? What if the hearer does not respond with faith and obedience to the proclaimed word of God despite the preacher's intention? Has the word of God been preached in such a situation? And what are the roles of the preacher, the hearer, and the Holy Spirit regarding the result of the preached word? The purpose of this chapter is to survey the intention and results of the human proclamation of the word of God in the biblical testimony.

The Intention of Preaching

This section will explore the intention of preaching by the Old Testament prophets, Jesus, the apostles, and the church.

The Old Testament Prophets

The word of God does not only convey information; there is a divine intention behind the word. It is an expression of God's will, which God purposes to accomplish. As Ruth B. Edwards notes, "The word . . . is never simply a piece of information, but rather the will of God in a particular situation. It may come as a message of salvation ... It may be, and often is, a sober message of warning or judgment."[1] Terence E. Fretheim also provides this analysis:

> *The word of God is always an intentional, never an idle word.* The word of God is the vehicle for the will of God; the word expresses what God intends. The intention of the word of God is to serve the purposes of God in the world, to move the world along toward the objectives God has for it. The word activates the will of God; it represents a decision by God to accomplish what God wants to accomplish in a specific situation ... The word makes available to the world what would not otherwise be available—an experience (including knowledge) of the will of God.[2]

As a result, when God commissions his prophets in the Old Testament to proclaim his word, he also commissions them, not only to convey his revelation, but also to express his divine will on his behalf, which God purposes to achieve. Thus, when the prophet speaks on behalf of God, there is a divinely commissioned intention behind the preached word.

For example, in the commissioning of Moses, God announces, "So now, go, I am sending you to Pharaoh to bring my people the Israelites out of Egypt" (Exod 3:10). Thus, in Moses' ensuing ministry, he brings God's word to Pharaoh in order to command Pharaoh to obey God's request to release the Israelites from slavery. The intention behind the preaching ministry of Moses is that God's purpose of freeing the Israelites will be achieved.

In God's subsequent promise to raise up an eschatological prophet "like Moses" in Deuteronomy 18, God commissions this prophet in the following manner:

> I will raise up for them a prophet like you from among their brothers; I will put my words in his mouth, and he will tell them everything I command him. If anyone does not listen to my words that the prophet speaks in my name, I myself will call him to account. (Deut 18:18–19)

Thus, the eschatological prophet "like Moses" will command God's people with the words that God will put in his mouth; the intention is that the people will obey.

In Jeremiah, God commissions his prophet in the following manner:

---

1. Edwards, "Word," 4:1102.
2. Fretheim, "Word of God," 6:963; my italics.

Then the Lord reached out his hand and touched my mouth and said to me, "Now, I have put my words in your mouth. See, today I appoint you over nations and kingdoms *to uproot and tear down, to destroy and overthrow, to build and to plant.*" [My emphasis] (Jer 1:9–10)

The intention behind Jeremiah's ensuing ministry of the word is that he will metaphorically uproot and tear down, destroy and overthrow, and build and plant, through the proclamation of the word of God. In other words, Jeremiah, on behalf of God, through his preaching, will bring both God's blessings and curses, salvation and judgment, to his hearers.

In Isaiah's call, God announces,

> Go and tell this people:
> "Be ever hearing, but never understanding;
> be ever seeing, but never perceiving."
> *Make the heart of this people calloused;*
> *make their ears dull*
> *and close their eyes.*
> Otherwise they might see with their eyes,
> hear with their ears,
> understand with their hearts,
> and turn to be healed. [My emphasis] (Isa 6:9–10)

The intention behind Isaiah's ensuing prophetic ministry is that he will not merely convey God's message to the people, but he will also confirm their disobedience towards God by preaching a message to the people that will "make their ears dull" and "close their eyes." In doing so, Isaiah's preaching will accomplish God's purpose by bringing judgment and curses upon his hearers.[3]

Later, in the context of Isaiah's oracles about God's eschatological salvation for his people, God promises:

---

3. This intention is a key component of Isaiah's commissioning. As Brueggemann observes, "The intention of the decree of Yahweh is that Judah and Jerusalem should be narcoticized so that they will not be healed. God wills an unhealed people!" in *Isaiah 1–39*, 61. Watts similarly comments, "[T]he messenger [plays] an active part in hardening and dulling so that repentance will not take place... This parallels the spirit's task in 1 Kgs 22:20–23. It is even closer to the 'hardening of Pharaoh's heart' (Exod 8:11, 28 [15, 32]; 9:7, 34)," in *Isaiah 1–33*, 75. And Evans, in his detailed analysis of Isaiah 6:9–10, suggests, "[Isaiah 6 is] a vision and commission of judgment and not simply a call to the prophetic vocation," in *To See and Not Perceive*, 22.

> As the rain and the snow come down from heaven
> and do not return to it without watering the earth
> and making it bud and flourish,
> so that it yields seed for the sower
> and bread for the eater,
> *so is my word that goes out from my mouth:*
> *It will not return to me empty,*
> *but will accomplish what I desire*
> *and achieve the purpose for which I sent it.* [My emphasis] (Isa 55:10–11)

The word of God is personified as something that "goes out" and "will not return . . . empty." God sends out his word "from my mouth," in this case through his messenger Isaiah, in order to "accomplish what I desire" and "achieve the purpose for which I sent it." This is not to attribute some magical or autonomous power behind the word.[4] Rather the word "accomplishes" what God desires because it is an expression of God's will; God's word expresses God's sovereign purpose, and thus the things spoken of will come to pass. As Buist M. Fanning comments:

> In the case of the faithful, sovereign God of the OT, what he says will occur and what he does to accomplish it can easily be conceptually conjoined. This does not indicate, however, that ancient Hebrews understood words to possess a magical power or concrete existence in themselves. The identity and reliability of the speaker and his or her authority and power to act in accordance with his/her word is all-important.[5]

Thus, in the specific context of Isaiah 55, God's word, which is his promise to save his people, will "accomplish" God's "desire" and "achieve" God's "purpose" because God himself will bring about the events that he has promised.

The commissioning of the eschatological servant-preacher is announced as follows:

---

4. Edwards notes, "[T]he effectiveness of God's word depends ultimately on the biblical concept of His character rather than anything intrinsic to words themselves," in "Word," 4:1102–3. Thiselton also provides an in-depth critique of this supposed power of the words in the Old Testament, and suggests that the effectiveness of the words comes from its "performance utterance," in "The Supposed Power of Words in the Biblical Writings."

5. Fanning, "Word," 848–49.

> The Spirit of the Sovereign Lord is on me,
> because the Lord has anointed me
> *to preach good news* to the poor.
> He has sent me *to bind up* the broken-hearted,
> *to proclaim* freedom for the captives
> and release from darkness for the prisoners,
> *to proclaim* the year of the Lord's favor
> and the day of vengeance of our God,
> *to comfort* all who mourn,
> and *provide* for those who grieve in Zion—
> *to bestow* on them a crown of beauty instead of ashes,
> the oil of gladness instead of mourning,
> and a garment of praise instead of a spirit of despair. [My emphasis] (Isa 61:1-3a)

There is a divinely commissioned intention behind the gospel preaching ministry of the servant; the servant-preacher is to "bind up the broken-hearted," set free, comfort, and provide joy.[6] God's will is to be accomplished through the servant's preaching.[7] Thus, in the announcement of God's salvation, the proclamation of the servant-preacher ushers in God's new age of salvation and provides comfort and healing.

Jesus

The Gospels of Matthew and Mark record that Jesus begins his preaching ministry with the words, "The time has come. The kingdom of God is near. *Repent and believe* the good news!" (Mark 1:15; cf. Matt 4:17). Jesus preaches the gospel (κηρύσσω and τό εὐαγγέλιον τοῦ θεοῦ; Mark 4:14) in order that his hearers will repent and believe. In the Gospel of Luke, Jesus begins his preaching ministry by quoting and claiming for himself the commissioning of the Isaianic servant-preacher (Luke 4:17-19). Jesus' intention is that his faithful preaching of God's word will set people free through the proclamation of the gospel.

---

6. In the Hebrew text, this is vividly expressed with a series of seven infinitives: "to preach . . . ; to bind up . . . ; to proclaim . . . ; to proclaim . . . ; to comfort . . . ; to provide . . . ; to give. . . ."

7. Knight, who identifies Israel as the servant in this passage, comments, "God himself then purposes to act in and through Israel his instrument so that his plan for humankind may bring about *shalom* in human society," in *Isaiah 56-66*, 51.

In Jesus' explanation of his parable of the sower, in which he establishes the paradigm for his own preaching ministry, he quotes and claims for himself the commissioning of Isaiah from Isaiah 6:

> The secret of the kingdom of God has been given to you. But to those on the outside everything is said in parables, *so that*,[8]
>
> "They may be ever seeing but never perceiving,
> and ever hearing but never understanding;
> otherwise they might turn and be forgiven!"
>
> [My emphasis] (Mark 4:11–12, quoting Isa 6:9–10; cf. Matt 13:11–17; Luke 8:10)

Thus, the intended purpose of Jesus' preaching, as the one who metaphorically sows the word, is that his preaching will reveal the secret of the kingdom of God to his faithful disciples; but it will also confirm the unbelief of those who are "on the outside" by blinding their perception and dulling their understanding.

The Apostles

The apostles preach with the same intention as that of Jesus. In the Synoptic Gospels, when the disciples are sent out by Jesus, their preaching is that "people should repent" (Mark 6:12), just as Jesus had also preached that people should repent (Mark 1:15). The disciples are to preach for a result. For example, in Matthew's Great Commission, the disciples are commissioned by Jesus to teach people to obey the commands of Jesus (Matt 28:20); and in Luke's Great Commission, the disciples are to preach "repentance and forgiveness" (Luke 24:47). Thus, there is an intention behind the preaching of the disciples, and this intention is commissioned by Jesus.

In Acts, the apostles routinely conclude their *kerygma* with an appeal to repent (e.g., Acts 2:38; 3:19; 17:30; 26:20). Paul explains his commissioning to King Agrippa, using the language and concepts of the Isaianic servant-preacher:

> I have appeared to you to appoint you as a servant and as a witness of what you have seen of me and what I will show you. I will rescue you from your own people and from the Gentiles. I am sending you to them *to open their eyes and turn them from*

---

8. Mark 4:12 and Luke 8:10 introduce the quotation from Isaiah 6 with ἵνα, which has a telic force ("in order that"). For a discussion of Mark's use of ἵνα and its theological implications, see Carson, "Matthew," 308–10.

darkness to light and from the power of Satan to God, so that they may receive forgiveness of sins and a place among those who are sanctified by faith in me. [My emphasis] (Acts 26:16b-19)

The intention behind Paul's preaching ministry is metaphorically to "open their eyes" and "turn them from darkness to light and from the power of Satan to God" so that his hearers might receive forgiveness of sins and become sanctified for God; and this intention is commissioned upon Paul's message by the risen Christ. As Paul further explains to King Agrippa, "I preached that they should repent and turn to God and prove their repentance by their deeds" (Acts 26:20b).

In Paul's epistles, Paul provides further insights into his preaching ministry. In 1 Corinthians, in response to criticisms about his style of preaching, Paul writes, "God was pleased through the foolishness of what was preached to save those who believe" (1 Cor 1:21). Thus, God's purpose for Paul's preaching is not that Paul might impress the hearers with "wise and persuasive words" (cf. 1 Cor 2:4), but to save those who believe the gospel message. In 2 Corinthians, Paul similarly explains his ministry as such: "We are therefore Christ's ambassadors, as though God were making his appeal through us. We implore you on Christ's behalf: Be reconciled to God" (2 Cor 5:20). And in Colossians 1:28, Paul explains, "We proclaim him, admonishing and teaching everyone with all wisdom, so that we may present everyone perfect[9] in Christ." Thus, the aim behind Paul's proclamation ministry is that the Colossians might reach Christian maturity.

The Christian Church

In the Synoptic Gospels, through the Great Commission, Jesus commissions not only his disciples, but the subsequent Christian church to proclaim the gospel so that hearers might obey the commands of Jesus (Matt 28:20) and repent (Luke 24:47). In Paul's epistles, he appeals for people to preach the gospel so that those who hear might believe in the message and call upon the name of the Lord and be saved (Rom 10). And Paul's charge to Timothy is expressed as follows: "Preach the Word; be prepared in season and out of season; *correct, rebuke and encourage . . .*" (2 Tim 4:2).

In the letter of Hebrews, which itself is a "word of exhortation" (Heb 13:22) and was probably to be read aloud in churches as the word of God,[10]

---

9. τέλειος. A better translation might be "mature" rather than "perfect."

10. Recent research identifies the letter of Hebrews as a "common form of Hellenistic-Jewish and early Christian oral sermon," and may be classified as a "paraenetic homily in the Hellenistic-Jewish synagogue tradition"; thus Lane notes, "[I]t is the oldest

the writer juxtaposes OT Scripture passages with his own passages of exhortation, in which the writer both encourages and warns the readers.[11] Within the argument of Hebrews, God continues to speak his "voice" to the readers today through the OT Scriptures and human proclamation of the gospel, in order to warn (e.g., 3:15), promise (e.g., 4:1), encourage (e.g., 6:9) and urge the readers to action (e.g., 6:10–12). The writer urges the readers to continue gathering (10:25a) around the heavenly Jerusalem where they hear God's "voice" (cf. 12:18–29) so that they might "spur one another on towards love and good deeds" and "encourage one another" (10:24, 25b). Thus, the intention behind preaching and reading God's word in the context of a church is that the hearers might be encouraged, rebuked, and urged towards love and good deeds.

Assessment

This section has examined the intention behind the preached word. In the Bible, God's human messengers are called to a preaching ministry where the intention is not that they only convey God's message, but that they urge the hearer to respond in belief and action. Through the preached message, the preachers might exhort their hearers by commanding, promising, encouraging, rebuking, and warning. In the end, the preachers are urging their hearers to believe and obey God, who is the source of their message. And the preacher does this on behalf of God; the intention comes not only from the preacher but ultimately from God, for it is God's purpose that the preached message moves the hearers to faith and repentance. Therefore, to preach God's word is to preach, on behalf of God, with the divinely commissioned intention that the hearer hears God's message and responds to God in faith and repentance. In this sense, human preaching is the word of God, for the human proclamation is not only conveying the message from God, but it is performing the divinely intended purpose of God's word. Thus, Buist M. Fanning also concludes:

> It is only right that this gospel which the early Christians proclaimed should be called "God's word". It is a message that comes from God and carries his authority and pledge, as though God himself were speaking through his messengers. It is also a message about God's work of salvation, a work planned, put into action, and ultimately accomplished by God himself. So at two

---

complete early Christian sermon that has been preserved," in "Hebrews," 450.

11. Ibid., 453–56, for a more detailed analysis of the purpose, plan, and structure of Hebrews.

levels this message or gospel comes from God; the proclamation and the reality it describes are both from God.[12]

The Results of Preaching

The above section examined the preached word and found that there is an intention behind it. Preaching is the word of God, because it performs a divinely intended purpose on behalf of God. But how does the actual result of such preaching relate to this? What if the hearer does not respond with faith and obedience to the proclaimed word of God, despite the preacher's intention? Has the word of God been preached in such a situation? And what are the roles of the preacher, the hearer, and the Holy Spirit regarding the result of the preached word? The purpose of this section is to survey the results of the human proclamation of the word of God in the biblical testimony.

The Response of the Hearer to the Preached Word

This sub-section will survey the pattern of responses by the hearers to the human proclamation of the word of God.

The Old Testament Prophets

In the Old Testament, the general pattern is one where the hearers reject the proclamation of God's word by God's commissioned, Spirit-anointed messengers; although some hearers might respond with belief and obedience (e.g., Isa 66:5), the typical response is unbelief and disobedience. For example, in Moses' preaching ministry, both his own people, the Israelites, and Pharaoh do not listen to him (e.g., Exod 6:9–12; 7:13). The Israelites typically respond as a "stiff necked" people (e.g., Exod 32:9; 33:3, 5; 34:9; Deut 9:6, 13; 10:16; 31:27) and Pharaoh typically responds with a "hardened heart" (e.g., Exod 7:13, 22; 8:15, 19, 32; 9:12, 35). Nonetheless, regardless of the reception of his ministry, at the end of his life, Moses is described as a "prophet" (Deut 34:10) because he had obediently fulfilled God's commission to be the messenger of his word.

In the commissioning of Ezekiel, God declares:

> Son of man, go now to the house of Israel and speak my words to them. You are not being sent to a people of obscure speech

---

12. Fanning, "Word," 851.

and difficult language, but to the house of Israel—not to many peoples of obscure speech and difficult language, whose words you cannot understand. Surely if I had sent you to them, they would have listened to you. *But the house of Israel is not willing to listen to you because they are not willing to listen to me, for the whole house of Israel is hardened and obstinate.* [My emphasis] (Ezek 3:4–7)

Thus, the ensuing pattern for Ezekiel's preaching ministry is one where his own people, the Israelites, will refuse to listen to him just as they refuse to listen to God. Similarly, in the commissioning of Isaiah, God sends his prophet Isaiah to proclaim the word to the people who will hear but never understand, see but never perceive; the people will not turn and be healed in response to Isaiah's preached message (Isa 6:9–10). And in the commissioning of Jeremiah, God sends his prophet Jeremiah "against the kings of Judah, its officials, its priests and the people of the land" who will "fight against" Jeremiah (Jer 1:18–19). The eschatological Isaianic servant-preacher will be similarly rejected: "[h]e was despised and rejected by men . . . he was despised, and we esteemed him not" (Isa 53:3).

The storyline of the Old Testament concludes with this summary assessment of the people:

> The Lord, the God of their fathers, sent word to them through his messengers again and again, because he had pity on his people and on his dwelling-place. *But they mocked God's messengers, despised his words and scoffed at his prophets* until the wrath of the Lord was aroused against his people and there was no remedy. [My emphasis] (2 Chr 36:15–16)

Thus, the overall pattern of the OT storyline is one where God graciously sends his word to his people through his faithful human proclaimers; and one where the people refuse to hear the word and respond instead with unbelief and disobedience. Yet, despite this, the Bible's assessment is that the word has been preached obediently and truthfully by God's messengers.

Jesus

In the Synoptic Gospels, a pervading theme is the unbelief and metaphorical blindness of the people to the preaching of Jesus (e.g., Mark 3:5–6; 6:1–6; 8:11–12, 17–18).[13] In this context, Jesus tells two significant parables, which

---

13. See also Evans, "Hardness of Heart," 298–99; Howard, "Blindness and Deafness," 81–82.

both serve as explanatory paradigms for the ministry of Jesus. The first is the parable of the sower (Mark 4:1-20; Matt 13:1-23; Luke 8:4-15). In this parable, the farmer faithfully sows the seed. However, only one out of the four types of soil produces a crop; this soil represents the small number who might hear and respond to the preached word. The significance is that, although a preacher might faithfully preach the word, not all will hear, repent, and obey, as was anticipated by Isa 6:9-10. Yet, whatever the outcome, in the same way that the seed has been sown by the hard-working farmer, the parable describes the word as being faithfully preached; that is, regardless of the results, the seed is still the word and the preacher has preached the word. The second is the parable of the tenants (Mark 12:1-12; Matt 21:33-46; Luke 20:9-19). In this parable, the vineyard owner sends servants in succession and finally his son to the tenants; but the tenants beat and kill each of the servants and, climactically, the son. The significance is that Jesus follows in the line of God's prophets who faithfully proclaim God's word to his people. But, just as the prophets were persecuted and their message rejected, Jesus and his message will be rejected. And the climactic act of rejection will be the crucifixion of the Son of God.

In the Gospel of John, the programmatic Prologue announces that the Word "came to that which was his own, *but his own did not receive him*" (John 1:11).[14] Thus, Jesus, the climactic revelation of God, the incarnate Word, would come to his own people, only to be rejected. Nonetheless, some would hear and believe, for "to all who received him, to those who believed in his name, he gave the right to become children of God" (John 1:12).

Therefore, Jesus is the prophet who faithfully preaches God's word; Jesus is the incarnate Word who is God's message to the world. Although some might hear Jesus and repent and believe, not all will hear and respond with faith and obedience. Indeed, the typical pattern is one of rejection towards Jesus and his message. Yet the word of God has been preached by Jesus; for, regardless of the results, the message is still the word and, not only has Jesus faithfully preached the word, he *is* the Word.

The Apostles

The typical pattern of persecution and rejection will continue in response to the preaching ministry of the apostles. In the book of Acts, one major theme

---

14. Although the first use of the term "his own" is neuter (ἴδια) and the second use (ἴδιοι) is masculine, the referent is probably the same—i.e., the Jewish nation. For example, see Carson, *The Gospel according to John*, 124-25.

is the inevitable progress of the word of God (e.g., Acts 6:7; 12:24; 13:49; 19:20) through the Spirit-anointed proclamation ministry of the apostles from Jerusalem to Judea, Samaria, and to the ends of the earth (cf. Acts 1:8). But another contrasting major theme is the opposition to the proclaimed gospel, especially by the people of Israel (e.g., Acts 4:13–22; 5:17–42; 6:8—8:3; 12:1–19; 13:50–51; 14:4–7, 19; 16:19–24; 17:5–9, 13, 32; 18:6, 12–17; 19:23–41; 21:27–36; 23:12–15; 28:24–28). This rejection of the gospel message was anticipated by Isaiah 6:9–10 (Acts 28:25–27) and the promise of the Isaianic servant-preacher (Acts 28:28).

Paul's ministry is also typified by the rejection of his person and message. In 2 Corinthians 2, he explains, "To the one we are the smell of death; to the other, the fragrance of life" (v. 16). Thus, although Paul's preaching ministry is one of spreading "the fragrance of the knowledge of [Christ]" (v. 14) with the result that some will be saved (v. 15), there will be those who are repulsed by Paul and his message. Nonetheless, Paul is confident that the word of God has still been preached, because "we speak before God with sincerity, like men sent from God" (v. 17).

The Christian Church

The pattern of persecution and rejection will also continue in response to the preaching of the word by the Christian church. For example, Paul exhorts Timothy to follow his model in the pattern of the rejected Isaianic servant-preacher: "So do not be ashamed to testify about our Lord . . . But join with me in suffering for the gospel, by the power of God" (1 Tim 1:8). And after Paul charges Timothy to "Preach the Word" (2 Tim 4:2), Paul adds:

> For the time will come when men will not put up with sound doctrine. Instead, to suit their own desires, they will gather around them a great number of teachers to say what their itching ears want to hear. *They will turn their ears away from the truth* and turn aside to myths. [my emphasis] (2 Tim 4:3–4)

Thus, although Timothy might faithfully "preach the word," many who hear will turn away from his preached message. Nonetheless, despite this rejection, Paul encourages Timothy: "But you, keep your head in all situations, endure hardship, do the work of an evangelist, discharge all the duties of your ministry" (2 Tim 4:5).

Assessment

The pattern in the Bible is one where the hearer frequently responds to the preached word by refusing to hear and obey the message. Of course, not all respond in this way, for many will indeed respond with faith and repentance. But the overall pattern in both the Old and New Testaments is one where the hearers typically reject the message of the prophets, Jesus, the apostles, and the Christian church. Nonetheless, the Bible still describes the word as being preached by the human messenger. Its status as the word of God that must be heard and obeyed is unaffected by the response to its message. For just as the farmer sowed the seed, and the seed was the word, the preacher has also preached the word independently of the outcome.

This mixed response to preaching does not indicate a failure of the word of God to be preached. Rather, the mixed response is the expected response to the faithful preaching of the word. Jesus explains his own person and ministry as one that divides "a man against his father; a daughter against her mother" (Matt 10:35; cf. Luke 12:49–53). And he warns that the ministry of his disciples will cause similar division, "Brother will betray brother to death, and a father his child; . . . All men will hate you because of me . . ." (Matt 10:21–22; cf. Mark 13:13; Luke 21:17). But this is to be expected, because Jesus notes, "If they persecuted me, they will persecute you also. If they obeyed my teaching, they will obey yours also. They will treat you this way because of my name, for they do not know the One who sent me" (John 15:20–21). Thus, the nature of the ministry of proclamation, specifically because it is performed on behalf of Christ, is one that engenders division and rejection. And the content of the proclaimed message is one that will also provoke a mixed response. As Paul notes:

> For the message of the cross is foolishness to those who are perishing, but to us who are being saved it is the power of God . . . [W]e preach Christ crucified: a stumbling-block to Jews and foolishness to Gentiles, but to those whom God has called, both Jews and Greeks, Christ the power of God and the wisdom of God. (1 Cor 1:18, 23–24).

Thus, although the preached message of the cross is "the power of God and the wisdom of God," it might be perceived as "foolishness" by the hearer.

The Roles of the Preacher, the Hearer, and the Spirit

When God's human messenger proclaims the word of God, the results will be mixed. Although some might hear and believe, many will reject the message and refuse to believe and obey. If so, then what are the various roles of the preacher, the hearer, and the Spirit regarding the result of the preached word of God?

The Human Preacher

God explains Ezekiel's commissioning in the following manner:

> Son of man, *I have made you a watchman* for the house of Israel; so hear the word I speak and give them warning from me. When I say to a wicked man, "you will surely die," and *you do not warn him* or speak out to dissuade him from his evil ways in order to save his life, that wicked man will die for his sin, and *I will hold you accountable for his blood. But if you do warn the wicked man* and he does not turn from his wickedness or from his evil ways, he will die for his sin; but *you will have saved yourself.*
>
> Again, when a righteous man turns from his righteousness and does evil, and I put a stumbling-block before him, he will die. *Since you did not warn him*, he will die for his sin. The righteous things he did will not be remembered, and *I will hold you accountable for his blood. But if you do warn the righteous man* not to sin and he does not sin, he will surely live because he took warning, and *you will have saved yourself.* [My emphasis] (Ezek 3:17–21)

God uses the metaphor of a "watchman" to explain Ezekiel's commissioning as God's Spirit-anointed human messenger. Ezekiel's responsibility is to proclaim obediently God's word, in order to warn the people. Although the hearers might refuse to listen to Ezekiel's message, Ezekiel cannot be held accountable for their response, as long as he obediently fulfills his role of preaching the word to the people. Conversely, if Ezekiel fails to warn the people then he is accountable for their doom.

When Jesus commissions his disciples for their mission of preaching the word, he tells them, "But when you enter a town and are not welcomed, go into its streets and say, 'Even the dust of your town that sticks to our feet we wipe off against you' . . . I tell you, it will be more bearable on that day for Sodom than for that town" (Luke 10:10–12; cf. Matt 10:14–15; Mark 6:11; Luke 9:5; Acts 13:51). The shaking of the dust from the feet is a symbol that the disciples are not accountable for whatever judgment might come upon the people who rejected their message; rather, the hearers are the ones accountable for their own responses.[15] Thus, although the disciples are re-

---

15. Carson explains, "A pious Jew, on leaving Gentile territory, might remove from

sponsible for preaching the word, they are not accountable for how their message is received.

Therefore, the role of the human preacher is to preach faithfully the word despite whatever persecution, opposition, or rejection the preacher might face. Moreover, as someone commissioned and entrusted with the word, the preacher must obediently fulfill this role by preaching the word. However, having preached the word, and precisely because the word has been preached, the preacher is not accountable for how the hearer might respond to the message.

The Hearer

The hearer is the one who is responsible and accountable for how the message is received. When God promises to raise up an eschatological prophet "like Moses," he also warns, "If anyone does not listen to my words that the prophet speaks in my name, I myself will call him to account" (Deut 18:19). This is an important theme that runs through the Bible. For example, Jesus introduces his parable of the sower with the command "Listen!" (Mark 4:3); and then he concludes the parable by urging the hearers, "He who has ears to hear, let him hear" (Mark 4:9; cf. Matt 13:9; Luke 8:8). Thus, Jesus' role is to preach the word, but the hearers' responsibility is to hear and obey the word. Similarly, at the end of Peter's sermon on the Day of Pentecost, the hearers ask the apostles, "Brothers, what shall we do?" to which Peter replies, "Repent and be baptized, every one of you . . ." (Acts 2:27–38). Luke, the writer of Acts, further emphasizes, "With many other words [Peter] warned them; and he pleaded with them, 'Save yourselves from this corrupt generation'" (Acts 2:40). In this way, the Spirit-anointed Peter faithfully preaches the word, with the divinely commissioned intent of warning and pleading with the people through the gospel, but it is now the hearers' responsibility to respond with belief and save themselves.

On the one hand, some will respond to the preached word with faith and repentance. They will recognize the message as the word of God and believe. For example, after Peter's sermon on the Day of Pentecost, Luke notes, "Those who accepted his message were baptized, and about three thousand were added to their number that day" (Acts 2:41). This response of belief

---

his feet and clothes all the dust of the pagan land now being left behind . . . *thus dissociating himself from* the pollution of those lands and *the judgment in store for them,*" in "Matthew," 246; my italics. Similarly, Wessell notes, "The significance of the act here is to declare the place to be heathen and to make it clear that those who rejected the message must now answer for themselves," in "Mark," 667.

and obedience is what distinguishes a Christian from a non-believer. For example, Paul reminds those in Ephesus, "And you also were included in Christ when you heard the word of truth, the gospel of your salvation. Having believed, you were marked in him with a seal, the promised Holy Spirit . . ." (Eph 1:13). Likewise, Peter reminds his readers, "For you have been born again, not of perishable seed, but of imperishable, through the living and enduring word of God . . . And this is the word that was preached to you" (1 Peter 1:23, 25b). And those who respond this way are commended. For example, Paul commends the Christians at Thessalonica, "[W]hen you received the word of God, which you heard from us, you accepted it not as the word of men, but as it actually is, the word of God, which is at work in you who believe" (1 Thess 2:13).

But, on the other hand, many will reject the preached word; they will refuse to hear it and obey. And for this they are condemned. As Jesus notes:

> The men of Ninevah will stand up at the judgment with this generation and condemn it; for they repented at the preaching of Jonah, and now one greater than Jonah is here. The Queen of the South will rise at the judgment with this generation and condemn it; for she came from the ends of the earth to listen to Solomon's wisdom, and now one greater than Solomon is here. (Matt 12:41–42; cf. Luke 11:32)

The stubborn hearer is condemned for not recognizing the status of Jesus' words as the climactic word of God. The preached word *is* the word of God; the hearer ought to have recognized this, and is condemned for failing to do so. Peter similarly observes:

> They think it strange that you do not plunge with them into the same flood of dissipation . . . *But they will have to give account to him* who is ready to judge the living and the dead. For this is the reason the gospel was preached even to those who are now dead, so that they might be judged according to men in regard to the body, but live according to God in regard to the spirit. [My emphasis] (1 Pet 4:4–6)

Thus, the hearer is the one responsible for hearing and believing the preached word of God. The hearer is held accountable for his or her response and will be judged accordingly. If the hearer rejects the preached message, then he or she is condemned, because the hearer failed to accept the preached message as it really was, the word of God.

The Holy Spirit

Previous chapters have noted that the Holy Spirit has the role of revealing the message and guiding the preacher to the truth, and of gifting and empowering the preacher to proclaim this message. But the Holy Spirit has an additional role with the hearer of the preached message.

In the Synoptic Gospels, although a prominent theme is the metaphorical blindness of the people to Jesus and his message (e.g., Mark 8:11–21, especially verse 18), another contrasting theme is the lifting of this blindness by God. For example, the juxtaposition of Jesus' curing of a blind man (Mark 8:22–26) and Peter's pivotal declaration that Jesus is the "Christ" (Mark 8:27–30) indicates that Peter's declaration was a result of God curing the man's spiritual blindness. As Jesus comments, "Blessed are you, Simon son of Jonah, *for this was not revealed to you by man, but by my Father in heaven*" (Matt 16:17). Thus, in order for the hearer to understand, God must first lift their spiritual blindness, otherwise the hearer will "be ever seeing but never perceiving, and ever hearing but never understanding" (Mark 4:12). Therefore, those who respond to the gospel, in the Synoptics, do so because of the work of the sovereign God.

The Spirit has an important role in overcoming the spiritual blindness (or deafness) of the hearers of the gospel. Jesus anticipates this illuminating work of the Spirit when he promises that the Spirit will "convict the world of guilt in regard to sin and righteousness and judgment" (John 16:8). Thus, the Spirit will accompany the disciples' future ministry by exposing the truth of the gospel to the hearers.[16] Indeed, Paul tells the Christians in Thessalonica, "[O]ur gospel came to you not simply with words, but also with power, *with the Holy Spirit* and with deep conviction . . . [Y]ou welcomed the message with the joy given *by the Holy Spirit*" (1 Thess 1:5, 6b). Thus, the gospel message is accompanied by the work of the Holy Spirit; those who respond to the gospel do so because of the illuminating work of the Holy Spirit, which accompanies the preached gospel of Jesus Christ. And the Holy Spirit continues this illuminating work in the life of the Christian believer. For example, Paul remarks to the Ephesians, "I keep asking that the God of our Lord Jesus Christ, the glorious Father, may give you *the Spirit of wisdom and revelation, so that you may know him better. I pray also that the eyes of your heart may be enlightened to know the hope* . . ." (Eph

---

16. As Carson notes, "Just as Jesus forced a division in the world (15:20) by showing that what it does is evil (7:7; 15:22), so the Paraclete continues this work. Indeed, he most commonly does so through the witness of disciples (15:26, 27); he always does so in connection with the truth of the gospel of Jesus Christ, since his whole purpose is to bring glory to him (16:14)," in *The Gospel according to John*, 537.

1:17–18a). Thus, the Holy Spirit provides "wisdom" and "revelation" so that the believer might be further "enlightened."

Conversely, those who do not respond do so because they have not been enlightened by the Holy Spirit. In Paul's letter to the Corinthians, after noting that the gospel message is "foolishness to those who are perishing" (1 Cor 1:18), he explains, "The man without the Spirit does not accept the things that come from the Spirit of God, for they are foolishness to him, and he cannot understand them, because they are spiritually discerned" (1 Cor 2:14). Thus, without the Spirit, the wisdom of the gospel message is hidden to the hearer. As Paul later comments, "And even if our gospel is veiled, it is veiled to those who are perishing. The god of this age has blinded the minds of unbelievers, so that they cannot see the light of the gospel of the glory of Christ, who is the image of God" (2 Cor 4:3–4). Without the work of divine illumination, the hearer remains a captive to the "god of this age" who has "blinded the minds of unbelievers."

Assessment

The preacher, the hearer, and the Holy Spirit have different roles regarding the result of the preached word. These roles may be complementary, but they are also to be distinguished from each other. The preacher's role is to preach faithfully the word despite persecution, opposition, or rejection. The hearer's role is to recognize the preached message as the word of God and respond to it in faith and obedience; the hearer will be accountable to God for his or her response to the preached word. The Holy Spirit's role is to enlighten the hearer so that he or she might recognize the wisdom and truth of the preached word; without this work of the Holy Spirit, the gospel message will be veiled and seem to be "foolishness" to the hearer.

Thus, when the word of God is preached, there are multiple and simultaneous roles. Each must play his or her own part. This is summarized by Paul to the Christians in Thessalonica:

> But we ought always to thank God for you, brothers loved by the Lord, because from the beginning God chose you to be saved through the sanctifying work of the Spirit and through belief in the truth. He called you to this through our gospel, that you might share in the glory of our Lord Jesus Christ. So then, brothers, stand firm and hold to the teachings we passed on to you, whether by word of mouth or by letter. (2 Thess 2:13–15)

In this passage Paul describes God's salvation as being accomplished through God choosing and calling, the Spirit sanctifying, the Thessalonians believing and standing firm, and Paul preaching the gospel and passing on the "teachings" (or "traditions") by "word of mouth or by letter." Therefore, there are many different roles that accompany the preaching of the word, and God ultimately oversees these complementary, but different, roles to achieve his salvation.

These multiple roles provide several important distinctions, which also help to explain several phenomena in the Bible. First, the status of the preached word of God is independent of its results. The preached gospel *is* the word of God independently of its outcome; it does not *become* the word of God when the hearer recognizes its validity and responds in faith.[17] Thus, if a preacher should preach the message of the gospel, then the word of God has been preached, even if no-one receives or responds to it. In the parable of the sower, the seed is the word of God, and the seed has been sown; this is independent of whichever soil the seed falls upon and its results. In a similar way, if a preacher preaches the gospel, then the word has been preached and the message *is* the word of God; this is independent of how the hearer responds to the word.

Second, although the Holy Spirit's work of illumination might be necessary for a hearer to recognize and respond to the preached word, the hearer is also accountable for his or her own response. For the hearer has an active role in choosing how to respond to the preached message. For example, although the Bible describes God hardening Pharaoh's heart towards the preached message of Moses (Exod 4:41; 7:3; 9:12; 10:1, 20, 27; 11:10; 14:4, 8), the Bible also describes Pharaoh as hardening his own heart (Exod 8:32; 9:34). And ultimately, Pharaoh was accountable and judged by God for his disobedience to the preached message. In Stephen's speech, he recounts, "You stiff-necked people, with uncircumcised hearts and ears! You are just like your fathers: You always resist the Holy Spirit! Was there ever a prophet your fathers did not persecute?" (Acts 7:51–52). Thus, although the people have "uncircumcised hearts and ears" because they have not been enlightened by the Holy Spirit (cf. Rom 2:29), they themselves also actively "resist the Holy Spirit" by refusing to accept the gospel. In the parable of the sower, the hearers might not be able to perceive or understand Jesus' message because the "secret" of the kingdom has not been revealed to them (cf. Mark 4:11), but, nonetheless, Jesus exhorts them to "Listen!" and "hear" (Mark 4:3, 9); and the parable itself is an illustration of the importance of

---

17. Thus, I cannot agree with Barth's proposal that the preached word of God only *becomes* the word of God in the event of proclamation, in *Church Dogmatics*, 1/1:106, 124–27.

hearing, believing, and holding firm to the word of God. Thus, in the Bible, the hearer is responsible and accountable to God for how he or she responds to the preached word.

Third, although the preacher's intention might be flawed, the hearer might still accept the message or the Holy Spirit might still work through the preached message to produce faith and repentance in the hearer. For example, although Jonah eventually preached the word of God to the Ninevites (Jonah 3:3), he only did so reluctantly because he did not want the Ninevites to repent and be spared from God's judgment (cf. Jonah 4:1–2). Yet, the Ninevites responded with remarkable belief and repentance to the preached word of God (Jonah 3:4–9). Thus, despite Jonah's flawed intentions, the hearers were still able to hear and respond obediently to the preached word. Similarly, Paul writes to the Christians in Philippi:

> It is true that some preach Christ out of envy and rivalry, but others out of good-will . . . The former preach Christ out of selfish ambition . . . But what does it matter? *The important thing is that in every way, whether from false motives or true, Christ is preached.* And because of this I rejoice. [My emphasis] (Phil 1:15–18)

Despite the false motives of some preachers, Paul rejoices because the gospel has still been preached. The primary importance is that the gospel message is preached. This is because the hearer might still believe, or the illuminating work of the Holy Spirit might still accompany the preached gospel, independently of the preacher's motivation.

Conclusion

This chapter has examined both the intention behind the preached word and the subsequent results of preaching. First, regarding the intention of preaching, God's messengers are called to preach God's message so that their hearers might respond in faith and action. The preachers might do this by exhorting, commanding, promising, warning, rebuking, or encouraging their hearers; but ultimately they are urging their hearers to believe in and obey God, who is the source of their message. The preacher does this on behalf of God who commissioned him or her. As such, the intention comes not from the preacher alone, but ultimately from God, for it is God's intention that the hearers respond to the preached message. Therefore, to preach God's word is to preach on behalf of God with the divinely commissioned intention that the hearer hears God's message and responds to God in faith and obedience. In this sense, preaching is the word of God, for it is not only conveying a message from God, but it is performing the divinely intended purpose of God's word. Second, regarding the results of preaching, although the preacher might faithfully preach the word, there will be mixed responses by the hearers—some might hear, believe, and obey, but others will not. Nonetheless, the status of the preached word as the word of God is not affected by the responses to it; for the word of God is still the word of God independently of how it is received. This is further explained by the different roles of the preacher, the hearer, and the Holy Spirit regarding the results of the preached word. For the preacher has the role of preaching faithfully the word of God, with the divinely intended purpose of that word; the hearer has the role of hearing and obeying this word; and the Holy Spirit has the role of illuminating the hearer to the word—and God works through these different roles to achieve his purpose. Thus, the roles complement each other. But the roles are also distinct and this explains how the status of the word of God is independent of its results, the preacher is not accountable for the response of the hearer, the hearer is accountable for his or her own response, and the preached message might still lead to faith and repentance despite the flawed motives of the preacher.

In this survey of the biblical testimony, various aspects of the preached word of God have been examined: God speaking his word, the human messengers, the content of the message, the intention of preaching, and the results. The next chapter will attempt to integrate this and construct a theological understanding of preaching as the word of God.

— 8 —

The Preached Gospel as the Word of God

In the previous chapters, the biblical testimony has been surveyed to examine the various aspects of preaching: God speaking his word, the human messenger proclaiming the word, the message of preaching, the intention of preaching, and the results of preaching. This allows our original problem to be once again addressed: can preaching be identified as the word of God? How can preaching be the word of God if it is being proclaimed by a human proclaimer? In this chapter, the observations from the previous chapters will be integrated in order to construct a theological understanding of preaching as the word of God, with a particular focus on the preached gospel as the word of God.

God Speaks His Word

The Bible reveals God to be a God who speaks—this is foundational for any theology of preaching. The God of the biblical testimony is an active and speaking God; this is what distinguishes God from other gods and idols. God is a God of revelation; he reveals himself to his created beings—humankind. Moreover God has not only spoken in the past, but he continues to speak in the present. The Bible employs the term "the word of God"—or similar terms—for the concept of a revealed message that comes from God.

Human Messengers

God speaks his word in various ways. Sometimes he speaks directly—hearers might hear a voice. But at other times God will speak through dreams, visions, angelic messengers, and even a donkey. God is sovereign, and he sovereignly chooses his own way to speak his word; God is not restricted to only one means of speaking his word. But in addition to these ways, God also uses human messengers to speak his word. In the Bible, human messengers might authoritatively introduce their message with the formula, "This is what the Lord says," or hearers might attribute a message heard as being that of "the word of God." Thus, there is a phenomenon in the Bible where a human messenger will speak the word of God.

The Bible describes human messengers who speak the word of God, such as Moses, the eschatological prophet of Deuteronomy 18, the prophets, the Isaianic servant-preacher, Jesus, the apostles, and the Christian church. All these messengers share several features. First, they are anointed by God's Spirit. As such, they are not only set apart for a specific ministry of proclamation, but they are also gifted and empowered by the Spirit, who authors God's word. Second, these messengers are commissioned by God. God raises and sends them to speak on his behalf. As a result, these human messengers represent God through their person, ministry, and message. They speak God's word because they speak on behalf of God, in God's name, and with God's authority. Third, the messengers receive their message from God. They do not author their own message; rather, they are the recipients of God's revelation. Thus, they speak God's word because their message comes from God and not themselves. Fourth, the messengers faithfully proclaim the God-revealed message by truthfully proclaiming it without changing or modifying it. Thus, they speak God's word because they have not modified the divinely authored word, which they have received from God and now accurately proclaim.

These four features are not necessary for the word of God to be preached, for the sovereign God was able to speak through a donkey. God's mode of revelation is not restricted to the faithful proclamation of a God-commissioned, Spirit-anointed human messenger. However, these four features would seem sufficient to guarantee that the word of God is preached by a human messenger. For a human preacher would be speaking the word of God if he or she is anointed, gifted, and empowered by the Spirit who authors God's word; the preacher is commissioned by God and to speak on behalf of God; the preacher receives the message from God's revelation; and the preacher preaches the message without modification. The significance of this observation is that the Christian church today can also claim to be preaching the authoritative word of God. For, in the present salvation-historical age, God similarly anoints Christians with his Spirit to be his divinely commissioned proclaimers of his word. The Christian church preaches the word because it speaks on behalf of God, in his name.

The Message of the Preached Word

Not every message comes from God. For if the preacher exhorts the hearers to "follow other gods," (Deut 13:1–5) or if the preacher's message does "not take place or come true," then those words are not the word of God (Deut 18:22). Therefore, an important criterion for assessing if a message is the revealed word of God is its actual content—that is, is it consistent with God's revelation, character, and will, and is it true?

In the Bible, the word of God can refer to any general message from God. But as the storyline of the Bible progresses, the word of God gradually refers more specifically to a special message regarding God's climactic act of salvation for his people and judgment upon the enemies of God and his people. It is a message of both hope and warning, blessing and cursing. Finally, in the New Testament, with the arrival of Jesus and the inauguration of a new eschatological age of salvation-history, the word of God will usually refer to the special message of the gospel—the news that God's Messiah has arrived to usher in the reign of God's kingdom.

On the one hand, the word of God—the gospel message—as proclaimed by Jesus and the apostles, is continuous with God's revelation to the Old Testament prophets, which was proclaimed orally by the prophets, and then subsequently inscripturated as Old Testament Scripture. This is something to which Jesus and the apostles will appeal, namely, that their message is consistent and continuous with God's revelation as heard through the Old Testament prophets and Scriptures; their message is not innovative but continuous with God's past revelation. On the other hand, the gospel message is new, because it was hidden in ages past, and is only now revealed by God through his Son Jesus. For this reason, the gospel message is described as a "secret" or a "mystery." This word of God is proclaimed by Jesus and the apostles; and the proclamation of Jesus and the apostles is also subsequently inscripturated as New Testament Scripture. The word of God is preserved and continues to speak today through these Scriptures.

This is significant in several ways. First, in the present church age, God continues to speak his word to the Christian church through the Scriptures—which preserve the testimony of the prophets, Christ, and the apostles—and the proclamation of the gospel. Thus, the Christian church receives God's word through the reading of Scriptures and the hearing of the proclamation of the gospel by other Christians. The Christian church, in turn, can pass on this same message by faithfully preaching the message of the Scriptures and the gospel.

Second, the preached message should correspond with God's revelation in the Scriptures. That is, the preacher's message should be consistent with the inscripturation of the proclamation of God's other messengers—the prophets, Christ, and the apostles—in the Scriptures. For example, Christ and the apostles appeal to Scriptures to demonstrate the validity of their message. And the Bereans are commended for not only receiving the message of the apostle Paul, but for also examining the Scriptures "to see if what Paul said was true" (Acts 17:11). Therefore, if a Christian preacher today preaches the word, the preached message should correspond to the message of the Bible; and the hearers are to examine the Scriptures to assess if the message is supported by the Scriptures.

Third, the Christocentric gospel message is an important component of the word of God. This is true of both the written and the preached word of God. With regard to the written word, the overarching storyline of the Bible is the Christocentric gospel message; this progressively unfolding storyline is a continuous thread that runs through the Bible and gives it its unity. Although the Bible is composed by different authors—from different backgrounds and contexts, writing in different languages, employing different literary genres, addressing different audiences, situated in different stages of salvation-history—the Bible is unified by its gospel storyline. Thus, each passage of the Bible, when it is located into its overarching storyline, is part of the Christocentric gospel message.[1]

Fourth, if the gospel message is preached, then the word of God is preached. For this reason, Paul's aim is to "preach Christ crucified" (1 Cor 1:23). And the content is more important than the form, for it is not necessary that Paul's message should be accompanied by "wise and persuasive words" (1 Cor 2:4), but it is necessary that the gospel is preached (1 Cor 2:2). Conversely, if the content is a "different gospel," then that is a guarantee that the word of God is not preached, no matter how persuasive or impressive the preacher might be (Gal 1:6–9). This does not mean that God's revelation is restricted only to the gospel message; for example, the Holy Spirit revealed through the prophet Agabus that there would be a severe famine (Acts 11:28)—a message that is not directly related to the gospel message. However, the gospel is the climactic word from God; and the gospel is the overarching storyline that unifies God's inscripturated revelation. Moreover, God's ultimate purpose is "the summing up of all things in Christ" (NASB, Eph 1:10); and the gospel—"the mystery" (Eph 1:9)—reveals this Christocentric purpose and calls all to live accordingly.

---

1. For a more detailed analysis of the related issue of *canonical exegesis*, refer to my treatment of this in Part C, chapter 10. And for a more detailed analysis on the overarching storyline of the Bible, see Goldsworthy's argument in *According to Plan*. Also useful are his "Gospel and Kingdom," "Gospel and Wisdom," and "The Gospel in Revelation," which are now reprinted in *The Goldsworthy Trilogy*.

Therefore, today, God reveals his message of the gospel to his commissioned, Spirit-anointed preachers through the reading of the word and the proclamation of the word. This word is a Christocentric word, namely, the gospel that calls all to recognize Jesus as the Christ and to live a life of trust and obedience in Christ. In turn, the Christian preacher is to proclaim this Christocentric gospel message, and in doing so, preach the word of God. This message should be consistent with the message of the gospel in Scripture; and the hearers can confirm this by examining the Scriptures. In this way, the preached gospel is the word of God, not only because it is the word *from* God (a subjective genitive) but also the word *about* God (an objective genitive).

The Intention of the Preached Word

When God speaks his word he is not merely conveying information. There is a divine purpose behind his word. For example, this purpose might be to save his people or it might be to judge; his word might bless or it might curse. Similarly, when God speaks his word through his human messengers, there remains a divine purpose behind this preached word. For it is through the preached word that God might save or judge, bless or curse. That is, God accomplishes his purposes through the human proclamation of his word.

Importantly, the preacher performs this intention on behalf of God. For example, the preacher might command, bless, curse, save, judge, or warn on behalf of God. As Paul notes, "We are therefore Christ's ambassadors, *as though God were making his appeal through us. We implore you on Christ's behalf...*" (2 Cor 5:20). Moreover, the preacher is commissioned by God to perform this intention. For example, Ezekiel is commissioned by God to be the "watchman" who warns the people with his proclamation. In this sense, preaching is the word of God, because the preacher is commissioned by God to preach with a divinely intended purpose on behalf of God.

However, there is a qualification that needs to be added to this observation. Just as there is an important distinction between the "revealed" and "hidden" wills of God,[2] there is a similar distinction regarding God's intention. For example, God's "revealed" intention might be that the proclaimed gospel message will save those who hear; but in his "hidden" intention he

---

2. This distinction explains the phenomenon where God openly reveals that his will is that he "wants all men to be saved and to come to a knowledge of the truth" (1 Tim 2:4), but yet the Bible also foresees that not all will be saved (e.g., Rev 20:15). Thus, in God's "hidden" will, only he knows whom he has purposed for salvation or judgment.

may have purposed the proclaimed gospel to harden those in rebellion against him.³ For example, in Jesus' explanation of the parable of the sower, Jesus preaches "so that" (ἵνα) some might not believe the word (Mark 4:12); God's intention is to confirm the unbelief of those who refuse to hear and obey the word. This would be the "hidden" intention behind the preaching of the word in the parable. This further explains why some in the parable will not respond to the seed, which is the word of God, despite the sower's intentions. Yet, the sower would have been faithfully sowing the seed, the word, with the intention that those who hear will be saved, in line with God's "revealed" intention.

The Results of the Preached Word

There will be a mixed response to the word of God. Although the Spirit-anointed preacher may have proclaimed the gospel message with a divinely commissioned intention on behalf of God, not all who hear will respond with faith and obedience. On the contrary, the Bible presents a typical pattern of rejection and persecution in response to the preached word. This does not indicate a failing to preach the word of God. For the status of the word of God is independent of its reception by the hearer. The sower has faithfully sown the seed, the word, irrespective of how the soil might respond to the seed.

However, the mixed response is indicative of the different roles of the human preacher, the hearer, and the Spirit regarding the result of the preached word. The preacher's role is to preach faithfully the word despite opposition or rejection. The hearer's role is to recognize the preached message as the word of God and respond to it with faith and obedience. The hearer will be the one accountable to God if the faithfully preached word of God is not obeyed. The Holy Spirit's role is to illuminate the hearer so that the message might be recognized as God's wisdom and truth; without this work of the Spirit, the hearer will perceive the message to be foolishness.

---

3. Fretheim similarly distinguishes between what he labels the "circumstantial" and the "absolute" will of God: "God's absolute will as expressed in the word has to do with God's will for the salvation of the community. While the word of God brings light and understanding (Ps 119:130), its goal and effect are more wide-ranging: it is a life-giving word upon which people depend for their very existence (Deut 8:3; 30:11–20; 32:46–47; Ps 119:25, 50, 116, 154). If the word is not heard, it is as if there were a famine in the land (Amos 8:11–12). God's circumstantial will is also expressed in the word; for example, God can speak of judgment (cf. Ps 50:7; Zeph 1:1–18). But this word of God is in the service of God's absolute will for the salvation of as many as possible (Ezek 18:23, 32; 33:11)," in "Word of God," 963.

God oversees the various roles and accomplishes his purpose through the preaching of the word. However, the distinction between the roles is important, for it explains that the preacher is not accountable for the response of the hearer, the hearer is accountable to God for his or her response, and the preached message might still lead to faith and repentance from the hearer despite any flawed motives from the preacher.

Therefore, because mixed results among the hearers are to be expected, and because there are important distinctions between the roles of the preacher, the hearer, and the Spirit, the response of the hearer is not a criterion for whether or not the word of God has been preached. If the preached word *is* the word of God, then its status as the word of God is independent of the response of the hearer to the preached message or the illuminating work of the Holy Spirit. It does not only *become* the word of God if a hearer responds with faith and obedience; it already *is* the word of God prior to any response from the hearer. If it were not so, the hearer would not be held accountable to God for failing to recognize it as the authoritative word of God.

A Proposal

How can the words of a human be identified as the word of God? In order to answer this question, I have surveyed the biblical testimony regarding the phenomenon of humans who proclaim the word of God. Having done so, I propose that preaching *is* the word of God because:

1. God is a God who speaks his word.
2. God raises, commissions, and sends human messengers to speak on his behalf.
3. These human messengers are anointed, gifted, and empowered by the Spirit, who is the author of the word of God.
4. These human messengers do not invent their own message, but receive it from God's revelation; these human messengers faithfully proclaim this received message by preaching the message without modification.
5. In a general sense, any message received from God would be the word of God. But, in a special sense, as a result of God's progressive revelation, an important content of the word of God is the Christocentric gospel. In this special sense, the word of God is now not only the word *from* God, it is the word *about* God, namely, his Son. This message is continuous with the message of the OT prophets, which was subsequently inscripturated as OT Scripture, but it is also a climactic

new message that has only now been revealed through the preaching of Jesus and the apostles, which has now been inscripturated as NT Scripture.

6. The human preacher preaches with a divinely commissioned intention, which is an expression of God's purposes, on behalf of God; and God achieves his purposes through this human proclamation.

7. Nonetheless, because of God's "hidden" intention, and because of the different roles of the preacher, the hearer, and the Spirit, the ultimate result of preaching among the hearers is not a criterion for determining if the word of God is preached. Thus, the status of the preached word as the word of God is independent of its results. It is precisely because the preached word *is* God's word that the preacher is not responsible for the hearer's response and the hearer is accountable to God for his or her own response.

Acts 8:26-40: A Case Study

The story of Philip preaching to the Ethiopian eunuch (Acts 8:26-40) is a useful case study that illustrates the above proposal. In this story, Philip is the Spirit-anointed messenger who is gifted and empowered by the Spirit (vv. 29, 39); he is commissioned and sent by God to preach (vv. 26, 29).[4] The content of Philip's message to the Ethiopian eunuch is the gospel about Christ (v. 35, cf. v. 40). Philip's gospel message is not innovative, but is continuous with the inscripturated message of the OT prophet Isaiah (vv. 32-33, quoting Isaiah 53); but Philip also follows the gospel storyline from the Old Testament to the climactic story of Jesus (v. 35). When Philip preaches the gospel, he is not only presenting information, but his intention is that his message will move the Ethiopian eunuch to belief and repentance. In response to Phillip's message, the Ethiopian requests to be baptized (v. 36).

A Further Problem

After this survey of the biblical testimony, it is legitimate to identify preaching as the word of God, and in particular, the preached gospel as the word of God. But this leads to a related problem: assuming that preaching can be the word of God, how can we recognize preaching that is the word of God?

---

4. As I have argued earlier, in the context of Luke-Acts, Philip and the apostles are also God's commissioned and Spirit-anointed messengers (cf. Acts 1:8) who fulfill the eschatological anticipation of a prophet and servant-preacher.

In particular, I have proposed that preaching is the word of God if God's message is "faithfully" preached. But what identifies "faithful" preaching?

This is no small problem. The Bible frequently warns against false preaching and urges people to distinguish false preaching from true preaching (e.g., Deut 13:1–5; 18:20–22; Mark 13:21–23; 1 John 4:1–6; Revelation 13). And the Reformers established the "true" or "pure" preaching of the word as the mark of a true church. At the conclusion of this part, I have granted that preaching—particularly the preached gospel—can be identified as the word of God. But I have not established how we might recognize "faithful" or "pure" preaching that is the word of God. This will be the subject of investigation for the next part of this book.

PART C

A Fresh Approach

The Application of Speech-Act Theory

Part A examined how Martin Luther and John Calvin equated the preached word as the word of God. For the two Reformers, preaching *is* the word of God. This resulted in not only a high view of preaching, but it also became foundational for their concept of the church, for they identified the preached word as a mark of the true church. But did the Reformers too readily equate preaching as the word of God? This introduced our problem: is preaching the word of God? Part B examined the biblical testimony regarding preaching. After a survey of the phenomenon of preaching in the Bible, I granted that it was legitimate to identify preaching as the word of God, and in particular the preached gospel as the word of God, for this is consistent with the Bible's own testimony. Moreover, the Christian church is commissioned by God to proclaim his word, for example, in the model of the prophet of Deuteronomy 18 and the Isaianic servant-preacher. But this leads to a related problem: assuming that the preached word is the word of God, how can we recognize preaching that is the word of God? In this part, I will approach this problem and explore if the application of speech-act theory might provide any valuable insights.

9

The Problem Revisited

The previous part examined the biblical testimony regarding preaching and the word of God. I granted that preaching can be equated with the word of God, for this was consistent with the phenomenon of preaching in the biblical testimony. However, this has led to our problem: how can preaching be identified as the word of God? This is no small problem. Surely not *all* preaching is the word of God. The Bible consistently warns against false messengers and false messages. For this reason the Reformers were forced to qualify that it was only "true" or "sincere" preaching that could be a mark of the church. But when is preaching the "true" preaching of the word of God? What preaching should be identified as the word of God? And what criteria can be used for deciding this? In this chapter I will revisit and explore this problem a bit further and then suggest a fresh way forward.

The Problem of Preaching and the Word of God Revisited

How can preaching be the word of God if it comes from the mouth of a fallible and finite human speaker? Klaas Runia articulates this problem well.[1] On the one hand, if preaching is to be the word of God, the preacher must proclaim the message of God as given to us in *Scripture*: "This is the one great and indispensable condition for all true preaching."[2] But would this not lead to "a mere repetition of the sacred words of the biblical passage" or "a careful exposition of the passage"? No, because, on the other hand, proc-

---

1. In his excellent examination of the New Testament phenomenon of preaching, Runia devotes the final section of his article to this problem, in "What Is Preaching According to the New Testament?," 38–48.

2. Ibid., 39.

lamation "has to be *applied* or, even better, *actualized* towards the hearers in their particular situation."³ But this requires the preacher to "actualize" the text towards the hearers, which would require human interpretation and subjectivity: "Naturally, this means that every sermon bears the marks of the preacher. It also suffers from his limitations, whether it be on the theological plane or on the psychological or spiritual."⁴ There will thus always be "an inner tension" with the Christian concept of preaching: "On the one hand, we must maintain that the preaching of the Word of God *is* the Word of God. On the other hand, we must admit that the human element can and often does obscure the message."⁵ However, for Runia, this "dialectical tension"⁶ is necessary:

> If we give up the essential nature of Christian preaching as the Word of God, we land in the morass of subjectivism. If we give up the humanity and fallibility of all Christian preaching we enter the road that leads to the objectivism of the Roman Catholic doctrine of the infallibility of the church.⁷

But how satisfactory is this "dialectical tension"? Although Runia might be content to leave us with this tension, other theologians attempt to resolve it.

Karl Barth

Karl Barth famously leads the contemporary discussion by suggesting that preaching can only *become* the word of God in *the event* of revelation. Barth makes a threefold distinction between the revealed word, the written word, and the preached word. The Bible (the written word) and the church's proclamation (the preached word) attest to revelation—Jesus Christ, the revealed incarnate Word—but themselves are not that revelation; but revelation takes place in the event of this attestation to Christ, and in doing so, the Bible and the proclamation become the word of God.⁸ Thus, when and if preaching

---

3. Ibid., 41; his italics.
4. Ibid.
5. Ibid., 43; his italics.
6. Ibid., 45, in which Runia terms it a "dialectical tension" between the *quia* ("because") and the *quatenus* ("in as far as"), as in: "We promise to adhere to the confession *because* we believe it to be in agreement with Scripture, but due to the inadequacies of all human documents the promise also implies that we shall adhere to it only *in as far as* the confession does agree with Scripture [his italics]."
7. Ibid., 44–45.
8. Barth, *Church Dogmatics*, 1/1:124–27. For Barth, humankind cannot know God

becomes the word of God are dependent upon God's sovereignty and not the preacher: "[W]e must not think of ourselves as uttering prophecies; if Christ deigns to be present when we are speaking, it is precisely because that action is God's, not ours. Since this is the way things happen, the preacher can make no claims for his own programme."[9]

Thus, Barth attempts to resolve the tension by suggesting that the human fallible witness is not the word of God, but only becomes the word of God in the event of the revelation of Jesus Christ. The strengths of this view are that it maintains a high view of preaching, while acknowledging the fallibility of the human preacher; and it rightly emphasizes the sovereignty of God and the necessity of the *illuminating* work of the Holy Spirit in the hearer.[10] However, Barth's view is not without problems. His view of preaching *becoming* the word of God does not adequately account for the phenomenon of preaching in the biblical testimony, where the word of God is preached. For example, in the parable of the sower, the seed *is* the word of God regardless of its reception by the different types of soil.

Helmut Thielicke

Helmut Thielicke suggests that the word of God is to be understood as such: the Spirit is concealed in the letter of the word, and the word contains the Spirit. God's word must not be understood as mere letter apart from the Spirit. The Spirit also performs a hermeneutical function by disclosing his testimony to the reader, making the reader a "new creature."[11] For Thielicke, there are three forms of the word of God, with three degrees of authority. First, there is the Word incarnate in Jesus Christ. This Word is a personal, not merely verbal event, an ontic being rather than a spoken entity. Second, the word is the message of the incarnate Word, in the form of the original human witness, which has come to us through the documents written by the evangelists and apostles. The word of God is actually present in these documents, because the incarnate Word reaches and is presented afresh to us. Third, the word of God is the witness given in later ages by witnesses of the word.[12] There is no qualitative difference between the sec-

---

apart from his revelation in Jesus Christ, who is the incarnation of God's eternal Word; see *Church Dogmatics*, 1/2:1–44.

9. Barth, *Prayer and Preaching*, 69. Similarly, his discussion of preaching in Barth, *Homiletics*, 47–55.

10. See my discussion on the Spirit's work of illumination in chapters 7 and 8.

11. Thielicke, *The Evangelical Faith*, 94–95.

12. Ibid., 106–7.

ond (i.e., the written word) and the third (i.e., the preached word) forms, for both proclaim God's word. The preached word, by becoming endowed with the Spirit, becomes God's own word. Thielicke notes, "[T]he Word that was published then and the Word that is preached today are one and the same Word of God."[13] In fact, written Scripture had its origin in the oral proclamation of the word, which was indwelt by the Spirit. Thus, Scripture is written to be preached, to be "put back into oral proclamation."[14]

Thus, Thielicke attempts to resolve the tension by emphasizing the work of the Spirit who indwells the word and works hermeneutically in the life of the hearer. The strength of this view is that it recognizes that the message of Scripture is to be proclaimed rather than only read; and it also maintains a high view of preaching by emphasizing the work of the Spirit. But the weakness is that preaching only becomes the word in the event of the Spirit's work. We could call this an "adoptionist" view of preaching, which requires the Spirit to indwell the preached word for it to become God's word. However, this does not adequately account for the phenomenon of preaching in the Bible where the preached message *is* the word of God.

David Buttrick

David Buttrick[15] suggests, "insofar as our [human] words are instigated by Jesus Christ, serve God's salvific purpose, and are ratified by the Spirit with a being-saved community, *they are the Word of God.*"[16] As Buttrick further explains:

> [W]e must modestly claim that preaching *is* "the Word of God." We may be two-legged little human beings, but we stand before the mysterious Presence-in-Absence and, through Christ, mediate understandings of God to a being-saved community in a most mysterious world ... Though we are quite aware of our humanness, nevertheless, by faith we preach as if we were means of grace, which we are! We believe that through our words God reaches out, claims, converts, and saves because we continue the preaching of Jesus Christ ... We are chronically bemused by our

---

13. Ibid., 107–8.
14. Ibid., 109.
15. David Buttrick is the Professor of Homiletics and Liturgy at Vanderbilt University Divinity School.
16. Buttrick, "A Brief Theology of Preaching," 325; his italics.

obvious inadequacy, our demonstrable humanity . . . and, at the same time, staggered by being *chosen* to preach.[17]

Buttrick has a few cautionary remarks. First, the work of the Spirit in the preacher must not be confused with moments of ecstasy or gifted rhetoric: "While the Spirit may give homiletic gifts . . . we cannot identify the Spirit with particular rhetoric or particular moments in preaching. The Spirit labors as much in our struggles as in our spontaneities."[18] Instead, "[t]he presence of the Spirit is not self-evident but it is, indeed, an article of faith—of *homiletic* faith. Wherever there is faith in Jesus Christ, the Spirit is with community and with speakers to community."[19] Second, quoting scriptural texts or ideas does not guarantee that the word of God is preached:

> The repetition of Scripture, or even the careful interpretation of Scripture, does not guarantee that preaching will be the Word of God . . . To so argue would be to insist that by *works* of fidelity we can take charge of God's Word. No, God is free even from our fidelities! So, let us be willing to say baldly that it is possible to preach the Word of God without so much as mentioning Scripture . . . [W]e must not say that preaching from Scripture is requisite for sermons to be the Word of God. An authority model descending from God to Christ to Scripture to sermon could lead to a terrifying arrogance that not only contradicts the gospel but destroys preaching.[20]

Thus, this approach attempts to resolve the tension by emphasizing the human task in preaching: the human words become the word of God because they continue the preaching of Jesus Christ, for God's purposes, and this is what the preacher has been *chosen* by God to do.[21] The strengths of this approach are that it attempts to maintain a high view of preaching and simultaneously not downplay the humanness of the preacher's role and work, and it also stresses the sovereignty of God in choosing preaching as a means of communicating his word. This view also rightly sees a continuity in the preached message of Jesus Christ and that of the preacher. But there are also weaknesses. First, in the emphasis upon the humanness of

---

17. Ibid., 324; his italics.
18. Ibid.
19. Ibid.; his italics.
20. Ibid.; his italics.
21. There is an emphasis on God's gracious *choosing* of the preacher to speak the word of God. For example, in his treatment on the theology of preaching, Buttrick concludes with the emphatic statement, "We have been *chosen* [his italics] to speak God's own Word," in "A Brief Theology of Preaching," 325.

the preacher's work and words, it is difficult to see how the preached word *is* the word of God. In this model, we can see how preaching might *become* the word through the work of the Spirit and God's sovereign choosing, but Buttrick fails to account for how preaching *is* the word of God. Second, Buttrick has created an unwise distinction between Scripture and the word of God. His claim that the "repetition" or "careful interpretation of Scripture" would "not guarantee that preaching will be the Word of God" implies that the Scriptures themselves are not the word of God but only become the word of God if God so chooses. Third, Buttrick defines preaching the word of God as *continuing the preaching of Jesus Christ*. But how can the preacher have access to the preaching of Jesus Christ except through the witness of Scripture?

The Expository "School" of Preaching

In contrast to Buttrick, other theologians and preachers emphasize the need to incorporate as much Scripture into preaching as possible. For, if Scripture is the word of God, then by essentially re-proclaiming Scripture, the word of God is preached. In his book on evangelistic preaching, John Chapman[22] explains Paul's command to "Preach the Word," in 2 Timothy 4:2, as: "[Paul] is speaking about the word of God, the Spirit-inspired Scriptures that are sufficient for God's person to be equipped for every good work."[23] Thus, Chapman concludes, "When we say accurately what the Bible says we will be the mouthpiece of God."[24] Such an approach is often self-consciously labeled "expository preaching" because it primarily aims to expound a scriptural text. As Bryan Chapell explains, "Biblical exposition binds the preacher and the people to the only source of true spiritual change. Because hearts are transformed when people are confronted with the word of God, expository preachers are committed to saying what God says."[25] John Piper gives an example of this approach:

---

22. John Chapman was a prominent and influential Bible teacher, preacher, and evangelist in the evangelical Christian community in Australia, the UK, and South Africa.

23. Chapman, *Setting Hearts on Fire*, 14–15.

24. Ibid., 28.

25. Chapell, *Christ-Centered Preaching*, 22. Similarly, Greidanus argues that "the essence of preaching" is "to preach the Scriptures," in *The Modern Preacher and the Ancient Text*, 15. Robinson notes, "Whether or not a man can be called an expositor starts with his purpose and with his honest answer to the question: 'Do you, as a preacher, endeavor to bend your thought to the Scriptures, or do you use the Scriptures to support your thought?'" *Biblical Preaching*, 20. And Wells explains, "[E]vangelical

> I say that good preaching is "saturated with Scripture" and not "based on Scripture" because Scripture is more (not less) than the basis for good preaching. Preaching that proclaims God's supremacy does not begin with Scripture as a basis and then wander off to other things. It oozes Scripture.
>
> My continual advice to beginning preachers is, "Quote the text! Quote the text! Say the actual words of the text again and again. Show the people where your ideas are coming from." Most people do not easily follow the connections a preacher sees between his words and the text. They must be shown again and again with actual quotes from Scripture.[26]

Thus, this approach attempts to resolve the tension by asking the preacher to say only what a scriptural passage is saying and to refer frequently to Scripture.[27] Although proponents of this approach would never suggest that preaching should be the mere quoting of Scripture passages *verbatim* (which would be akin to a "dictation" theory of preaching), they are not too far from asking a preacher to merely paraphrase a Scripture passage. The merits of this approach are that it is founded upon a high view of Scripture—for Scripture *is* the word of God—and it emphasizes the need for objective controls in preaching, namely, Scripture itself. However, this approach is not without problems. First, this approach does little to explain how the preacher's human interpretation and appropriation of Scripture does not detract from his or her preaching still being the word of God. For the preacher, unless he or she is merely repeating passages from Scripture, is now preaching humanly *interpreted* passages from Scripture.[28] Second, often, this approach is somewhat dependent upon a "propositional" view of revelation, for the preacher is essentially gleaning ideas, concepts, principles, and propositions from the scriptural text.[29] But this reliance upon a

---

preaching aims to change lives by bringing a congregation face to face with the living God through the interpreted, biblical word," in "The Theology of Preaching," 66–67.

26. To be fair, Piper would not say that this is *all* that there is to preaching, but nonetheless I think that this quotation properly captures his emphasis on the use of Scripture in preaching. See *The Supremacy of God in Preaching*, 86.

27. For example, Chapman advises: "It is highly likely that at most evangelistic gatherings people will not have their Bibles with them . . . It is a good idea [then] to have the organisers print the Bible passage so that people will be able to read it as it is being read aloud, and refer to it later," in *Setting Hearts on Fire*, 95.

28. Further, the way that a preacher approaches, interprets, and applies Scripture is related to the traditions and theological positions of the preacher. A good examination of this is found in McKim, *The Bible in Theology and Preaching*.

29. This is illustrated by Piper's complaint that "the power and authority of biblical preaching [is] undercut" by "subjectivist epistemologies that belittle propositional

"propositional" view of revelation would share some of the weaknesses of such a reductionist approach.[30] Further, much of the literary genres of the Bible are not easily reduced to propositions or principles. Is such preaching, then, committing the so-called "heresy of propositional paraphrase"?[31] Third, it also cannot adequately explain the phenomenon of preaching in the biblical testimony. For not all proclamation in the New Testament is the quoting or explanation of scriptural passages. When Paul asks Timothy to "preach the Word" (2 Tim 4:2), is he really asking him to expound a scriptural passage? Fourth, this approach is also open to a *reductio ad absurdum* type of argument. For why have preaching at all if we already have Scripture? And why explain or expound Scripture, when it could be easily repeated *verbatim* instead?

Peter Adam

Peter Adam[32] represents another approach. Adam provides three "biblical foundations" of preaching: *God has spoken, It is written,* and *Preach the Word*.[33] First, *God has spoken* through his self-revelation, which is expressed in words. It is by these words that God has revealed to us who he is, that he made the universe, and his saving acts. It is also by these words that we know Jesus Christ, the gospel, and his plan of salvation. Further, it is by these words that we know how to respond to him in faith as we hear his voice. Second, *It is written* because God has caused his words to be recorded for future generations. For example, Moses not only preaches his sermons, but writes them down for subsequent generations to read and obey. In this way, God's words are preserved or "inscripturated." Third, there is a call in the Bible to *Preach the Word*. For example, in the Old Testament, prophets, priests, kings, and wise men are called to speak the words of God. In

revelation," in *The Supremacy of God in Preaching*, 40.

In McKim's survey of different approaches to the Bible, he reproduces a sermon by James Borland as an example of preaching that is wedded to a "propositional" approach to Scripture; the sermon takes principles from scriptural texts and weaves them into a three point sermon, in *The Bible in Theology and Preaching*, 60–62.

30. It is unfortunately not within the scope of this book to examine the issue of propositional revelation. For a convincing overview and analysis, see Vanhoozer, "The Semantics of Biblical Literature, especially 56–75; and Vanhoozer, "God's Mighty Speech Acts," 132–39.

31. To borrow Vanhoozer's term, from "The Semantics of Biblical Literature," 67.

32. Peter Adam is a prominent theologian and preacher in Australia, especially in the evangelical Anglican context of Sydney and Melbourne.

33. Adam, *Speaking God's Words*, 15–56; Adam, "Preaching and Biblical Theology," 104–5.

the New Testament, the pastors and teachers in the post-apostolic church are encouraged to teach the truth and refute error, and ordinary believers have the responsibility of encouraging one another with God's words. Peter Adam concludes, "Those who receive the biblical revelation also receive the command to become speakers of God's word."[34]

But Adam also acknowledges the problem of equating preaching with the word of God: "This high view of preaching as the Word of God may in fact cause problems. If we begin to understand any one sermon as a Word of God, we are beginning to treat human explanations and ideas as God's words."[35] As a response to this, Adam cautions against directly equating our preaching as the word of God. Although Paul could claim this, in passages such as 1 Thessalonians 2:13, we who are not apostles may not.[36] And although Romans 10:14 shows that Christ may be heard through preaching and 2 Corinthians 5:19–20 claims that God makes his appeal through preaching, this is not the same as claiming that preaching itself is the word of God.[37] Instead, Adam prefers to think of the relationship between preaching and the word of God as such:

> Perhaps the best way of describing [the claim that preaching the word of God is the word of God] is to say that when human beings explain the Word of God, preach it, teach it, and urge people to accept it, then the Word of God achieves its purpose, and this is one of the normal ways in which God brings his Word to human beings. It is perhaps helpful to describe this in terms of the work of the Spirit. We must assert that the Spirit was involved in the creation of the Word of God, that is, Scripture... We must also recognize the work of the Spirit in the activity of the preacher, and the activity of the Spirit in the minds, hearts and wills of the hearers. The Scripture itself is a product of the Spirit, and when the Spirit works in the preacher and in the hearers, the words of God are mediated and bear fruit in the lives of those who hear.[38]

---

34. Adam, *Speaking God's Words*, 105.

35. Ibid., 115, where Adam also adds, "This looks to me like the beginning of Protestant tradition."

36. Ibid.

37. Ibid., 117–18.

38. Ibid., 118.

Thus, preaching is "the work of the Spirit in the preacher as well as in the hearer that God uses to bring his Spirit-inspired Word to effect in human lives."[39]

So, in answer to the question, "Is preaching itself the word of God?" Adam replies, "[O]ur preaching conveys the message of God when we preach and teach the words of Scripture."[40] That is, preaching itself is not the word of God, but by preaching, teaching, and urging people to accept the written word of God, God's message is conveyed. Adam approvingly quotes David Bast, "The only kind of preaching worthy of the name is that in which the truth of a Scripture text is explained and applied to the lives of the hearers."[41] From this Adam concludes, "If our preaching is true to Scripture it will be the means by which God brings the Word of God to those who hear us."[42]

Thus, Adam resolves the tension by not privileging preaching with the status of the word of God. The strengths of Adam's approach are that he has emphasized a high view of Scripture and the necessary role of the Holy Spirit in preaching, and he has protected against spurious human claims to speak God's word. However, there are several weaknesses. First, by claiming that preaching is something less than the word of God he cannot adequately explain the phenomenon of preaching according to the Bible. For what is Paul asking Timothy when he urges "Preach the Word"? And what is the sower sowing in the Jesus' parable of the sower if not the word of God?

Second, Adam places an emphasis upon teaching and explanation of Scriptures as the essence of preaching. It is significant that Adam prefers the metaphor of the "teacher" to that of the "prophet" or "poet" for the preacher.[43] But such a reductionist model can skew one's view of preaching. For the Bible itself consists of a rich array of different presentations of God's word through different literary genres, such as poems, songs, parables, visions, dreams, and drama, in addition to straightforward didactic material. And throughout the Bible, God's human messengers did not only teach, but they were also prophets, poets, psalmists, "heralds," "ambassadors," and proclaimers; and, as demonstrated in my survey of the Bible, two important models of preaching are the prophet of Deuteronomy 18 and the Isaianic servant-preacher. It is difficult to see how "teaching" or "explaining" can adequately capture the essence of what it is to "preach" or "proclaim."

---

39. Ibid., 119.
40. Ibid., 120.
41. Ibid., 119.
42. Ibid., 120.
43. Ibid., 117.

Third, Adam's approach is quasi-Barthian. For, in Adam's proposal, although the human words themselves are not the word of God, they convey God's message. And God uses this human explanation of Scripture "to bring his Spirit-inspired Word *to effect* in human lives."[44] Thus, it is in the event of proclamation, in the achieving of God's purposes, through the work of God's Spirit, that the word of God is heard.

Fourth, Adam also creates a problematic distinction between the word of God and its message. In Adam's model, preaching is the "conveying of God's message," through the explaining and teaching of Scripture, that is, the word of God written. Yet Adam cannot grant that this would be the equivalent of preaching the word of God. But in order to do this, Adam has to create a distinction between "God's message" and "God's word," thereby restricting the locus of God's revelation to the actual words in Scripture and not to their message. But how legitimate is this distinction? For it is the truth of what has been affirmed that is the key. That is, if both the message and the written words are affirming the same truth, then how can one be equated with the word of God but not the other? If we grant this distinction, then we would correspondingly not be able to recognize any translated Scripture as being the word of God.

A Fresh Approach?

The problem of preaching is how to maintain a high view of preaching that acknowledges that human preaching *is* the word of God, because this would seem to be consistent with the biblical phenomenon of preaching where, in Jesus' parable of the sower, the sower sows the word of God, and Paul's exhortation to Timothy is to "Preach the Word." But how can this high view be maintained when there is a tension between God speaking and a human speaking, God's word as propositional or personal, preaching as the word or becoming the word, didactic or poetic, verbal utterance or an event, an assertion or its effect, propositional statements or existential encounter, words or the message conveyed by the words? Is there a way forward from here? Perhaps it is time for a fresh approach to this problem.

Conclusion

In this chapter the problem of preaching was revisited, namely, if preaching is the word of God, how can the word of God be spoken by a human

---

44. Ibid., 119; my italics.

preacher? How might we theologically articulate such a concept? And how can we tell when and if preaching is the word of God? In response to these questions, different contemporary attempts at answering this question were surveyed. For Klaas Runia, preaching must be a "dialectical tension" between the objective written word of God and the subjective human interpretation of this word; for Karl Barth, human preaching becomes the word of God in the event of its witness to Jesus Christ, the Word incarnate; for Helmut Thielicke, human preaching becomes the Spirit-endowed word of God; for David Buttrick, human preaching becomes the word of God by continuing the preaching of Jesus Christ; for the expository "school" of preaching, human preaching is the word of God because it expounds the message of the written word of God; and for Peter Adam, human preaching is not the word of God, but it does convey God's message by the explanation and application of the written word of God. At the end of this survey, I concluded that each of these explanations had strengths, but ultimately failed in adequately explaining the phenomenon of preaching where human preaching *is* the word of God. At this stage, having revisited the problem, I will suggest a way forward through the analysis and application of speech-act theory. In the next chapter, I will explore what contributions speech-act theory might make to our examination of preaching and the word of God.

10

Speech-Act Theory, the Preached Word of God, and Discernment

In the previous chapter, I revisited the problem of preaching, namely, if preaching is the word of God, how can the word of God be spoken by a human preacher? How might we theologically articulate such a concept? And how can we tell when and if preaching is the word of God? I then surveyed different contemporary attempts to answer such questions, noting their strengths and weaknesses. This leads now, in this chapter, to the exploration of speech-act theory and its possible application to our problem of preaching to see if this may provide any helpful and fresh insights.

Speech-Act Theory

Speech-act theory is a theory about the use of language. It was initially developed by John Langshaw Austin (1911–1960), in *How To Do Things with Words*,[1] and subsequently refined and systematized by his student John Searle (born 1932).[2] At its very heart, it proposes that a speaker is not merely uttering sounds, words, or statements, but is performing an action—hence the name, *speech act*.

---

1. What is remarkable is that this was published posthumously and is the product of reconstructed lecture notes. Austin, *How to Do Things with Words*.

2. Searle, "Austin on Locutionary and Illocutionary Acts," 405–24; Searle, *Speech Acts*; Searle, *Expression and Meaning*. Vanhoozer observes, "If Austin is the Luther of speech act philosophy, John Searle may be considered its Melanchthon—its systematic theologian." *Is There a Meaning in This Text?*, 209. For a concise overview of speech-act theory, see Bach, "Speech-Act Theory," 868–69.

Austin's initial insight is that in addition to statements that describe facts—which Austin labels "constatives"—language is also used to perform actions—labeled "performatives." Examples of performatives are saying "I do" (in a marriage ceremony), "I name this ship the *Queen Elizabeth*" (in christening a ship), "I give and bequeath my watch to my brother" (in a will), or "I bet you sixpence [*sic*] it will rain tomorrow" (in a bet).[3] Austin tentatively proposes that the difference is that a constative can be assessed to be true or false, whereas a performative is assessed to be "happy" or "unhappy."[4] But later, Austin shows that even this distinction fails,[5] because, on the one hand, even performatives need to correspond with fact (for example, to warn "I warn you that the bull is about to charge" requires the fact that the bull is truly about to charge).[6] And, on the other hand, *all* uses of language perform an action, even the act of making a statement.

So how does the use of language perform an action? Austin formulates that a speech act can be divided into three components: the locutionary, the illocutionary, and the perlocutionary act. First, the locutionary act (A) is the performance of an act *of* saying something. It corresponds to the *meaning*—i.e., the sense and reference—of what has been said. There are three further distinctions within the locutionary act, namely, the phonetic act, the phatic act, and the rhetic act:

> The phonetic act is merely the act of uttering certain noises. The phatic act is the uttering of certain vocables or word, i.e. noises of certain types, belonging to and as belonging to, a certain vocabulary, conforming to and as conforming to a certain grammar. The rhetic act is the performance of an act of using those vocables with a certain more-or-less definite sense and reference.[7]

Second, the illocutionary act (B) is the performance of an act *in* saying something. It corresponds to the *force* of what has been said. Third, the perlocutionary act (C) is the performance of an act *by* saying something. It corresponds to the *effect* of what has been said:

> Saying something will often, or even normally, *produce certain consequential effects* [my italics] upon the feelings, thoughts, or

---

3. Austin, *How to Do Things with Words*, 4–5.

4. A performative is "unhappy" when it goes wrong or "misfires." This occurs because of "infelicities," in Austin, *How to Do Things with Words*, 12–45.

5. Ibid., 45–91.

6. Ibid., 55.

7. Austin, *How to Do Things with Words*, 95.

actions of the audience, or of the speaker, or of other persons: and it may be done with the design, intention, or purpose of producing them; and we may then say, thinking of this, that the speaker has performed an act in the nomenclature of which reference is made either (C. *a*), only obliquely, or even (C. *b*), not at all, to the performance of the locutionary or illocutionary act. We shall call the performance of an act of this kind the performance of a 'perlocutionary' act.[8]

Austin provides two examples:

(E. 1)

Act (A) or Locution

He said to me "Shoot her!" meaning by "shoot" shoot and referring by "her" to *her*.

Act (B) or Illocution

He urged (or advised, ordered, &c.) me to shoot her.

Act (C. *a*) or Perlocution

He persuaded me to shoot her.

Act (C. *b*)

He got me to (or made me, &c.) shoot her.

(E. 2)

Act (A) or Locution

He said to me, "You can't do that."

Act (B) or Illocution

He protested against my doing it.

Act (C. *a*) or Perlocution

He pulled me up, checked me.

Act (C. *b*)

He stopped me, he brought me to my senses, &c.

He annoyed me.[9]

Austin further divides illocutionary acts into five classes: verdictives, exercitives, commissives, behabitives, and expositives.[10] First, the verdictives are typified by the giving of a verdict, such as to estimate, reckon, or appraise. Second, the exercitives are the exercising of powers, rights, or

8. Ibid., 101.
9. Ibid., 101–2.
10. Ibid., 151.

influence, such as to appoint, vote, order, urge, advise, or warn. Third, the commissives are typified by promising, that is, they commit you to do something. Fourth, the behabitives are to do with attitudes and social behavior, such as apologizing, congratulating, commending, condoling, cursing, and challenging. Fifth, the expositives explain how we are using our words, such as when we say, "I reply," "I argue," "I concede," or "I postulate." However, Austin concedes that this classification is far from precise, and that there will be "overlaps" and "awkward cases."[11]

John R. Searle develops Austin's analysis of speech acts. In *Speech Acts: An Essay in the Philosophy of Language*, Searle proposes that "[t]he unit of linguistic communication is not, as has generally been supposed, the symbol, word or sentence, or even the token of the symbol, word or sentence, but rather the . . . performance of the speech act."[12] Searle subsequently suggests the following hypothesis:

> The form that this hypothesis will take is that speaking a language is *performing speech acts*, acts such as making statements, giving commands, asking questions, making promises, and so on; and more abstractly, acts such as referring and predicating; and secondly, that these acts are in general made possible by and are performed *in accordance with certain rules* for the use of linguistic elements.[13]

Or, in short, "speaking is a rule-governed form of behavior."[14]

There are two elements to Searle's hypothesis. First, to speak a language is to perform a speech act. For Searle, when a speaker utters a sentence, he is performing at least three different kinds of acts: (a) "utterance acts," that is, to utter words (morphemes and sentences), (b) "propositional acts," that is, to refer and predicate,[15] and (c) "illocutionary acts," that is, to state, question, command, promise, and so on.[16] A propositional act cannot occur alone.[17] Searle notes, "One cannot just express a proposition while

---

11. Ibid., 151.
12. Searle, *Speech Acts*, 16.
13. Ibid.; my italics.
14. Ibid., 17.
15. Searle prefers to understand "meaning" as comprised of "reference" and "predication," in contrast to Austin's understanding of "meaning" as "sense" and "reference."
16. Searle, *Speech Acts*, 24.
17. In his article "Austin on Locutionary and Illocutionary Acts," 413, Searle demonstrates that Austin's distinction between locutionary and illocutionary acts does not hold. For, in Searle's analysis, every rhetic act is an illocutionary act: "no utterance of a sentence with its meaning is completely force-neutral."

doing nothing else and have thereby performed a complete speech act . . . When a proposition is expressed it is always expressed in the performance of an illocutionary act."[18] The correlation is that most illocutionary acts will have propositional content.[19] The general form of illocutionary acts can thus be represented as *F(p)* where "F" is the illocutionary force and "p" is the proposition.[20]

Second, speech acts are performed by uttering expressions in accordance with certain "constitutive" rules. "Constitutive" rules constitute and regulate activities, and often have the form: "*X* counts as *Y* in context *C*."[21] For example, under the constitutive rules of baseball, hitting a ball over the fence *counts as* a home-run. Similarly, there are constitutive rules that govern human behavior and language. Searle gives the example of the speech act of making a promise. One can make a promise (and be bound by it) only because there exist certain conventions and rules of behavior under which the utterance *counts as* a promise.[22] Why else would making a promise create an obligation? Thus, Searle concludes that rules are required in order to perform most illocutionary acts.

Searle expands on his hypothesis in his discussion on meaning. Searle critiques a notion of meaning that proposes: "To say that a speaker *S* meant something by *X* is to say that *S* intended the utterance of *X* to produce some effect in a hearer *H* by means of the recognition of this intention."[23] Instead, Searle proposes that in the case of illocutionary acts, the speaker succeeds by getting the hearer to recognize what he or she is trying to do. For the intended "effect" of meaning is not a belief or response, instead it is understanding, which is not a perlocutionary effect.[24] For, understanding is knowing what a sentence *means* and what it *counts as*.[25]

In a later work, Searle also introduces an insightful comparison between the logic of promise and the logic of assertion. In the logic of assertion, the illocutionary force is to get the words (that is, their propositional

---

18. Searle, *Speech Acts*, 29.

19. Ibid., 30, where Searle notes that there would be no propositional content in utterances such as "Hurrah" or "Ouch."

20. Ibid., 31.

21. Ibid., 35.

22. Ibid., 37.

23. Ibid., 43, as proposed by Paul Grice.

24. Ibid., 49–50.

25. So also Vanhoozer's analysis of Searle, in Vanhoozer, "The Semantics of Biblical Literature," 89.

content) to match the world; but in the logic of promise or commands, the force is to get the world to match the words.[26]

In summary, on the basis of Austin's and Searle's work, speech-act theory makes three important contributions. First, to speak is to perform an act. It is a false dichotomy to distinguish between stating facts and performing an action, for, on the one hand, even the stating of facts is an action, and, on the other hand, speech acts require correspondence with truth to be "happy" or "felicitous." Second, speech acts are composed of three components: the act *of* saying something (locution); the act performed *in* saying something (illocution); and the act performed *by* saying something (perlocution). Third, speech acts require "constitutive rules" for them to *count as* an action.

The Application of Speech-Act Theory in Theological and Biblical Studies

In the last several decades, theologians and biblical scholars have applied the contributions of Austin and Searle.[27] In theological studies, Donald Evans applies speech-act theory to the analysis of the biblical language of creation. Specifically, what action is a person performing when he or she utters, "God is my Creator"? Evans suggests that the speaker is logically both acknowledging and committing themself to a status and role as God's steward and worshipper.[28] Anthony Thiselton utilizes Austin's speech-act theory to debunk the notion that biblical words, such as blessings and curses, operated because of a primitive notion of the magical power of words. Instead, the supposed "power" of words rests upon the nature of the speaking agent, and the illocutionary force of what is uttered, in line with the accepted convention of the situation.[29] Nicholas Wolterstorff suggests that the text of the Bible itself is a speech act, that is, a locutionary act through which God's illocutionary acts are performed. In this sense, the theist is entitled to claim that God *speaks*.[30] Further, the Bible belongs more appropriately in the category of "speaking" rather than "revelation."[31] Gordon McConville

---

26. Searle, *Expression and Meaning*, 3.

27. For a comprehensive review, see Briggs, "The Uses of Speech-Act Theory in Biblical Interpretation," 229–76.

28. Evans, *The Logic of Self-Involvement*.

29. Thiselton, "The Supposed Power of Words in the Biblical Writings," 283–99.

30. Wolterstorff, *Divine Discourse*. For to speak is to perform an illocutionary action, as argued earlier by Wolterstorff, "Why Animals Don't Speak," 463–85.

31. Wolterstorff, *Divine Discourse*, 19–36.

applies Wolterstorff's theory to the book of Jeremiah and argues, "The book of Jeremiah, dependent on underlying speech-acts [of God through the prophet], becomes in itself a speech-act to the community that hears and preserves it."[32]

In hermeneutical studies, Thiselton proposes that biblical language can be understood as speech acts.[33] Thiselton notes that, as a result, the "overworn dualism" between objective propositional description, on the one hand, and subjective existential self-involvement, on the other hand, can be removed. For if biblical texts are speech acts (i.e., $F(p)$, using Searle's notation), then they embody both a propositional content and involvement. For example, to say, "Jesus is Lord" (1 Cor 12:3) is "neither simply p nor simply F but $F(p)$, or more specifically a commissive which entails the assertion of a state of affairs."[34] Kevin J. Vanhoozer, in *Is There a Meaning in This Text?*, proposes that the biblical text and its meaning should be understood as "communicative-action," for the "basic unit of meaning is not the word but the speech act."[35] Based upon this premise, Vanhoozer argues that it is valid to speak of "a meaning in the text." In "The Hermeneutics of I-Witness Testimony,"[36] Vanhoozer argues that "testimony" is a speech act,[37] which is not only a valuable source of knowledge, but which itself is "as basic a means of knowledge as are perception and memory."[38]

In the fields of biblical criticism, interpretation, and exegesis, speech-act theory has also been applied.[39] Peter W. Macky argues that the Bible's writers' purpose was not only to inform but to perform a "variety of speech

---

32. McConville, "Divine Speech and the Book of Jeremiah," 37.

33. Thiselton, *New Horizons in Hermeneutics*, 272–312. See also Haarbeck et al., "Word, Tongue, Utterance," 1078–146; Thiselton, "The Parables as Language-Event," 437–68; Thiselton, "The Supposed Power of Words in the Biblical Writings," 283–99; Thiselton, "Communicative Action and Promise in Interdisciplinary, Biblical and Theological Hermeneutics," 133–239.

34. Thiselton, *New Horizons in Hermeneutics*, 294.

35. Vanhoozer, *Is There a Meaning in This Text?*, 209.

36. Vanhoozer, "The Hermeneutics of I-Witness Testimony," 366–87. This is reprinted in Vanhoozer, "The Hermeneutics of I-Witness Testimony," in *First Theology: God, Scripture and Hermeneutics*, 257–74.

37. In the article, although Vanhoozer never formally invokes the categories and terminology of speech-act theory, nevertheless, the foundation of his argument is that the Fourth Gospel should be understood as "testimony" from the author to the reader.

38. Vanhoozer, "The Hermeneutics of I-Witness Testimony," 270.

39. The entire edition of *Semeia* 41 (1988), edited by Hugh C. White, is devoted to exploring the possible uses of speech-act theory, although Thiselton complains, "[W]ith the exception of one or two articles," it was "like an orchestra tuning up for a concert which was never played," in Thiselton, "Speech-Act Theory and the Claim that God Speaks," 97n3.

act purposes" such as "relational, dynamic, and exploratory speech acts," which "have not been adequately recognized by many readers of the Bible."[40] Vanhoozer, in "The Semantics of Biblical Literature," suggests, *"[T]here is a correlation between a text's genre, or literary form, and a text's illocutionary point and force."*[41] From this, he argues:

> As Christian readers, we ought to be interested not only in the propositions themselves but in the manifold ways these propositions are presented for our consideration. In the context of Scripture's various genres, these propositions count as warnings, commands, prayers, questions, etc. as well as assertions.[42]

Walter Houston applies speech-act theory to the prophetic discourse in the Old Testament, specifically the pronouncements of "doom," that is, judgment.[43] Houston suggests that "the power of the prophetic word could be understood as due to its illocutionary force"[44] and in pronouncements of doom, the distinction between illocution and perlocution is crucial:

> [A]s long as the prophets' hearers understood that they were warning them, calling for repentance or whatever the particular speech act might be, and understood the content of the warning or whatever it might be, then the prophets had *done* what they set out to do, even if they had not achieved the effect they had hoped for.[45]

Thiselton regularly applies the tools of speech-act theory in his commentary on 1 Corinthians. For example, he claims that the "proclamation of the cross" is rightly viewed as a speech act.[46] Dietmar Neufeld, in his recent application of speech-act theory to 1 Corinthians 6:1–11, concludes, "Paul used speech acts of admonition and rebuke with the illocutionary force of the *directive* and *expressive* to provoke a transformation of conduct."[47] And Pamela M. Eisenbaum uses speech-act theory to examine the locution and

---

40. Macky, "The Multiple Purposes of Biblical Speech Acts," 61.
41. Vanhoozer, "The Semantics of Biblical Literature," 91; his italics.
42. Ibid., 92.
43. Houston, "What Did the Prophets Think They Were Doing?," 133–53.
44. Houston cautionarily adds, "[A]ssuming that that idea does not cover words with supernatural power," in "What Did the Prophets Think They Were Doing?," 141.
45. Ibid., 143; his italics.
46. Thiselton, *The First Epistle to the Corinthians*, 52.
47. Neufeld, "Acts of Admonition and Rebuke," 399.

illocution of the kerygmatic proclamation of the risen Christ by the early church.[48]

Therefore, over the last few decades, speech-act theory has been used in the disciplines of theological and biblical studies. Although such application is only recent, there is already much promise in the usefulness of speech-act theory in providing fresh insights. As a result, Richard S. Briggs comments:

> Indeed, in the course of this survey [of the uses of speech-act theory in biblical interpretation] it has been noted repeatedly that the use of speech-act categories to approach questions of biblical interpretation leads one easily into adjacent inter-disciplinary pursuits ... [T]here are obvious areas of overlap with questions in the philosophy of religion, of liturgical language and of theological conceptualization of the God who speaks. *It is also evident that studies of particular phenomena in the Bible which can themselves be called speech-acts (such as blessing and cursing, binding and loosing, oaths, promises, preaching and so forth) are all germane to the topic of speech acts and biblical interpretation.* [My italics][49]

And, along with Briggs, I feel that this is where my study of preaching is also heading. Perhaps the use of speech-act theory may provide fresh insights into the conceptualization of the biblical phenomena of preaching, just as it has in other fields of theological and biblical studies.

Thus, for the rest of this chapter, I will turn my attention to the application of speech-act theory to our problem of how preaching is the word of God. I will explore the possibilities of conceptualizing preaching as a speech act where God is the divine speech agent; the preacher is the human speech agent; preaching is the locution, illocution, and perlocution of the word of God; and where there are "happy" and "unhappy" cases of preaching.

God: The Divine Speech Agent

In chapter 4, I explored how God is presented in the Bible as *the God who speaks his word*. Now, in view of speech-act theory, God can be understood as a divine speech agent.[50] For to speak is to perform a speech act. From

---

48. Eisenbaum, "A Speech Act of Faith," 24–45.

49. Briggs, "The Uses of Speech-Act Theory in Biblical Interpretation," 257–58.

50. Vanhoozer pursues this further by suggesting, "[O]ne fruitful way forward for systematic theology is to conceive of God as a communicative agent," and thus advocates a "communicative theism," in "Effectual Call or Causal Effect?," 250–51.

this, further suggestions follow. First, God can perform speech acts without having to utter audible sounds or words. According to Searle, the basic unit of linguistic communication is not the word or the sentence but the speech act,[51] and the essence of speaking is the illocutionary act.[52] Accordingly, it is possible for God to "speak" by performing illocutionary acts with or without audible sounds or words. Here, Wolterstorff's analysis is helpful:

> Once illocutionary acts are thus distinguished from locutionary acts, then it immediately occurs to one that though of course such actions as asking, asserting, commanding, and promising, can be performed by way of uttering or inscribing sentences, they can be performed in many other ways as well. One can say something by producing a blaze, or smoke, or a sequence of light-flashes. Even more interesting: one can tell somebody something by deputizing someone else to speak on one's behalf. In short, contemporary speech-action theory opens up the possibility of a whole new way of thinking about God speaking: perhaps the attribution of speech to God by Jews, Christians, and Muslims, should be understood as the attribution to God of *illocutionary actions,* leaving it open how God performs those actions—maybe by bringing about the sounds or characters of some natural language, maybe not.[53]

Vanhoozer incorporates this into his most recent proposal for a *dramatic* construal for systematic theology, in *The Drama of Doctrine,* 44–48.

51. "The unit of linguistic communication is not, as has generally been supposed, the symbol, word or sentence, or even the token of the symbol, word or sentence, but rather the production or issuance of the symbol or word or sentence in the performance of the speech act ... More precisely, the production or issuance of a sentence token under certain conditions is a speech act, and speech acts ... are the basic or minimal units of linguistic communication," in Searle, *Speech Acts,* 16.

52. The essence of speaking is the illocutionary act because, first, locution can never occur by itself and exists for the purpose of illocution. As Searle rightfully notes, "When a proposition is expressed [i.e., Austin's locutionary act] it is always expressed in the performance of an illocutionary act," in Searle, *Speech Acts,* 29. For this reason, Searle prefers to understand a speech act as: (a) Uttering words = *utterance act*; (b) Referring and predicating = *propositional act*; and (c) Stating, questioning, commanding, promising, etc. = *illocutionary* act. See Searle, *Speech Acts,* 24.

Second, "meaning" is the result of the illocutionary force and "understanding" occurs when a hearer recognizes the illocutionary force of the utterance. Accordingly, Vanhoozer notes, "If analytic philosophy conducts an anatomy of communicative action, then the notion of illocution must be judged to be its heart," in "From Speech Acts to Scripture Acts," 173. For further discussions regarding "meaning" and "understanding" as the result of illocution, see Alston, *Illocutionary Acts and Sentence Meaning,* 147–310; Searle, *Speech Acts,* 42–53; Vanhoozer, "From Speech Acts to Scripture Acts," 173–82.

53. Wolterstorff, *Divine Discourse,* 13; his italics.

In other words, God can "speak" because illocutionary acts are possible with or without sounds. If so, then there are a variety of ways in which God might possibly speak. As Wolterstorff further notes:

> Once upon a time Morse Code was used for saying things at a distance, and semaphores, for communicating between ships. And we all know of the sign language used by and for those who are deaf. Actually all of us use conventional gestures of various sorts to say things: winks, nudges, shrugs, nods, and so forth. The media of divine discourse are even more diverse, or so at least the biblical writers claim. Words, yes; but beyond that, happenings of all sorts: dreams, visions, apparitions, burning bushes, illnesses, national calamities, national deliverances, droughts—on and on. When reflecting on discourse, be it human or divine, it's important to keep in mind this diversity of media—especially important to keep in mind that one doesn't need words to say things.[54]

This diversity of "media of divine discourse" certainly opens up the possibility that God may indeed speak through a human preacher. But more about that later.

Second, the "word of God" can be understood as a speech act. As Searle suggests, a speech act may be formulated as $F(p)$ where F is the illocutionary force and p is the propositional content of the utterance. If so, then the "word of God" is composed of *both* the propositional content from God (the action *of* saying something by God) and an illocutionary force from God (the action *in* saying something by God). And if this analysis is correct, then the dichotomy between God *saying* and God *doing* is no longer valid, for God is performing both when he speaks his word. Vanhoozer's insights are relevant for our present discussion:

> [The concept of speech acts] allows us to transcend the debilitating dichotomy between revelation as "God saying" and as "God doing." For the category of *speech act* acknowledges that saying too is doing, and that persons can do many things by "saying."[55]

And other similar dichotomies would no longer hold. As Vanhoozer notes further:

> The Word of God is God in communicative act, and there is no reason that some communicative acts cannot be verbal. This implies that the dichotomy between propositional and personal

---

54. Ibid., 38.
55. Vanhoozer, "God's Mighty Speech Acts," 130; his italics.

revelation is not as hard and fast as almost a century of debate has implied.[56]

Interestingly, Thiselton makes a similar observation:

> Searle's distinction [between *F* and *p*] sheds light on the logical fallacy reflected in the overworn dualism ... between on the one hand, description, objectification, report, and proposition, and on the other hand, address, promise, understanding and self-involvement.[57]

Although Vanhoozer's and Thiselton's comments address the specific issue of how to construct a doctrine of Scripture as the word of God, and a corresponding hermeneutical approach, their analyses hold for our more general discussion of God speaking his word. As such, the word of God, as a speech act, is *both* propositional and personal, saying and doing, cognitive information and existential encounter.

Third, Scripture, although it is a text, is also a speech act.[58] But more than this, it is a *divine* speech act. Accordingly, as Vanhoozer notes, "[S]peech act categories have the potential to help us appreciate what it means to call the Scriptures God's Word."[59] Or, as Vanhoozer elaborates:

> ... we may say that the Bible is divine-human communicative action: its locutions and illocutions are the result of double-agency, what Austin Farrer calls the "causal joint." The warnings, promises, assertions, prophecies, songs and so forth in Scripture are divine as well as human communicative acts. God's Word really is written. However, whereas human discourse relies on rhetoric to achieve the intended perlocutionary effects, Scripture's perlocutionary effects depend on the Spirit's agency.[60]

Thus, we can understand Scripture as a divine-human speech act. Or as Wolterstorff argues, the Bible is "divinely appropriated human discourse."[61]

Fourth, God's speech acts occur within the context of a covenant that he has established between himself and creation. According to Searle, "speaking is a rule-governed form of behavior."[62] That is, the illocution con-

---

56. Ibid., 131.
57. Thiselton, *New Horizons in Hermeneutics*, 294.
58. This is the foundational argument of Vanhoozer, *Is There a Meaning in This Text?*, 201–366.
59. Vanhoozer, "From Speech Acts to Scripture Acts," 163.
60. Vanhoozer, "God's Mighty Speech Acts," 155–56.
61. Wolterstorff, *Divine Discourse*, 53.
62. Searle, *Speech Acts*, 17.

sists of both the speaker's intention and the convention within which the utterance is expressed. As Searle explains:

> In our analysis of illocutionary acts, we must capture *both the intentional and the conventional aspects* and especially the relationship between them. In the performance of an illocutionary act in the literal utterance of a sentence, the speaker intends to produce a certain effect by means of getting the hearer to recognize his *intention* to produce that effect; and furthermore, if he is using words literally, he intends this recognition to be achieved in virtue of the fact that the *rules* for using the expressions he utters associate the expression with the production of that effect [my italics].[63]

In other words, speech acts are only meaningful because they occur within a *context* or *convention*. I suggest, then, that the *context* or *convention* within which God performs his speech acts is the divinely established covenant between God and his creation.

This above point is worth exploring further. An important contribution of speech-act theory is the observation that an utterance actually *counts as* something, such as a promise, or blessing, or commandment, or curse, and so forth. But how can this be explained? What is it that makes an utterance *count as* something? There have been various attempts to account for this. For Searle, speech acts are performed by uttering expressions in accordance with certain "constitutive" rules. "Constitutive" rules constitute and regulate activities, and often have the form: "*X* counts as *Y* in context *C*."[64] For example, in the same way that, under the constitutive rules of baseball, hitting a ball over the fence *counts as* a home-run, there are constitutive rules that govern human behavior and language, where an utterance *counts as*, say, a promise.[65] Conversely, in the absence of such constitutive rules, behavior and language would not *count as* something.

According to Wolterstorff, in his "Why Animals Don't Speak" and *Divine Discourse,* an utterance *counts as* a speech action because it acquires "a certain *normative standing* in one's society, a standing constituted in part by a certain complex of rights and/or responsibilities."[66] Thus, to speak is

---

63. Ibid., 45.
64. Ibid., 35.
65. Ibid., 37.

66. Wolterstorff, "Why Animals Don't Speak," 471; his italics. Wolterstorff repeats the argument of this article in chapter 5, titled "What It Is to Speak," in *Divine Discourse,* 75–94.

to "[take] up a certain sort of *normative stance*."⁶⁷ In other words, when a speaker makes a request, he or she takes up the *normative stance* or *status* as the one who makes a request; or if the speaker makes a promise, he or she takes up the *normative stance* as the one who makes a promise, which entails necessary obligations and responsibilities. Correspondingly, the hearer acquires the *normative stance* as the person on whom a request or promise has been made, with its entailing obligations and responsibilities.⁶⁸ As Wolterstorff explains, "Speech presents us with [a] profoundly different phenomenon: that of acquiring rights and responsibilities and of doing so in accord with, or in violation of, obligations."⁶⁹ If so, then if we are to conceive of God as a speech agent, it follows that, according to Wolterstorff, God is similarly acquiring the *normative status* of the speech agent who asserts, requests, commands, blesses, promises, judges, condemns, forgives, and so forth.⁷⁰ And conversely, the person who hears God speak acquires the *normative status* of someone upon whom an assertion, request, command, blessing, promise, judgment, condemnation, or act of forgiveness has been made.

Vanhoozer advances the discussion by suggesting that it is the presence of a *covenant* that makes an utterance *count as* a speech act. In other words, the speech act is a *covenant act*. As Vanhoozer explains:

> . . . I tend to see *all* communicative action in covenantal terms. Philosophers are generally more comfortable speaking of cultural and social conventions than of covenants. However, only if we allow our theological convictions to deepen philosophy at this point by invoking the design plan of language will a more adequate description of communication as a species of *covenantal* action be possible. Communicative privileges and responsibilities are best seen in a covenantal framework. Language is a divinely appointed covenantal institution . . . What we need to see is that all discourse is a form of interpersonal, communicative—which is to say covenantal—action. The parties to

---

67. Wolterstorff, *Divine Discourse*, 35. Alston holds the same view: "An utterance is most basically made into an illocutionary act of a certain type by virtue of a *normative stance* [my italics] on the part of the speaker," in *Illocutionary Acts and Sentence Meaning*, 71.

68. This is essentially the argument of Wolterstorff in "Why Animals Don't Speak," 463–85; Wolterstorff, *Divine Discourse*, 75–94.

69. Wolterstorff, *Divine Discourse*, 93.

70. Ibid., 95–113, where Wolterstorff uses this as the justification for the claim that God can speak.

the covenant of discourse, the communicants, are essentially two: speaker and hearer . . .[71]

Thus, a pre-existing covenant between the speaker and the hearer operates so that the speaker and the hearer have normative standings, with entailing obligations and responsibilities, with regard to discourse, so that an utterance counts as a promise, command, warning, request, blessing or curse. But where did this covenant come from? It is a divinely ordained institution.[72] As Vanhoozer further explains:

> Genesis recounts the beginnings of many human institutions: marriage, the family, work. These are not merely social but *created* [his italics] institutions, God-ordained orders intended to structure human experience every bit as much as those other divine orders, space and time. For our purposes, however, perhaps the most important institution initiated by God is the covenant. In speaking, God commits both himself and his addressees to certain obligations. *In short, God establishes a personal relationship with men and women by communicating covenants* [my italics]. Subsequent communicative acts of God also take the form of covenants: to Noah (Gen 9:8), to Abraham (Gen 15:18), to David (2 Sam 7). Promising and sentencing[73] are constitutive of the covenant Yahweh instituted with Israel as recounted in the book of Deuteronomy.[74]

Vanhoozer's insights are helpful, and if they are correct (and I believe them to be so) then the God in the Bible who speaks is a divine speech agent, who engages in interpersonal discourse, within the context of a divinely ordained covenant between himself and creation, so that his utterances are to be counted as promises, commands, warnings, requests, blessings, curses and judgments. And it is within this covenant that both God and his creation have normative standings ascribed to them as, respectively, the one who speaks and the ones who hear.

---

71. Vanhoozer, "From Speech Acts to Scripture Acts," 173; his italics.

72. Thus, one of his subheadings is titled, "Language: A Convention Made in Heaven?," in Vanhoozer, *Is There a Meaning in This Text?*, 213.

73. Vanhoozer singles out promising and sentencing as paradigmatic illocutionary acts, which any theory of speech acts therefore needs to be able to explain adequately.

74. Vanhoozer, "From Speech Acts to Scripture Acts," 188.

The Preacher: The Human Speech Agent

In chapter 5, I examined how God commissions *human messengers* to proclaim his word. In view of speech-act theory, this human messenger can also be understood as a speech agent who speaks on behalf of God. From this, the following observations can be made. First, when the human speech agent speaks the word of God, there is a dual divine-human agency operating. This is an example of what Wolterstorff terms *double agency discourse*.[75] Such double agency discourse is common in everyday life. For example, a president or executive might *superintend* what his or her secretary says by "dictating," or indicating the substance of what should be said, or even by the secretary "knowing the mind" of the president. Or the president might *authorize* what the secretary writes by signing the text, or even getting the secretary to sign on his or her behalf, thereby indicating that what the secretary says *counts as* the president's illocutionary act. Or the president might *deputize* an ambassador by commissioning him or her to represent one's state and speak on its behalf. A deputized person does not necessarily receive the words to say, but still *speaks in the name of* the deputizer: "the deputy has, as it were, power of attorney."[76] Thus, "the listener is presented not merely with locutionary acts of the ambassador but with locutionary acts which *count as* illocutionary acts performed by the ambassador's head of state."[77] But this leads to an interesting question: granted that the head of state performs illocutionary acts by the ambassador's locutionary acts, does the ambassador himself perform illocutionary acts by way of his locutionary acts? That is, does he speak discourse in his own voice? Wolterstorff's answers thus:

> [I]t might sometimes be the case that the very same utterings [of the ambassador] count both as the performance of speech actions by the ambassador and as the performance of speech actions by his head of state; these might be the very same speech actions, or somewhat different. Probably the most common occurrence, though, is that in the course of issuing the warning, the ambassador moves back and forth between speaking in the name of his head of state and speaking in his own voice; and sometimes part of what he does when speaking in his own voice consists of communicating a message from his head of state.[78]

---

75. Wolterstorff, *Divine Discourse*, 38.
76. Ibid., 44.
77. Ibid., 45.
78. Ibid.

Wolterstorff extends his analysis to the phenomenon of discourse in the Bible where Old Testament prophets were commissioned and deputized, and New Testament apostles were similarly commissioned and perhaps also deputized by God.[79] This is consistent with the observation in chapter 5 that human messengers (such as Moses, the prophet of Deuteronomy 18, the Isaianic servant-preacher, Jesus, the apostles, and the Christian church) have been commissioned by God to speak his word. Having been thus commissioned and deputized by God, they engage in double agency discourse. And this would explain the Bible's emphasis upon the necessity of commissioning for a human proclaimer of the word of God.

Second, the human speech agent speaks within the context of a divinely ordained convention. As Searle suggests, an utterance or behavior requires a convention to *count as* a certain action. Or as Wolterstorff suggests, normative stances are ascribed to the speech agent so that an utterance *counts as* a speech act. Thus, a queen is able to christen a ship, or a husband-to-be is able to pronounce, "I do," or a judge can pronounce, "Guilty." I suggest that, with regard to a human proclaimer of the word of God, God ordains it so that the human's proclamation is to be *counted as* God's own speech act. And this is something that Calvin recognized—see chapter 2 of this book—that the preaching ministry exists only within the context of a God-ordained office of preaching. And, although Vanhoozer does not directly discuss the proclamation of the word of God, this would be consistent with his analysis that God performs his speech acts within a divinely ordained covenant between himself and creation.

Thus, God's commissioning of the human proclaimer also exists within a divinely ordained convention or institution where the messenger's proclamation is to be *counted as* a divine speech act. The messenger is ascribed the normative status of one who performs God's speech acts. That is, as a result of this divinely ordained convention the messenger is ascribed the status where he or she really can issue a command, or warning, or blessing, or curse, or judgment as God's command, warning, etc. Further, the hearers *ought* to recognize the normative status of the proclaimer, and they *ought* to recognize their own normative status as persons upon whom God has performed a speech act. This would be consistent with the Bible's emphasis upon the commissioning of a human proclaimer who speaks the word of God. For example, it explains Paul's repeated appeals to his apostleship in his letters to the Corinthian church. For Paul is claiming the normative status of the one sent by God to perform God's speech act towards the Corinthians;

---

79. Ibid., 45–51.

and they in turn ought to recognize their normative status as the church to whom a divine speech act has been performed.

The Locution of the Word of God

So far, I have suggested that the human proclamation of the word of God can be understood as a speech act—an example of double agency discourse—where the human's proclamation is to be *counted as* God's speech act. If so, then the word of God consists of locution, illocution, and perlocution. I begin by exploring its locutionary act.

Austin suggests that the locutionary act is the act *of* saying something, that is, the uttering of a sentence with a meaning (sense and reference).[80] This is to be distinguished from the illocutionary act that is the act *in* saying something, that is, the force behind the utterance. Searle, who notes that even the act of locution is itself an illocution, prefers instead the notation of $F(p)$ to describe a speech act, where p is the propositional content (reference and predication) and F is the illocutionary force.[81]

What then is the *locution* (using Austin's terminology) or the *propositional content* (using Searle's terminology) of the human proclamation of the word of God? In chapter 6 of this book, I concluded that, although in a general sense any message from God is the word of God, there also exists a special sense in which the preached gospel is the word of God. In this special sense, *the content of proclamation is the message of the gospel*, namely, that God has sent his Son to redeem the world and now all must repent, believe, and live as followers of Christ. It was also recognized by Luther and Calvin, as noted in chapter 2 of this book, that the preaching of the gospel is synonymous with the preaching of the word. If so, the following observations regarding the preached gospel can also be made. First, the locution of proclamation that is the word of God, in this special sense, is the gospel. In other words, the human proclaimer is to locute the gospel message. As Paul expresses it, "We preach Christ crucified" (1 Cor 1:23). Moreover, to locute a different gospel would not be to locute the word of God. As Paul warns, "But even if we or an angel from heaven should preach a gospel other than the one we preached to you, let him be eternally condemned!" (Gal 1:8; cf. 2 Cor 11:4). And this is what Luther recognized: "But is the doctrine [*sic*] different and even proposes another way by which to be delivered from sin

---

80. Austin, *How to Do Things with Words*, 94–98, 109.
81. Searle, *Speech Acts*, 21–33.

than through Christ, the falsity of it appears at once. For such teachers do not speak the word of God, and the hearers do not hear it . . ."[82]

Second, the locution originates from God. In Deuteronomy 18, God promises of the eschatological prophet, "I will put my words in his mouth" (Deut 18:18). Thus, the human proclaimer is to receive his or her locution from God. The proclaimer is not free to make up his or her own message. It is for this reason that Paul must claim regarding his message, "I did not receive it from any man . . . rather, I received it by revelation from Jesus Christ" (Gal 1:12). Hence Paul calls it "the gospel *of God*" (Rom 1:1).

Third, the locution of proclamation is identical to the locution of Scripture. For what was once proclaimed by the prophets, Jesus, and the apostles has also been inscripturated. And what is now inscripturated is to be once again proclaimed. This was something that the Reformers also recognized. Thus, the proclaimer's access to the locution of the gospel is through the locution of Scripture. Moreover, the Spirit who "carried" the prophets and apostles to speak and write, and who is responsible for the "inspiration" of Scripture, is the same Spirit who anoints, empowers, and gifts the human proclaimer. Thus, there will be an identity in the Spirit-inspired locution of Scripture and the Spirit-empowered locution of the proclaimer.

Fourth, the locution of the human proclaimer sits under the authority of the locution of Scripture. The locution of the proclaimer cannot contradict the locution of Scripture. The Spirit who locutes his message in Scripture will not locute a contradictory message in a human proclaimer. From this, Calvin's assertions that "Word and Spirit belong inseparably together" and "we insist that [the church's authority] be attached to the Word, and do not allow it to be separated from it" would seem to be correct.[83] As a result, the hearers of the proclaimed word of God also have the responsibility to check if the locution of the proclaimed message is the same as that of Scripture. For example, this is what the Bereans did in Acts 17:11. And it is what Paul commands the Corinthians to do regarding prophecy, that is, "weigh carefully what is said," in 1 Corinthians 14:29.[84]

Fifth, at this stage, a brief explanatory excursus needs to be made. It has been suggested above that a preacher's locution ought to be the gospel message, but it has also been suggested above that the preacher's locution

---

82. Luther, *Commentary on the Epistles of Peter and Jude*, 192.

83. In *Institutes*, IV.viii.13, in which Calvin also approvingly quotes Chrysostom: "As Christ testified that he spoke not from himself, because he spoke from the Law and the Prophets, so let us not believe anything that is thrust in under the title of the Spirit *apart from the Gospel* [my italics]."

84. For a more detailed discussion on the relationship between preaching and New Testament prophecy, refer to the appendix.

should be identical to that of Scripture, and that Scripture is the primary means by which the preacher might receive his or her locution from God. But what about those passages of Scripture that don't directly locute the gospel message? Does this mean that the preacher is to appeal to *sensus plenior* or resort to innovative (and illegitimate) methods of exegesis in order to locute the gospel?

One answer is to note that this is a phenomenon of the dual authorship of Scripture. On the one hand, there is a diversity inherent in the message of Scripture because of the diversity of human authors who wrote in their own particular salvation-historical, social, religious, historical, geographical, cultural, literary, and linguistic contexts, and thus would not have necessarily referred to the gospel directly. But on the other hand, there is a unity founded upon the single divine author who acts in a unified way to bring salvation to the world and superintended the process of inscripturation, which reveals the single message of this salvation.[85]

Another answer is to note that although each particular passage of Scripture (either an oracle, pericope, psalm, poem, paragraph, vision, parable, etc.) may not directly refer to the gospel message, each passage of the Bible is located ultimately in a canonical framework that is gospel-centric. For the meaning of a passage is not only discovered through grammatico-historical exegesis, but it is ultimately discovered through grammatico-historico-*canonical* exegesis.[86] This is consistent with Douglas J. Moo's observations regarding the use of Old Testament texts by the New Testament authors:

> The meaning intended by the human author of a particular text can take on a "fuller" meaning, legitimately developed from his meaning, in the light of *the text's ultimate canonical context* [my italics]. Without necessarily appealing to the divine author as intending a meaning separate from, and hidden from, the human author at the point of inspiration, we would appeal to the divine author as providing the larger context of the developing canon as the framework within which the New Testament writers read the Old Testament. What is involved is not just the ultimate significance of a text, or its valid manifold applications, but the meaning of the text, not fully understood by the human author.[87]

---

85. This is the foundation of the argument in Goldsworthy, *Preaching the Whole Bible as Christian Scripture*, 63–80.

86. Thus, in this section, I am not suggesting that a preacher needs to appeal to *sensus plenior*; rather I am proposing that the preacher can appeal to a *canonical* exegesis.

87. Moo, "The Problem of *Sensus Plenior*," 210.

And this is also consistent with the earlier discussion in chapter 6 regarding Paul's use of the word "mystery" to refer to the gospel message. For the gospel message was "hidden" in ages past in the writings of Old Testament Scripture, but has been "revealed," especially in the context of the complete revelation of the canon.

The application of speech-act theory may prove helpful here in bringing together the above two answers by recognizing the whole of canonical Scripture, as authored through double agency discourse, as a unified speech act. As Wolterstorff suggests:

> All that is necessary for the whole to be God's book is that all the human discourse it contains has been *appropriated* [my italics] by God, as one single book, for God's discourse. If it is the Christian Bible we are speaking of, the event which *counts as* God's appropriating this totality as the medium of God's own discourse is presumably that rather drawn out event consisting of the church's settling on this totality as its canon.[88]

In other words, the "writings which saw the day as a sizable number of independent books, and still retain that separate identity, are all together appropriated into a text which is one single book."[89] Further, the canon is unified in its locutionary act. As Vanhoozer notes:

> A text must be read in light of its intentional context . . . For it is in relation to its intentional context that a text yields its maximal sense, its fullest meaning. *If we are reading the Bible as the Word of God, therefore, I suggest that the context that yields this maximal sense is the canon, taken as a unified communicative act.* The books of Scripture, taken individually, may anticipate the whole, but the canon alone is its instantiation.
>
> If God is taken to be the divine author, in other words, then it is the canon as a whole that becomes the communicative act that needs to be described . . . The problem of the "fuller meaning" of Scripture and of determining the divine author's intent is precisely the problem of choosing the intentional context that best enables one maximally to describe the communicative action embodied in Scripture. That is, to say that the Bible has a "fuller meaning" is to focus on the (divine) author's intended meaning at the level of the *canonical* act. Better said, *the canon as a whole becomes the unified act for which the divine intention serves as the unifying principle.* The divine intention *supervenes*

---

88. Wolterstorff, *Divine Discourse*, 54.
89. Ibid.

on the intention of the human authors . . . That Jesus is the referent of the whole relies on, but cannot be reduced to, the intended meaning of the individual books; yet the unity of Scripture emerges only at the canonical level. [His italics.][90]

All this is to say that the locution of the Bible consists of diverse locutions of human authors and proclaimers, speaking *in the name of God* within their particular contexts. But, each particular locution is also divinely *appropriated* and ultimately located within the whole of the canon, and is one of many components of the unified locution of the gospel message, whose referent is Christ. To only see a locution of a particular passage of Scripture without seeing the overarching canonical locution of the gospel and its christological referent is, so to say, to miss the wood for the trees.[91]

The Illocution of the Word of God

Austin suggests that the illocutionary act is the performance of an act *in* saying something; it is the *force* of what has been said.[92] It corresponds to the F in Searle's formula $F(p)$ where F is the "illocutionary force indicator" and p the "propositional indicator."[93] And it is the illocutionary act that is the essence of speaking; to speak is to illocute. For although Austin initially locates "meaning" with the locutionary act, in which sense and reference are uttered,[94] Searle's analysis demonstrates that "meaning" is tied up just as much with the illocutionary act as it is with the locutionary act.[95] For example, if a speaker warns, "the paint is wet," the meaning cannot be re-

---

90. Vanhoozer, *Is There a Meaning in This Text?*, 265.

91. As Goldsworthy notes, "It is grossly irresponsible for a preacher to moralize on isolated texts and to convey the notion that the real issue is finding self-esteem, happiness, health, self-fulfillment, or any other desirable quality in life, as if these were valuable in themselves. All these good qualities need to be put in perspective through the gospel and its framework of salvation history," in *Preaching the Whole Bible as Christian Scripture*, 79–80.

92. Austin, *How to Do Things with Words*, 98–101.

93. Searle, *Speech Acts*, 29–33.

94. Austin summarizes a locutionary act as "roughly equivalent to uttering a certain sentence with a certain sense and reference, which again is roughly equivalent to 'meaning' in the traditional sense," in Austin, *How to Do Things with Words*, 109.

95. Ibid., 103, where this is something that Austin later recognizes: "[T]he expressions 'meaning' and 'use of sentence' can blur the distinction between locutionary and illocutionary acts." Alston later builds upon Searle's work and provides a detailed analysis of the relationship between meaning and illocution, where meaning is to be understood as illocutionary *potential*, in *Illocutionary Acts and Sentence Meaning*, esp. 147–309.

stricted to sense and reference, that is, the proposition that the paint is wet, but is ultimately related to the intentionality of the utterance, that is, the illocutionary force of warning.

Thus, if the aim of speaking is that a hearer "understands" the "meaning" of what has been said, then, according to speech-act theory, the aim of speaking is that the hearer recognizes the illocutionary force of the speech act. Going back to the example of the speaker's warning that "the paint is wet," a hearer has not understood the speech act if he or she perceives it as, say, a promise rather than a warning, despite understanding the propositional content. This is something that Austin recognizes. For "the performance of an illocutionary act involves the securing of *uptake* [his italics]," that is, "bringing about the understanding of the meaning and of the force of the locution."[96] Searle develops this by suggesting that in the case of illocutionary acts, the speaker succeeds by getting the hearer to recognize what he or she is trying to do. For the intended "effect" of meaning is not a belief or response, instead it is "understanding," which is not a perlocutionary effect.[97] For, understanding is knowing what a sentence *means* and what it *counts as*.[98]

In chapter 7 of this book I explored how there is an *intention* behind the proclamation of the word of God. And, in chapter 2, I noted that Luther insisted that there is always a purpose behind preaching: "[I]t is not enough just to take the life and work of Christ, and, in preaching, merely tell the story and the chronicle of events."[99] The application of speech-act theory here would suggest that a proclaimer is not only locuting but also illocuting the word of God. If so, then the following suggestions can be made. First, the word of God has both a locutionary and an illocutionary force, that is, $F(p)$. In the case of the preached gospel, the propositional content p of the word of God is the gospel, that is, "Christ died for our sins . . . [and] was raised on the third day" (1 Cor 15:3–4). But p is also accompanied by an illocutionary force F. On the one hand, p is always expressed with F, the illocutionary force, for a propositional act cannot occur alone. But on the other hand, F requires that there is p, namely the gospel message to proclaim.

Perhaps this insight, that p cannot be proclaimed without an F would explain why Paul rejoices that, although "some preach Christ out of envy and rivalry," nonetheless, "whether from false motives or true, Christ is

96. Austin, *How to Do Things with Words*, 117.

97. Searle, *Speech Acts*, 49–50.

98. So also Vanhoozer's analysis of Searle, in Vanhoozer, "The Semantics of Biblical Literature," 89. For further discussion, see also Vanhoozer, "From Speech Acts to Scripture Acts," 178–82.

99. Luther, "The Freedom of a Christian," 367.

preached" (Phil 1:15–18). For despite false motives of the proclaimers, the gospel *p* has been locuted, and in being locuted, it has also necessarily carried an illocutionary force *F*. As a result, "Christ is preached," or *F(p)*.

Second, the proclaimer of the word of God is not only commissioned by God to locute the divine message, but also to illocute the divine speech act on behalf of God. Thus, the proclaimer is not only *speaking* but *doing* God's speech act on his behalf. This is what it means to be an "ambassador," "servant," or "witness" for the gospel. In other words, the proclamation of the gospel involves not only locuting the message but also performing God's illocutionary force of warning, commanding, blessing, cursing, and so on. The so-called "power" of the preached word comes from its illocutionary force.[100] This was recognized by Calvin, as was noted in chapter 2, who urged pastors to "*do* [my emphasis] all things in God's word."[101]

Third, there is a variety of illocutionary forces that may accompany the locuted word of God. For the proposition "Jesus is Lord" can be a warning to those who refuse to submit to Jesus, a command to accept Jesus as Lord, an appeal to believe in Jesus, a prayer to the Lord Jesus, a promise to those who hope in Jesus, an encouragement to believers who suffer, a blessing to those who believe, a curse to those who disbelieve, a confession of faith, an assertion, and so on. Thus, the word of God cannot be restricted to only one illocutionary force. Nor, would it seem, that one illocutionary force should be privileged over another.

Fourth, the inscripturation of the word of God preserves not only the locution but the illocution of God's speech acts.[102] What was once illocuted in the past by prophets, Jesus, and the apostles has been inscripturated so that God continues to illocute to contemporary audiences through Scripture. But what is the illocutionary force of Scripture? It is here that we must recognize that Scripture has a *variety* of illocutionary forces. And this operates at many levels. It may operate at the level of each individual passage of Scripture. For example, Thiselton routinely applies the analysis of speech-act theory to various passages in 1 Corinthians in his commentary.[103] And it can operate at the level of each book or literary genre. For example,

---

100. As according to the insights of Thiselton, "The Supposed Power of Words in the Biblical Writings," 283–99.

101. *Institutes*, IV.viii.9.

102. For more discussion, see Vanhoozer, "From Speech Acts to Scripture Acts," 190.

103. Thiselton, *The First Epistle to the Corinthians*. And this is anticipated by an earlier work by Peter W. Macky, in which he concludes that a "variety of speech act purposes . . . can plausibly be discerned as lying behind the words the biblical writers uttered," in Macky, "The Multiple Purposes of Biblical Speech Acts," 61.

Vanhoozer's thesis is that there is a *"correlation between a text's genre, or literary form, and a text's illocutionary point and force."*[104] And, ultimately, it can operate at the level of the canon. That is, just as there was a canonical locution of the Christocentric gospel message, there is also a *canonical illocution*. But what is the illocutionary force of the unified canon? Vanhoozer suggests that it is the illocutionary act of *covenanting*,[105] and then probingly asks, "Could it be that certain illocutions come to light only when we describe what God is doing at the canonical level?"[106]

Fifth, the preacher has access to the illocution of the word of God by careful exegesis and interpretation of Scripture.[107] And in doing so, the preacher will be receiving his or her illocution from God. Thus, if the preacher in turn proclaims not only the locution of Scripture but also its illocution, then the preacher will be performing a speech act on behalf of God. In this way, the word of God, which was illocuted in the past by the prophets, Jesus, and the apostles, whose illocution is preserved by inscripturation, continues to illocute to present day hearers through the proclamation of the gospel.

The Perlocution of the Word of God

Austin suggests that the perlocutionary act is the performance of an act *by* saying something; it is the *effect* of what has been said.[108] Here Austin notes, "It is the distinction between illocutions and perlocutions which seems likeliest to give trouble."[109] Austin suggests that the distinction is

---

104. Vanhoozer, "The Semantics of Biblical Literature," 91; his italics. In a later work, Vanhoozer develops this: "[T]he author's illocutionary intentions come to light only at the level of the literary whole ... I maintain that we should recognize *generic illocutions* [his italics]: the narrative act, the parabolic act, the apocalyptic act, the historical act, the prophetic act and so on. In other words, each of the major forms of biblical literature has its own characteristic illocutionary forces: wisdom ('commending a way'), apocalyptic ('encouraging endurance'), prophecy ('recalling covenant promises and obligations') and so on. To describe and ascribe generic illocutionary acts, then, is to say what an author is doing in his text considered as a whole," in "From Speech Acts to Scripture Acts," 193.

105. Vanhoozer, "From Speech Acts to Scripture Acts," 194.

106. Ibid., 195.

107. Indeed, Vanhoozer's thesis is that it is not only possible but warranted for the reader to secure illocutionary uptake of the word of God in Scripture, in *Is There a Meaning in This Text?*, esp. 197–366. See also Vanhoozer, "From Speech Acts to Scripture Acts," 173–85.

108. Austin, *How to Do Things with Words*, 101.

109. Ibid., 110.

that the illocutionary act achieves effects such as securing uptake, taking effect, or inviting a response, in which case the illocutionary act is "happily, successfully performed";[110] whereas the perlocutionary act produces effects such as the achievement of a perlocutionary object (convincing, persuading) or a perlocutionary sequel.[111]

The distinction between illocution and perlocution is important. However, Austin finds it difficult to properly make this distinction because he errs by making illocutionary uptake a condition for the "happy" or "successful" performance of an illocutionary act. But this does not have to be so. As Alston notes:

> Whether I told you that the dean is coming to dinner or asked you to bring me a towel does not hang on whether you heard or understood me. If you didn't, my communicative purpose has been frustrated. *But it doesn't follow that I didn't tell you or ask you.* [My italics.][112]

Thus, it is important to distinguish between illocution and its effects. For an illocutionary act can by "happy" or "successful" regardless of the effects upon the hearer; instead, the latter are perlocutionary effects. Thus, Searle modifies Austin's work by distinguishing "understanding," which is an illocutionary effect,[113] from belief or response, which would be perlocutionary effects.[114]

So what is the relationship between the locutionary, illocutionary, and perlocutionary act? Here, Alston's insights are particularly helpful. Alston observes that there is an asymmetrical hierarchy between "sentential acts" (his term for locutionary acts), illocutionary acts, and perlocutionary acts.[115] That is: (1) Illocutionary acts presuppose sentential acts,[116] but not vice versa. In other words, there can be no illocutionary force if there is no utterance of some form; but conversely, there can be an utterance with no content[117]

---

110. Ibid., 116–18.

111. Ibid., 118.

112. Alston, *Illocutionary Acts and Sentence Meaning*, 24.

113. The hearer understands the speaker when he or she recognizes the utterance of the speaker and what the speaker is trying to do, Searle, *Speech Acts*, 47.

114. Ibid.

115. Alston, *Illocutionary Acts and Sentence Meaning*, 26–32.

116. Ibid., 27–28, where Alston enlarges the concept of "sentential acts" to cover not only verbal utterances (such as a sentence) but also elliptical utterances (such as "Left" in response to a request for directions) and non-verbal communication (such as a nod or wink), which he terms "sentence surrogates."

117. For example, "Wow!"

or illocutionary force. (2) Perlocutionary acts presuppose sentential acts, but not vice versa. In other words, there can be no perlocutionary effect on a hearer without the issuing of an utterance of some form; but there can be an utterance with no effect upon a hearer. And (3) Perlocutionary acts may be based on illocutionary acts, but not vice versa. In other words, "a perlocutionary act *consists* in the production of some effect, whereas an illocutionary act does not."[118]

In chapter 7 of this book I explored the *results* of preaching. If the analysis of speech-act theory is applied here, the following suggestions can be made. First, in the proclamation of the word of God, it is important to distinguish between the illocution of the word and the perlocutionary effects. It is this distinction that provides the foundation to Walter Houston's thesis that the Old Testament prophets were successful in their proclamations of judgment and doom:

> The *illocutionary* act of giving an order has been successfully performed, even though the *perlocutionary* effect of getting them to obey it has not . . . In these terms, as long as the prophets' hearers understood that they were warning them, calling for repentance or whatever the particular speech act might be, and understood the content of the warning or whatever it might be, then the prophets had *done* what they set out to do, even if they had not achieved the effect they had hoped for.[119]

And this distinction between illocution and its perlocutionary effects is just as valid in conceptualizing the proclamation of the word of God. That is, on the one hand, the word is proclaimed when it is illocuted; but on the other hand, it does not follow that it must result in belief or obedience to qualify as a proclamation of God's word, for those effects are perlocutionary effects. Therefore, one can have "happy" or "successful" illocution of the word independently of the effects upon the hearer.

Second, the perlocutionary effects are beyond the control of the proclaimer. The proclaimer cannot coerce, manipulate, or force a hearer to believe or obey. That is, although the proclaimer must ensure that the gospel is illocuted, the speaker cannot ensure that the hearer responds with faith and repentance. The hearer is responsible for his or her response, not the proclaimer. Thus, a proclaimer is to illocute "Christ crucified" (1 Cor 1:23) without resorting to "wise and persuasive words" (1 Cor 2:4), that is, to coerce or manipulate. For that would be to confuse the illocutionary with the perlocutionary act. Here, Thiselton's comments are helpful:

118. Alston, *Illocutionary Acts and Sentence Meaning*, 26–32.
119. Houston, "What Did the Prophets Think They Were Doing?," 143; his italics.

> . . . I distinguish between *"illocutionary" speech-acts*, which depend for their effectiveness *on a combination of situation and recognition*, and *"perlocutionary" speech-acts*, which depend for their effectiveness on *sheer causal (psychological or rhetorical) persuasive power*. This also holds for the distinction between the nature of *apostolic* rhetoric and the *pragmatic, audience-determined rhetoric of Corinth* . . . [His italics.][120]

Third, whereas the proclaimer is not responsible, the Holy Spirit is active and responsible for the perlocutionary effects of the proclamation of the word of God. Or, as Vanhoozer notes, "The Spirit 'advenes' on truth to make it efficacious."[121] That is:

> There is a connection, I submit, between pneumatology and perlocutions . . . [A] perlocution is what one brings about *by* one's speech act. Speech frequently presents an argument, but arguments are intended to produce assent. Perlocutions have to do with the effect on the hearer of a speech act. Now, the primary role of the Holy Spirit, I believe, is to *minister the Word*. The application of salvation is first and foremost a matter of applying both the propositional content and the illocutionary force of the gospel in such a way as to bring about perlocutionary effects: effects which, in this case, include regeneration, understanding, and union with Christ . . . It is not simply the impartation of information, nor the transfer of mechanical energy, but the impact of a total speech act . . . that is required for a summons to be efficacious . . . The effectual call is best understood in terms of a conjunction of Word and Spirit, illocution and perlocution.[122]

Therefore, while the human proclaimer illocutes the word, it is the Spirit who works in the life of the hearer to achieve the perlocutionary effects. Or, to use the categories suggested by the Reformers, the illocution of the word would correspond with the "external" or "open" call, and the perlocution of the word would correspond with the "internal" or "hidden" call of the gospel.

Fourth, perlocution requires illocution and locution. That is, for people to be saved, the gospel must be proclaimed. In Alston's hierarchical analysis of the relationship between locution, illocution, and perlocution it was noted that illocution requires locution, and perlocution requires locution and illocution. Thus, any so-called belief or repentance in the absence

---

120. Thiselton, *The First Epistle to the Corinthians*, 51.
121. Vanhoozer, "Effectual Call or Causal Effect?," 249.
122. Ibid., 248; his italics.

of the proper locution and illocution of the gospel cannot be a legitimate perlocutionary effect. For it is an effect in response to some other locution, such as a wrong message (a "different gospel" or "no gospel at all"), or some other illocution, such as the use of manipulation or rhetoric (with "wise and persuasive words"). Or, another way of expressing this is that the subjective aspect of the word of God (inner belief and repentance) requires the objective aspect of the word of God (the outward proclamation of the gospel). That is, in the theological terms of the Reformers, the inner call of the Spirit requires the external call of human proclamation.

Fifth, perlocution is difficult, if not impossible, to quantify, qualify, or measure objectively. For, while the locutionary and illocutionary acts are external to the hearer, the perlocutionary effect is internal to the hearer. Thus, for an outside observer, it is impossible to assess objectively the perlocutionary effect. Interestingly, the Reformers introduced the concept of the "marks" of the church in order to outline criteria with which to distinguish a true church from a false one. The first two "marks"—proclamation and sacraments—are external criteria, which, according to the analysis of speech-act theory, correspond with the locution and illocution of the gospel. But the additional third "mark" of church discipline is an internal criteria, which corresponds with perlocution. Thus, by adding the "mark" of church discipline, the Reformers added a mark that is both not necessary to the preaching of the word and impossible to assess objectively. But, they were forced to add this "mark" when they recognized that a gathering of people around the proclamation of the gospel might not guarantee a true church, for the gathered "sheep" may not be the true sheep.

Discernment: "Happy" and "Unhappy" Speech Acts

Austin distinguishes between "happy" and "unhappy" performative utterances. An "unhappy" performative utterance occurs in the case of an "infelicity." Examples of "infelicities" would be "misfires," "misinvocations," "misexecutions," "misapplications," "hitches," "abuses," or "insincerities."[123] In order for a performative utterance to be "happy" there are certain "rules" that must not be infringed. Examples of such rules are: a conventional procedure exists, the appropriate person performs the procedure, the procedure is executed correctly, and the procedure is executed completely.[124] In addition, the speaker is to be sincere,[125] and the utterance must be "true,"

---

123. Austin, *How to Do Things with Words*, 12–24.
124. Ibid., 25–38.
125. Ibid., 39–45.

that is, it must correspond with the facts.[126] For example, one cannot *warn*, "The bull is about to charge," if in fact there is no bull about to charge. Or one cannot *request*, "Close the door," if the door is already closed.

Searle similarly suggests that there are conventional or constitutive rules that are required for the successful performance of illocutionary acts.[127] Further, there are "defects" (Searle's preferred term for Austin's "infelicities")[128] if the following "rules" are not followed: (1) the *propositional content rule*, which refers to the propositional content of the illocutionary act; (2) the *preparatory rule*, which refers to the conditions surrounding the illocutionary act; (3) the *sincerity rule*, which refers to the sincerity of the speaker; and (4) the *essential rule*, which refers to what the illocutionary act *counts as*.[129] For example, if speaker S performs an illocutionary act of *promising* to hearer H a future act A of S, then it is necessary that (1) the *propositional content condition* is the future act A of S; (2) the *preparatory condition* is that (a) H would prefer S's doing A to his not doing A, and S believes H would prefer S's doing A to his not doing A, and (b) it is not obvious to both S and H that S will do A in the normal course of events; (3) the *sincerity condition* is that S intends to do A; and (4) the *essential condition* is that the utterance counts as the undertaking of an obligation to do A.[130]

If the proclaimed word of God can be understood as a speech act, then we can also talk of "happy" and "unhappy" proclamation. If certain "rules" are not followed, or if certain "conditions" are not present, then the proclamation is an "infelicity" (Austin's term) or "defective" (Searle's term). In such cases, the proclamation has "misfired" and should not be ascribed the status of the word of God. But what might these rules or conditions be? I suggest the following:

1. There exists a *divinely ordained convention* that the proclaimer is able to speak on behalf of God. This convention exists because in God's covenant, which he has established with creation, he has ordained affairs in such a way that he will speak to humankind through divinely commissioned messengers. For example, in the Old Testament, in Deuteronomy 18, God ordains it that he will "raise up . . . a prophet" who will speak his words to the people (v. 18a); conversely, a *false* prophet is one who has not undergone this divinely ordained convention of being commissioned by God (cf. Jer

---

126. Ibid., 45.
127. Searle, *Speech Acts*, 33–71.
128. Ibid., 54.
129. Ibid., 62–71.

130. For Searle, promising is the paradigmatic illocutionary act. However, he also extends the analysis of the four "rules" to acts of requesting, asserting, and questioning, in Searle, *Speech Acts*, 62–71.

23:21–22). And in the New Testament, Jesus commissions and sends his disciples: "As the Father has sent me, I am sending you" (John 20:21). It is for this reason that the Bible places such a high emphasis on the divine commissioning of God's messengers, be they the OT prophets, Jesus, the NT apostles, or the Christian church. For example, Paul repeatedly appeals to his commissioning in order to claim that his message is legitimately the word of God (1 Cor 7:40b; 14:36–38; Gal 1:11—2:10). For the divine commissioning ascribes upon the proclaimer the *normative status* of a speech agent who performs God's speech acts on his behalf. The divine commissioning gives the speaker the *warrant* to claim such a *normative stance*. Conversely, those who do not have this divine commissioning cannot claim this *normative status*; they cannot presume to speak "in the name of" God (cf. Deut 18:20). Instead, their speech acts are "defective."[131]

2. There exists a *divinely ordained procedure* that must be executed correctly. According to this procedure, the proclaimer must receive his or her message from God, and it is this divinely authored message that must be proclaimed by the speaker. For example, in the Old Testament, in Deuteronomy 18, the divinely ordained procedure is that God will put his "words" in the prophet's "mouth" and the prophet will "tell them everything I command him" (v. 18b); conversely, a *false* prophet is one who has not undergone this divinely ordained procedure of receiving "words" from God (cf. Jer 23:18, 21–22). And, in the New Testament, Jesus gives his "words" to the disciples prior to sending them into the world (John 17:8, 14). And it is for this reason that Paul must claim to the Galatians regarding his message: "I did not receive it from any man, nor was I taught it; rather, I received it by revelation from Jesus Christ" (Gal 1:12).

Thus, the proclaimer receives his or her speech act from God and must re-proclaim this same speech act. Today, the proclaimer has access to this speech act from the text of Scripture, which is the inscripturated speech act of God. Therefore, the proclaimer must aim towards both a correct interpretation of Scripture and a correct re-proclamation of the message of Scripture. In speech-act terms, the proclaimer must recognize the illocutionary act that is ascribed to the author of the scriptural text (i.e., "interpretation");[132] and then the proclaimer must perform the same illocutionary act upon the hearers (i.e., "re-proclamation"). In doing so, the

---

131. At this point, one might legitimately ask how one can know if one is commissioned. Does this point not beg the need for further criteria? This is indeed a valid question. However, it is one that is beyond the scope of my present project.

132. Vanhoozer helpfully demonstrates that "interpretation" is the process of "inferring authorial intentions" and "ascribing illocutionary acts," in Vanhoozer, "From Speech Acts to Scripture Acts," 182–85.

proclaimer is performing the same illocutionary act as the scriptural text, and is thus performing the divine speech act on behalf of God.

3. There exists a *divinely revealed propositional content*. In the case of the preached gospel, this propositional content is the gospel. That is, the locution (in Austin's terms) or *p* (in Searle's terms) should be the divinely revealed gospel message. This locutionary act should correspond with God's revealed truth. For example, in the Old Testament, in Deuteronomy 13, a *false* locutionary act is one that locutes a false god (v. 2); and in Deuteronomy 18, a *false* locutionary act is one that "has not been spoken by the Lord" (v. 21) and therefore "does not take place or come true" (v. 22). And, in the New Testament, Paul warns against those who falsely locute "a different gospel," which is really "no gospel at all" (Gal 1:6–9; cf. 2 Cor 11:4). It is for this reason that the Bible places such a strong emphasis on the message of preaching. For Paul, a criterion of true proclamation was that "we preach Christ crucified" (1 Cor 1:23). Thus, the proclaimer today must locute the gospel message. And the proclaimer has access to this locution in the locution of Scripture.

The analysis of speech acts has provided these three helpful "rules" or criteria for discerning if and when proclamation is the word of God. If these "rules" are followed, then we could say that the proclamation is "happy" (in Austin's terms) or "pure" or "true" (in the Reformer's terms). That is to say, if these "rules" or criteria are followed, although we could not say that we have the *necessary* conditions for the word of God to be preached because, as we have noted previously, the sovereign God may reveal his word through visions, angels, or even a donkey, yet we can say that we have the *sufficient* conditions to recognize the preached word as the word of God, because the speech act has been performed within a divinely ordained convention, according to a divinely ordained procedure, and it has locuted a divinely revealed message. If these conditions are followed, then it is sufficient that the preacher is ascribed the normative status as one who performs a divine speech act, and the hearer is ascribed the normative status as one who receives a divine speech act.

The above three "rules" are objective criteria; that is, they exist externally to the hearer. But what about the perlocutionary effect as a criterion, which would be subjective, or internal, to the hearer? After all, is this not what the Reformers refer to when they speak of a sheep recognizing the voice of the shepherd? In answer to this question, I refer back to the earlier discussion, where the distinction between illocution and perlocution was noted. That is, an illocutionary act can be "happy" or "successful" regardless of the perlocutionary effects upon the hearer. Thus, it does not follow that the absence of illumination, faith, and obedience equates with an "unhappy" speech act. But what if there is indeed illumination, faith, and obedience?

Would this be sufficient to guarantee that the speech act has been "happily" performed? Here, once again, I refer back to the earlier discussion regarding the asymmetrical relationship between locution, illocution, and perlocution. That is, although locution and illocution do not require perlocution, perlocution requires locution and illocution. Thus, *only* perlocution that follows from the "happy" locution and illocution of a speech act would guarantee that a speech act has been "happy"; but perlocution that follows from an "unhappy" locution and illocution of a speech act would not guarantee a "happy" speech act. Therefore, we still end up returning to our three "rules" or objective criteria as the sufficient conditions that guarantee that the preached word is the word of God.

Conclusion

In this chapter I explored the possible application of speech-act theory to our problem of how to conceptualize adequately preaching as the word of God. I began by examining speech-act theory. Speech-act theory is a theory about the use of language; it was initially developed by J. L. Austin and subsequently refined and systematized by his student John Searle. Speech-act theory makes three important contributions: first, a speaker is not merely uttering sounds, words, or statements, but is performing an action, namely, a *speech act*; second, speech acts are composed of locution (the act *of* saying something), illocution (the act *in* saying something), and perlocution (the act performed *by* saying something); and third, speech acts require "constitutive rules" for them to *count as* an action. I then surveyed the recent application of speech-act theory in theological and biblical studies. There is already much promise in the usefulness of speech-act theory in providing fresh insights in areas such as exegesis, hermeneutics, and the doctrine of Scripture. Finally, I turned to the application of speech-act theory to our problem of the preached word as the word of God. In particular, I explored the possibility of conceptualizing God as a divine speech agent, the proclaimer as a human speech agent, and the word of God as a speech act consisting of locutionary, illocutionary, and perlocutionary acts. In addition, speech-act theory was helpful in suggesting "rules" or criteria for discerning if preaching is "happy" or, to use the language of the Reformers, the "pure" preaching of the word. All that remains now is to summarize, refine, and synthesize my findings. This will be the task of the next chapter.

11

The Problem Addressed
A Final Synthesis

In the previous chapter, the application of speech-act theory helped to conceive how proclamation could be *counted as* a divine speech act, that is, the word of God. Further, the application of speech-act theory helped to provide criteria for discerning if and when proclamation is to be counted as the word of God. In doing so, I have almost finished what I set out to accomplish, that is, to construct an adequate conceptualization of preaching as the word of God. The next task would be to summarize, refine, and synthesize my findings. This will be the subject of this penultimate chapter.

Summary of the Argument Thus Far

In the previous chapter, I applied the tools of speech-act theory to the biblical phenomenon of the human proclamation of the word of God. In particular, I examined the concepts of God as a divine speech agent, the proclaimer as a human speech agent, and the word of God as a speech act (locution, illocution, and perlocution). So, in response to our question, "How can human proclamation be the word of God?" my findings can be summarized as:

1. God is a divine speech agent (locuter, illocuter, and perlocuter).
2. The human proclaimer performs God's speech act on God's behalf:
    a. this is an example of double agency discourse
    b. the proclaimer is authorized and deputized by God
    c. in God's covenant with his creation, the conventional rules are such that God's commissioned speech agent is ascribed the normative status of someone who speaks on behalf of God.
3. The word of God is a divine speech act:

a. in the preached gospel, the locution is the gospel message
   b. there is a variety of illocutionary forces
   c. the desired perlocutionary effect is belief and obedience.
4. The proclaimer has access to the locution and illocution of the word of God from Scripture.
5. The proclaimer re-locutes and re-illocutes the gospel message on behalf of God.
6. The proclamation sits under the authority of the locution and illocution of Scripture.
7. The proclaimer is not responsible for the perlocutionary effects. However, the Holy Spirit is active in achieving the perlocutionary effects.

Thus, the analysis of speech-act theory helps to conceive how the human proclamation of the gospel can be *counted as* the word of God. The proclaimer is ascribed the normative status of one who speaks a double agency (divine-human) discourse; and the hearers are ascribed the normative status of people who should recognize that a divine speech act has been performed upon them.

Nonetheless, surely not all proclamation is the word of God. Here the further application of speech-act theory provided criteria for discerning whether or not a particular proclamation is "happy" or "unhappy." Here is a summary of the findings:

1. There exists a *divinely ordained convention*: if a proclaimer has been commissioned by God, then this proclaimer has been ascribed the *normative status* of a speech agent who performs God's speech acts on God's behalf.
2. There exists a *divinely ordained procedure*: the proclaimer must receive his or her speech act from God and must re-proclaim this same speech act. Today, the proclaimer has access to God's speech act from Scripture, which is the inscripturated speech act of God.
3. There exists a *divinely revealed propositional content*: in the case of the preached gospel, the propositional content of proclamation is the gospel.

If these three criteria are fulfilled, then the proclaimer's speech act is a "happy" one, that is, one that can be ascribed the status of the word of God. I should note that these criteria are not *necessary* to ensure that proclamation is the word of God. God may sovereignly choose to speak his word some other way, for example, through a donkey, angels, dreams, and visions. Additionally, the word of God as a category is a broad category that includes *any* message from God, and thus cannot be restricted to *only* the gospel message. However, the criteria outlined above are *sufficient* to *guarantee* that such proclamation is the word of God. In other words, if the proclaimer is commissioned by God, locutes and illocutes God's speech act, that is, the gospel, then we can discern such proclamation to be the word of God.

Further Observations

The application of the tools of speech-act theory to the biblical phenomenon of the preaching of the word of God, in the special sense of the preached gospel, has helped to conceptualize what it is to proclaim the gospel as the word of God and to suggest criteria for discerning proclamation of the gospel that claims to be the word of God. The basic conclusion has been this: *to preach the gospel as the word of God is to re-locute and re-illocute the divine speech act, the gospel, which itself was once locuted and illocuted by the prophets, Jesus, and the apostles, and which now continues to be locuted and illocuted in the canonical Scriptures.*

But some additional issues still need addressing. Earlier, in chapter 9 of this book, I briefly surveyed different contemporary accounts of preaching by Barth, Thielicke, the expository "school" (e.g., Chapman), Buttrick, and Peter Adam. Each approach emphasizes one aspect of the speech act, but is ultimately inadequate by failing to account for all aspects of the speech act. For example, Barth reduces the whole speech act to the perlocutionary act by identifying the "event" of belief and obedience in the hearer through the sovereign work of the Holy Spirit as the word of God. Similarly, Thielicke emphasizes the perlocutionary act in which the Spirit advenes upon the preached word to make it the word of God. Buttrick reduces the whole speech act to the illocutionary act in which the preacher continues the illocutionary act of Christ; but for Buttrick the locutionary act is not essential for the speech act. For expository preachers, the whole speech act is reduced to the locutionary act, where the text of Scripture is essentially re-quoted or paraphrased, but there is little attempt to recapture the illocutionary act of Scripture. For Peter Adam, the illocutionary act is often reduced to only teaching or explanation.

In response to this and other unfinished business, the analysis of speech-act theory permits some further observations. First, a holistic understanding of preaching as a speech act, composed of all *three* components of locution, illocution, and perlocution, will be helpful. There is a message to be preached—the locution. But there is also a force behind the message that aims to affect the hearer—the illocution. And there may indeed be a response from the hearer—the perlocution. All three components are legitimate aspects of the entire *event* of preaching, for preaching is essentially a speech act.

Second, nonetheless, out of the three components, the locutionary aspect has priority. According to speech-act theory, both illocution and perlocution *presuppose* locution. In the special case of the preached gospel, the locution of the gospel is logically prior to its illocutionary or perlocutionary acts. The entire event of gospel preaching is dependent upon the locutionary act, namely that the gospel was indeed preached. If the gospel message was not preached, then the locutionary act has failed, and it follows that any illocutionary or perlocutionary act is "defective." And this is something that Luther recognized, when he complained about preachers who did not locute the gospel but instead locuted "a fable of the old ass or a story about Dietrich of Bern" or "the pagan teachers."[1]

Third, the locution of proclamation comes from Scripture. The preacher receives his or her locution from God; and the preacher's access to God's revelation is from Scripture. The preacher therefore needs to demonstrate that his or her speech act is indeed "happy" by demonstrating that it is the same locution as that of Scripture. For the authority and authenticity of the proclamation resides in its identity of locution with that of Scripture. Moreover, the hearers also have the responsibility to check that the locution of the proclamation is indeed identical to that of Scripture. It is here that expository preaching is correct in emphasizing the need on the part of the preacher to demonstrate, and the need on the part of the hearers to authenticate, that the preached message corresponds with the message of Scripture.

Fourth, preaching must recognize that locution is always accompanied by an illocutionary force. And not only that, it must recognize that there is a *variety* of illocutionary acts that accompanies the single locutionary act of the gospel. In the proclamation of the apostles, the gospel message ("we preach Christ crucified") is accompanied by a variety of illocutionary forces.

---

1. The quotation is from a sermon preached at Erfurt in 1521. I have already quoted it in chapter 2 of this book, but will once again provide it here: "In Germany, there may be altogether perhaps three thousand pastors, but not four men of the right sort—God have mercy on us in this woeful state of affairs! As soon as a good preacher appears, he deals briefly with the gospel and then follows it up with a fable of the old ass or a story about Dietrich of Bern. Or else, he dabbles in the pagan teachers, Aristotle, Plato, Socrates, and others, who are all quite contrary to the gospel. They are also contrary to God, for they have no knowledge of the light we possess," from Luther, "Three Sermons Preached after the Summons to Worms," 113.

For example, it is a promise to those who believe, an urge to repentance to those who don't believe, a blessing to the faithful, a curse to the unfaithful, an encouragement to those who suffer, a warning to those about to fall away, a command to persevere, an assertion of a historical fact, an explanation to those who ask, an apology against the attackers of Christianity, and so on. And as mentioned, in the previous chapter, there is a variety of illocutionary forces at the level of a single passage of Scripture, the level of a single book and its genre, and at the level of the entire canon. Thus, it also follows that there is a variety of illocutionary forces that accompanies the single locutionary act of the preached gospel. And a holistic understanding of preaching will appreciate this. In other words, it is important to maintain the distinction between the locutionary and the illocutionary act; for although there is only one locutionary message, there can be multiple illocutionary acts that accompany it. Thus, an approach that emphasizes one particular illocutionary act, such as "teaching" or "explanation," and equates this with "true preaching," has unfortunately confused the distinction between the locutionary and illocutionary act, and has become reductionistic in its use of illocutionary forces.

Fifth, the recognition that locution is accompanied by illocution and that illocution presupposes locution, or, in Searle's formula, that the illocutionary act requires both F and p helps to resolve the dichotomy between the usual conceptualizations of preaching as propositional or personal, as *is* or *becoming* the word, didactic or poetic, verbal utterance or an event, an assertion or its effect, propositional statements or existential encounter, words or the message conveyed by the words. For preaching as illocution requires *both* locution and illocution, p and F.

Sixth, a traditional sermon is not the only means of illocuting the word of God. Although the essence of a speech act is its illocution, it does not follow that illocution (or locution) requires verbal utterance. For example, the "wink" of an eye can illocute a message through the locution (or "blinking") of an eyelid. Similarly, a "thumbs-up" gesture can illocute through the locutionary action of a thumb movement. Thus, the word of God can also be illocuted through other means besides preaching. In the Old Testament, prophets sometimes illocuted God's message through dramatic prophetic-acts (e.g., Ezekiel lying on his left and right sides, in Ezekiel 4). In the New Testament, Jesus performed miracles as "signs" that illocuted a message (cf. John 2:11; 20:30–31). In the history of the church, paintings or stained-glass windows have illocuted the gospel message. Similarly today, the gospel can be illocuted through other media besides the formal sermon, such as, songs, poetry, and drama. In fact, such media are often accompanied by powerful illocutionary forces. Thus, although my study has tried to argue that the traditional sermon is a legitimate means of locuting and illocuting the word of God, I cannot grant that it is the *only* legitimate means of locuting and illocuting the word of God.

Seventh, the distinction between the illocutionary act and the perlocutionary act is crucial. The preacher is responsible for the illocutionary act, which in turn is dependent upon the locutionary act. But the preacher is not responsible for the perlocutionary act. Instead, it is the Holy Spirit and the hearer who have the dual responsibility for the perlocutionary act, that is, belief and obedience. Or, as Luther observed, "We have the *jus verbi* [right to speak], but not the *executio* [power to do]; we should preach the word, but the consequences must be left to God's own good pleasure."[2] Thus, regardless of the outcome in the life of the hearer, if the preacher has "happily" (or "faithfully") illocuted the speech act, then we can say that the word of God has been preached. Further, a recognition that the Holy Spirit is responsible for the perlocutionary act, and not the preacher, should keep the preacher humble and motivate the preacher to pray for the sovereign work of the Holy Spirit.

Eighth, the hearers have the dual responsibility of assessing and responding to the locutionary and illocutionary act of the preacher. For example, in the Old Testament, the Israelites are commanded to assess the prophets (e.g., Deuteronomy 13 and 18); and, in the New Testament, the Bereans are commended for examining the Scriptures every day to "see if what Paul said was true" (Acts 17:11), and the Corinthians are commanded to "weigh carefully what is said" by those who prophesy (1 Cor 14:29). Thus, the hearers are to assess if the preacher's speech act corresponds with the locution and illocution of Scripture. And once it is recognized that the preacher is indeed proclaiming the word of God, the hearers then have the obligation to respond accordingly to the preached word. For the *normative status* of one who preaches the word of God has been ascribed to the preacher; and the *normative status* of one who has heard the word of God has been ascribed to the hearer.

I am arguing therefore for a holistic understanding of preaching that recognizes it as a speech act composed of its three aspects of locution, illocution, and perlocution—where God, through the Holy Spirit, is responsible for locution, illocution, and perlocution, and the preacher is responsible for locution and illocution. Preaching that emphasizes one aspect of the speech act is reductionistic and unhelpful. For example, preaching that aims to quote Scripture almost word-for-word because it equates this with "preaching," might emphasize the locutionary act at the expense of the illocutionary

---

2. Luther, "The Eight Wittenberg Sermons (1522)," 398.

act. But this fails to recognize that a locutionary act cannot exist alone; a locutionary act is always accompanied by illocution. For, in the end, both the scriptural text and preaching are not only *saying* something but also *doing* something to the hearer. But another example would be preaching that emphasizes the illocutionary or perlocutionary acts at the expense of the locutionary act. An example of this would be preaching that aims for emotional or existential impact that is achieved through rhetoric or manipulation (which confuses the distinction between illocution and perlocution), or it is achieved without the prior preaching of the gospel (which forgets that illocution and perlocution presuppose locution). But, in contrast to the above approaches, preaching should recognize all three components as legitimate aspects of the entire *event* of preaching.

Further Inquiries

This book has concentrated on the limited task of conceptualizing the preached *gospel* as the word of God, which is the more special sense of the preached word. But what about the more general sense of the preached word, where the message from God may refer to a message that is not directly identified as the gospel? For example, in the New Testament, Paul speaks "[a]ccording to the Lord's own word" regarding the future events relating to Christians at Christ's second coming (1 Thess 4:15); here, the content of the word is not directly related to the gospel message. In this general sense of the preached word, how would we discern claims to have preached a word from God? Or, as would be relevant in our contemporary churches, how are we to understand the case of a preacher who preaches "from the Bible," by expounding a Bible passage, as in the case of expository preaching,[3] and claims to have preached the word of God? How are we to conceptualize and discern this more general sense of the preached word?

This would be certainly a fruitful area for future research; and, although it is beyond the scope of this present project, it would not be too unrelated to the discussion in this book. So perhaps, for the moment at least, I can put forward a few tentative preliminary proposals. In the contemporary case of expository preaching, the preached word can be conceptualized as the word of God because:

3. The school of so-called "expository preaching" aims to preach the message of the Bible for a contemporary audience. For example, Robinson defines "expository preaching" as, "Expository preaching is the communication of a biblical concept, derived from and transmitted through a historical, grammatical, and literary study of a passage in its context, which the Holy Spirit first applies to the personality and experience of the preacher, then through him to his hearers," in *Biblical Preaching*, 20.

1. God is a divine speech agent (locuter, illocuter, and perlocuter).
2. The human proclaimer performs God's speech act on God's behalf:
   a. this is an example of double agency discourse
   b. the proclaimer is authorized and deputized by God
   c. in God's covenant with his creation, the conventional rules are such that God's commissioned speech agent is ascribed the normative status of someone who speaks on behalf of God.
3. The word of God, as illocuted in Scripture, is a divine speech act:
   a. Scripture performs a locutionary act
   b. Scripture performs an illocutionary act
   c. the perlocutionary effect is belief and obedience
4. The proclaimer has access to the locution and illocution of the word of God from Scripture. The "faithful" interpretation of Scripture by the preacher is the illocutionary uptake of Scripture by the preacher.
5. The proclaimer re-locutes and re-illocutes the speech act of Scripture on behalf of God. That is, the proclaimer re-performs the original speech act of Scripture. In this way, Scripture once again "speaks" to the hearer.
6. The proclamation sits under the authority of the locution and illocution of Scripture.
7. The proclaimer is not responsible for the perlocutionary effects. However the Holy Spirit is active in achieving the perlocutionary effects.

This above utilization of speech-act theory would help to conceive how preaching "from the Bible" can be *counted as* the word of God. The preacher is ascribed the normative status of one who speaks a double-agency (divine-human) discourse; and the hearers are ascribed the normative status of people who should recognize that a divine speech act has been performed upon them.

Further, the hearers would have the responsibility to "sift" or "weigh" the preacher's speech act (as the Corinthians were to do in 1 Cor 14:29) by assessing if the preacher's speech act is the same as the speech act—locution and illocution—of the Scripture passage that is being "expounded" (in a similar manner to that of the Bereans in Acts 17:11). If the speech act is not that of Scripture, then the hearers could refute the preacher's claim to have preached "from the Bible"; they would not be under the normative status of people to whom a divine speech act has been performed. But if the speech act is the equivalent of that of Scripture, then the hearers are ascribed the normative status of people to whom a divine speech act has been performed.

Here, as in the case of the preached gospel, the distinction between the perlocutionary effect and the illocutionary act is crucial. For the status of the word being preached is dependent upon the illocutionary act and the presupposed locutionary act, but it is independent of the perlocutionary effect. Thus, even in the absence of belief and obedience to the preached word, if the illocutionary act has been "happy," then we can say that the preached word *is* the word of God.

Similarly, the asymmetrical relationship between locution, illocution, and perlocution would be crucial. For although illocution does not require perlocution, perlocution requires illocution and, with it, locution. Thus, even if the sheep supposedly hear the voice of their Shepherd, which is a perlocutionary effect, this perlocutionary effect cannot exist in isolation from a "happy" illocutionary act. Thus, it is necessary that the locution and illocution are indeed "faithful" to the speech act of Scripture for this to be a "happy" speech act.

The following would be criteria for assessing if the Bible has been "faithfully" preached:

1. There exists a *divinely ordained convention*: if a proclaimer has been commissioned by God, then this proclaimer has been ascribed the *normative status* of a speech agent who performs God's speech acts on God's behalf..

2. There exists a *divinely ordained procedure*: the proclaimer must receive his or her speech act from God and must re-proclaim this same speech act. In the case of preaching "from the Bible," as in expository preaching, the proclaimer has access to God's speech act from Scripture, which is the inscripturated speech act of God.

3. There exists a *divinely revealed propositional content*: in the case of expository preaching, the propositional content is that of the Bible passage being expounded.

If these three criteria are fulfilled, then the proclaimer's speech act is a "happy" one, that is, one that can be ascribed the status of the word of God. I should note again that these criteria are not *necessary* to ensure that proclamation is the word of God, for God may sovereignly choose to speak his word some other way, for example, through a donkey, angels, dreams, and visions, and not necessarily through an expository-style sermon. However, the criteria outlined above are *sufficient* to *guarantee* that such proclamation is the word of God. In other words, if the proclaimer is commissioned by God, and if the proclaimer re-locutes and re-illocutes the inscripturated divine speech act, then we can discern such proclamation to be the word of God.

Therefore, in the more general case of expository preaching: *to preach the word of God is to re-locute and re-illocute the inscripturated divine speech act, which itself was once locuted and illocuted by the prophets, Jesus, and the apostles, and which now continues to be locuted and illocuted in the canonical Scriptures.*

A Way Forward

So far, I have recognized a theological problem raised by the Reformers, surveyed the biblical data, and utilized the philosophical tool of speech-act theory. Is there a way forward from here? I will once again restate our problem: if we enter a church, and there is a preacher who preaches a message, how can we determine if this is a church in which the pure word of God is preached?

Let us again restrict ourselves to the preached word of God in its specific sense, that is, the gospel. In the light of the preceding findings, analysis, and discussion, I now make the following proposals. First, we must recognize that there exists a real possibility that we are hearing the word of God, albeit through a human preacher. For there exists a divinely ordained convention (whereby the preacher is commissioned by God and thus has been ascribed the normative status of a speech agent who performs God's speech acts on God's behalf); there exists a divinely ordained procedure (whereby the preacher receives and has access to God's speech act from Scripture, which is the inscripturated speech act of God, and the preacher re-performs this speech act); and there exists a divinely revealed propositional content (whereby the propositional content is the gospel) in order to preach the word of God. And if these three criteria are fulfilled, then it is sufficient, though not necessary, to guarantee that the word of God is being preached. Thus, the Reformers are right to suggest the possibility that the sheep may gather around the voice of God—their Shepherd—and hear him speak to them through the preached word.

Second, we might ask, "Does the preacher's locution correspond with that of the gospel message of Scripture?" In other words, what is the message, or the propositional content, being locuted? Or, in Searle's formulation—$F(p)$—what is the p that is being preached? If the locution corresponds with the gospel message of Scripture, for example, that Christ died for sins and was raised on the third day (cf. 1 Cor 15:3–4; 1 Pet 3:18), then the preacher has faithfully re-locuted the gospel message. Alternatively, if the locution does not correspond with the gospel message of Scripture, for example, that Christ did *not* die for sins *nor* was he raised on the third day, then the preacher has failed to re-locute faithfully the gospel message (cf. Gal 1:8–9; 2 Cor 11:4). In the latter case, we cannot say that the word of God has been preached. Therefore, in the case of gospel preaching as the word of God, it is necessary and sufficient that the gospel message, as locuted by Scripture, is re-locuted.

Third, we might ask, "Does the preacher's illocution correspond with that of the gospel message of Scripture?" What is the illocutionary force? Or, in Searle's formulation—$F(p)$—what is the F? As noted earlier, when the gospel was preached by Jesus and the apostles, it was accompanied by a variety of illocutionary forces—promise, exhortation, encouragement, command, warning, blessing, assertion, explanation, judgment, etc. Thus, here, the preacher has a choice of a variety of illocutionary forces with which to preach the gospel; the preacher is not restricted to only one particular illocutionary force. In the same way that Jesus and the apostles used different illocutionary forces for different audiences and contexts, the contemporary preacher might also choose to use different illocutionary forces. Therefore, we cannot say that there is only one illocutionary force that is necessary for the preached gospel to be the word of God; there exists a variety of illocutionary forces that may accompany the preached gospel as the word of God.

But, as a brief excursus, in the more general case of expository gospel preaching,[4] if the preacher were to choose a particular Bible passage from which to expound the gospel, then the preacher should secure illocutionary uptake from the Bible passage, and then re-illocute the gospel message from the Bible passage with the same illocutionary force as the Bible passage. This is the aim of expository preaching. Similarly, the hearer should also secure illocutionary uptake from the Bible passage and assess if the preacher's illocution corresponds with that of the Bible passage.

But how necessary is it for the preacher's illocution F to correspond with that of the Bible passage, if the gospel message p has been preached anyway? What if, say, the preacher's illocutionary force is one of promising when the biblical passage's illocutionary force is that of warning? That is, despite the preacher's best intentions, he or she has failed to secure illocutionary uptake of the passage and thus has failed to re-illocute the Bible passage; yet the locution, the gospel message, has still been preached. A similar (but not exactly the same) scenario is found in Philipians 1:15–18 where some preach Christ from false motives, yet Paul still rejoices because

---

4. I am using the term "expository gospel preaching" to refer to the case where a preacher aims to preach the gospel message by expounding a particular passage in the Bible.

"whether from false motives or true, Christ is preached" (v. 18). Despite the preachers' wrong motives, Paul can still conceptualize their preaching as the word of God because the gospel message has been preached.[5] If so, then in the case of expository preaching, even if the well-meaning preacher fails in re-illocuting the Bible passage, yet still locutes the Bible passage, then we would have to grant that the gospel has still been preached, and thus the word of God has been preached. Thus, in the case of expository gospel preaching, in order for the preached gospel to be the word of God, although it would be sufficient for the preacher to secure illocutionary uptake and re-illocute the gospel message from the Bible passage, it is not necessary, as long as the gospel message is still preached.

But, as in the above case of expository gospel preaching, why should a preacher faithfully re-illocute a Bible passage if it is not necessary for the word of God to be preached? The answer lies in the aim and claim of preaching, and in particular, expository preaching. The aim of preaching, as I have argued, is to perform a speech act on behalf of God; and in the case of expository preaching, it is to re-perform the inscripturated speech act on behalf of God. And in order to perform a speech act on behalf of God, the preacher's locution and illocution are to correspond with God's locution and illocution. If so, then this is a "happy" speech act, which is sufficient to guarantee that the word of God is preached; that is, the preacher can claim that his or her proclamation is the same speech act as that of the biblical passage. But if the preacher has failed to re-illocute God's illocution, then this is an "unhappy" speech act because there is a failure to secure and effect illocutionary uptake by the preacher. The preacher cannot claim to preach "from the Bible" because the preacher's speech act does not correspond with the inscripturated speech act. But how can it be an "unhappy" speech act if the word of God might still be preached, as in the case of the well-meaning preacher who fails to re-illocute but still locutes the inscripturated gospel speech act? Because in this counter-case, the preacher's speech act still locutes the gospel, albeit not with the corresponding illocutionary force of the expounded biblical passage and is thus still a gospel message, *but* it is not the same speech act as that of the biblical passage, which is the aim and claim of the preacher. That is, although the preacher has preached *a* message (because the preacher's p corresponds with the p of the passage), the preacher has failed to preach *the* message of the Bible passage (because the preacher's F does not correspond with the F of the passage); although *a* speech act has been performed, it is not *the* speech act of the Bible passage.

5. Notice that Paul juxtaposes the brothers' faithful preaching of the "word of God" (v. 14) with those who preach "Christ" from false motives (v. 18); thus, for Paul, both are preaching the "word of God."

Thus, the preacher fails in both the aim and claim of expository gospel preaching, that is, to preach "from the Bible."

Fourth, it is not necessary to ask, "What is the perlocutionary effect of the proclamation?" in order to assess if the word of God has been preached. For the perlocutionary effect is both not necessary for the preached gospel to be the word of God and it is impossible to assess objectively because it is the result of the work of the hidden and inner working of the Spirit in the life of the hearer. Further, the preacher cannot be held responsible for the hearer's refusal to respond; this is something for which the hearer is responsible before God. Thus, regardless of the absence or presence of the perlocutionary effect, in the presence of the faithful re-locution and re-illocution of the gospel message, we are to grant that the preacher has preached the word of God.

Nonetheless, a related and insightful question might be to ask, "What is the preacher's intended perlocutionary effect?" For if the preacher's illocutionary force is the same as that of the gospel or the Bible passage being expounded, then it follows that the preacher's intended perlocutionary effect is also the same. That is, if the preacher's intended perlocutionary effect corresponds with that of the gospel's intended perlocutionary effect, then this would suggest that the preacher has indeed secured illocutionary uptake of the gospel and is re-illocuting the gospel with the original illocutionary force. Or, to use the language of the Reformers, the preacher's intended perlocutionary effect should correspond with God's open and revealed will that all respond to the divine speech act in faith and obedience, even though the preacher has no access to God's hidden and secret will, and thus will not know what the actual perlocutionary effect will be.

Conclusion

In this chapter, I have summarized, refined, and synthesized my findings. The analysis of speech-act theory helped to conceptualize the preached gospel as the word of God, where the preacher re-locutes and re-illocutes the gospel message on behalf of God. Speech-act theory also provided criteria or rules for discerning what proclamation ought to be counted as a divine speech act. Such rules would be: (1) there exists a divinely ordained convention such that the proclaimer is commissioned to speak on behalf of God; (2) there exists a divinely ordained procedure where the proclaimer receives his or her message from God, and it is this received message that is subsequently proclaimed; and (3) there exists a divinely revealed propositional content, which, in the case of the preached gospel, is the inscripturated gospel. Although such rules are not necessary, they are sufficient to guarantee that the preached gospel is the word of God. Thus, if these rules are followed, then the preacher is ascribed the normative status of one who has performed a divine speech act, and the hearers are ascribed the normative status of ones upon whom a divine speech act has been performed. A basic conclusion was then suggested: *to preach the gospel as the word of God is to re-locute and re-illocute the divine speech act, the gospel, which itself was once locuted and illocuted by the prophets, Jesus, and the apostles, and which now continues to be locuted and illocuted in the canonical Scriptures.* A holistic understanding of preaching thus recognizes it as a speech act composed of its three aspects of locution, illocution, and perlocution—where God, through the Holy Spirit, is responsible for locution, illocution, and perlocution, and the preacher is responsible for locution and illocution.

In response to our problem, the four suggestions were these: (1) there exists the possibility that preaching is the word of God; God may indeed be speaking through the preaching of a human. In order to assess if this really is so, then we may ask (2) "Does the speaker's locution correspond with the gospel message of Scripture?" and (3) "Does the speaker's illocution correspond with that of the gospel message of Scripture?" or, in the more general case of expository preaching, "Does the speaker's illocution correspond with that of the Bible passage being expounded?" If the answers to these questions are "Yes," then it is sufficient to guarantee that the preached gospel is the word of God. A further helpful question is (4) "What is the preacher's intended perlocutionary effect?" For, if the preacher's intended perlocutionary effect corresponds with that of the gospel, then this would suggest that the preacher has secured illocutionary uptake of the gospel and is re-illocuting the gospel with the original illocutionary force.

Thus, the criteria are basically that the preacher faithfully re-locutes and re-illocutes the gospel with the same intended perlocutionary effect as that of the inscripturated gospel message, although the preacher is not responsible for the actual perlocutionary effect. Or, to use the categories of form and material, *formally* speaking, the source of preaching ought to be Scripture, and *materially* speaking, the preaching ought to have the same locutionary force, illocutionary force, and intended perlocutionary effect (according to God's open and revealed will) as that of the Bible passage being expounded, although the perlocutionary effect is ultimately the work of God's Spirit (according to God's hidden and secret will).

PART D

Conclusion

In the previous section, the analysis of speech-act theory helped to conceptualize the preached gospel as the word of God, where God is a divine speech agent and the human performs God's speech act on God's behalf by re-locuting and re-illocuting the gospel. Speech-act theory also provided criteria for discerning what proclamation ought to be counted as a divine speech act. In this final part, I aim to conclude this project.

Our initial problem was the conceptualization of the preached gospel as the word of God, and just as importantly, criteria for assessing when this is the case. This is a theological problem that was raised by the Reformation era, for the Reformers identified the preached word as a "mark" of the true church. Thus, the legitimacy of the Reformation and subsequent Christian churches that emerge from the Reformation tradition is grounded upon the fact that preaching *is* the word of God. And it is a theological problem that continues today, with many contemporary preachers claiming to speak the word of God.

The purpose of this book was to explore this theological problem, namely, how can we conceptualize preaching to be the word of God, and what conditions would be necessary or sufficient to guarantee that the word of God has been preached? The methodology was to survey the theological stance of the Reformers; examine the biblical revelation regarding the phenomenon of the preached word; and utilize a contemporary philosophical tool carefully appropriated for theological use in order to answer our problem. This philosophical tool was speech-act theory, as developed by J. L. Austin and systematized by John Searle. At its very heart, speech-act theory proposes that a speaker is not merely uttering sounds, words, or statements, but is performing an action. The hope was that the use of speech-act theory might provide fresh insights in the conceptualization of the biblical phenomenon of the preached word, just as it has in other fields of theological and biblical studies.

From the start, the task was limited in two ways. First, the term "preaching" referred to the proclamation of a message. Thus, while acknowledging that a message might be communicated through a wide variety of media, such as drama or written text, the task was to examine the specific medium of oral transmission, that is, the proclamation of a message. Second, the examination of the "word of God" was limited to the special sense of the preached word, that of the preached gospel. Thus, although there is a more general sense of the preached word, for example, that of contemporary expository preaching, the task was limited to the conceptualization of the phenomenon of gospel preaching, that is, preaching whose content would be the specific gospel message, which announces that Christ has come as the Savior and Lord, and that all must respond with a life of faith and obedience. This focus was warranted because the New Testament often refers to this more specialized sense in its use of the term "word of God"; and the Reformers usually referred to this sense when they equated preaching to be the word of God. Therefore, the focus of this task was limited to the particular concept of the *preached gospel as the word of God* (in the special sense), rather than the preached word (in the general sense) as the word of God. Nonetheless, the hope is that what has been discovered with the application of speech-act theory to the concept of the preached gospel as the word of God may be applied fruitfully and more widely in the future to any general message that is preached as the word of God, especially in the case of expository preaching that aims to preach a message derived faithfully from Scripture. Thus, at the end of my discussion, I have suggested some possible ways to explore this further in future inquiries.

In Part A of this book, I surveyed the theological stance of the Reformers, in particular, Martin Luther and John Calvin. Luther and Calvin equated the preached word as the word of God; for them, preaching *is* the word of God. This resulted in not only a high view of preaching, but it also became a foundational concept for their concept of the church, for they identified the preached word as a mark of the true church. But did the Reformers too readily equate preaching as the word of God? This introduced the problem: when is preaching the word of God?

In Part B, I responded by examining the biblical testimony regarding preaching. After this survey of the phenomenon of the preached gospel in the Bible, I granted that it was legitimate to identify the preached gospel as the word of God, for this is consistent with the Bible's own testimony. Moreover, the Christian church is commissioned by God to proclaim his word, for example, in the model of the prophet of Deuteronomy 18 and the Isaianic servant-preacher. But this led to a related problem: assuming that preaching is the word of God, how can we recognize preaching that is the word of God?

In Part C, I responded with the application of speech-act theory to the problem of how to conceptualize and discern preaching that is the word of God. The analysis of speech-act theory helped to conceptualize the preached gospel as the word of God, where (1) God is a divine speech agent (locuter, illocuter, and perlocuter); (2) the proclaimer is a human speech agent who performs God's speech act on God's behalf; (3) the word of God is a divine speech act; (4) the proclaimer has access to the locution and illocution of the word of God from Scripture; (5) the proclaimer re-locutes and re-illocutes the gospel message on behalf of God; (6) the proclamation sits under the authority of the locution and illocution of Scripture; and (7) the proclaimer is not responsible for the perlocutionary effects, which are achieved by the work of the Holy Spirit. Further, speech-act theory provided criteria or rules for discerning what proclamation ought to be counted as a divine speech act. Such rules would be: (1) there exists a divinely ordained convention such that the proclaimer is commissioned to speak on behalf of God; (2) there exists a divinely ordained procedure where the proclaimer receives his or her message from God, and it is this received message that is subsequently proclaimed; and (3) there exists a divinely revealed propositional content, which, in the case of the preached gospel, is the inscripturated gospel. Although such rules are not necessary, they are sufficient to guarantee that the preached gospel is the word of God. Thus, if these rules are followed, then the preacher is ascribed the normative status of one who has performed a divine speech act, and the hearers are ascribed the normative status of ones upon whom a divine speech act has been performed.

As a result, I arrived at a basic conclusion: *to preach the gospel as the word of God is to re-locute and re-illocute the divine speech act, the gospel, which itself was once locuted and illocuted by the prophets, Jesus, and the apostles, and which now continues to be locuted and illocuted in the canonical Scriptures.* A holistic understanding of preaching thus recognizes it as a speech act composed of its three aspects of locution, illocution, and perlocution—where God, through the Holy Spirit, is responsible for locution, illocution, and perlocution, and the preacher is responsible for locution and illocution. Although it was not within the scope of this project, speech-act theory also helped to conceptualize the more general case of expository preaching as the *re-locution and re-illocution of the inscripturated divine speech act, which itself was once locuted and illocuted by the prophets, Jesus, and the apostles, and which continues to be locuted and illocuted in the canonical Scriptures.*

In the light of these findings, speech-act theory provides the following responses to our initial problem: first, we must recognize that there exists the real possibility that one might hear the word of God, albeit through a human preacher; second, the preacher's locution, that is p, should correspond with the p of the gospel message of Scripture; and third, the preacher's illocution, that is F, should correspond with the F of the gospel message of Scripture. If so, then that is sufficient to guarantee that the preached gospel is the word of God. Fourth, an additional helpful criterion is if the preacher's intended perlocutionary effect corresponds with that of the gospel, for this means that the preacher has secured illocutionary uptake and is re-illocuting the gospel with its original illocutionary force. Thus, the criteria are basically that the preacher re-locutes and re-illocutes the gospel with the same intended perlocutionary effect as that of the inscripturated gospel message, although the preacher is not responsible for the actual perlocutionary effect.

I end this project by restating the conclusion. To proclaim the gospel as the word of God is *to re-locute and re-illocute the gospel message, as once locuted and illocuted by the prophets, Jesus, and the apostles, and that continues to be locuted and illocuted in Scripture.* And in doing so, I end where I began, with the observations of Martin Luther, from his treatise "The Freedom of a Christian":

> You may ask, however: "What then is that word which gives such signal grace, and how shall I use it?" The answer is: It is nothing else than the message proclaimed by Jesus, as contained in the gospel; and this should be, and, in fact, is, so presented that you hear your God speak to you.[6]

---

6. Luther, "The Freedom of a Christian," 359.

Appendix
Prophecy and Preaching

In this book's treatment of preaching, I have had to refer to several texts that refer to the New Testament phenomenon of "prophecy." This introduces the question of whether or not preaching is the same as prophecy as described in the New Testament. The purpose of this appendix is to examine in more detail the relationship between preaching and prophecy.

Paul and Prophecy

It is not easy to pinpoint what Paul identifies as "prophecy" because the term is used by Paul, other New Testament writers, and first-century writers to cover a wide range of phenomena.[1] Paul uses the term "prophecy" and its cognates in many of his letters (1 Cor 11:4–5; 12:10, 28–29; 13:2, 8–9; 14:1–6, 22–25, 29–33, 37–39; Rom 12:6; 1 Thess 5:19–21; 1 Tim 1:18; 4:14; Eph 2:20; 3:5; 4:11). The activity of "prophecy" is a "gift" (χάρισμα) from God (Rom 12:6) or the Holy Spirit (1 Cor 12:4), or a "gift" (δωρεά) "given" (δίδωμι) by Christ (Eph 4:7, 11); it is a "work" (ἐνεργέω) of the Holy Spirit

---

1. For a detailed overview of the use of "prophecy" in extra-biblical works, the Bible, and 1 Corinthians, see Thiselton, *The First Epistle to the Corinthians*, 956–65. For a more comprehensive study, see Aune, *Prophecy in Early Christianity and the Ancient Mediterranean World*, esp. pages 248–64, which deal with Pauline texts. Aune himself identifies "Christian prophetic speech forms" or "oracular material" in the NT with these five "objective criteria": the saying (1) is attributed to a supernatural being; (2) consists of special knowledge, such as a prediction of the future, which the speaker could not have known by ordinary sensory means; (3) is introduced or concluded by a formula; (4) makes reference to the inspiration of the speaker; and (5) does not fit comfortably in its present literary setting, because of its oracular origins, in *Prophecy in Early Christianity and the Ancient Mediterranean World*, 247–48, 317. However, Aune's methodology is problematic because he has *a priori* presupposed a certain form of speech to be prophetic.

(1 Cor 12:11). It is a gift that is enjoyed by both men and women (1 Cor 11:4, 5; cf. Acts 21:9). Prophecy, along with other spiritual gifts, is used in the context of the community of Christian believers, the body of Christ (1 Cor 12:27–31; Rom 12:5), particularly to prepare God's people for works of service (Eph 4:11) so that the church might be strengthened, edified, and comforted (Eph 4:12; 1 Cor 14:3–4). But if an unbeliever should wander into the Christian community and hear such prophecy, then "he will be convinced by all that he is a sinner and will be judged by all, and the secrets of his heart will be laid bare. So he will fall down and worship God, exclaiming, 'God is really among you!'" (1 Cor 14:24–25).

In Paul's letters, he employs a nuanced "yes ... but ..." type of argument when it comes to the issue of prophecy.[2] Paul tells the Corinthians, "[B]e eager to prophesy," (1 Cor 14:39). But, in the context of a Corinthian church, where Corinthian Christians displayed an immature and self-serving approach to spiritual gifts, such as prophecy, Paul also follows with a warning about how such gifts must be used, "But everything should be done in a fitting and orderly way" (1 Cor 14:40). Similarly, on the one hand, Paul exhorts the Thessalonians, "Do not put out the Spirit's fire; do not treat prophecies with contempt" (1 Thess 5:19–20). But, on the other hand, Paul also follows with a warning, "Test everything" (1 Thess 5:21), for, as the Thessalonians themselves will find out, not all so-called prophecy is genuine (cf. 2 Thess 2:2) and one should not be deceived by them (cf. 2 Thess 2:3).

As a result of the improper or false uses of prophecy, Paul provides certain guidelines regarding the activity of prophecy. First, as a work of the Holy Spirit, it must be consistent with God's purposes and character. Thus, prophecy is used to edify and comfort the Christian community (1 Cor 14:4); it operates out of love (1 Cor 14:1; cf. 13:1–13) for the good of others (1 Cor 12:7; 14:26) rather than for selfish ambition or pride. And it submits to the requirement for orderly gatherings (1 Cor 14:40), so that only one person should prophesy at a time (1 Cor 14:29–32), for "God is not a God of disorder but of peace" (1 Cor 14:33). Second, those who prophesy are still subservient to the apostolic word of apostles such as Paul. For, as Paul warns, "If anybody thinks he is a prophet or spiritually gifted, let him acknowledge that what I am writing to you is the Lord's command. If he ignores this, he himself will be ignored" (1 Cor 14:37–38). Third, the words of those who prophesy are to be "weighed carefully" (διακρίνω)[3] by "the

---

2. Much of 1 Corinthians, especially chapters 7–12, follows the "yes ... but ..." form of argument, in Carson, *Showing the Spirit*, 17.

3. It is the prophecy rather than the prophet that is to be "weighed carefully" (contra Robertson, *The Final Word*, 98–100). For a fuller discussion regarding this, see Carson, *Showing the Spirit*, 95–96.

others" (οἱ ἄλλοι), namely, the community of Christians who are being addressed (1 Cor 14:29).[4] Moreover, the prophet needs to evaluate critically his or her own words; for one should only prophesy "in proportion to his faith" (Rom 12:6).[5]

But the problem for us today is: to what is Paul referring when he speaks of "prophecy"? And what is its relationship to the preaching of the word of God? And what is the relationship between prophecy and the canonical Scriptures?

Prophecy as Preaching

One camp might equate what Paul calls "prophecy" with what we would today call "expository preaching," that is, the expounding of Scripture. This position is often traced back to the Reformers.[6] And it is still the approach of some today. For example, J. I. Packer writes:

> ... the essence of the [OT] prophetic ministry was forthtelling God's present word to his people, and this regularly meant application of revealed truth rather than augmentation of it. As Old Testament prophets preached the law and recalled Israel to face God's covenant claim on their obedience, with promise of blessing if they complied and cursing if not, so it appears that New Testament prophets preached the gospel and the life of faith for conversion, edification and encouragement ... By parity of reasoning, therefore, any verbal enforcement of biblical teaching as it applies to one's present hearers may properly be called prophecy today, for that in truth is what it is.[7]

---

4. "The others" (οἱ ἄλλοι) in 1 Cor 14:29 refers to the gathering of listeners, rather than the other prophets, in Grudem, *The Gift of Prophecy in 1 Corinthians*, 60–62. So also Carson, who notes, "This does not mean that everyone in the congregation should participate equally in the evaluating process ... but only that the responsibility for evaluation is not permitted to rest with the prophets, but is extended to the broader community," in *Showing the Spirit*, 121.

5. The phrase in Rom 12:6, κατὰ τὴν ἀναλογίαν τῆς πίστεως ("according to the proportion of faith"), is open to several interpretations: the prophet is to speak according to (1) his or her *own personal* faith in God, or (2) *the faith*—i.e., the set of Christian beliefs. For a discussion of this phrase, consult Moo, *The Epistle to the Romans*, 765–66; Morris, *The Epistle to the Romans*, 440–41.

6. For example, Robeck Jr. claims, "The Reformers, Luther and Calvin, limited the spontaneous character of the Scriptures, hence, they popularized the idea of prophecy as preaching," in "Prophecy, Prophesying," 761. Though, later, we shall see that this is an oversimplification of what the Reformers actually believed.

7. Packer, *Keep in Step with the Spirit*, 215.

The advantage of this approach is that it safeguards the canon from extra-biblical revelation, which might supersede or contradict the canon. But the disadvantage is that it limits God's revelation to only the canon, and it risks "putting out the Spirit's fire" (cf. 1 Thess 5:19).

Prophecy as Revelation

The other camp might recognize a *revelatory* element to "prophecy" that clearly distinguishes it from "preaching." For example, Michael Green writes:

> [O]ne commonly hears it said that prophecy is the same as preaching or teaching . . . The two were quite different. Prophets and teachers are distinguished in passages such as Acts 13:1, 1 Corinthians 12:29. It is one thing to prepare one's address in dependence on the Spirit and to preach it in the power of that same Spirit; it is quite another thing to find the Spirit taking over and speaking directly from Christ through you, in words that you had never intended to use at all.[8]

Some who recognize this revelatory element would believe that the gift of prophecy still operates today. The advantage of this approach is that it "[does] not treat prophecies with contempt," as Paul urges (cf. 1 Thess 5:20). However, the disadvantage is that there is little to distinguish the utterances of a modern-day "prophet" from that of the Old Testament prophets and New Testament apostles, which might lead to questions regarding the status of the canon.[9] In response, some argue that any contemporary gift of prophecy is discontinuous with that of NT prophecy.[10] Or others might argue that the gift of prophecy ceased completely with the death of the apostles and the

---

8. Green, *I Believe in the Holy Spirit*, 171.

9. This is essentially the argument of MacArthur Jr. For example, he argues, "We must not undermine the uniqueness of God's revelation in the Bible. We cannot abandon *sola Scriptura* without defying the Bible's own claim for itself. If we dare to insist we are receiving revelation from God that matches or exceeds the Scriptures, we travel a perilous path that can only lead to theological chaos and spiritual disaster," in *The Charismatics*, 38–39.

10. For example, Prior acknowledges that there is contemporary prophecy, but carefully distinguishes it from the phenomenon of NT prophecy: "[W]e must stress that, as with the ministry of the first apostles, so with the prophets who with them became the foundation of the church, their authority is *unique and unrepeatable* [my emphasis]," in *The Message of 1 Corinthians*, 235. The problem with this is that it is difficult to see how Paul was making this same distinction, for example, to the Corinthian church.

closure of the canon; such a view was championed by B. B. Warfield[11] and is often called the "cessationist" view.[12]

Grudem's Thesis

Wayne A. Grudem has recently offered an alternative position, which I shall now explore in more detail.[13] On the one hand, in his survey of the New Testament material, Grudem understands prophecy to be essentially revelatory. For Grudem, the "essential nature of prophecy" is that it is: (1) a revelation from the Holy Spirit, that is (2) reported publicly.[14] Further, although Grudem doesn't formally state it, he regards spontaneity as an important, if not essential, element in the prophetic revelation from the Holy Spirit. For example, he will later distinguish between "teaching" and "a *spontaneous* revelation," and he also explains, "a prophecy must be the report of a *spontaneous* revelation from the Holy Spirit."[15] Therefore, prophecy cannot be equated with teaching, which is "often simply an explanation or application of Scripture";[16] nor can prophecy be equated with preaching.[17]

But, on the other hand, according to Grudem, the New Testament phenomenon of prophecy is not the same as that of Old Testament prophecy; it is of a lower ranking in authority status to the pronouncements of the OT prophets, the NT apostles, or canonical Scripture. To support this thesis, Grudem notes NT examples of "prophecy" where Paul disobeys the prophecy of Acts 21:4; Agabus' prophecy in Acts 21:10–11 is inaccurate; the

---

11. In a chapter titled "The Cessation of the Charismata," Warfield's aim is "to convince us that the possession of the charismata was confined to the apostolic age," in *Counterfeit Miracles*, 6.

12. For example, Gaffin Jr., "A Cessationist View," in *Are Miraculous Gifts for Today? Four Views*, 25–64. Similarly, Robertson, who argues, "If revelation has been completed with the perfection of the New Testament Scriptures, then prophecy as the principal revelational gift has now ceased ... [The modern preacher] must beware of claiming for himself either the revelational experience of the prophet or the foundational position of the apostle," in *The Final Word*, 20.

13. This has been published in several works: Grudem, *The Gift of Prophecy in 1 Corinthians* (this is reproduction of his 1978 doctoral dissertation for the University of Cambridge, England); Grudem, *The Gift of Prophecy: In the New Testament and Today*; and Grudem, "Prophecy, Prophets," 701–10.

14. Grudem, *The Gift of Prophecy: In the New Testament and Today*, 135–40.

15. Ibid., 140–43; my italics.

16. Ibid., 140.

17. Grudem equates "teaching" with "preaching": "In modern English, the word 'preaching' is generally used to mean the same thing as the New Testament meant by 'teaching,'" in *The Gift of Prophecy*, 143.

Thessalonians, who "received" and "accepted" God's word "with joy inspired by the Holy Spirit" (1 Thess 1:6; 2:13; cf. 4:15) need to be told by Paul to "not despise prophesying" (1 Thess 5:20); the Corinthians need to be told by Paul to value prophecy over other gifts such as tongues (1 Cor 14); prophecy is to be evaluated critically (1 Cor 14:29); and the prophet, unlike Paul, can not claim to speak God's very words (1 Cor 14:36).[18] Thus, Grudem concludes "NT prophecy did not have the authority of God's very words."[19] Accordingly, in his *The Gift of Prophecy*, the chapter headings repeatedly refer to prophecy as "Speaking Merely Human Words to Report Something God Brings to Mind," whereas OT prophets and NT apostles are "Speaking God's Very Words."[20]

The strengths of Grudem's thesis are that it recognizes the revelatory element of prophecy, the diverse ways that prophecy might be manifested, and the need for prophecy to submit to apostolic authority. However, there are some weaknesses.[21] First, Grudem distinguishes between Old Testament prophets who spoke "God's very words" and New Testament prophecy that uses "merely human words" to report a divinely revealed idea.[22] Such a distinction is based on a very narrow view of revelation.[23] For, although the divinely superintended *results* of inscripturated revelation are the "very words of God,"[24] this does not mean that the *mode* of revelation[25] needs to be one where God revealed the "very words of God" to the OT prophet or NT apostle.[26] Surely the OT prophets and NT apostles would also have

18. Grudem, "Prophecy, Prophets," 708. Carson also provides a detailed summary of Grudem's argument in Carson, *Showing the Spirit*, 94–98.

19. Grudem, "Prophecy, Prophets," 708.

20. Grudem, *The Gift of Prophecy*, 7–8.

21. I will proceed to list these weaknesses despite Carson's claim: "That Grudem has rightly delineated some distinguishing limitations of New Testament prophecy is in my judgment beyond cavil. It will not do to question his entire synthesis because we have questions about some of his formulations," in *Showing the Spirit*, 99.

22. Ibid., 160–61, where Carson claims that Grudem has been inaccurately understood on this point. Yet, in Grudem's dictionary article, dated as recently as 2000, Grudem repeatedly contrasts NT prophecy with "God's very words." For example, "[Paul] surely would not have done this if the prophecy had been *God's very words* . . ."; "thus implying that NT prophecy did not have the authority of *God's very words*"; "If prophecy does not contain *God's very words*, then what is it?" [my emphases]. Thus, Grudem, even now, consistently makes the distinction between prophecy and "God's very words," in "Prophecy, Prophets," 706–7.

23. For a similar critique, see Turner, "Spiritual Gifts Then and Now," 16.

24. Such would be Jesus' view of the words of Scripture, in Matt 5:18.

25. For a more detailed discussion on the valid distinction between the *mode* and *result* of revelation, see Carson, *Showing the Spirit*, 161.

26. Such a view would be close to a "dictation" theory of revelation.

received ideas and concepts from God. For example, Scripture often consists of the OT prophets' reports of dreams and visions, which can not be classified as "words" revealed by God that were to be quoted verbatim. Such a distinction also creates a false dichotomy between "God's very words" and "merely human words." One immediately wonders what words the OT prophets and the NT apostles used if they were not also "human words."[27] For example, the apostle Paul uses very human words to write his letter to Philemon. Moreover, such a distinction presents problems regarding one's view of Scripture and the use of translations. For example, the LXX is often not an exact word-for-word translation of the Hebrew text. And, similarly, what are we to do with our modern-day English translations? Grudem's view of revelation would lead one to question whether or not such translations are "God's very words."

Second, Grudem emphasizes the spontaneous element in the revelation of prophecy. This is largely because Grudem uses 1 Corinthians 14 as the grid by which all New Testament prophecy is to be understood. And in his analysis, 1 Corinthians 14:30 depicts prophetic revelation as coming "*quite spontaneously,* for it comes while the first speaker is talking."[28] This leads him to conclude, "So this prophecy does not seem to be a sermon or lesson which had been prepared beforehand; it is much more spontaneous than that."[29] And for Grudem, this is an important distinction between prophecy, which is based upon spontaneous revelation, and teaching (or preaching), which is based upon careful and conscious reflection:

> [I]f a message is the result of conscious reflection on the text of Scripture, containing interpretation of the text and application to life, then it is (in New Testament terms) a *teaching*. But if the message is the report of something God brings suddenly to mind, then it is a *prophecy*.[30]

However, Grudem's insistence upon spontaneity is misguided. For, the essence of revelation is simply that something is *revealed* to the recipient; it is unnecessary for it to be spontaneous or instantaneous.[31] It is hard to conceive that all prophetic revelation should be characterized by spontaneity. This, again, is too narrow a view of revelation. In the end, Grudem's analysis

27. Such a view would be akin to a "docetic" view of Scripture.
28. Grudem, *The Gift of Prophecy in 1 Corinthians*, 117; his emphasis.
29. Ibid.
30. Grudem, *The Gift of Prophecy: In the New Testament and Today*, 143; his italics.
31. "Why must 'revelation' be instantaneous rather than the result of sustained prayer and sustained prayerful contemplation, meditation, and rational reflection?," asks Thiselton, *The First Epistle to the Corinthians*, 962.

places too much weight on 1 Corinthians 14:30, where Paul's point has more to do with teaching orderly and peaceful worship than the spontaneous nature of prophetic revelation.

Third, as Carson notes, Grudem's thesis "oversimplifies the contrast between Old Testament prophets and New Testament prophets," for in the Old Testament, there also existed "schools" of the prophets, and such schools did not enjoy the status of, say, Amos or Isaiah; thus, "[t]here is no single, stereotypical Old Testament prophecy and a different stereotypical New Testament prophecy."[32] Perhaps New Testament prophets could be similarly described as belonging to the prophetic "school" of Christ or the apostles? Thus, New Testament prophets are dependent upon sayings of Christ and the apostles, and do not enjoy the status of Christ or the apostles, but they are still proclaiming the revealed word of God.

Fourth, Grudem's thesis oversimplifies the contrast between the New Testament apostles and the New Testament prophets. This forces him to argue that the phrase "the apostles and prophets" (τῶν ἀποστόλων καὶ προφητῶν; Eph 2:20; cf. 3:5; 4:11)[33] is speaking of the one and same group—"the apostles *who are also prophets*"—rather than two groups of people—"the apostles and prophets."[34] Although Grudem's interpretation is plausible,[35] there are exegetical difficulties with Grudem's interpretation, not the least being Paul's distinction between the apostles and prophets in Ephesians 4:11.[36] Thus, if Ephesians 2:20 uses the phrase "the apostles and prophets" to refer to *both* the apostles and New Testament prophets, then, as O'Brien comments:

---

32. Carson, *Showing the Spirit*, 98. This point is also noted by O'Brien, *The Letter to the Ephesians*, 215-16.

33. In Eph 2:20, Paul states that "God's household" is built upon the "foundation of the apostles and prophets." The term "prophets" cannot refer to OT prophets, but refers instead to NT prophets. For a discussion on this, see O'Brien, *The Letter to the Ephesians*, 214, esp. n44.

34. Grudem, *The Gift of Prophecy in 1 Corinthians*, 82-105. Carson supports Grudem's suggestion, and adds, "If we conclude, against Grudem, that the 'prophets' in question here enjoy a role with the apostles in providing the revelatory foundation for Christianity (although that is not quite what is said), we must hasten to admit that this is an anomalous use of 'prophets' in the New Testament," in Carson, *Showing the Spirit*, 96-7. However, against Carson, (1) by accepting "prophets" as a separate group from the "apostles" one is not also saying that the "prophets" provide "the revelatory foundation for Christianity" (which Carson himself seems to admit with his concession, "although that is not quite what is said"); and (2) one wonders why such a use of "prophets" in Eph 2:20 and 3:5 should be the "anomalous use"; surely such a judgment needs to be made upon other grounds.

35. So Carson, *Showing the Spirit*, 96-97, esp. n73.

36. O'Brien, *The Letter to the Ephesians*, 215-16.

APPENDIX

Together with the apostles, prophets were the first authoritative recipients and proclaimers of God's revelation in Christ. If the single article [τῶν] before the two nouns "apostles" and "prophets" does not indicate an identity, then it may focus on a certain unity. "The apostles and Christian prophets are both seen as those to whom God made known the revelation of the gospel,"[37] and who were the first proclaimers of it.[38]

Fifth, Grudem's thesis downplays the need to evaluate critically the message of the Old Testament prophets and New Testament apostles. Although Grudem acknowledges the need in the Old Testament to test a prophet (Deut 18:20; 13:5), he claims that once it is established that a person is a true Old Testament prophet, his words are always to be considered as God's words:

> [W]e do not find in the Old Testament any instance where the prophecy of someone who is acknowledged to be a true prophet is "evaluated" or "sifted" so that the good might be sorted from the bad, the true from the false . . .
>
> So what we find in the Old Testament is that every *prophet* is judged or evaluated, but not the various parts of every *prophecy*.[39]

And, in Grudem's argument, the New Testament apostles enjoy the same privileged status of the Old Testament prophets.[40] But this is a bit of an oversimplification. For the apostles were not free from critical evaluation. For example, in Acts 17:11 the Bereans are commended for having "received the message with great eagerness and examined the Scriptures every day to see if what Paul said was true." In Galatians 1:8, Paul warns, "[E]ven if we or an angel from heaven should preach a gospel other than the one we preached to you, let him be eternally condemned." And in Galatians 2:14, Paul is compelled to publicly rebuke the apostle Peter for "not acting in line with the truth of the gospel." Thus, even the apostles needed to submit their own person and message under the authority of the Scriptures and the gospel message; this is partly why the apostles themselves appeal so frequently to Old Testament Scripture to demonstrate the truth of their message. The so-called "apostolic authority" does not reside so much in the office or

---

37. O'Brien is quoting Sandnes, *Paul—One of the Prophets?*, 235–36.

38. O'Brien, *The Letter to the Ephesians*, 216.

39. Grudem, *The Gift of Prophecy: In the New Testament and Today*, 20–21; his italics.

40. Ibid., 32, where Grudem states, "The apostles are the New Testament counterpart of the divinely authoritative Old Testament prophets."

person of the apostle, but in the Christ-revealed and Christ-commissioned gospel message that is proclaimed by them.

Sixth, Grudem along with others who insist that the phenomenon of New Testament prophecy can not be equated with preaching have too restrictive a view of what constitutes "preaching." For example, Grudem writes:

> ... *teaching*[41] in terms of the New Testament epistles consisted of repeating and explaining the words of Scripture (or the equally authoritative teachings of Jesus and of the apostles) and applying them to the hearers ... [It] is something very much like what is described by our phrase "Bible teaching" today.[42]

Similarly, Turner explains:

> Charismatic *teaching* includes exposition that relates scripture and tradition to the immediate needs of a congregation, while prophecy primarily denotes the declaration by a man of material revealed to him *directly* by the supernatural source rather than mediated through consideration of scripture.[43]

And it is worthwhile to quote Green again:

> It is one thing to prepare one's address in dependence on the Spirit and to preach it in the power of that same Spirit; it is quite another thing to find the Spirit taking over and speaking directly from Christ through you, in words that you had never intended to use at all.[44]

Such understandings of preaching are reductionistic, by limiting the essence of preaching to the explanation and application of Scriptures, and anachronistic, by construing preaching mainly in modern-day concepts of an expository sermon. However, the essence of preaching should be better understood as *proclamation*, namely, the forthtelling of a God-revealed word. Such understandings of preaching also restrict the place of Scripture in preaching, for they limit the preacher's use of Scripture to only explanation and application. But, for the preacher, Scripture is also used for *revelation*—that is, the Spirit speaks to the preacher in the words of Scripture—and, for the hearers, Scripture is used for *critical evaluation*—that is, in the model of the Bereans, the audience examines the preached message

---

41. His italics; and for Grudem, "teaching" is the same as "preaching."
42. Grudem, *The Gift of Prophecy: In the New Testament and Today*, 142.
43. Turner, "Spiritual Gifts Then and Now," 14; his italics.
44. Green, *I Believe in the Holy Spirit*, 171.

to see if it corresponds with the Scriptures and the gospel message. And, most importantly, such understandings of preaching downplay the *revelatory* aspect of preaching. When Paul instructs Timothy to "preach the Word," he is surely asking Timothy to preach a divinely revealed message. For the message of the preacher has indeed been revealed to him or her by the Holy Spirit; the Holy Spirit superintends the whole process and activity of preaching. And, even if it has been revealed after hours of careful reflection upon the Scriptures, it is still no less than revelation from the Holy Spirit. The prophetic element of preaching does not need to be limited to only the "inspired," "ecstatic," or "unplanned" moments of preaching, as Grudem and others attempt.[45] Thus, Grudem's distinction between teaching (or preaching), which is "the result of conscious reflection on the text of Scripture," and prophecy, which is "the report of something God brings *suddenly* to mind" cannot be sustained.[46]

Assessment

While I welcome Grudem's thesis because it has emphasized the *revelatory* aspect of New Testament prophecy, its diversity, and its subservience to apostolic authority and thus the canonical Scriptures, I especially find his formulation of what constitutes "revelatory" problematic. I also cannot understand the need to differentiate so sharply between preaching and prophecy, for the two activities have much more in common than not—for example, they are both the proclamation of a Holy-Spirit revealed message, typically for the edification of the church.[47] Those, such as Grudem, who try to differentiate between preaching and prophecy, emphasize the non-spontaneity of preaching and its reliance upon the text of Scripture to differentiate it from prophecy. But, even if we accept these caricatures and construals of preaching, why should they disqualify preaching as prophecy?

---

45. "[E]ven prepared teachings can be interrupted by unplanned additional material which the Bible teacher suddenly felt God was bringing to his mind—in that case, it would be a 'teaching' with some prophecy mixed in," in Grudem, *The Gift of Prophecy: In the New Testament and Today*, 143.

46. Ibid.; my italics.

47. Carson might counter by saying that the problem is that I have formulated "prophecy" as a function—what it *does*—and thus it is too easy to find something else (such as preaching) with the same function and equate the two: "When Paul says that prophecy is for the 'strengthening, encouragement and comfort' ([1 Cor]14:3) of the congregation, he does not thereby *define* prophecy, for exposition, prayer and teaching might serve the same ends," in *Showing the Spirit*, 91. In response, I have not defined prophecy by what it does, but by what it is, namely, the proclamation of a message revealed by the Holy Spirit.

Nonetheless, having expressed our reservations with Grudem's thesis, if we accept "prophecy" as revelatory but subservient to Scripture, what is its relationship to preaching? There are three plausible options: (1) prophecy and preaching are the same; (2) prophecy and preaching are different; or (3) preaching is a subset of prophecy. Some contemporary evangelical scholars, such as Packer, argue for the first option: prophecy and preaching are synonymous because they are essentially the same thing—both are forthtelling the word of God. Many contemporary evangelical scholars, such as Carson and Grudem argue for the second option. Although both prophecy and preaching might convey the word of God, they are not the same. For, to confuse the two would be the same as arguing: "For just as a cat is an animal, and a dog is an animal, so a cat is a dog."[48]

But a case can be made for the third option, namely, that preaching is a subset of prophecy. For, both prophecy and preaching are essentially the "forthtelling" of the divinely revealed word of God. However, phenomenologically, in the New Testament and first century, the semantic range of "prophecy" is so diverse that it can cover something such as the predictions—*foretelling*—of Agabus (Acts 11:28; 21:10–11), and it can cover the proclamation—*forthtelling*—of the gospel upon which the church is founded (Eph 2:20; 3:5).[49] We should not be surprised by this diversity, because God's revelation is diverse, and accordingly there will be diverse manifestations of prophecy, both in form and content.

However, in the Pauline corpus, the semantic range is not so wide. Paul primarily uses the term "prophets" and "prophesy" to describe persons who proclaim—*forthtell*—the word of God.[50] Such proclamation is a spiritual gift (Rom 12:6; 1 Cor 12:10; Eph 4:11) to be preferred over speaking in tongues (1 Cor 14:5). It is a joint working by the Holy Spirit and a human proclaimer (1 Cor 12:11; 1 Thess 5:19), which results in orderly and intelligible communication (1 Cor 14:19, 29–33), operating out of love (1 Cor 14:1). It edifies the church (1 Cor 14:4) and reveals God to the non-believer (1 Cor 14:24–25). It is upon such Spirit-revealed proclamation (Eph 3:5) that the church is founded (Eph 2:20). Nonetheless, such proclamation is always to be tested (1 Thess 5:21); it is to be "weighed carefully" and "sifted" (1 Cor 14:29), for it is subservient to the Scriptures and apostolic authority

---

48. Carson, "The Corinthian Correspondence."

49. For a good summary of the diverse referents of "prophet" and "prophecy" by NT writers, see Green, *I Believe in the Holy Spirit*, 168–70.

50. Although Paul might be using "prophecy" in the sense of *foretelling* in 1 Tim 1:18 and 4:14, "prophecy" probably refers to a proclamation that Timothy was gifted by the Holy Spirit, similar to how Paul and Barnabas were identified by the Holy Spirit (cf. Acts 13:2). See Stott, *Guard the Truth*, 56, 122–23.

(1 Cor 14:37-38), and the prophet must speak only according to one's faith (Rom 12:6). Although, in one sense, all Christians are "prophets" because they have received and proclaim the gospel (e.g., 1 Thess 1:4-8; cf. 1 Pet 1:23; 2:9-10), in another sense, a smaller selection of Christians will be particularly gifted to prophesy. For this reason, Paul instructs the Corinthians to "eagerly desire spiritual gifts, especially the gift of prophecy" (1 Cor 14:1) but warns against too quickly presuming to be a "prophet" (1 Cor 14:37).

If so, then it is hard to see how preaching can be essentially different from Paul's primary understanding of prophecy. For, if we recognize the revelatory aspect of preaching and do not enforce rigid and anachronistic construals upon what "preaching" should be, and if we understand that Paul primarily uses "prophecy" in a narrower sense than some other first-century usages, then preaching and prophecy are the same. Nonetheless, because the phenomena of prophecy are so diverse, "preaching" is a subset under the wider phenomenological umbrella of "prophecy." In other words, our conclusion is that *although "prophecy" is not restricted to "preaching," it primarily denotes "preaching."* Anthony C. Thiselton, after his extensive study of "prophecy," seems to arrive at a similar conclusion:

> In summary, *prophesying* in Paul's theology and in his argument in [1 Corinthians 14] *is the performing of intelligible, articulate, communicative speech-acts, the operative currency of which depends on the active agency of the Holy Spirit mediated through human minds and lives to build up, to encourage, to judge, to exhort, and to comfort others in the context of interpersonal relations.* Such a definition is not comprehensive. It allows for short utterances or, in accordance with Paul's own wishes, for longer stretches of speech to which the nearest modern parallel is probably that of an informed pastoral sermon which proclaims grace and judgment, or requires change of life, but which also remains open to question and correction by others.[51]

And this seems to be what John Calvin was also originally arguing:

> I am certain, in my own mind, that [Paul] means by prophets, not those endowed with the gift of foretelling, but those who were blessed with the unique gift of dealing with Scripture, not only by interpreting it, but also by the wisdom they showed in making it meet the needs of the hour ... From this let us therefore learn that prophets are (1) outstanding interpreters of Scripture; and (2) men endowed with extraordinary wisdom and aptitude for grasping what the immediate need of the church is,

---

51. Thiselton, *The First Epistle to the Corinthians*, 1094; his italics.

and speaking the right word to meet it. That is why they are, so to speak, messengers who bring news of what God wants.

... In a word my view is that prophets . . . are those who are skilful and experienced in making known the will of God, by applying prophecies, threats, promises, and all the teaching of Scripture to the current needs of the church.[52]

Calvin acknowledges that "prophets" can be used to describe those with "the gift of foretelling," but then asserts that this is not what Paul means by the term. Instead, Paul's usage is restricted to those who make known the will of God and apply it to the needs of the church. Perhaps we can still learn from Calvin's insight here, and, not the least, from his concession: "Should anyone be of a different opinion, I am willing to acknowledge that there is room for it, and will not pick a quarrel with him because of it."[53]

---

52. In his comments on 1 Cor 12:28, in Calvin, *The First Epistle of Paul the Apostle to the Corinthians*, 271.

53. Ibid.

Bibliography

Adam, Peter. "The Preacher and the Sufficient Word: Presuppositions of Biblical Preaching." In *When God's Word Is Heard: Essays on Preaching Presented to Dick Lucas*, edited by Christopher Green and David Jackman, 27–42. Leicester: InterVarsity, 1995.

———. "Preaching and Biblical Theology." In *New Dictionary of Biblical Theology*, edited by T. Desmond Alexander and Brian S. Rosner, 104–12. Downers Grove: InterVarsity, 2000.

———. *Speaking God's Words: A Practical Theology of Preaching*. Leicester: InterVarsity, 1996.

Allister, Donald. "Ecclesiology: A Reformed Understanding of the Church." *Churchman* 103 (1989) 249–61.

Alston, William P. *Illocutionary Acts and Sentence Meaning*. Ithaca: Cornell University, 2000.

Ames, Frank Ritchel, "דבר." In *New International Dictionary of Old Testament Theology and Exegesis*, edited by Willem A. VanGemeren, 1:912–15. Grand Rapids: Zondervan, 1997.

Anderson, Marvin. "John Calvin: Biblical Preacher (1539–1564)." *Scottish Journal of Theology* 42 (1989) 167–81.

Attridge, Harold W. *The Epistle to the Hebrews: A Commentary on the Epistle to the Hebrews*. Hermeneia. Philadelphia: Fortress, 1989.

Aune, David E. *Prophecy in Early Christianity and the Ancient Mediterranean World*. Grand Rapids: Eerdmans, 1983.

Austin, J. L. *How to Do Things with Words: The Williams James Lectures Delivered at Harvard University in 1955*. Edited by J. O. Urmson and Marina Sbisa. Cambridge, MA: Harvard University Press, 1962.

Avis, Paul. "Luther's Theology of the Church." *Churchman* 97 (1983) 104–11.

Bach, Kent. "Speech Act Theory." In *The Cambridge Dictionary of Philosophy*, edited by Robert Audi, 869. New York: Cambridge University Press, 1999.

Barth, Karl. *Church Dogmatics*. Edited by G. W. Bromiley and T. F. Torrance. Translated by G. T. Thomson. 4 vols. Edinburgh: T. & T. Clark, 1936. Repr., New York: Scribners, 1955–69.

———. *Homiletics*. Translated by Geoffrey W. Bromiley and Donald E. Daniels. Louisville: Westminster John Knox, 1991.

———. *Prayer and Preaching*. London: Student Christian Movement, 1964.
Baue, Frederic W. "Luther on Preaching as Explanation and Exclamation." *Lutheran Quarterly* 9 (1995) 405–18.
Bauer, David R. "Son of God." In *Dictionary of Jesus and the Gospels*, edited by Joel B. Green and Scot McKnight, 769–75. Downers Grove: InterVarsity, 1992.
Beale, G. K. *The Book of Revelation: A Commentary of the Greek Text*. New International Greek Testament Commentary. Grand Rapids: Eerdmans, 1999.
Bergman, J. et al. "דבר." In *Theological Dictionary of the Old Testament*, edited by G. Johannes Botterweck and Helmer Ringgren, 3:84–125. Grand Rapids: Eerdmans, 1978.
Blaser, Klauspeter. "Calvin's Vision of the Church." *Ecumenical Review* 45 (1993) 316–27.
Botterweck, G. Johannes, and Helmer Ringgren, eds. *Theological Dictionary of the Old Testament*. 11 vols. Grand Rapids: Eerdmans, 1978.
Briggs, Richard S. "The Uses of Speech-Act Theory in Biblical Interpretation." *Currents in Research: Biblical Studies* 9 (2001) 229–76.
Brooks, Peter Newman. "Luther the Preacher." *Expository Times* 95 (1983) 37–41.
Bruce, F. F. *The Epistle to the Hebrews*. New International Commentary on the New Testament. Grand Rapids: Eerdmans, 1990.
———. "Interpretation of the Bible." In *New Dictionary of Theology*, edited by Sinclair B. Ferguson and David F. Wright, 565–68. Downers Grove: InterVarsity, 1988.
Brueggemann, Walter. *Isaiah 1–39*. Westminster Bible Companion. Louisville: Westminster John Knox, 1998.
Buttrick, David. "A Brief Theology of Preaching." In *Major Themes in the Reformed Tradition*, edited by Donald K. McKim, 318–25. Grand Rapids: Eerdmans, 1992.
Calvin, John. *Calvin's Commentaries: The Epistles of Paul the Apostle to the Romans and to the Thessalonians*. Edited by David W. Torrance and Thomas F. Torrance. Translated by Ross MacKenzie. Grand Rapids: Eerdmans, 1961.
———. *The First Epistle of Paul the Apostle to the Corinthians*. Translated by John W. Fraser. Grand Rapids: Eerdmans, 1960.
———. *Institutes of the Christian Religion*. Edited by John T. McNeill. Translated by Ford Lewis Battles. 2 vols. Library of Christian Classics 20–21. Philadelphia: Westminster, 1960.
Carson, D. A. "The Corinthian Correspondence." NT 707 Lectures. Trinity Evangelical Divinity School. Deerfield, IL, 2001.
———. *The Gospel According to John*. Leicester: InterVarsity, 1991.
———. "Matthew." In *The Expositor's Bible Commentary*, edited by Frank E. Gaebelein, 8:1–599. Grand Rapids: Zondervan, 1984.
———. *Showing the Spirit: A Theological Exposition of 1 Corinthians 12–14*. Homebush West: Lancer, 1988.
Chapell, Bryan. *Christ-Centered Preaching: Redeeming the Expository Sermon*. Grand Rapids: Baker, 1994.
Chapman, John. *Setting Hearts on Fire: A Guide to Giving Evangelistic Talks*. Kingsford: Matthias Media, 1999.
Childs, Brevard S. *Isaiah*. Old Testament Library. Louisville: Westminster John Knox, 2001.
Christensen, Duane L. *Deuteronomy 21:10—34:10*. Word Biblical Commentary 6B. Nashville: Nelson, 2002.

Clowney, Edmund P. *The Church*. Contours of Christian Theology. Downers Grove: InterVarsity, 1995.
Craddock, Fred B. "Preaching." In *The Anchor Bible Dictionary*, edited by David Noel Freedman, 5:451-54. New York: Doubleday, 1992.
Cranfield, C. E. B. *The Gospel according to Saint Mark*. Cambridge: Cambridge University Press, 1959.
Dodd, C. H. *The Apostolic Preaching and Its Developments*. London: Hodder and Stoughton, 1936.
Edwards, Ruth B. "Word." In *The International Standard Bible Encyclopedia*, edited by Geoffrey W. Bromiley, 4:1101-7. Grand Rapids: Eerdmans, 1988.
Eisenbaum, Pamela M. "A Speech Act of Faith: The Early Proclamation of the Resurrection of Jesus." In *Putting Body and Soul Together: Essays in Honor of Robin Scroggs*, edited by Virginia Wiles et al., 24-45. Valley Forge, PA: Trinity, 1997.
Evans, Craig A. "Hardness of Heart." In *Dictionary of Jesus and the Gospels*, edited by Joel B. Green and Scot McKnight, 298-99. Downers Grove: InterVarsity, 1992.
———. "Prophet, Paul as." In *Dictionary of Paul and His Letters*, edited by Gerald F. Hawthorne and Ralph P. Martin, 763-65. Downers Grove: InterVarsity, 1993.
———. *To See and Not Perceive: Isaiah 6.9-10 in Early Jewish and Christian Interpretation*. Sheffield: Journal for the Study of the Old Testament, 1989.
Evans, D. D. *The Logic of Self-Involvement: A Philosophical Study of Everyday Language with Special Reference to the Christian Use of Language about God as Creator*. London: Student Christian Movement, 1963.
Fanning, Buist M. "Word." In *New Dictionary of Biblical Theology*, edited by T. Desmond Alexander and Brian S. Rosner, 848-53. Downers Grove: InterVarsity, 2000.
Feinberg, John S. *No One Like Him: The Doctrine of God*. Wheaton: Crossway, 2001.
Ferry, Patrick. "Martin Luther on Preaching: Promises and Problems of the Sermon as a Source of Reformation History and as an Instrument of the Reformation." *Concordia Theological Quarterly* 54 (1990) 265-80.
Feuillet, André, and Pierre Grelot. "Word of God." In *Dictionary of Biblical Theology*, edited by Xavier Léon-Dufour, 666-70. New York: Seabury, 1962.
Fretheim, Terence E. "Word of God." In *The Anchor Bible Dictionary*, edited by David Noel Freedman, 6:961-68. New York: Doubleday, 1992.
Gaffin, Richard B., Jr. "A Cessationist View." In *Are Miraculous Gifts for Today? Four Views*, edited by Wayne A. Grudem, 25-64. Grand Rapids: Zondervan, 1996.
Garvie, Alfred Ernest. *The Christian Preacher*. New York: Scribner's Sons, 1921.
Goldsworthy, Graeme. *According to Plan: The Unfolding Revelation of God in the Bible*. Leicester: InterVarsity, 1991.
———. *The Goldsworthy Trilogy*. Carlisle: Paternoster, 2000.
———. *Preaching the Whole Bible as Christian Scripture*. Grand Rapids: Eerdmans, 2000.
———. "Relationship of Old Testament and New Testament." In *New Dictionary of Biblical Theology*, edited by T. Desmond Alexander and Brian S. Rosner, 81-89. Downers Grove: InterVarsity, 2000.
Green, Michael. *I Believe in the Holy Spirit*. London: Hodder and Stoughton, 1975.
Greidanus, Sidney. *The Modern Preacher and the Ancient Text: Interpreting and Preaching Biblical Literature*. Grand Rapids: Eerdmans, 1988. Repr., Grand Rapids: Eerdmans, 1999.

Grudem, Wayne A. *The Gift of Prophecy in 1 Corinthians*. Washington, DC: University Press of America, 1982.

———. *The Gift of Prophecy: In the New Testament and Today*. Eastbourne: Kingsway, 1988.

———. "Prophecy, Prophets." In *New Dictionary of Biblical Theology*, edited by T. Desmond Alexander and Brian S. Rosner, 701–10. Downers Grove: InterVarsity, 2000.

———. "Scripture's Self-Attestation and the Problem of Formulating a Doctrine of Scripture." In *Scripture and Truth*, edited by D. A. Carson and John D. Woodbridge, 19–59. Grand Rapids: Baker, 1992.

Haarbeck, Hermann, et al. "Word, Tongue, Utterance." In *The New International Dictionary of New Testament Theology*, edited by Colin Brown, 3:1078–1146. Grand Rapids: Zondervan, 1971.

Hawthorne, Gerald F. "Prophets, Prophecy." In *Dictionary of Jesus and the Gospels*, edited by Joel B. Green and Scot McKnight, 636–42. Downers Grove: InterVarsity, 1992.

Henry, Carl F. H. *God, Revelation and Authority: Volume 2: God Who Speaks and Shows: Fifteen Theses, Part One*. Waco: Word, 1976.

Houston, Walter. "What Did the Prophets Think They Were Doing? Speech Acts and Prophetic Discourse in the Old Testament." *Biblical Interpretation* 1 (1993) 167–88.

———. "What Did the Prophets Think They Were Doing? Speech Acts and Prophetic Discourse in the Old Testament." In *The Place Is Too Small For Us: The Israelite Prophets in Recent Scholarship*, edited by Robert P. Gordon, 133–53. Winona Lake: Eerdmans, 1995.

Howard, Carol D. C. "Blindness and Deafness." In *Dictionary of Jesus and the Gospels*, edited by Joel B. Green and Scot McKnight, 81–82. Downers Grove: InterVarsity, 1992.

Hugenberger, Gordon P. "Preach." In *The International Standard Bible Encyclopedia*, edited by Geoffrey W. Bromiley, 3:940–43. Grand Rapids: Eerdmans, 1986.

Johnson, David H. "Logos." In *Dictionary of Jesus and the Gospels*, edited by Joel B. Green and Scot McKnight, 481–84. Downers Grove: InterVarsity, 1992.

Kistner, Wolfram, and Manas Buthelezi. "The Proclamation of the Gospel and Other Marks of the Church." *Lutheran World* 23 (1976) 21–32.

Klauber, Martin I. "Calvin on Fundamental Articles and Ecclesiastical Union." *Westminster Theological Journal* 54 (1992) 341–48.

Klug, Eugene F. "Luther on the Church." *Concordia Theological Quarterly* 47 (1983) 193–207.

———. "Luther's Understanding of 'Church' in His Treatise *On the Councils and the Church* of 1539." *Concordia Theological Quarterly* 44 (1980) 27–38.

Knight, George A. *Isaiah 56-66: The New Israel: A Commentary on the Book of Isaiah 56-66*. International Theological Commentary. Grand Rapids: Eerdmans, 1985.

Koester, Craig R. *Hebrews*. Anchor Bible 36. New York: Doubleday, 2001.

Kruse, Colin G. "Servant, Service." In *Dictionary of Paul and His Letters*, edited by Gerald F. Hawthorne and Ralph P. Martin, 869–71. Downers Grove: InterVarsity, 1993.

Ladd, George Eldon. "Kingdom of God." In *The International Standard Bible Encyclopedia*, edited by Geoffrey W. Bromiley, 3:23-29. Grand Rapids: Eerdmans, 1986.

———. *A Theology of the New Testament*. Grand Rapids: Eerdmans, 1974.

Lane, William L. *Hebrews 1-8*. Word Biblical Commentary 47A. Dallas: Word, 1991.

———. *Hebrews 9-13*. Word Biblical Commentary 47B. Dallas: Word, 1991.

———. "Hebrews." In *Dictionary of the Later New Testament and Its Developments*, edited by Ralph P. Martin and Peter H. Davids, 443-58. Downers Grove: InterVarsity, 1997.

Leith, John H., ed. *Creeds of the Churches: A Reader in Christian Doctrine from the Bible to the Present*. Louisville: Westminster John Knox, 1982.

Leske, Adrian M. "Isaiah and Matthew: The Prophetic Influence in the First Gospel: A Report on Current Research." In *Jesus and the Suffering Servant: Isaiah 53 and Christian Origins*, edited by William H. Bellinger Jr. and William R. Farmer, 152-69. Harrisburg, PA: Trinity, 1998.

Lewis, Alan. "Ecclesia ex Auditu: A Reformed View of the Church as the Community of the Word." *Scottish Journal of Theology* 35 (1982) 13-31.

Lincoln, Andrew T. *Ephesians*. Word Biblical Commentary 42. Dallas: Word, 1990.

Lose, David J. "Luther and the Evangelical Clarity of Scripture and Sermon." *Lutheran Forum* 31 (1997) 32-35.

Luther, Martin. "Answer to the Superchristian, Superspiritual, and Superlearned Book of Goat Emser (1521)." Translated by A. Steimle. In *Works of Martin Luther*, 3:307-401. Philadelphia: Muhlenberg, 1930.

———. "A Brief Explanation of the Ten Commandments, the Creed, and the Lord's Prayer (1520)." Translated by A. Steimle. In *Works of Martin Luther*, 2:351-84. Philadelphia: Muhlenberg, 1930.

———. *Commentary on the Epistle to the Romans*. Translated by J. Theodore Mueller. Grand Rapids: Zondervan, 1954.

———. *Commentary on the Epistles of Peter and Jude*. Edited by Paul W. Bennehoff. Translated by John Nichols Lenker. Grand Rapids: Kregel, 1982.

———. *A Compend of Luther's Theology*. Edited by Hugh Thomson Kerr. Philadelphia: Westminster, 1943.

———. "Concerning the Ordering of Divine Worship in the Congregation (1523)." Translated by P. Z. Strodach. In *Works of Martin Luther*, 6:49-64. Philadelphia: Muhlenberg, 1932.

———. "That Doctrines of Men Are To Be Rejected (1522)." Translated by W. A. Lambert. In *Works of Martin Luther*, 2:429-55. Philadelphia: Muhlenberg, 1943.

———. "The Eight Wittenberg Sermons (1522)." Translated by A. Steimle. In *Works of Martin Luther*, 2:387-425. Philadelphia: Muhlenberg, 1943.

———. "An Exposition of the Eighty-Second Psalm (1530)." Translated by C. M. Jacobs. In *Works of Martin Luther*, 4:285-323. Philadelphia: Muhlenberg, 1931.

———. "The Freedom of a Christian." In *Reformation Writings of Martin Luther*, edited by Bertram Lee Woolf, 1:349-79. New York: Philosophical Library, 1953-56.

———. "The German Mass and Order of Service (1526)." Translated by A. Steimle. In *Works of Martin Luther*, 6:151-89. Philadelphia: Muhlenberg, 1932.

———. *Luther: Lectures on Romans*. Translated by Wilhelm Pauck. Library of Christian Classics. Philadelphia: Westminster, 1961.

———. *Luther's Works*. Edited by Jaroslav Pelikan (vols. 1–30) and Helmut T. Lehmann (vols. 31–55). 55 vols. American ed. St. Louis and Philadelphia: Concordia and Fortress, 1955–1986.

———. "The Magnificat (1520–1)." Translated by A. T. W. Steinhauser. In *Works of Martin Luther*, 3:117–200. Philadelphia: Muhlenberg, 1930.

———. "On the Councils and the Churches (1539)." Translated by C. M. Jacobs. In *Works of Martin Luther*, 5:125–300. Philadelphia: Muhlenberg, 1931.

———. "An Open Letter Concerning the Hard Book against the Peasants (1525)." Translated by C. M. Jacobs. In *Works of Martin Luther*, 4:257–81. Philadelphia: Muhlenberg, 1931.

———. "The Pagan Servitude of the Church: A First Inquiry (De Captivitate Babylonica Ecclesiae Praeludium)." In *Reformation Writings of Martin Luther*, edited by Bertram Lee Woolf, 1:201–29. New York: Philosophical Library, 1953–56.

———. "The Right and Power of a Christian Congregation or Community to Judge All Teaching and to Call, Appoint, and Dismiss Teachers, Established and Proved from Scripture (1523)." Translated by A. T. W. Steinhauser. In *Works of Martin Luther*, 4:73–85. Philadelphia: Muhlenberg, 1931.

———. *The Table-Talk of Martin Luther*. Translated by William Hazlitt. Philadelphia: Lutheran Publication Society, 1900.

———. "Three Sermons Preached after the Summons to Worms." In *Reformation Writings of Martin Luther*, edited by Bertram Lee Woolf, 2:99–125. New York: Philosophical Library, 1953–56.

———. "Treatise on Good Works (1520)." Translated by W. A. Lambert. In *Works of Martin Luther*, 1:173–285. Philadelphia: Muhlenberg, 1943.

MacArthur, John F., Jr. *The Charismatics: A Doctrinal Perspective*. Grand Rapids: Zondervan, 1978.

Macky, Peter W. "The Multiple Purposes of Biblical Speech Acts." *The Princeton Seminary Bulletin* 8 (1987) 50–61.

McConville, Gordon. "Divine Speech and the Book of Jeremiah." In *Trustworthiness of God: Perspectives on the Nature of Scripture*, edited by Paul Helm and Carl R. Trueman, 18–38. Grand Rapids: Eerdmans, 2002.

McKim, Donald K. *The Bible in Theology and Preaching*. Eugene: Wipf and Stock, 1999.

McNeill, John T. "John Calvin: Doctor Ecclesiae." In *The Heritage of John Calvin: Heritage Hall Lectures 1960–1970*, edited by John H. Bratt, 9–22. Grand Rapids: Eerdmans, 1973.

Metzger, Bruce M. *A Textual Commentary on the Greek New Testament*. New York: United Bible Societies, 1971.

Michaels, J. Ramsey. *1 Peter*. Word Biblical Commentary 49. Waco: Word, 1988.

Moo, Douglas J. "The Problem of *Sensus Plenior*." In *Hermeneutics, Authority, and Canon*, edited by D. A. Carson and John D. Woodbridge, 175–211. Grand Rapids: Academie, 1986.

———. *The Epistle to the Romans*. New International Commentary on the New Testament. Grand Rapids: Eerdmans, 1996.

Moore, T. M. "The Pastor's Glory and Crown: Calvin on the Marks of the Church, Revisited." *Reformation and Revival* 10, no.4 (2001) 61–80.

Morris, Leon. *The Epistle to the Romans*. Pillar New Testament Commentary. Grand Rapids: Eerdmans, 1988.

———. *The Gospel according to John*. New International Commentary on the New Testament. Grand Rapids: Eerdmans, 1995.
Morrison, John D. "John Calvin's Christological Assertion of Word Authority in the Context of Sixteenth-Century Ecclesiological Polemics." *Scottish Journal of Theology* 45 (1992) 465-86.
Mounce, Robert H. "Preaching, Kerygma." In *Dictionary of Paul and His Letters*, edited by Gerald F. Hawthorne and Ralph P. Martin, 735-37. Downers Grove: InterVarsity, 1993.
Nestingen, James Arne. "Challenges and Responses in the Reformation." *Interpretation* 46 (1992) 250-60.
Neufeld, Dietmar. "Acts of Admonition and Rebuke: A Speech Act Approach to 1 Corinthians 6:1-11." *Biblical Interpretation* 8 (2000) 375-99.
Noll, Mark A. "Martin Luther and the Concept of a 'True' Church." *Evangelical Quarterly* 50 (1976) 79-85.
O'Brien, Peter T. *The Letter to the Ephesians*. Pillar New Testament Commentary. Grand Rapids: Eerdmans, 1999.
———. "Mystery." In *Dictionary of Paul and His Letters*, edited by Gerald F. Hawthorne and Ralph P. Martin, 621-23. Downers Grove: InterVarsity, 1993.
Osborne, Grant R. *Revelation*. Baker Exegetical Commentary of the New Testament. Grand Rapids: Baker, 2002.
Packer, J. I. *Keep in Step with the Spirit*. Leicester: InterVarsity, 1984.
Peterson, David. *Engaging with God: A Biblical Theology of Worship*. Leicester: Apollos, 1992.
Piper, John. "The Divine Majesty of the Word: John Calvin, The Man and His Preaching." *Southern Baptist Journal of Theology* 3, no. 2 (1999) 4-15.
———. *The Supremacy of God in Preaching*. Grand Rapids: Baker, 1990.
Pless, John T. "Martin Luther: Preacher of the Cross." *Concordia Theological Quarterly* 51 (1987) 83-101.
Polhill, John B. "Kerygma and Didache." In *Dictionary of the Later New Testament and Its Development*, edited by Ralph P. Martin and Peter H. Davids, 626-29. Downers Grove: InterVarsity, 1997.
Prior, David. *The Message of 1 Corinthians: Life in the Local Church*. Bible Speaks Today. Leicester: InterVarsity, 1985.
Robeck, C. M., Jr. "Prophecy, Prophesying." In *Dictionary of Paul and His Letters*, edited by Gerald F. Hawthorne and Ralph P. Martin, 755-62. Downers Grove: InterVarsity, 1993.
Robertson, O. Palmer. *The Final Word: A Biblical Response to the Case for Tongues and Prophecy Today*. Edinburgh: Banner of Truth, 1993.
Robinson, Haddon W. *Biblical Preaching: The Development and Delivery of Expository Messages*. Grand Rapids: Baker, 1980.
Rogge, Joachim. "Luther and the One Church." *Evangelical Review of Theology* 8 (1984) 100-109.
Runia, Klaas. "Preaching, Theology of." In *New Dictionary of Theology*, edited by Sinclair B. Ferguson and David F. Wright, 527-28. Downers Grove: InterVarsity, 1988.
———. "What Is Preaching According to the New Testament?" *Tyndale Bulletin* 29 (1978) 3-48.
Ryrie, Charles C. *Dispensationalism*. Chicago: Moody, 1995.

Sandnes, K. O. *Paul—One of the Prophets? A Contribution to the Apostle's Self-Understanding*. Tübingen: Mohr/Siebeck, 1991.

Scharf, Greg R. "Was Bullinger Right about the Preached Word?" *Trinity Journal* 26 (2005) 3–10.

Schmitt, John J. "Prophecy (Preexilic)." In *The Anchor Bible Dictionary*, 6 vols, edited by David Noel Freedman, 5:482–89. New York: Doubleday, 1992.

Schwöbel, Christoph. "The Creature of the Word: Recovering the Ecclesiology of the Reformers." In *On Being the Church: Essays on the Christian Community*, edited by Colin E. Gunton and Daniel W. Hardy, 110–55. Edinburgh: T. & T. Clark, 1989.

Searle, John R. "Austin on Locutionary and Illocutionary Acts." *Philosophical Review* 77 (1968) 405–24.

———. *Expression and Meaning: Studies in the Theory of Speech Acts*. Cambridge: Cambridge University Press, 1979.

———. *Speech Acts: An Essay in the Philosophy of Language*. New York: Cambridge University Press, 1969.

Smith, Gary V. "Prophet; Prophecy." In *The International Standard Bible Encyclopedia*, edited by Geoffrey W. Bromiley, 3:986–1004. Grand Rapids: Eerdmans, 1986.

Sparn, Walter. "Preaching and the Course of the Reformation." In *Transmission of Ideas in the Lutheran Reformation*, edited by Helga Robinson-Hammerstein, 173–82. Dublin: Irish Academic, 1989.

Stott, John R. W. *Guard the Gospel: The Message of 2 Timothy*. Bible Speaks Today. London: Inter-Varsity, 1973.

———. *Guard the Truth: The Message of 1 Timothy and Titus*. Bible Speaks Today. Downers Grove: InterVarsity, 1996.

Strodach, P. Z. "Luther's Liturgical Writings." In *Works of Martin Luther*, 6:1–47. Philadelphia: Muhlenberg, 1932.

Tappert, Theodore G. *The Book of Concord: The Confessions of the Evangelical Lutheran Church*. Edited and translated by Theodore G. Tappert. Philadelphia: Fortress, 1959.

Thielicke, Helmut. *The Evangelical Faith*. Edited and translated by Geoffrey W. Bromiley. 3 vols. Tübingen: Mohr/Siebeck, 1978. Repr., Grand Rapids: Eerdmans, 1982.

Thiselton, Anthony C. "Communicative Action and Promise in Interdisciplinary, Biblical and Theological Hermeneutics." In *The Promise of Hermeneutics*, edited by Roger Lundin et al., 133–239. Grand Rapids: Eerdmans, 1999.

———. *The First Epistle to the Corinthians*. New International Greek Testament Commentary. Grand Rapids: Eerdmans, 2000.

———. *New Horizons in Hermeneutics: The Theory and Practice of Transforming Biblical Reading*. Grand Rapids: Zondervan, 1992.

———. "The Parables as Language-Event: Some Comments on Fuchs's Hermeneutics in the Light of Linguistic Philosophy." *Scottish Journal of Theology* 23 (1970) 437–68.

———. "Speech-Act Theory and the Claim that God Speaks: Nicholas Wolterstorff's *Divine Discourse*." *Scottish Journal of Theology* 50 (1997) 97–110.

———. "The Supposed Power of Words in the Biblical Writings." *Journal of Theological Studies* 25 (1974) 283–99.

Torrance, Iain R. "*Mysterium Christi* and *Mysterium Ecclesiae*: The Christological Ecclesiology of John Calvin." *Greek Orthodox Theological Review* 43 (1998) 459–67.

Trites, Allison A. "Witness, Testimony (part)." In *The New International Dictionary of New Testament Theology*, edited by Colin Brown, 3:1047–52. Exeter: Paternoster, 1979.
Turner, Max. "Spiritual Gifts Then and Now." *Vox evangelica* 15 (1985) 7–64.
van der Walt, A. G. P. "Calvin on Preaching." In *John Calvin's Institutes: His Opus Magnum: Proceedings of the Second South African Congress for Calvin Research, July 31–August 3, 1984*, 326–49. Potchefstroom: Potchefstroom University, 1986.
VanGemeren, Willem A. *Interpreting the Prophetic Word: An Introduction to the Prophetic Literature of the Old Testament*. Grand Rapids: Zondervan, 1990.
———. *The Progress of Redemption: The Story of Salvation from Creation to the New Jerusalem*. Grand Rapids: Academie, 1988.
VanGemeren, Willem A., ed. *New International Dictionary of Old Testament Theology and Exegesis*. 5 vols. Grand Rapids: Zondervan, 1997.
Vanhoozer, Kevin J. *The Drama of Doctrine: A Canonical-Linguistic Approach to Christian Theology*. Louisville: Westminster John Knox, 2005.
———. "Effectual Call or Causal Effect? Summons, Sovereignty and Supervenient Grace." *Tyndale Bulletin* 49 (1998) 213–51.
———. "From Speech Acts to Scripture Acts: The Covenant of Discourse and the Discourse of the Covenant." In *First Theology: God, Scripture, and Hermeneutics*, 159–203. Downers Grove: InterVarsity, 2002.
———. "God's Mighty Speech Acts: The Doctrine of Scripture Today." In *First Theology: God, Scripture, and Hermeneutics*, 127–58. Downers Grove: InterVarsity, 2002.
———. "The Hermeneutics of I-Witness Testimony: John 21:20–24 and the Death of the Author." In *First Theology: God, Scripture, and Hermeneutics*, 257–74. Downers Grove: InterVarsity, 2002.
———. "The Hermeneutics of I-Witness Testimony: John 21:20–24 and the Death of the Author." In *Understanding Poets and Prophets: Essays in Honour of George Wishart Anderson*, edited by Graeme A. Auld, 366–84. Sheffield: Journal for the Study of the Old Testament, 1993.
———. *Is There a Meaning in This Text? The Bible, The Reader, and the Morality of Literary Knowledge*. Grand Rapids: Zondervan, 1998.
———. "The Semantics of Biblical Literature: Truth and Scripture's Diverse Literary Forms." In *Hermeneutics, Authority, and Canon*, edited by D. A. Carson and John D. Woodbridge, 49–104. Grand Rapids: Academie, 1986.
Vawter, Bruce. *Biblical Inspiration*. Philadelphia: Westminster, 1972.
Wagner, J. Ross. "The Heralds of Isaiah and the Mission of Paul: An Investigation of Paul's Use of Isaiah 51–55 in Romans." In *Jesus and the Suffering Servant: Isaiah 53 and Christian Origins*, edited by William H. Bellinger Jr. and William R. Farmer, 193–222. Harrisburg, PA: Trinity, 1998.
Warfield, Benjamin B. *Counterfeit Miracles*. New York: Scribner's Sons, 1918.
Watts, John D. W. *Isaiah 1–33*. Word Biblical Commentary 24. Waco: Word, 1985.
Wells, David F. "The Theology of Preaching." In *God's Living Word: Orthodox and Evangelical Essays on Preaching*, edited by Theodore G. Stylianopoulos, 57–70. Brookline, MA: Holy Cross Orthodox, 1983.
Wessell, Walter W. "Mark." In *The Expositor's Bible Commentary*, edited by Frank E. Gaebelein, 8:601–793. Grand Rapids: Zondervan, 1984.
Westphal, Charles. "The Marks of the Church: A Protestant Viewpoint." *Anglican Theological Review* 42 (1960) 91–100.

Williamson, Joseph Crawford. "The Marks of the Church: A Recurring Protestant Dilemma." *Andover Newton Quarterly* 6N (1965) 24–34.

Wolterstorff, Nicholas. *Divine Discourse: Philosophical Reflections on the Claim That God Speaks*. New York: Cambridge University Press, 1995.

———. "Why Animals Don't Speak." *Faith and Philosophy* 4 (1987) 463–85.

Wood, Arthur Skevington. "Luther as a Preacher." *Evangelical Quarterly* 21 (1949) 109–21.

Author Index

Adam, Peter, 8, 82n2, 86n11, 87n12, 172–75, 176, 212
Allister, Donald, 64n20
Alston, William P., 190n67, 198n95, 202–3, 204
Ames, Frank Ritchel, 84n7
Anderson, Marvin, 15n9
Attridge, Harold W., 102n24
Aune, David E., 229n1
Austin, John Langshaw, 2, 8, 9, 177–79, 182, 194, 198, 201–2, 205–6, 225
Avis, Paul, 59n7, 61n15, 64n20, 66

Bach, Kent, 177n2
Barth, Karl, 8, 151n17, 166–67, 176, 212
Bast, David, 174
Baue, Frederic W., 15n13
Bauer, David R., 102n22, 103n25
Beale, G. K., 130n50
Bergman, J., 84n7
Blaser, Klauspeter, 50, 69n37
Briggs, Richard S., 182n27, 185
Brooks, Peter Newman, 14n8
Bruce, F.F., 5n6, 127n34, 128n40, 129n42, 130n46
Brueggemann, Walter, 135n3
Bullinger, Heinrich, 57, 58n3
Bultman, Rudolf, 118n13
Buthelezi, Manas, 64n20, 76n67
Buttrick, David, 8, 168–70, 176, 210

Calvin, John, 6, 11, 13, 14–15, 39–56, 57–59, 68–78, 193, 194, 195, 200, 226, 241–42
Carson, D. A., 99n15, 100n16, 103n30, 104, 138n8, 143n14, 146n15, 149n16, 230n2, 231n4, 234n21, 236, 239n47, 240
Chapell, Bryan, 170
Chapman, John, 170, 171n27
Childs, Brevard S., 96n6, 101n19
Christensen, Duane L., 95n4
Clowney, Edmund P., 76
Craddock, Fred B., 115n3
Cranach, Lucas, 14
Cranfield, C. E. B., 115n7, 116n9

Dodd, C. H., 111n48, 118n13

Edwards, Ruth B., 85n8, 86n10, 124, 133–34, 136n4
Eisenbaum, Pamela M., 184–185
Evans, Craig A., 107n39, 135n3, 142n13
Evans, Donald D., 182

Fanning, Buist M., 82n3, 124–25, 136, 140–41
Farrar, Austin, 188
Feinberg, John S., 103n27
Ferry, Patrick, 13n1, 31
Feuillet, André, and Pierre Grelot, 83n5
Fretheim, Terence E., 86n9, 134, 159n3

Gaffin, Richard B., Jr., 233n12

AUTHOR INDEX

Garvie, Alfred Earnest, 13, 14n5, 15n11
Goldsworthy, Graeme, 5n5, 157n1, 196n85, 198n91
Green, Michael, 232, 238, 240n49
Greidanus, Sidney, 170n25
Grudem, Wayne, A., 10, 87n12, 94n1, 231n4, 233–40

Haarbeck, Hermann, et al, 84n7
Hanson, A. T., 127n34
Hawthorne, Gerald F., 101n19,
Henry, Carl F. H., 4n3
Houston, Walter, 184, 203
Howard, Carol D. C., 142n13
Hugenberger, Gordon P., 100n45

Johnson, David H. 88n14,

Kistner, Wolfram, 64n20, 76n67
Klauber, Martin I., 71n44
Klug, Eugene F., 67
Knight, George A., 137n7
Koester, Craig R., 103n24, 127n34, 128n40, 129n44
Kruse, Colin G., 109n43

Ladd, George Eldon, 103, 115n6, 116n9
Lane, William L., 128n37, 129n41, 130n48, 139n10
Leith, John H., 57n1, 58n3, 59n5, 77n73
Leske, Adrian M., 100n17
Lincoln, Andrew T., 100n18
Lose, David J., 14n8, 26
Luther, Martin, 6, 11, 13–14, 15–38, 55–56, 57–68, 75–78, 194–95, 199, 213, 215, 226, 228

MacArthur, John F., Jr, 232n9
Macky, Peter W., 183–84, 200n103
McConville, Gordon, 182–83
McKim, Donald K., 171n28, 172n29
McNeill, John T., 50n104, 69n35
Metzger, Bruce M., 99n15, 103n27
Michaels, J. Ramsey, 126n31
Moo, Douglas J., 196, 122n21, 231n5
Moore, T. M., 76n63
Morris, Leon, 99n15, 103n28, 231n5
Morrison, John D., 73

Mounce, Robert H., 118n13, 121n19

Nestingen, James Arne, 68n32
Neufeld, Dietmar, 184
Noll, Mark A., 60n10, 61n12

O'Brien, Peter T., 110n46, 236–37
Osborne, Grant R., 130n50

Packer, J. I., 231, 240
Peterson, David, 129n41
Piper, John, 15n9, 46n94, 170–71
Pless, John T., 14n3, 15n9
Polhill, John B., 111n48, 118n13
Prior, David, 232n10

Robeck, C. M., Jr., 231n6
Robertson, O. Palmer, 230n3, 233n12
Robinson, Haddon W., 170n25, 216n3
Runia, Klaas, 8, 111n48, 124n27, 165, 166, 176
Ryrie, Charles C., 115n6

Sandnes, K. O., 237n37
Scharf, Greg R., 57n1
Schmitt, John J., 95n3
Schwöbel, Christoph, 50, 68n31, 69n35
Searle, John, 3, 8, 177, 180–82, 186, 188–89, 193, 194, 198, 199, 202, 206, 214, 225
Smith, Gary V., 114n1
Sparn, Walter, 13n1
Strodach, P.Z., 66
Stott, John R. W., 125n29

Thielicke, Helmut, 8, 167–68, 176, 212
Thiselton, Anthony, 86n9, 136n4, 182, 183, 184, 188, 200, 203–4, 229n1, 235n31, 241
Torrance, Iain R., 71n47
Trites, Allison A., 103n49
Turner, Max, 234n23, 238

van der Walt, A. G. P., 15n9, 46n93
VanGemeren, Willem A., 94, 101n20, 114
Vanhoozer, Kevin J., 183, 184, 172n31, 177n2, 181n25, 185n50, 187–88,

190–91, 193, 197, 198n90, 199n98, 200n102, 201, 204, 207n132

Wagner, J. Ross, 109n43, 110n44
Warfield, B. B., 232–33
Watts, John D. W., 135n3
Wells, David F., 170n25
Wessell, Walter W., 147n15
White, Hugh C., 183n39
Williamson, Joseph Crawford, 76n63
Wolterstorff, Nicholas, 182, 183, 186–87, 188, 189–90, 192–93, 197–98
Wood, Arthur Skevington, 13, 14n4, 26

Zwingli, Ulrich, 58n3

Subject Index

Abraham, 86
Adam and Eve, 86
Apply, Application (of Scripture), 5, 8, 41, 84n6, 110, 166, 171n28, 174, 176, 196, 204, 205, 216, 231, 233, 235, 238, 242
Apollos, 16
Apostles, 7, 17, 20, 21–22, 29, 35, 41, 43–44, 47, 49, 71, 89, 105–9, 117–25, 138–39, 143–44, 193, 195, 213–14, 230, 232, 236–37
    Apostolic authority, 28, 41, 46, 104, 106, 131, 234, 237–38
    Apostolic kerygma (preaching of the gospel), 11, 89, 90, 111n48, 118, 138–39, 117–25, 144
    Apostolic succession, 11
    'Fishers of men', 105
Augsberg Confession, 59, 77

Bible, *see* Scripture; Word of God

Catholic Mass, 14
Cessationist, 232
Christ, the, 43, 61, 99n13, 100n18, 102, 115–120, 126n33, 149 158 *see also* Jesus Christ
Chrysostom, 195n83
Church,
    False, 60, 70
    Faults, 72
    As God's work, 65, 67
    Iinvisible, 60–61, 68–69
    Marks, 1, 6, 10, 39, 57–59, 61–64, 65, 71–78, 205, 225, 226
    Maturity, 52
    Offices, 30–31, 49–50, 61, 193
    Preacher of the word, 109–10, 112, 125–31, 155, 156, 226–27
    True, 2, 57–64, 70–71
    Visible 60–61, 69 *see also above*
Church service, 14, 15, 17, 62, 65–66
Congregation, 62, 63–64, 65–66, 72–73, 125, 231n4
Covenant, 45, 91, 97, 114, 188–91, 193, 201, 206, 210, 217

Daniel, 86
David, 91, 95, 113
Deacon, 50
Doctrine, 19–20, 27–32 passim, 39–52 passim, 60–63, 66–67, 69–71, 75, 144, 166, 194
    Of Scripture, 9, 188, 209

Elder, 50
Election, 69, 75
Elijah, 99n13, 113
Emser of Leipzig, Goat (Jerome), 19, 34
Eternal promise, 25
Eunuch, Ethiopian, 161
Evangelist, 17, 52, 105, 115n7, 138–39, 144, 157 *see also* Preaching, Evangelistic
Exegesis, 5, 103n29, 104, 196, 201

SUBJECT INDEX

Expound, expounding (Scripture), 8, 18, 26, 43, 45–46, 170–72, 176, 216–18, 220–23 passim, 231
Ezekiel, 141–42, 146, 158, 214

Faith, 18–19, 21, 33, 36, 38, 48, 51, 58, 61, 67, 69, 77, 109, 139, 141, 168, 169, 200, 231, 241
From hearing, 19, 24, 31–32, 36–37, 49, 51–2, 54, 90, 127, 140, 147–49, 151–53, 159–60, 172, 203, 226

God
Speaks, 81–84, 154, 182, 185–91
Trinitarian, 83, 89, 104
God's will, 48, 52, 74, 85, 133–34, 136, 137, 153, 158–59, 222, 242
Voice of God, 11, 15, 127–29, 139–140
Gospel,
Message of the gospel, 3, 7, 18–20, 39–40, 59, 89–90, 115–32, 145, 150, 156, 160, 194, 199, 213, 226
Preached gospel as word of God, 1, 3, 7, 8, 9, 16–27, 32–56, 57, 77–78, 88–90, 114–32, 133, 154–62, 194–98, 211, 219–23, 226–28
Great Commission, 105n35, 106, 107, 138

Hhearer, 36, 38, 54, 83, 128n37, 129n45, 141–48, 173–74, 190, 191, 193, 199
Hearer's responsibility, 36–37, 146, 147–53, 159–60, 213, 215, 217
Holy Spirit, 4, 9, 15, 17, 24, 75–76, 83–84, 106, 121, 155, 188, 212, 215, 223
Illuminating work of, 5,6, 13, 24–25, 37, 38, 53, 54, 56, 149–50, 151–53, 159, 160, 167–70, 173–75, 176, 239, 241
Iinspiring scripture, 4, 42–43, 173, 195
Ministry of, 34–35, 52, 55, 229
And prophets, 92, 95–96, 98–99, 104, 106, 146

Hosea, 18

Idols, 82–83, 113–14
Illocution, 9–10, 178–89, 190n67, 191n73, 192, 194, 198–206, 208–18, 220–28
Interpreter, 5, 47–48
Isaiah, 96–97, 113, 135–36, 142
Isaianic servant-preacher, *See* Preaching, Eschatological Isaianic servant-preacher

Jeremiah, 134–135
Jesus Christ, 3, 5, 6–7, 13, 17, 18, 19–20, 32, 39, 43, 52, 58, 59, 61, 63, 69, 70, 73, 82, 83, 87, 88–89, 90, 97–112, 117–32, 146, 130, 131, 145, 169, 195, 199–200, 207, 234n24, 226
Climax of God's word, 7, 26, 44–45, 88, 98, 100, 112, 115, 117, 124n26, 128, 143, 148, 157, 160, 161
Incarnate, 8, 22, 61, 88, 98, 100–101, 103, 117, 143, 166, 167, 176
As preacher, 7, 8, 9, 18, 20–22, 25, 35, 37, 38, 41, 44, 67n30, 83, 94, 97, 98, 99n12, 100–112, 115–17, 124, 131–32, 137–38, 142–43, 145, 147, 148, 149, 151–52, 155, 156–57, 159, 161, 168–70, 176, 195, 212, 214, 219, 220, 223, 227–28, 232, 238
As the message of the gospel, *see* Word of God, Christocentric,
Joel, 95
Jonah, 152
John, 103, 104
John the Baptist, 99n13, 102, 117
Josiah, 87

Laity, 31
Law, 19–20, 23, 30, 32, 35, 42, 45–46, 48, 86–87, 122, 231
Locution, 9–10, 178–79, 182–185, 188, 192, 194–98, 202, 208–9, 210–11, 212–19, 221–28
Luke, 16, 20, 116, 118–19

Malachi, 95
Matthew, 116
Mark, 20, 115
Moses, 7, 47–48, 85, 86, 92–96, 112, 134, 141, 172

Nathan, 91, 95, 113
Nations, 97, 107, 108n42

Pastor, 29–31, 50
Paul, 1, 10, 16, 18, 22, 33–35, 44, 52, 65, 70, 74, 83, 87, 89, 107n39, 108–9, 110, 111, 118, 121–124, 125, 138–139, 144, 145, 148, 149, 150–151, 152, 157, 158, 173, 184, 193, 194, 195, 197, 199, 207, 208, 216, 220–221, 229–231, 234, 235, 236, 237, 239, 240–242
Perlocution, 9–10, 178–179, 182–185, 188, 199, 201–205, 208–218, 222–228
Peter, 35, 46, 104, 118, 119–120, 125–126, 147, 148, 149, 237
Pharaoh, 93, 134, 141, 151
Philip, 161
Pope, 14, 22, 73
    Papal authority, 1, 6, 63, 78
Preacher, 18, 27–31, 47–51
    Authority, 47, 49–50, 63–64, 74
    Calling, 27–30, 37, 47, 50–51, 53, 111n49, 169, 206–207, 211
    Clarity, 26
    Commissioned, see Preacher, Calling
    Eschatological Isaianic servant-preacher, 7, 96–112, 119–120, 130–131, 136–137, 138, 142, 144, 155, 163, 174, 193, 227
    Fallibility, 5, 165–170
    Gifting, 30–31, 110–111
    Humility, 29, 215
    Ordination, 29, 49, 50
    Power, 52
    Purpose, 74 see also Preaching, Purpose
    Responsibility, 146–147, 150–153, 160, 211, 215, 222, 228
Preaching,
    Application, see Apply; Word of God, Applied
    Christ's, see Jesus Christ, As preacher
    Content, 16, 40–41, 46–47, 48, 49, 55, 89, 117–32, 156, 157, 165, 169, 170–72, 194–98, 201, 207–8, 211, 213, 215–18, 226, 228, 232, 238
    Expository, 38, 170–72, 176, 210, 213, 216–19, 220, 226, 227–28, 231
    Evangelistic, 66, 88–89, 138–39, 158–59, 170–71, 200
    Faithful, see Preaching, Pure
    Form, 1, 22, 131, 139, 214
    Human, 1, 7, 8, 13, 24, 33–34, 51, 56, 74, 160–61, 165–76
    Intention, 7, 10, 133–140, 152, 214, 220–21
    Office, 50, 55, 193
    Pure, 77, 162, 165, 174, 208, 214, 218–19
    Purpose, 13, 20, 23, 31–32, 51–53, 55, 74, 111, 199
    Result, 8, 33–34, 67n30, 133, 141–45, 151–53, 159, 175, 203–5, 211, 213, 216, 222, 228
    Source, 6, 13, 26–27, 37, 38, 55, 140, 152, 213, 217–18, 223
    As speech act, 185, 213, 215–16, 217–18, 221
    True, see Preaching, Pure
Priest, 20, 23, 29–31, 42, 45, 48–49, 50, 70, 172
Priesthood of believers, 20, 23, 30–31, 32, 50, 110, 127n34
Prophecy, 10, 24, 65, 76, 92, 94, 95–96, 109, 111n47, 114, 123, 126n30, 130n50, 131, 184, 195, 201n104, 214, 229–42

Prophet, 7, 9, 22–29 passim, 38, 40–49 passim, 58, 70–71, 76, 81, 85, 88, 90, 91–112 passim,113–14, 120, 122–25, 131, 133–37, 141–43, 145, 147, 151, 156, 160, 163, 172, 174, 184, 193,195, 200, 201, 203, 206, 207, 212, 214, 215, 219, 223, 227, 227–28, 233–37
   Eschatological, 7, 94–96, 98–99, 101, 105, 106, 110, 114, 134, 147, 155, 163, 174, 193, 195, 206, 207, 208, 227
   Of Deuteronomy 18, *see* Prophet, Eschatological
   New Testament, 23, 229–42

Reformers, 1–2, 3, 6, 9, 10, 13, 14, 57–59, 76, 78, 204, 205, 208, 219, 225, 231n6
Roman Catholic Church, 6, 14, 59n5, 60, 64, 66, 67, 70, 77n74, 166

Sacraments, 30, 39, 48, 58–62, 66, 70–73, 205
Scripture 235n27 *see also* Word of God
   Canon, 5, 120, 197–98, 201
   Clarity, 26, 35
   Continuity, 5, 122–23, 156, 157, 198
   Expounding, *see* Expound
   References to, 27, 38, 169
   Translated, 175, 235
Second Helvetic Confession, 57, 58, 77
Sermon, 14, 17, 26, 139n10, 214–15, 232, 235
Servant, 29, 48, 86, 92, 94, 96–97, 100–103, 105, 107n41, 108–12, 124n25, 130, 143, 200 *see also* Isaiah, Isaianic servant-preacher
Shepherd, 1–2, 20, 59, 63–64, 73, 219
Solomon, 91, 95
Speaker, 3, 9, 129, 136, 169, 173, 177–82 passim, 189, 190–91, 198–99, 202–9 passim, 223, 225, 229, 235
Speech-act, 3, 9, 76 , 177, 182–86
   Divine, 9, 183, 185–91, 207, 210–12, 223, 227
   Within a covenant, 190–91, 193, 206

speech-act theory, 2, 3, 8–9, 177–85, 197, 198–99, 201–3, 206, 209, 223, 225
   Constitutive rules, 9, 182, 189, 206–7, 225–26
Speech agent, 182
   Divine, 9, 185, 191, 209, 210, 217, 219, 225, 227
   Double agency discourse, 192, 193, 194, 197, 210, 211, 217
   Human, 9, 185, 192, 193, 209, 210, 227
Stephen, 87, 151

Teach or teachings, 15, 16–17, 20–24, 27, 31, 34, 40–51, 58, 60, 63–65, 70–71, 74–75, 87, 93–94, 98, 101, 109, 111, 166n8, 130n47, 138, 139, 145, 150–51, 173–75, 212, 214, 231–39 passim, 242
Teacher, 18, 20–24, 45, 47–54, 114, 173–75, 195, 213, 232
Testimony, 6, 13, 27, 28, 34, 39, 44, 47, 51, 55, 89, 111, 119–20, 127, 130, 144, 156, 167
   Biblical, 79–162, 226
Timothy, 111, 125
Truth, 4, 44, 70

Witness, 97n8, 107n41, 117, 120n17, 130, 167–68, 200
Word of God, 1–2, 3, 81–90, 154
   Applied, 5, 8, 41, 166, 174, 176, 231, 233, 235, 238, 241–42
   Authoritative, 86
   Christocentric, 6, 13, 22–25, 26, 37, 55, 88, 90, 117, 120, 122, 124, 130–31, 157–58, 197–98
   Complete, 40, 44–46
   Contemporary, 84n6, 87, 156, 200
   Effective, 85–86, 136
   Eternal, 25, 33, 44, 126, 167n8
   Form, 4n3, 14, 122, 154–55, 174, 184, 187
   Heard, 83, 86, 87, 126–32
   Human messenger, 1, 7, 85, 86–87, 88, 91–97, 102, 105–12, 113, 131, 133, 140, 142, 145–47,

154–155, 158, 160–61, 165–76,
192–95, 204, 210–11, 217, 219,
228, 240
Human proclaimer, *see above*
Illocution, 9, 182–89, 198–201, 204,
207–9, 210–23, 227–28
Incarnate, 8, 22, 24–25, 59, 83, 88,
104–5, 143, 167
Inscripturated, 4, 6, 10, 13, 26, 38,
40, 41, 42, 46, 55, 86–87, 89, 90,
122, 124, 125, 131, 156–57, 160,
161, 172, 218–19, 221, 222–223,
227–28
Interpreted, 5, 42, 45, 48–49, 166,
169, 171, 173, 176, 185, 201,
207, 217, 235, 241

Locution, 9, 182, 184, 194–98,
208, 209, 210–23, 227–28
Mystery, 123–24, 156, 196–97
Perlocution, 9, 184, 185, 188, 203–5,
208, 209, 210–23, 227–28
Proclaimed by Christ, *see* Jesus, As
preacher
Pure, 77–78
Purpose, 87, 89, 158–59, 183, 199
Read, 15, 65–66, 74–75
Rejected, 99n123, 106n38, 128n40,
141–45, 159
As a speech-act, 182, 185, 187, 194,
241
Title for Christ, 8, 24, 88, 104, 117
Written, 15, 25–27, 40–46, 65, 87,
89, 90, 166, 167–68

Scripture Index

Genesis

3:1	86
3:9	82
9:8	191
12:1–7	86
12:1–3	82
15:1	91
15:18	191
16:7–13	91
20:3–7	91
21:17–19	91
22:1–18	86
22:11–12	91
31:10–13	91
31:11–13	91
31:24	91
46:2	91

Exodus

3–4	92
3	82
3:4	47
3:6	87
3:10	134
3:14–15a	93
3:15	94
3:16–17	127n34
3:18	93
4:41	151
4:10	93
4:11–16	93
4:16	93
4:12	33
4:22	86, 94
4:27–31	127n34
5:1	86, 94
5:23	93
6:1–9	127n34
6:6	94
6:9–12	141
6:11	94
6:28—7:2	93
7:1	93
7:2	94
7:3	151
7:13	141
7:15–16	94
7:16	94
7:17	86, 94
7:22	141
8:1	86, 94
8:11	135n3
8:15	135n3, 141
8:19	141
8:20	86, 94
8:28	135n3
8:32	135n3, 141, 151
9:1	86, 94
9:7	135n3
9:12	141, 151
9:13	86, 94
9:34	135n3, 151
9:35	141

Exodus (continued)

10:1	151
10:3	86, 94
10:20	151
10:27	151
11:4	86, 94
11:10	151
14:31	48
14:4	151
14:8	151
15:26	82
19	99n12
19:3–6	127n34
19:3	94
19:19	82
19:21	94
20	35
23:20–33	127n34
30:31	94
32:27	86, 94
34:27	86
34:28	86

Leviticus

1:2	94
19:31	48
25	101n19
26	99n12

Numbers

7:89	82, 91
11:17–30	92
11:25–29	92
11:29	96n5
12:6	91
12:7–8	94
12:7	96
22:28	91

Deuteronomy

4:2	42
4:10–14	99n12
4:12–33	85
4:12	82, 91
4:13	86
4:33	82, 83
4:35–36	83
4:39	83
5:5	85
5:22–26	82
5:22	91
5:23–32	99n12
5:30	94
5:32	45
6:4	86
8:3	159n3
9:6	141
9:13	141
10:4	86
10:16	141
13	208, 215
13:1–5	156, 162
13:1–3	114
13:1	42
13:2	208
13:5	237
17:10–11	48
18	94–96, 95n4, 97, 99n13, 101, 105, 106, 110, 134, 155, 174, 193, 195, 206, 208, 215, 227
18:10–11	48
18:15–22	94
18:15	48, 95
18:16	82
18:18–19	134
18:18	95, 195, 206, 207
18:19	95, 147
18:20–22	162
18:20	95, 207, 237
18:21	208
18:22	95, 114, 156, 208
27–28	86
28	99n12
30:11–20	159n3
30:20	82, 86
31:9–13	86
31:9	86

SCRIPTURE INDEX

31:24	86	20:5–6	113
31:27	141	22:20–23	135n3
32:1–2	86		
32:9	141		
33:3	141	## 2 Kings	
33:5	141		
34	95n4	1:3–4	91
34:9	141	1:8	99n13
34:10	94, 141	2:21–22	99n13
		4:8–37	99n13
		4:42–44	99n13
## Joshua		5	99n13
		22–23	87
24:2	86		

2 Chronicles

Judges

		6:4	82
2:4	91	6:16	91
6:11–12	91	36:15–16	142

1 Samuel

Nehemiah

3	82	8:12	87
3:1	91		

Job

2 Samuel

		11:5	82
7	191	37:5	82
7:4–17	91	40:9	82
7:28	91		
12:1–10	113		
22:14	82	## Psalms	

		2	100
## 1 Kings		3:13	84
		4:1	84n6
3:5	91	4:7	84n6
8:15	82	4:8–11	84n6
8:26	91	18:13	82
17:2	99n13	29:3–9	82
17:8	99n13	33:6	82, 85, 86
17:14	86, 99n13, 113	50:7	159n3
17:16	99n13	68:11	86
17:17–24	99n13	81:10	33
17:24	86, 99n13	82	30
19:13	82		

Psalms (continued)

89:19	91
94:8	54
95	84
95:7	54, 82
101	65
115:3-5	82
119:9-16	87
119:25	159n3
119:50	159n3
119:116	159n3
119:130	159n3
119:154	159n3
138:4	82
147:19-20	86

Proverbs

2:6	82

Isaiah

1:1	91
1:2	86
1:10	86
1:20	82
2:3	86
6	135n3, 138
6:8	82
6:9-10	135, 135n3, 138, 142, 143, 144
6:9	54
9:2	100, 109
11:1-3	97n7
30:27	82
30:30-31	82
30:8	86
32:15-20	97n7
34:16	82
35:5-6	101
26:19	101
29:18-19	101
40-48	83n4
40	116n8
40:1-5	97, 99n13
40:5	82
40:9	96, 126n32
41:8-9	107n40, 108
41:9	107n40
41:27	96, 97
42:1	100, 107n40, 108
42:1-4	97, 100, 101n20
42:6-7	109
42:6	100, 107n40
42:7	109
42:10	107n40
42:19	97, 107n40
43:9-10	108
43:10-12	107n40
43:10	97n8, 108
43:12	97n8
43:21	97, 97n8
44:1-2	107n40
44:1	97, 108
44:2	108
44:3	97
44:8	107n40
44:21	107n40
44:26	97, 107n40
45:1	108n42
45:4	107n40, 108
45:20-21	83
48:16	97
48:20	107n40
49:1	108
49:3-7	107n40
49:6-7	108
49:6	100, 107n40, 108, 109
49:7	108
49:22-23	108
50:10	107n40
51-55	109n43
52:7-10	108
52:7	47, 97, 100, 110n44
52:10	107n40, 108n42
52:13—53:12	108
52:13	107n40
52:15	108
53	161
53:3	142
53:4	101n20

53:11	107n40	**Jeremiah**		
53:12	101n20			
54:17	97, 107n40	1:9–10		135
55	62, 63, 136	1:18–19		142
55:3	54	2:2		85
55:4–5	107n40	2:4		85
55:5	108	6:1–3		85
55:10–11	85, 136	7:4		73
56–66	96n6	9:20		82
56:6	97	10:5		83
57:19	100	16:16		105n35
58:14	82	23:16		82
59:21	97, 97n7	23:18		207
60:3	108n42	23:21–22		206–7
60:10–16	108n42	23:28		40
	60:21–22 97n7	30:1		86
61	96n6, 100, 101, 101n19	36:27–32		86
61:1–11	97, 97n7	**Ezekiel**		
61:1–3	96, 108, 137			
61:1–2	96	1:1		91
61:1	96, 100n17	3:4–7		141–42
61:2	96	3:17–21		146
61:6	108	3:17		40
61:8–9	97n7	4		214
61:9	97, 108	10:5		82
61:11	108	18:23		159n3
62:2	82, 108n42	18:32		159n3
62:10–12	108	33:11		159n3
62:10	108	43:2		82
63:17	97, 107n40			
64:2	108	**Daniel**		
65:8–9	107n40			
65:8	97	7		91
65:9	97	12:4		86
65:13–15	107n40			
65:13	97			
65:23	97	**Joel**		
66:5	141			
66:12	108n42	2:28–32		96
66:14	97, 107n40	2:28		91
66:15	97			
66:18–19	108n42			
66:19–20	108	**Amos**		
66:19	97n8			
66:22	97	8:11–12		159n3

Obadiah

1:1	91

Jonah

3:3	152
3:4–9	152
4:1–2	152

Micah

1:1	91

Zephaniah

1:1–18	159n3

Haggai

1:12	82

Zechariah

1:14	91
3:6–7	91

Malachi

2	30
2:7	15, 42, 29
3	116n8
3:1	99n13

Matthew

1:11–15	99n13
1:18	98n9
1:20	91, 98n9
2:13	91
3:3	115n5
3:11–12	99n13
3:11	98n9, 106
3:13–17	100
3:16—4:1	98
3:17	105
3:22	105
3:31	102
4	21
4:1	98n9
4:16	100
4:17	116n9, 116n10, 137
4:19	105
4:23	106n36, 115n5, 116n10
5–7	99n12
5:13–14	47
5:13	105n35
5:14–16	105n35, 107
5:18	234n24
5:21	99n12
5:27	99n12
5:31–32	99n12
5:33–34	99n12
5:38–39	99n12
5:43–44	99n12
7:24–27	99n12
7:29	106n37
8:17	101n20
9:35	106n36, 115n5, 116n10
9:37–38	106
10:1–4	106n36
10:1	107
10:5–42	106n36
10:5	106
10:6–42	105n35
10:7–8	107, 116n9
10:7	115n5, 117
10:14–15	146
10:16	106
10:18	107
10:19–20	106
10:21–22	145
10:35	105, 145
10:40–42	106
10:40	98
11:1	106n36
11:5	106n36, 115n5
11:10	99n13

11:11	116n9
11:27	43, 103, 103n30
12:18–21	100, 101n20
12:31–32	98
12:41–42	148
12:41	98
13:1–23	143
13:11–17	138
13:9	147
13:11	116n9
13:19	115n5, 116n10
13:20	116n10
13:21	116n10
13:22	116n10
13:23	116n10
13:24–30	107n41
13:24	116n10
13:31	116n10
13:33	116n10
13:44	116n10
13:45	116n10
13:47	116n10
13:52	116n10
15:24	98
16:14	102
16:16	102
16:17	149
17:5	45, 100, 105
17:11–13	99n13
18:20	72
18:23–35	107n41
20:31	102
20:26–28	107n41
21:23–27	106n37
21:33–46	98, 102, 143
21:33–42	107n41
21:37	98
22:1–14	107n41
22:31	87
23:8	43
23:9–10	43
23:10	43
24:9–14	107
24:14	115n5, 117
24:42–51	107n41
25:14–30	107n41
25:21	107n41
25:23	107n41
26:11	74
26:13	115n5
28:5–7	91
28:16–29	106n36
28:18–20	106, 107
28:19–20	22, 41, 43, 109
28:19	105n35
28:20	110, 138, 139

Mark

1:1	116n8, 126n32
1:2–3	116n8
1:1–8	99n13
1:7–8	99n13
1:1	102
1:2	99n13
1:6	99n13
1:8	98n9, 106
1:9–14	99n13
1:9–13	98
1:9–11	89
1:11	82, 83, 91, 105
1:12	98n9
1:14–15	83, 105n36, 115n5, 116, 116n8, 126n32
1:14	116n8, 116n10
1:15	89, 115n5, 116n8, 116n9, 117, 137, 138
1:17	105
1:22	106n37
1:27	106n37
1:34	105n36
1:38–39	83, 105n36
1:40–45	99n13
2:2	83, 88, 99n13, 115n5, 116n8
3:5–6	142
3:13–18	105n36
3:14–15	107
3:14	106
3:24	116n9
4	116n8
4:1–20	143
4:3	147, 151

Mark (continued)

4:9	89, 116, 147, 151
4:11–12	138
4:11	116n9, 151
4:12	138n8, 149, 159
4:14	115n5, 116n8, 137
4:15	116n8
4:16	116n8
4:17–19	137
4:17	116n8
4:18	116n8, 116n11
4:19	116n8
4:20	110, 116n8
4:26	116n8
4:30	116n8
4:33	88, 115n5, 116n8
6:1–6	142
6:6–13	105n36
6:7	106
6:11	146
6:12–13	107
6:12	89, 117, 138
6:30–44	99n13
8:11–21	149
8:11–12	142
8:17–18	142
8:22–26	149
8:27–30	149
8:28	102
9:2–8	99
9:7	82, 83, 89, 91, 105
9:37	98, 106
10:43–45	107n41
11:28–33	106n37
12:1–12	98, 102
12:1–11	107n41
12:1–12	143
12:6	98
13:9–11	107
13:9	107
13:10	115n5, 117
13:11	106
13:13	145
13:21–23	162
13:32–37	107n41
14:9	115n5
15:39	102
15:61	116n9
16:15	22

Luke

1:1–4	89
1:2	107n41
1:13–17	91
1:15–17	99n13
1:32–35	102
1:35	98n9
1:38	107n41
1:46–65	37
1:46–48	107n41
1:54	107n41
1:69	107n41
2:9–12	91
2:29	107n41
2:32	100
3:2–18	99n13
3:4–6	99n13
3:13–17	99n13
3:15–17	99n13
3:2	99n13
3:16	98n9, 106
3:21–22	99n13, 100
3:22	98
3:29	98
4:1	98, 98n9
4:14	98
4:16–21	83, 100
4:18–19	101, 106n36
4:18	98, 115n5
4:24–27	99n13
4:31–44	101
4:32	106n37
4:36	106n37
4:43–44	106n36
4:43	98, 115n5
5:1	88, 115n5, 117n11
5:8–11	105
5:15	101
5:17	101
6:6	101
6:7	119

6:12–16	106n36	12:49–53	145
6:17–19	101	13:10–13	101
7:12–17	99n13	13:22	101
7:16	99n13	13:32–33	101
7:21–22	101	13:49	119
7:22	101, 106n36, 115n5, 117n11	14:15–24	107n41
		14:34	105n35
7:27	99n13	15:18	116n9
7:28	116n9	16:13	107n41
8:1	106n36, 115n5	16:16	115n5, 117
8:4–15	143	17:7–10	107n41
8:8	147	19:11–27	107n41
8:10	138, 138n8	19:17	107n41
8:11	115n5, 117n11	19:20	119
8:12	117n11	19:47	101
8:13	117n11	20:1	101, 106n36, 115n5, 117n11
8:15	117n11		
9:1–6	106n36	20:2–8	106n37
9:6	117	20:9–19	98, 102, 143
9:1–2	106	20:13	98
9:2	106, 107, 115n5, 116n9, 117	21:12–15	107
		21:13	107
9:5	146	21:17	145
9:6	107, 115n5	21:37–38	101
9:11	101, 115n5, 117n11	22:37	100, 101 n20
		24:27	89, 120n18
9:19	102	24:44–49	120n18
9:35	100	24:44	89
9:48	106	24:45–49	106n36
9:60	115n5, 117	24:47–48	105n35, 107
10:1–24	106n36	24:47	106, 138, 139
10:1–3	106	24:48	107
10:2	106	24:49	106
10:9	107, 115n5, 117		
10:10–12	146		
10:16	47, 98, 106		

John

10:21–22	103
10:21	98
10:39	115n5
11:4–5	101
11:28	115n5, 117n11
11:32	98, 148
11:48–49	106n38
12:10	98
12:12	106
12:24	119
12:28	98n9
12:35–48	107n41

1:1–18	88, 104, 117
1:6–9	99n13
1:6–8	117
1:11	143
1:12	143
1:15	99n13, 117
1:18	103
1:19–27	99n13
1:29–34	99n13
1:32–33	99n14
1:38	99n14

John (continued)

1:49	99n14	8:43	104
2:11	214	8:47	71
3:2	99n14	8:51	104
3:3	99n14	9:2	99n14
3:5	99n14	9:4	98n10
3:12–13	103n30	9:17	99
3:17	98n10	10	63
3:27–30	99n13	10:27	104
3:34	98, 98n10, 104	10:36	98n10
3:36	104	11	21
4	117	11:8	99n14
4:19	99	11:42	98n10
4:25	46	12:28	83, 91
4:31	99n14	12:38–41	100
4:34	98n10	12:44–50	98n10
4:39–41	117	12:44	98
4:41–42	104	12:48	104
5:19	99n14	13:16	106
5:23–24	98n10	13:20	98n10, 106
5:24	99n14	14	21
5:25	82, 99n14	14:6–10	103
5:36–38	98n10	14:10	98, 103
5:30	98n10	14:23	104
5:37	89, 98n10	14:24	98n10, 104
5:39	89	14:26	43
6:14	99	15:3	104
6:25	99n14	15:20–21	145
6:29	98n10	15:20	104, 149n16
6:30–34	100	15:21	98n10
6:38–39	98n10	15:22	149n16
6:44	98n10	15:26–27	106
6:46	103	15:26	89, 149n16
6:57	98n10	15:27	149n16
6:68	104	16:5	98n10
7:7	149n16	16:8	149
	7:16–33: 98n10	16:13	43
7:16	41	16:14	149n16
7:26–29	98n10	17:3–25	98n10
7:29	98n10	17:6–8	106
7:40	99, 104	17:6	104
7:52	99, 99n14	17:8	103, 207
8:14–18	98n10	17:14	98, 106, 207
8:18	89	17:18	106
8:31	104	17:17	104
8:37	104	19:23	45
8:42	98n10	19:35	117
		20:16	99n14
		20:21	98n10, 207

20:22	104
20:23	104
20:30–31	89, 214
20:31	54, 117
21:24	117

Acts

1:1	117n12
1:4–8	108
1:8	108, 144, 161n4
1:21–22	108
2:4	108
2:11	117n12, 119n16
2:14–41	89, 118n14
2:16–21	109
2:17	44
2:27–38	147
2:32	108, 120
2:36	118
2:38	89, 118, 138
2:40	117n12, 147
2:41	147
3:11–26	89
3:12–26	118n14
3:13	107
3:15	108, 120
3:18	120
3:19	138
3:21	120
3:24	117n12, 120
3:26	107
4:1	117n12
4:2	117n12, 119n16
4:4	119n16
4:8–20	89
4:8–12	118n14
4:13–22	144
4:17	117n12
4:18	117n12, 119n16
4:27	107
4:29	107, 117n12, 119n16
4:30	107
4:31	89, 117n12, 119n16, 130n50
4:33	108, 118n15, 120
5:17–42	144
5:20	117n12, 119n16
5:21	117n12
5:25	117n12
5:28	117n12, 119n16
5:30–32	120
5:32	108
5:40	117n12, 119n16
5:41	108
5:42	117n12, 118n15, 119n16
6:2	89, 119n16, 130n50
6:3	117n12
6:4	119n16
6:7	88, 89, 119n16, 144
6:8—8:3	144
6:10	117n12
7:2–53	118n14
7:31	82
7:38	87
7:51–52	151
8:4	117n12, 119n16, 125
8:5	117n12, 118n15, 119n16
8:12	117n12, 118n15, 119n16
8:14	119n16, 130n50
8:25	89, 108, 117n12, 119n16, 120n17
8:26–40	161
8:26	91, 161
8:29	161
8:32	161
8:33	161
8:35	89, 117n12, 118n15, 119n16, 161
8:36	161
8:39	161
8:40	117n12, 119n16, 161
9:1–6	88
9:3–6	83
9:10	91
9:15–16	108

Acts (continued)

9:16	108
9:20	117n12, 118n15, 119n16
9:22	118n15
9:27	118n12, 119n16
9:28	118n12, 119n16
10:1–20	88
10:3–6	91
10:34–43	89, 118n14
10:36	117n12, 119n16
10:37	117n12
10:39–43	108, 119–20, 120
10:39–42	120
10:41	120
10:42	117n12, 120
10:43	117n12, 120
10:44	117n12, 119n16
11:1	119n16, 130n50
11:14–15	117n12
11:19	117n12, 119n16
11:20	117n12, 118n12, 118n15, 119n16
11:26	117n12
11:28	157, 240
12:1–19	144
12:24	88, 89, 119n16, 144
13:1	232
13:2	240n50
13:5	89, 117n12, 119n16
13:7	89, 119n16
13:16–48	89
13:16–41	118n14
13:22	117n12
13:26	119n16, 120n17
13:27	120
13:30–31	120
13:31	108
13:32–33	120
13:32	117n12, 119n16, 120n17
13:38	117n12, 119n16
13:42	118n12
13:44	89, 119n16
13:45	118n12
13:46	89, 118n12, 119n16
13:47	108
13:48	89, 119n16
13:49	88, 89, 119n16, 144
13:50–51	144
13:51	146
14:1	118n12
14:3	108, 117n12, 118n12, 119n16, 120n17
14:4–7	144
14:7	117n12, 119n16
14:9	118n12
14:14–17	89, 118n14
14:15	117n12, 119n16
14:19	144
14:21	117n12, 119n16
14:25	118n12, 119n16
14:27	117n12
15:4	117n12
15:7	119n16
15:8	117n12
15:15	120
15:21	117n12
15:35	89, 117n12, 119n16
15:36	89, 117n12, 119n16
16:6	118n12, 119n16
16:10	117n12, 119n16
16:13	118n12
16:14	118n12
16:17	107, 117n12, 119n16
16:19–24	144
16:32	89, 118n12, 119n16
17:3	117n12, 118n14, 118n15, 119n16
17:5–9	144
17:7	118n15
17:11	119n16, 157, 195, 215, 217, 237
17:13	89, 117n12, 119n16, 144

17:18	117n12, 118n15, 119n16	25:19	118n15
17:19	118n12	26:2–23	118n14
17:22–31	89, 118n14	26:15–18	109
17:23	117n12	26:16b–19	138–139
17:30	138	26:16	108
17:32	119n16, 144	26:20	117n12, 119n16, 138
18:5	117n12, 118n15, 119n16	26:20	139
18:6	144	26:22	118n12, 120
18:9	118n12	26:23	109, 117n12
18:11	89, 117n12, 119n16	26:26	118n12
18:12–17	144	27:23–24	91
18:25	117n12, 118n12, 118n15	28:23	89, 117n12, 118n12, 118n15, 119n16, 120
18:26	118n12, 119n16	28:24–28	144
18:28	118n15	28:25–27	144
19:4	118n15	28:28	120n17, 144
19:8	118n12, 119n16	28:31	117n12, 118n15, 119n16
19:10	89, 119n16		
19:13	117n12, 119n16		
19:20	88, 89, 119n16, 144		

Romans

19:23–41	144
20:7	119n16
20:20	117n12
20:21	117n12, 118, 120
20:24	108, 119n16, 120n17
20:25	117n12
20:27	117n12, 119n16
20:32	119n16
21:4	233
21:8	125
21:9	230
21:10–11	233, 240
21:21	117n12
21:27–36	144
21:28	117n12
22:1–21	118n14
22:14–15	108
22:14	82
22:20	108
23:11	108, 117n12
23:12–15	144
24:24	118n15, 119n16
24:45–49	88

1	18
1:1	24, 111n49, 195
1:2–3a	122
1:2	22, 25, 28
1:1–4	22
1:3–4	16, 122n20
1:5	29, 111n49
1:6	111n49
1:7	111n49
1:16	31, 51
1:17	122n21
2:16	16
2:29	151
3:11	36
3:21	89, 122
3:24	51
5:10	39
10	18, 139
10:8	110n44, 121n19
10:13–15	27
10:14–15	110n44
10:14–21	32
10:14	36, 173
10:15	22, 36, 110

Romans (continued)

10:16	36
10:17	36, 51, 121n19
12:5	230
12:6–8	110, 110n46
12:6	111n47, 229, 231, 231n5, 241
12:8	110n46
15:4	87
16:25	22, 121n19
16:25–27	123n24
16:25–26	89, 123
16:26	122

1 Corinthians

1:1	112n49
1:2	112n49
1:17	121
1:18–25	121
1:18	121n19, 145, 150
1:21	139
1:23–24	145
1:23	89, 121n19, 157, 194, 203, 208
2:1–4	121
2:1	121n19
2:2	121, 121n19, 157
2:4	121, 139, 157, 203
2:6–10	122
2:14	150
4	30
6:1–11	184
7:40	207
10:6	87
11:2	121n19
11:4–5	229
11:4	230
11:5	230
11:23	121n19
11:26	67
12:1–11	110
12:3	183
12:4	229
12:7	230
12:8–10	110n46
12:10	111n47, 229, 240
12:11	230, 240
12:27–31	230
12:28–31	110
12:28–30	110n46
12:28–29	229
12:28	111n47
12:29	232
13:1–13	230
13:2	229
13:8–9	229
14	65, 234, 235, 241
14:1–6	229
14:1–5	111n47
14:1	230, 240, 241
14:3–4	230
14:4	230, 240
14:5	240
14:19	240
14:22–25	111n47, 229
14:24–25	230, 240
14:26	230
14:29–33	229, 240
14:29–32	230
14:29	195, 215, 217, 231n4, 234, 240
14:30	235, 236
14:31	24
14:33	230
14:35–38	230
14:36–38	207
14:36	234
14:37–39	229
14:37–38	241
14:37	241
14:39	111n47, 230
14:40	230
15:1–8	121
15:3–4	199, 219
15:12	121n19

2 Corinthians

2	144
2:14	144
2:15	144
2:16	53, 144

2:17	121n19, 144
3:3–6	35
3:9	52
3:18	43
4:2	121n19
4:3–4	150
4:5	121n19
4:6	52, 74
5:19–20	173
5:19	121n19
5:20	139, 158
11:4	122, 194, 208, 220
12:1	91

Galatians

1:6–9	122, 157, 208
1:8–9	220
1:8	194, 237
1:11—2:10	207
1:11–12	106
1:12	195, 207
1:16	121n19
2:14	237
3:1	39
3:13	39

Ephesians

1:9	157
1:10	157
1:13	69, 110, 121n19, 148
1:17–18a	149–50
2:17	100
2:20	70, 71, 229, 236, 236n33, 236n34, 240
3:1–13	123n25
3:2	123n25
3:4	121n19
3:3	123n25
3:5	123n25, 229, 236, 236n34, 240
3:6	123n25
3:7	123n25
3:8–9	110
3:8	121n19, 123n25
3:9	124n25
3:10	110, 123n25
4:7	229
4:10–13	52
4:11–12	110, 110n46
4:11	48, 111n47, 229, 229, 230, 236, 240
4:12	74, 230
6:19	121n19

Philippians

1:14	121n19
1:15–18	121n19, 152, 199, 220, 221
2:6–11	121
2:16	121n19

Colossians

1:5	121n19
1:24–27	124n25
1:25	121n19, 124n25
1:26–27	124n25
1:28	121n19, 139
2:3	45
3:16	121n19
4:3	121n19

1 Thessalonians

1:4–8	241
1:4–6	110
1:5	149
1:6	121n19, 149, 234
1:8	121n19
2:13	1, 34, 110, 121n19, 148, 173, 234
2:14n-15a	122n22
4:15	115n4, 215, 234
5:19–21	111n47, 229
5:19–20	230

1 Thessalonians (continued)

5:19	232, 240
5:20	232, 234
5:21	230, 240

2 Thessalonians

2:2	230
2:3	230
2:13–15	150
2:15	121n19
3:1	121n19
3:6	121n19

1 Timothy

1:8	144
1:18	229, 240n50
2:4	158n2
3:15	70
3:16	121n19
4:1	44, 83
4:6	121n19
4:14	229, 240n50

2 Timothy

1:8–11	125
1:8	111, 121n19, 125
1:9–10	124n26, 125
2:2	111
2:9	121n19
2:11–13	121
2:15	111, 121n19
2:19	69
3:1	44
3:16	4
4:2	1, 111, 121n19, 125, 139, 170, 172
4:3–4	144
4:5	144
4:17	121n19

Titus

1:3	121n19
1:9	121n19

Hebrews

1:1–2	44, 81, 102
2:1–4	127, 128n39
2:2	91
2:3–4	126n32
2:3	130n46
3–4	129
3:1–4:13	128
3:1–5	94
3:3–11	84
3:5–6	103
3:6	103n24
3:7	83, 127, 128
3:12	129n43
3:13	128n39
3:15	127, 128, 140
4:1	140
4:2–3a	127
4:2	127
4:6	127
4:7	127, 128
4:12–13	128
4:12	128, 128n39
5:8	103n24
6:1	128n39
5:12	128n39
6:5	110, 128n39
6:9	140
6:10–12	140
7:28	103n24
10:10	39
10:19–25	129n41
10:19–22	129n41
10:23–25	129n41
10:25	129n42, 140
12	129
12:18–29	140
12:18–27	129
12:19	129
12:24	140
12:25	129, 129n43, 140

13:7	128n39, 130	1:20	125n30
13:9	130n47	1:21	125n30
13:17	130n46	3:3	44
13:22	128n39, 139		

1 Peter

1 John

		1:1–5	110
	1:3	1:1–4	89
1:10–12	89, 125, 126n31	2:18	44
1:10	125	4:1–6	162
1:12	24, 125		
1:18–25	126		
1:20	44		

Revelation

1:22–24	126n33		
1:23–35	110	1:1–2	89
1:23–25	126	1:1	91
1:23	16, 34, 126, 148, 241	1:2	130, 130n50
		1:5	39
1:25	18, 33, 36, 126, 126n32, 148	1:9	130, 130n50
		1:10	82
2	30	2:7	84
2:9–10	241	2:11	84
2:9	110	2:17	84
3:1	67, 126	2:29	84
3:18	219	3:6	84
3:19–22	35	3:13	84
4:1–2	126n33	3:22	84
4:4–6	148	6:9	130, 130n50
4:6	126, 126n33	13	162
4:10–11	110, 110n46	17:17	130n50
4:11	20, 47	19:9	130n50
		19:10	130
		19:13	88, 130n50

2 Peter

		20:4	130, 130n50
		20:15	158n2
1:16–18	21	21:5–8	82
1:17–18	91	21:5	84, 89
1:17	82	22:7	84
1:19	17, 23	22:12–16	84
1:19–21	4, 125n30	22:17	84
1:16–18	16	22:20	84

www.ingramcontent.com/pod-product-compliance
Lightning Source LLC
Chambersburg PA
CBHW071240230426
43668CB00011B/1523